Politics and Government in Hong Kong

This book examines the government of Hong Kong since its handover to mainland China in 1997, focusing in particular on the anti-government mass protests and mobilizations in the years since 2003. It argues that Hong Kong has been poorly governed since transferring to Chinese rule, and that public frustration with governmental performance, including anti-subversion laws and slow democratization, has resulted in the regular and massive protests, which have been rare in Hong Kong's past political development. The book then assesses different explanations for Hong Kong's government problems, including lack of social cohesion, incomplete economic restructuring, structural budgetary deficit, severe social inequality, intensifying cronyism, and deficiencies within the political system itself. It goes on to discuss the implications of poor governance for legislative elections, civil society and constitutional development, and considers the prospects for the future. It argues that although in the short term the Hong Kong government has managed to maintain its popular support ratings, in the longer run it is unlikely to be able to maintain its legitimacy in dealing with the fundamental challenges of government unless the current system is replaced by popular election of the government with appropriate institutional capacity and political powers.

Ming Sing is Associate Professor at Hong Kong University of Science and Technology. His publications include *Hong Kong's Tortuous Democratization: a Comparative Analysis* (2004), and *Hong Kong Government and Politics* (2003).

Routledge contemporary China series

Politics and Government in Hong Kong

Crisis under Chinese sovereignty

Edited by Ming Sing

Routledge
Taylor & Francis Group

LONDON AND NEW YORK

First published 2009
by Routledge
2 Park Square, Milton Park, Abingdon, Oxon OX14 4RN

Simultaneously published in the USA and Canada
by Routledge
711 Third Avenue Avenue, New York, NY 10017

Routledge is an imprint of the Taylor & Francis Group, an informa business

Typeset in Times by Wearset Ltd, Boldon, Tyne and Wear

British Library Cataloguing in Publication Data
A catalogue record for this book is available from the British Library

Library of Congress Cataloging in Publication Data
Politics and government in Hong Kong: crisis under Chinese sovereignty/edited by Ming Sing.
p. cm.
Includes bibliographical references and index.
1. Hong Kong (China)–Politics and government–1997– 2. Legitimacy of governments–China–Hong Kong. I. Sing, Ming, 1960–
JQ1539.5.A58P67 2008
320.95125–dc22
2008017923

ISBN10: 0-415-46960-6 (hbk)
ISBN10: 0-203-88897-9 (ebk)

ISBN13: 978-0-415-46940-1 (hbk)
ISBN13: 978-0-203-88897-1 (ebk)
ISBN13: 978-0-415-54303-3 (pbk)

Contents

Illustrations

Contributors

Joseph M. Chan is a Professor of Journalism and Communication at the Chinese University of Hong Kong. His research interests are international communication and cultural globalization, political communication, media development in Greater China, and the social impact of the internet. He is the author of *Mass Media and Political Transition: The Hong Kong Press in China's Orbit* (New York, 1991) (co-authored with C.C. Lee) and *Global Media Spectacle* (Buffalo, 2002) (co-authored with C.C. Lee, Zhongdang Pan and Clement So).

Joseph C.W. Chan is a Professor of Politics and Public Administration at the University of Hong Kong. His research interests include contemporary liberalism and perfectionism, Confucian political philosophy, the theory and practice of human rights, civil society and NGOs, and social cohesion. His representative publications include "Democracy and Meritocracy: Toward a Confucian Perspective," *Journal of Chinese Philosophy* (2007), "Moral Autonomy, Civil Liberties, and Confucianism," *Philosophy East and West* (2002), and "Legitimacy, Unanimity, and Perfectionism," *Philosophy and Public Affairs* (2000).

Shun-hing Chan is an Associate Professor of Religion and Philosophy at Hong Kong Baptist University. He focuses on sociology of religion, religions in Hong Kong and China, political theology, and contextual theology. He is the author of *Changing Church and State Relations in Hong Kong, 1950–2000* (Hong Kong, 2003) (co-authored with Beatrice Leung).

Elaine Chan is an Honorary Associate Professor and Research Officer of Politics and Public Administration at the University of Hong Kong. Her research interests include political culture, national identity, social movements, and cultural sociology. Her representative publications include "Beyond Pedagogy: Language and Identity in Post-colonial Hong Kong," *British Journal of Sociology of Education* (2002), "Defining Fellow Compatriots as 'Others' – National Identity in Hong Kong," *Government and Opposition* (2000), and "Structural and Symbolic Centers: Center Displacement in the 1989 Chinese Student Movement," *International Sociology* (1999).

Lucy M. Cummings was a former Honorary Assistant Professor of Politics and Public Administration at the University of Hong Kong. Her research interests lie at the intersection of ethics and contemporary affairs, which stem not only from her academic training, but from her work experience at various NGOs in the U.S.A., Taiwan, and Hong Kong. She is the author of *A Consultancy Study on Improved Governance in the Hong Kong Special Administrative Region* (Hong Kong General Chamber of Commerce, 2005) (co-authored with Ming Sing).

Michael E. DeGolyer is a Professor of Government and International Studies at Hong Kong Baptist University. His research interests are comparative/historical political development and political economy, Hong Kong political development, and technology and learning. He is the author of *The Outlook for US–China Trade and Cultural Exchange Relations Following the 1997–98 Summits: Chinese and American Perspectives* (Hong Kong, 1998).

Agnes Shuk-mei Ku is Associate Professor of Social Sciences at the Hong Kong University of Science and Technology. She is affiliated with the Center for Cultural Sociology at Yale University. Her research focuses on civil society and the public sphere, Hong Kong culture and politics, citizenship, gender, and disability issues. She is the author of *Narratives, Politics, and the Public Sphere: Struggles over Political Reform in the Final Transitional Years in Hong Kong (1992–1994)* (Ashgate, 1999).

Eliza W.Y. Lee is Associate Professor of Politics and Public Administration at the University of Hong Kong. Her current research interests are the politics of social policy development, civil society organizations, participatory governance, public management and gender, with particular focus on Hong Kong and its comparison with selected Asian states. Her representative publications are "Welfare Restructuring in Asian Newly Industrialized Countries: A Comparison of Hong Kong and Singapore," *Policy and Politics* (2006), "Individualism and Patriarchy: The Identity of Entrepreneurial Women Lawyers in Hong Kong," *Gender and Change in Hong Kong: Globalization, Postcolonialism, and Chinese Patriarchy* (2003), and "The Political Economy of Public Sector Reform in Hong Kong: The Case of a Colonial-Developmental State," *International Review of Administrative Sciences* (1998).

Francis L.F. Lee is an Assistant Professor of English and Communication at the City University of Hong Kong. His representative publications include "Strategic Interaction, Cultural Co-orientation, and Press Freedom in Hong Kong," *Asian Journal of Communication* (2007), "Objectivity as Self-censorship? Hong Kong Citizens' Beliefs in Media Neutrality and Perceptions of Press Freedom," *Asian Survey* (2007), "Collective Efficacy, Support for Democracy, and Political Participation in Hong Kong," *International Journal of Public Opinion Research* (2006), and "Radio Phone-in Talk Shows as Politically Significant Infotainment in Hong Kong," *Harvard International Journal of Press/Politics* (2002).

Ming Sing is Associate Professor of Social Sciences at the Hong Kong University of Science and Technology. His research focuses on comparing political culture in Asia, democratic development in Asia and the world, politics and government in Hong Kong, and institutional engineering and democratic governance. His representative publications include *Hong Kong's Tortuous Democratization* (2004), *Hong Kong Government and Politics* (2003), and "Public Support for Democracy in Hong Kong," *Democratization* (2005).

Benny Y.T. Tai is Associate Professor and Associate Dean of Law at the University of Hong Kong. His research focuses on constitutional law, administrative law, law and religion, and human rights. His major publications include "The Development of Constitutionalism in Hong Kong" in Raymond Wacks (ed.) *The New Legal Order in Hong Kong* (Hong Kong, 1999), and "The Advent of Substantive Legitimate Expectations in Hong Kong: Two Competing Visions" (2002).

James T.H. Tang is Professor of Politics and Public Administration at the University of Hong Kong. He specializes in international relations, and his research and teaching interests include Chinese foreign policy, international political economy in the Asia-Pacific region, and political transition in Hong Kong. His representative publications include "The Internet and Civil Society: Environmental and Labour Organizations in Hong Kong," *International Journal of Urban and Regional Research* (with Cindy Y.W. Chu, 2005), "Business as Usual: The Dynamics of Government–Business Relations in the Hong Kong Special Administrative Region," *Journal of Contemporary China* (1999), and "The First Hong Kong Special Administrative Region Legislative Council Elections," *Chinese Law and Government* (1999).

Wilson Wong is Associate Professor of Government and Public Administration at the Chinese University of Hong Kong. His research focuses on public budgeting and finance, public management and organization theory, public policy analysis and implementation, and Hong Kong politics and governance. His representative publications include *Contemporary Hong Kong Politics: Governance in the Post-1997 Era.* (Hong Kong 2007) (co-edited with Lam Waiman, Percy Lui, and Ian Holliday); and "What Drives Global E-government? An Exploratory Assessment of Existing E-government Performance Measures," in George Boyne, Kenneth Meier, Laurence O'Toole, and Richard Walker (eds) *Public Service Performance: Perspectives on Measurement and Management* (2006).

Acknowledgments

First of all, I am deeply indebted to Ming Chan and Gerald Postiglione for their initiation of this entire book project. The volume grew out of a workshop held at the City University of Hong Kong in 2005 as an effort to understand the multi-faceted causes of Hong Kong's post-handover governance crisis epitomized by the large-scale mass rally of 2003. Both Ming Chan and Gerald have provided unfailing support throughout different critical stages and managed to contribute to its final production. I am also grateful to Alvin So, Ngok Ma, Wai Ting, Denny Gittings, and two anonymous reviewers for Routledge, who have provided critical and constructive comments at various stages to improve this volume.

Some of the chapters have been supported by the Research Grant Council of Hong Kong Special Administrative Region, and I am grateful for its assistance.

I am also very grateful to Tom Bates of Routledge. He has been extremely helpful throughout the process of publishing this volume. I also thank Sophia Yanjun Hua, who has provided last-minute assistance in formatting and other clerical work. Eventually, my greatest gratitude is to the authors of the different chapters. Without their patience, this book would never have come out as it did.

Introduction

Hong Kong in crisis under Chinese sovereignty

Ming Sing

This book attempts to explore the causes of Hong Kong's poor governance and to evaluate its prospects since the early 2000s. On July 1, 2003, over half a million Hong Kong people joined in a mass protest against the poor governance of the post-handover Hong Kong government, the likely legislation of draconian anti-subversion laws, and for speedier democratization. The scale of the July 1 rally was the largest seen since 1989 in Hong Kong, a city of 6.8 million people. Although the protests in 1989 exceeded the scale of the 2003 marches, the Tiananmen protesters demonstrated against abuse of human rights in China, rather than poor governance within Hong Kong.[1]

The size of the participants, the huge diversity of the social groups involved, and the robust demands they voiced, powerfully underscored the pervasive public frustration with governmental performance. Groups involved in the protests included journalists, academics, workers, human rights, actors and artists, students, negative-equity homeowners, social welfare recipients, professionals, political parties, and Christian churches. The collective demand for more democracy and better governance is reminiscent of the explosion of civil society amid democratic transitions in various parts of the world.

Despite Beijing's economic sweeteners, and the ensuing economic rebound in Hong Kong from the last quarter of 2003 onward, only 34 percent of Hong Kong people trusted their government in late February, 2004.[2] The July 1, 2003 march, plus the over 200,000-strong pro-democracy rally on July 1, 2004, differed conspicuously with the tiny participation in pro-democratic rallies in the 1980s and 1990s, the largest of which had only 5,000 protesters in 1987. Of no less importance, the record-breaking voter turnout for local elections held on November 23, 2003, and the ensuing landslide victory of the pro-democratic camp over pro-China parties, upset Beijing because of the latter's possible loss of control over Hong Kong.[3]

Public sees poor governance in post-handover Hong Kong

Stability and prosperity demands good governance. In today's interdependent world, where markets and political liberalization, instead of government planning, are often the key engines of economic and social changes, political freedoms and participation are taken as crucial elements of stable and prosperous societies.[4] Accordingly, the World Bank has designed widely recognized barometers for gauging good governance, including: voice and accountability, political stability, government effectiveness, regulatory burden, rule of law, and clean government.[5] Since the handover, Hong Kong has been beset with questions on virtually every aspect of governance mentioned above.

Political voice through democratic participation is a core World Bank governance indicator and a key source of legitimacy. Hong Kong's pre-1997 colonial government attempted to maintain popular legitimacy by meeting performance targets that included high rates of economic prosperity, political stability, and the protection of civil liberties. Given the success of the colonial model,[6] there were strong arguments in favor of maintaining a similar political framework for the SAR after 1997.[7] Yet, this performance-based legitimacy formula seemingly no longer meets the expectations of the Hong Kong populace, especially since limited electoral and competitive politics have become part of the political landscape. In recent years, Hong Kong's popular demands for democratic participation in government have been vividly highlighted in public demonstrations and electoral results. Further credible and consistent evidence for the depth of Hong Kong's democratic aspirations may also be found in post-1997 popular survey data, which this study will now examine.[8]

Post-1997 opinion survey results have demonstrated consistent and strong support for democratic political reforms. In four representative surveys conducted between March, 2003 and January, 2004, between 70 percent and 80 percent of Hong Kong people supported the implementation of constitutional reform with universal suffrage by 2008. Even in the face of the central government's January, 2004 opposition to constitutional reform, popular support for constitutional reform – with universal suffrage by 2008 – remained at 58.5 percent in early March, 2004.[9] Similarly, in a survey conducted in June, 2005, after the central government's rejection of universal suffrage by 2008, 61 percent and 62 percent of the public still preferred universal suffrage as a method for electing the legislature and the chief executive respectively in 2012.[10] These survey results suggest that Hong Kong people will not be satisfied with anything less than a government based on the basic law promises of universal suffrage.

Thus, existing survey data and research evidence suggest clearly that public demands for universal suffrage in Hong Kong will remain strong, even with improved economic growth. In fact, if the patterns in Hong Kong follow those of other developed countries, we should expect stronger popular demand for democratic participation as Hong Kong's economic performance improves further. Several authors in this book argue that a popularly elected government, with appropriate institutional capacity and political power, would better confront fundamental challenges and implement policies for the long-term development of Hong Kong, and thus fundamentally improve its quality of governance.

In short, the recent departure of Tung Chee-hwa is unlikely to signal the end of the legitimacy and governance problem for the non-democratic government.

The new chief executive, Donald Tsang, who has been indirectly elected by a mere 800-strong Election Committee, will deprive him of the sorely needed public support derived from a free and fair election. The paucity of legitimacy may continue to make the government shy away from boldly confronting squarely short-term and long-term challenges confronting Hong Kong, including the aging population, pollution, medical finance, fair competition, social inequality, and the high ways for some civil servants and employees in publicly subsidized sectors. The latter issue will continue to foil the government's attempt to resolve the structural budget deficit, forcing the government to reduce its expenditures for various public policies in order to strike a balanced budget. The cutbacks may trigger wider state–society conflicts and forge a spirally downward cycle of declining public support for the Hong Kong government and the political system as a whole. Although the new government shepherded by Donald Tsang may continue to show better performance in terms of decisiveness and soundness in policy-making vis-à-vis that of Tung's era, if and when some of the fundamental challenges remain unresolved, mass mobilizations for democratization and better governance may happen again in the medium and long run, only to be compounded further by future cyclical economic downturns.

Arguments of the book chapters: poor governance triggers mass mobilizations

To reiterate, this book attempts to explore the causes of Hong Kong's poor governance and to evaluate its prospects. It will set out to delineate those causes by, first, focusing on the origins of its political instability, that is, mass mobilizations since mid-2003, with Chan and Lee's chapter using the quantitative approach and Agnes Kuk's using an interpretive one. It will then move on to Shun-hing Chan's as well as Elaine Chan and Joseph Chan's chapters, analyzing respectively the mobilization of Christian churches and the roots of Hong Kong's poor "social cohesion." They offer plenty of insights on various aspects of Hong Kong's poor governance since the handover. After that, Sing's chapter highlights five major institutional and cultural factors underlying Hong Kong's governance problems. Concerning the five major factors, one of them has been the unresolved budgetary crisis arising from incomplete economic restructuring. Wilson Wong devotes an entire chapter to put the issue under the microscope. Next, Eliza Lee argues forcefully that the remedial welfare system in Hong Kong has been found wanting under the severe and prolonged economic crisis in Hong Kong post-handover.

In order to improve Hong Kong's governance, in addition to building up full democracy and addressing internal problems, Lucy Cummings and James Tang propose that attention be given to the neglected international dimension of Hong Kong. Following that, the way in which the poor governance in the post-handover Hong Kong has shaped the elections for legislature in 2004 will be studied by Michael DeGolyer. Finally, Benny Tai will use a game-theory-like framework to illuminate how the chief executive, Chinese government and an increasingly robust civil society have interacted and shaped Hong Kong's contentious constitutional development.

As for the prospects of Hong Kong's governance as summed up in Sing's chapter, in the short run, a rebound in the personal supporting rating for the chief executive after the resumption of the office by Donald Tsang has been witnessed. Yet it is highly doubtful that Hong Kong's non-democratic system can avert its legitimation problem in the medium and long term owing to the entanglement of some unresolved structural factors. What follows will be a summary of the ensuing chapters.

The causes and implications of landmark mass mobilizations

We begin with Joseph Man Chan and Francis Lee's analysis of causes of the three mass protests held on July 1, 2003, January, 2004, and July 1, 2004. The authors have based their analyses on data obtained from some onsite surveys conducted during the three large-scale rallies and two post-rally population surveys. They aim to explore the identities of those who participated in the rallies and why they participated. Predicated on an extensive literature review, they focus their research on the effects of three possible types of mobilizing agencies: social and political groups, mass media, and individuals' social and political attitudes.

Concerning the identities of the participants, they have found that while people from all walks of life of different social strata took part in the rallies, a typical demonstrator could be characterized mainly as male, young, college educated, professional/semi-professional, and middle class. Given that this fits the group that is Hong Kong's economic "backbone," their collective action carries heightened political significance. Regarding the causes of mass participation in rallies in Hong Kong, both the onsite and population surveys demonstrate clearly that organizational affiliation is unimportant. Instead, the interaction between mass communication and interpersonal communication is more relevant. The demonstrators usually did not participate in the rallies alone. Instead they brought along family members, friends, or acquaintances. Many respondents to the surveys admitted the importance of the calls to action from friends and family.

Practically speaking, this research has once again underscored the significance of a free and responsible media in Hong Kong, which definitely help shape public opinion. Media outlets like *Apple Daily* and several prominent radio talk shows have served the important function of activating more private and public political discussion among citizens. Furthermore, despite the huge policy impact of the rallies at the individual level, it was found the mobilizations did not reach beyond the group of citizens who have harbored highly negative opinions toward the government.

Following Joseph Man Chan and Francis Lee's research on mass mobilizations is another chapter on a similar theme by Agnes Ku. Instead of providing causes for the mass rally of July 1, 2003, Ku endeavors to uncover the changes in the social and political meanings attached to the event, which were represented, contested and developed in the public sphere(s).

The author concludes her analysis by focusing on the useful conceptual edifice built on "hegemony," a process-oriented perspective that records the process of conflicts as they appear through a chain of events. She stresses that this enables us to examine the dynamics of contention and mobilization and illuminate the affinities and fissures both between the state and civil society and within the latter. The contestation reveals a question that is often ignored in the public sphere: whose civil society is it? This results in an improved appreciation of civil society that draws on and yet goes beyond the crude dichotomy of state versus civil society.

As mentioned above, still another chapter that deals with the causes or meanings of the mass protests since 2003 centers on the local Christian churches by Shun-hing Chan. Chan starts with a general note that in sociological literature, researchers have argued that the Christian churches are a constructive force facilitating democratization. He studies the relationship between Christianity and democracy in Hong Kong from 2001 to 2006, focusing particularly on the sociopolitical issues and the response of the Christian churches to the Hong Kong SAR government from 2003 to 2006.

Chan argues that social environment, international church organizations, models of the churches, and para-church organizations are four crucial factors shaping the churches' sociopolitical engagement in Hong Kong. More importantly, para-church organizations in both the Catholic church and the mainline Protestant churches do matter for the development of social movements and the building of civil society in Hong Kong.

While these mass protests reflect the dire consequences of bad governance in Hong Kong, Elaine Chan and Joseph C.W. Chan deal squarely with a root problem of Hong Kong's poor governance – its low level of social cohesion. Following in the footsteps of their analysis, they have drawn implications on the ways to improve Hong Kong's governance during the post-Tung era.

Low social cohesion has contributed to poor governance

Chan and Chan provide a pioneering empirical survey in Hong Kong to chart its state of social cohesion in 2003. Drawn from their survey results, they offer a few lessons regarding governance and social cohesion in Hong Kong along the aspects of leadership, politics, and policies.

Regarding leadership, their findings show that respondents were most frustrated with the political leadership. They attribute weak social cohesion to the poor leadership of the former chief executive Tung Chee-hwa – his poor governance style, his selection of incompetent principal officials, and his controversial public policies. They also regard conflicts between the government and citizens as the most detrimental to social cohesion. The fact that Tung was an inexperienced politician, and failed to establish transparency and openness when interacting with the public during the policy-making process, meant that social cohesion was sorely tested. Accordingly, the authors have argued that Hong Kong's chief executive and officials should discard their old colonial mindsets, be ready to face the public, and legitimize their policies through the legislature.

As for politics, the authors discover that political issues, especially the debate on the pacing of democratization, have been a source that has emasculated social cohesion. The contention over the pace of democratization has been the principal source of conflict between pro-China and pro-democracy groups, and more damaging to social cohesion than the socioeconomic issues among different classes. Tung was dismissive of political affairs and tried to deflect society's attention to social and economic concerns. Paradoxically, his strategy of depoliticization has gained no ground and instead delayed policy implementation owing to diluted social and political backing.[11]

The authors conclude that as liberty, democracy, and the rule of law are taken by the respondents as core values of Hong Kong, to truly implement people-based governance, the new chief executive will be under pressure to earnestly uphold those values in policy-making. Although an economic rebound may reduce some social frustration, they believe a high degree of social cohesion will not be achieved if principal societal values are continually defied and trampled on.

Can legitimacy by performance still work?

Given the preeminent importance of democracy in bettering good governance for Hong Kong, Ming Sing's chapter deciphers factors that have delegitimized Hong Kong's non-democratic system in assessing the readiness of Hong Kong for full democracy, and the implications of implementing full democracy on its governance.

He first argues that the mass protests from mid-2003 onward have suggested a withdrawal of public backing for the non-democratic system and a strong support for greater democracy. He then explicates how five major challenges have sapped the legitimacy of Hong Kong's non-democratic system since the handover. He expects the five challenges to continually weaken the public support for the non-democratic system, and maintain steadfast pressure for speedier democratization of Hong Kong.

Coinciding with these five major challenges has been the presence of the ethos of "post-materialist activism," which has figured as the most powerful explanation for mass support for universal suffrage among over a dozen possible explanatory factors in a survey conducted in June, 2003; that is, less than a month before the July 1, 2003 rally. Next, based on local and international data, the author contends that comparatively speaking, Hong Kong is long overdue for a transition to full democracy, and will probably enjoy a stable democracy should Beijing allow its implementation. Drawing on international experience, Sing offers arguments that the establishment of democracy in Hong Kong will enhance Hong Kong's governance and enable it to better weather major delegitimating challenges.

In Sing's analysis, one of the five major factors that have delegitimized the non-democratic structure has been the structural budget deficit and its aftermath. Wilson Wong has devoted a chapter to the causes and consequences of budget deficit in Hong Kong, given its detrimental effects on Hong Kong's governance.

Budget deficit and welfare cutting: deepening problems of governance

Wong argues that what the Asian financial crisis means to Hong Kong is not only a fleeting economic setback but the watershed of a new and tough economic era. The crisis, he alleges, has characterized the termination of a long period of enviable economic growth driven by economic bubbles and underscored the urgent need for restructuring its economy in order to lay a more solid economic foundation. He regards its fiscal system, which has been cleverly designed to fully exploit the advantages of the economic bloom by minimizing the tax burden and maximizing political stability, as ill preparing Hong Kong for facing up to structural change in the economy. The economic crisis has therefore quickly triggered a severe budget crisis.[12]

However, he claims, the doggedness of Hong Kong's fiscal problems cannot be attributed entirely to the paucity of technically sound fiscal options. He stresses that the root of the Hong Kong situation has been closely connected with the constraints of its new institutional setting created by the transfer of its sovereignty to China. The existing institutional setting of governance, particularly the lack of legitimacy of its non-democratic system in Hong Kong, has failed to endow its policy-makers with the required capacity and incentives to resolve the budget crisis with the requisite fiscal reform. Consequently, addressing the worsening budget problem becomes a prolonged and difficult process. He believes that the institutional setting of post-1997 Hong Kong has frustrated fiscal reform in at least three key ways.

Accordingly, the author argues that unless the current economic recovery rests on a more solid ground of a successful economic restructuring, Hong Kong will certainly experience another severe budget crisis once the economy sags again. Of no less worry, Wong projects a gloomy prospect for resolving the budget deficit in the absence of further democratic reform. He says that, apparently, the Chinese government hopes Donald Tsang can significantly promote the legitimacy of the Hong Kong government. However, Wong holds the view that Hong Kong needs more than a change of a man, but a change of system, to make its fiscal reform possible: "As long as the unbalanced fiscal structure and the lop-sized governance system do not change, the problems and constraints described in this chapter should remain relevant."

Similar to the main thrust of Wong's argument, Eliza Lee's chapter on welfare restructuring has also attributed the government's maintenance of an outdated welfare system and debatable welfare retrenchment to the lack of a democratic system. Lee makes it clear at the outset that the Hong Kong government, similar to other Asian newly industrialized countries, has openly rejected a high level of social spending and refused to recognize welfare as a set of social rights. Yet, in the aftermath of the Asian financial crisis, the financial capability of Hong Kong's residual welfare state was besieged with the challenge of overall budget deficit. As a result, she says the government has enforced budget cuts across all policy areas, including social welfare programs. In short, economic globalization and socioeconomic changes have forced Hong Kong to adopt a largely budget-driven approach to welfare restructuring and a retreat of the residual welfare state.

Lee finds that several structural limitations have existed in Hong Kong that reduce the impact of ordinary citizens resistance to the budget cuts. First, the lack of a high degree of democracy in Hong Kong has left the legislature and political parties little power to check the government. The absence of genuinely competitive elections have deprived welfare recipients from restraining the government from imposing unpopular welfare policies. Anther structural constraint has been that collective action has failed to be highly cohesive in the absence of strong civil society organizations. She notes that unconventional forms of political participation such as mass rallies are common in Hong Kong, but the average participation rate of citizens in civil society organizations has been far from high. Consequently, in the realm of social policies, for most welfare services, the well-organized groups are the public service professionals rather than ordinary welfare recipients. A corollary has been that the popular pressure has not been strong enough to bring about enormous concessions from the government, and that the government can shift the burden of blame.

Finally, Lee concludes that the liberal autocratic state of Hong Kong does not have enough legitimacy and capacity to integrate various social interests to effect major reforms in the present welfare system, despite the fact that the system is out of phase with its socioeconomic development. A case in point has been the incapacity of the state in reforming the public healthcare system, regardless of a pervasive appreciation that the current system is not financially sustainable. Likewise, the state has encountered grave difficulty in implementing reforms in the taxation system to buttress any further institutionalization of the welfare state. Such incapability, she claims, has not only worsened the crisis in the residual welfare state, but also entailed that the solution to the problem lies in further democratization.

While the Hong Kong community in general and the aforementioned chapters in particular have focused on internal reforms to address its governance challenges, Lucy Cummings and James Tang's chapter has contended that the external relations strategy of Hong Kong can also critically enhance Hong Kong's governance.

Improving Hong Kong's governance strengthening external relations

Cummings and Tang argue that Hong Kong's international character has always been a significant part of what makes it unique. They suggest that Hong Kong should adopt a more noticeable and globally responsible external agenda to strengthen local pride of place by showing Hong Kong's contribution to national and international stability and prosperity. In other words, Hong Kong should consider the global perspective in its efforts to improve governance locally.

To back up their arguments, their study rests on its own research into Hong Kong's external relations' performance by a 2004 telephone survey of global attitudes in Hong Kong. Their data reveal popular support for a more globally proactive Hong Kong, for enhancing Hong Kong's international reach and fulfilling its "Asia's World City" aspirations.

Cummings and Tang challenge critics who hold the position that encouraging Hong Kong's global moral obligations will sap obligations felt toward the Chinese nation or that globally responsible agendas have little relevance for the Hong Kong people. They argue that extending Hong Kong's "radius of responsibility" to the global level will not only promote national objectives, but also provide a hedge against the possibility that cohesion in Hong Kong will come at the expense of cohesion at the national or global level. They also contend that Hong Kong people would support a globally responsible agenda, and the governance of the SAR would be enhanced by advancing such an agenda given that it is a significant source of pride for the local population.

In addition, the authors argue, Hong Kong's political leaders have been too timid in exercising this basic law-given autonomy to manage Hong Kong's external relations. Both the Tung and Tsang administrations have limited their international outreach focus to advancing Hong Kong's value as a regional economic hub.

Poor governance and attitudes of voters

Next, we will explore Michael DeGolyer's chapter, which questions whether poor governance has impacted on voter orientation during elections. He first contextualizes his analysis by underscoring how Hong Kong people in general, and the democratic movement in particular, had long hoped and expected to directly elect all legislators in 2008.

Based on surveys of public attitudes and elections, DeGolyer charts the main outlines of public opinion in the context of the deteriorating governance in Hong Kong around 2004. He first notes that dissatisfaction with Tung seemed to be clearly affected by how he handled relations with the Mainland. Generally speaking, it appeared that inviting Beijing to intervene in Hong Kong's affairs was a primary cause of public dissatisfaction. The peak of dissatisfaction with the Hong Kong government's dealings with the Mainland came in June and July, 2004 following the Standing Committee of the National People's Congress interpretation of the basic law, which effectively blocked the transition to full democracy by 2008.

In the light of the poor governance amid Hong Kong's low degree of democracy, many respondents treated the elections in 2004 as a referendum asking for faster democratization. For example, it was found that the proportion supporting or opposing direct election of all the legislature's seats, the strategic focus of the electoral campaign among the democrats in the September election, was nearly identical to that of the votes taken up by pan-democrats.

So far, various contributors have dissected Hong Kong's governance problems by focusing on the causes of the mass rallies, the low social cohesion, and major issues with current institutions, including budget deficits and outdated social welfare models, among other things. Poor governance has created a palpable social division among the general public, with most pro-democratic camp voters aspiring to faster and fuller democratization in Hong Kong to address the issue. The final chapter rounds up the book by focusing on interactions between three important political actors to illuminate the macroscopic factors shaping not just the constitutional development of Hong Kong, but many other aspects of governance developed in this book.

Benny Tai first explains that he prefers to use a metaphor of a power game to help demystify the sacredness of the so-called "legal meaning" of constitutional texts. He notes that in almost all the constitutional controversies in Hong Kong, quarrels focused on the interpretation of some provisions of the Basic Law. By using the interactive game approach, Tai hopes to establish that constitutional interpretation is not rule-based, but player-based. Depending on the relative powers and limitations in the constitutional game, a player may have to adjust even its rule of interpretation as a result of strategic interactions with the interpretations of other players.

In short, Tai highlights three crucial actors engaged in the constitutional game from the early 2000s up until 2005 for Hong Kong. These actors are former chief executive Tung Chee-hwa, civil society in Hong Kong, and the Chinese government.

Tai notes that Beijing, as the third major player in the constitutional game, has become more actively engaged in Hong Kong's constitutional development in the wake of the July 1, 2003 rally. After the event, Beijing needed to reexamine the effectiveness of its strategies toward Hong Kong amid the sustained popular demands for further democratization, the decline in legitimacy of the Hong Kong government, and the incessant challenges to Tung's rule. All in all, Tai's analysis is that the new page in Hong Kong's constitutional development will hinge on the interactions of Beijing's renewed strategies toward Hong Kong, the strength of its civil society, and the tactics of Hong Kong's new chief executive, Donald Tsang.

Can Hong Kong's governance improve without democratic reform?

Remarkably, besides exposing the causes of Hong Kong's governance problems, several authors in this volume have concurred that further democratic reform is crucial to fundamentally resolving the issues of budget deficit, welfare retrenchment, low social cohesion, unsteady legitimacy, and challenges to political stability. In the short run, we have witnessed a rebound in personal support for the chief executive following the elevation to office by Donald Tsang. Yet it is highly doubtful that Hong Kong's non-democratic system can overcome its legitimation problem in the medium and long term owing to the following factors.

First, the distressing economic restructuring, structural fiscal deficits, severe social inequality, widely perceived cronyism, and grave executive–legislative tensions are very likely to continue to sap public support for the non-democratic system and maintain pressure for speedier democratization of Hong Kong at least in the medium term. Second, despite the economic vibrancy of mainland China, given the drastically growing economic dependence of Hong Kong on China since the handover, any economic downturn in China will significantly endanger Hong Kong's economy.

In short, the recent departure of Tung Chee-hwa is unlikely to bring an end to the legitimacy problem for the non-democratic government. The new chief executive, who has been indirectly elected by the 800-strong Election Committee, will deprive him of the much-needed public support derived from a free and fair election. The lack of a legitimacy system may continue to prevent the government from bluntly facing short-term and long-term challenges confronting Hong Kong, including the aging population, pollution, medical finance, fair competition, social inequality, and the excessive remuneration for some overpaid civil servants and employees in the publicly subsidized sectors. Though the new Hong Kong government shepherded by Donald Tsang may indicate better performance in terms of decisiveness and soundness in policy-making vis-à-vis that of Tung's era, while some of the aforementioned five major challenges remain unresolved, mass mobilizations for democratization may resurface in the medium and long run.

Notes

1 According to a survey conducted during the July 1 mass rally, the top two most important reasons for joining the protest pertained to the overall poor performance of the government, which were affirmed by about 92 percent (Chung, R. and Joseph M. Chan. "A Revelation of July 1. In that Mobilization Gives New Life to Democracy." 2005. see hkupop.hku.hk/, accessed July 3, 2005).
2 See the survey data from the University of Hong Kong (hkupop.hku.hk/).
3 The Democratic Party of Hong Kong has scored a record-breaking winning rate of close to 80 percent and won 92 seats amid the backdrop of a sharply rising voter turnout rate from 33.82 percent to 44.06 percent (*Ming Pao*, November 24, 2003). The 1.07 million voters who cast their votes represented a record of 44 percent of eligible voters, compared with a 36 percent turnout in the last election held in 1999. The Beijing-backed Democratic Alliance for Betterment of Hong Kong (DAB) won only 62 seats, a sharp decrease from the 83 scored during the same election of 1999 (*Asian Wall Street Journal*, November 25, 2003).
4 United Nations Development Programme (2002), Human Development Report, New York: Oxford University Press.
5 D. Kaufmann, A. Kraay, and M. Mastruzzi, "Governance Matters IV: Governance Indicators for 1996–2004" (World Bank Institute, 2005). This paper presents the latest update of our estimates of six dimensions of governance covering 209

countries and territories for five time periods: 1996, 1998, 2000, 2002 and 2004 (www.worldbank.org/wbi/governance/govdata/, accessed July 2, 2006). For a useful review of governance indicators see *Governance Indicators: A Users' Guide Joint* (United Nations Development Programme, European Commission publication, 2003) (www.undp.org/oslocentre/docs04/UserGuide.pdf).

6   Between 1960 and 1982, Hong Kong achieved a staggering average growth rate of 7 percent per year, ranked fifth in the world. Between 1980 and 1992, Hong Kong's average economic growth rate still rattled along at 6.7 percent per year. In 1995, Hong Kong's GDP per person gauged in purchasing power parity was the third highest globally. See World Bank, *World Development Report*. (New York: Oxford University Press, 1984): 218; Frederic C. Deyo, *Beneath the Miracle: Labor Subordination in the New Asian Industrialism* (Berkeley:University of California Press, 1989): 26.

7   In fact, the colonial government had already begun to face a legitimacy problem toward the end of colonial rule. See, for example, discussions in Ian Scott's *Political Change and the Crisis of Legitimacy in Hong Kong* (Hong Kong: Oxford University Press, 1989).

8   This and the above paragraph come from Sing *et al.* (2005).

9   See the poll conducted by the Chinese University of Hong Kong between March 1 and 8 (*Ming Pao*, March 24, 2004).

10   See the unpublished report by Sing *et al.* (2005).

11   Siu-kai Lau "Tung Chee-hwa's Governing Strategy: The Shortfall in Politics," in Lau Siu-kai (ed.) *The First Tung Chee-hwa Administration: The First Five Years of the Hong Kong Special Administrative Region* (Hong Kong: The Chinese University Press, 2002): 1–39.

12   This notion is used by Francis Fukuyama ("Social Capital, Civil Society and Development." *Third World Quarterly* 22, 1, 2001) who borrows it from Lawrence Harrison (1985).

References

Deyo, Frederic C. *Beneath the Miracle: Labor Subordination in the New Asian Industrialism*. Berkeley: University of California Press, 1989.

Fukuyama, Francis. "Social Capital, Civil Society and Development." *Third World Quarterly* 22 (February, 2001): 7–20.

Harrison, Lawrence E. *Underdevelopment is a State of Mind*. Cambridge: Center for International Affairs, Harvard University, 1985.

HKU Pop Site. July 1 Rally Feature Page (hkupop.hku.hk/, accessed July 3, 2005), 2003.

HKU Pop Site. People's trust in the HKSAR Government (hkupop.hku.hk/, accessed January 9, 2007), 2004.

Kaufmann, D., A. Kraay, and M. Mastruzzi. *Governance Matters IV: Governance Indicators for 1996–2004*. (papers.ssrn.com/sol3/papers.cfm?abstract_id=718081, accessed January 9, 2007), 2005.

Kuan, Hsin-Chi, and Lau Siu Kai. "Between Liberal Autocracy and Democracy: Democratic Legitimacy in Hong Kong." *Democratization* 9 (winter 2002): 58–76.

Lau, Siu-kai. "Tung Chee-hwa's Governing Strategy: The Shortfall in Politics." In *The First Tung Chee-hwa Administration: The First Five Years of the Hong Kong Special Administrative Region*, ed. Lau Siu-kai, pp. 1–39. Hong Kong: The Chinese University Press, 2002.

Scott, Ian. *Political Change and the Crisis of Legitimacy in Hong Kong*. Hong Kong: Oxford University Press, 1989.

Sing, Ming, Lucy Cummings, and James Tang. "A Roadmap for Good Governance in the Hong Kong Special Administrative Region." Unpublished paper, 2005.

Sing, Ming. "Public Support for Democracy in Hong Kong." *Democratization* 12 (April, 2005): 244–261.

United Nations Development Programme. *Governance Indicators: A Users' Guide Joint* (www.undp.org/oslocentre/docs04/UserGuide.pdf, accessed January 9, 2007), 2003.

World Bank. *World Development Report*. New York: Oxford University Press, 1984.

1 Who can mobilize Hong Kong people to protest?

A survey-based study of three large-scale rallies

Joseph M. Chan and Francis L. F. Lee

Introduction

To many government officials, politicians, and commentators, the July 1 demonstration in 2003 was a huge, pleasant, or unpleasant, surprise. Hong Kong used to have a good share of protests, but it is unprecedented to find more than half a million people taking to the streets to protest against the local government. The date "July 1" acquired new meanings, and the so-called "July 1 effect," no matter whether it really exists or what it can be referred to, has become part of the political discourse in Hong Kong. The demonstration also seems to have sparked off a pro-democracy movement. In the year that followed, a number of large-scale pro-democracy demonstrations were held.

The occurrence of these large-scale rallies raises a number of questions about Hong Kong people's political participation and mobilization. To state just a few: What are the social conditions that generate the large-scale rallies? How should we understand the rallies in relation to the history of political development in Hong Kong? Do they signify historical breaks or simply the expression of already existing undercurrents in Hong Kong society? Who participated in these rallies and why? How were they mobilized and by whom?

This chapter addresses the latter two questions by drawing upon onsite surveys of participants in the three rallies and two population surveys. Of particular interest is the effectiveness of a number of potentially significant mobilizing agencies – social and political groups, the mass media, and interpersonal networks. We believe the analysis should give us a better understanding of the contemporary social forces that work to shape the future of Hong Kong. It may provide clues to a better understanding of the past as well. In addition, the analysis allows us to revisit several arguments made by some commentators and stakeholders after the July 1 protest. For example, did people protest simply because they were unhappy with the economic situation? Did specific media outlets drive people to protest?

This chapter, in other words, focuses mainly on individual level analysis and on some of the micro-processes involved in the formation of protests. Nevertheless, we begin with a brief review of scholarly discussion about political participation and social mobilization in Hong Kong in order to put the protests into a larger, historical perspective. We then further explicate the focus of our empirical analysis, describe the survey methods, and present the findings. The implications of the results are discussed in the concluding section.

The rallies in historical perspectives

If the July 1 protest was a surprise to many, it was largely because the scene of thousands of protesters shouting slogans provided a stark contrast to the traditional image of Hong Kong citizens who shied away from political activism. This image of an apathetic public originated in the 1970s as part of an attempt to explain the enduring social stability of Hong Kong at the time. One account of this extraordinary stability attributed it to the prevalence of the refugee mentality among citizens, many of whom were themselves refugees from communist China. In spite of the dissatisfaction people might have with the colonial government, Hong Kong was for them the lifeboat. No one would risk rocking it. Other sociologists have come up with more systematic explanations. Most notably, King (1975) attributed the long stability of Hong Kong to the practice of what he labeled "the administrative absorption of politics," a process by which the colonial government co-opted local political elites into the decision-making and consultative bodies, thereby fostering an elite integration on the one hand and legitimation of political authority on the other. A second major explanation was offered by Lau (1982) who, taking a macro-level approach, identified the lack of integration between society and polity as the cornerstone of social stability in Hong Kong. To him, the "minimally-integrated social-political system" was the result of the colonial government's self-limitation in its exercise of power on the one hand, and the low expectations of the Hong Kong Chinese toward the government on the other. Social problems were seldom politicized and were often confined to families where private resources were mobilized for their resolution.

With these theories as the bases, Siu-kai Lau and Hsin-chi Kuan, among others, have conducted a series of survey studies of political culture in Hong Kong since the mid-1980s. The prevailing image of Hong Kong citizens derived from such studies is marked by political inefficacy, partial understanding of democracy, a negative view about "politics," distrust of politicians, inclination toward solving problems through personal means, and emphasis on social stability (e.g., Lau 1982, 1994, 1998, 2000; Lau and Kuan 1988, 1995, 1998; Kuan and Lau 2000, 2002; Wong and Lui 2000). As Ku (2002: 348–349) put it, the traditional characterization of Hong Kong people (which she does not agree with) derived from these studies is as follows:

> [Hong Kong people are] placing personal gain first, poor in morality and civic mindedness, ignoring or participating reservedly and intermittently in social activities not directly related to their personal interest, resorting to personalized approach and effort to solve their life problems or to improve their living standard rather than employing political or collective action.

Certainly, over the years, researchers have recognized gradual developments in Hong Kong's political culture. By the early 1990s, Lau and Kuan (1995) argued that many Hong Kong people had already become "attentive spectators" in politics. By the late 1990s, Kuan (1998) acknowledged that years of political transition had given rise to a vibrant political society in Hong Kong. Following this line of research and thinking, public participation in the large-scale protests in 2003 and 2004 may be regarded as signifying a new stage of development in Hong Kong's civic culture, especially in its participatory dimension.

However, not all scholars share the emphasis on stability and gradual evolution. Lui and Chiu (2000b), for instance, have observed that researchers tend to neglect the social undercurrents for change because of their statistical approaches. Such undercurrents would be more recognizable if more attention was paid to collective actions and social conflicts in Hong Kong. As Hong Kong society is pluralistic and there is a lack of a democratic system that can effectively handle the pluralism, the outbreak of conflicts results. Since the 1970s, Hong Kong has witnessed the growth of collective behaviors as a means for the expression of public opinion and the struggle for interests and rights (Cheung and Louie 1991; Lau and Wan 1997; Lui 1989, 2002).

While recognizing that social movement is subject to the confines of the political environment, Lui and Chiu (2000a) argued that collective behavior can act to change the establishment. Unlike collective behavior in the 1970s that arose in response to purely domestic factors, collective behaviors became more political in orientation during the transition period and in post-handover Hong Kong. The undercurrent for change is also detected in the public sphere where discursive battles are constantly fought. In a study of the public discourse on democracy and handover, Ku (2002) found that Hong Kong people do not just care about economics and ignore politics and that society and polity are not at a safe distance from one another.

In fact, political scientists dissatisfied with the "psycho-cultural approach" to political participation have also pointed out that a large part of Hong Kong people's apparent voting apathy was actually the result of people's understanding of the limitations of the political system (Tse 1997). Political culture is not so much a cause as an effect of institutional change (or the lack of it) (Lo 1999). At the same time, scholars argued that the conception of political participation should be broadened to include various forms of informal or non-institutionalized political activity. As Lam (2004: 43) defined it, political participation can be referred:

> to lawful or unlawful activities of support, making demands, debates, and other forms of expression communicated verbally and/or through the media targeted at the PRC government, and/or the ROC government, and the Hong Kong government ... acts of political participation ... also include those targeted at private institutions, such as university administrations and businesses that are designed to pose challenges to existing standards. In terms of the sites where this type of politics takes place, they are relatively

peripheral. In terms of the variety of their targets, they are relatively plural. When such a broad definition is adopted, researchers have pointed out that Hong Kong people's level of participation can be regarded as high even by international standards (DeGolyer and Scott 1996). A "tradition" of political participation during "major events" can also be recognized as stretching back into the 1950s.

If we follow these latter views, then the July 1 protest in 2003 and the subsequent large-scale rallies may actually be understood as manifestations of the undercurrents and social conflicts that have been existing and deepening in Hong Kong society over the past three decades. From this perspective we may even turn the usual question about mobilization on its head. Instead of asking why people can be mobilized in a certain case, we may actually need to ask why people are not mobilized more often. It is our contention that analysis of the actual mobilization processes and the influences of various mobilizing agencies (or the lack thereof) can inform the above perspectives which have structured previous academic analysis on political participation and mobilization in Hong Kong.

Mobilization and mobilizing agencies

Theorists studying social movements have recognized that protests may be best understood as produced by a confluence of macro-, meso-, and micro-level factors (McAdam *et al.* 1988; Snow and Benford 1992; Zuo and Benford 1995). Adverse macro-level social and political conditions would lead to grievances among citizens, which in turn become the bases for protests. At the same time, the characteristics of the political system would structure the range of opportunities and possible routes of actions for citizens. At the meso-level, the role of civic associations, social organizations, political parties, and media institutions in the formation of protests have to be considered. At the micro-level, individuals' decisions to participate in demonstrations are likely to be driven by a number of social and psychological factors. At the same time, interpersonal communication among citizens within their social networks may facilitate the flow of social influence and information related to the protests.

Macro- and meso-level factors are certainly important in explaining the occurrence of the three large-scale demonstrations concerned. Since the Asian Financial turmoil in late 1997, Hong Kong citizens have experienced years of continual economic decline. The Hong Kong government was generally considered as incompetent in dealing with a range of social and political crises. In early 2003, Hong Kong citizens' grievances were further aggravated by the SARS outbreak and government performance throughout the controversy on national security legislation. Before the first July 1 demonstration, a deep legitimacy crisis of the Hong Kong government had been in place (Chan and So 2003; Ku 2001, 2002). These situational factors constituted the macro-level conditions for the large-scale demonstrations to take place.

At the meso-level, years of political development in Hong Kong have con-tributed to the rise of a political society in the city (Kuan 1998). A key part of this political society is a range of civic associations, pressure groups, and polit-ical parties (Lui 1999). Some of these groups act as organizers of political activ-ities for citizens to participate. However, a widely recognized weakness of many pressure groups and political parties in Hong Kong is that they have neither large memberships nor strong group or party "machines" (Choy 1999). Apart from a few leftist organizations and political parties, the mobilizing power of pressure groups and political parties in Hong Kong is very limited.

Nevertheless, this weakness is partially compensated by the news media. As the media treat pressure groups and political parties as major news sources, they legitimize the groups and parties as spokespersons on social and political matters (Chan 1992; Fung 1995). At the same time, researchers have found that Hong Kong people, no matter whether they are politically active or not, do pay close attention to public affairs via the mass media (Chan and Lee 1992; Lau and Kuan 1995). Information and persuasive messages from social and political groups, therefore, can be effectively transmitted to the wider public via the media.

The above paragraphs, admittedly have provided only a very brief description of the macro- and meso-level conditions for the large-scale demonstrations in Hong Kong in 2003 and 2004. Yet they provide the context for the current study, which focuses on the micro-level processes that occurred under such conditions.

Every rally has a formation process. Central to the formation process are social interactions and various kinds of communications. Information has to be transmitted; common frames of reference and shared meanings have to be con-structed; the rights and wrongs of controversies have to be debated; calls to action have to be issued and listened to. Given certain macro- and meso-level conditions, social interactions and communications can create a "mobilizing social atmosphere" that generates large-scale participation among the populace. Arguably, this social atmosphere existed before the July 1 protest in 2003.

Mobilizing agencies are key actors in the pre-protest social communication processes. In this chapter, mobilizing agencies are broadly defined as any indi-viduals, groups, or organizations which act to encourage other people to participate in a political activity. Different mobilizing agencies could have many different reasons or motivations to mobilize others. A political party may want more people to show up to support a political cause, while some people may call upon friends to participate just because they want companions. But no matter what their interests are, their abilities to call upon others to act would largely affect the scale of a political activity.

As stated at the beginning, the current analysis pays special attention to three types of mobilizing agencies. First, by being the organizers of rallies, social and political groups make citizens' collective actions outside formal political institu-tions possible. But whether social and political groups are powerful mobilizing agencies would depend upon a number of factors, including their membership sizes, the connections between the groups and their supporters, and whether the group supporters are likely to pay attention to the group leaders' opinions and calls to action.

Second, mass media also have an important role in the formation of large-scale rallies. They are the most important platform for the communication of political information and influence in a modern society. However, a distinction may be drawn between the media being mobilizers and the media being facilitators (Chan and Lee 2007). Information and persuasive messages from the media are the basis upon which citizens form their political opinions and decide whether to participate in political activities. In this sense, the media are always important in facilitating citizens' participation. Yet specific media outlets may go a step further and act as mobilizers by directly encouraging their audience members to participate in certain activities. For the three large-scale rallies, the Chinese government has recognized a few media outlets in Hong Kong, such as the *Apple Daily* and a number of prominent radio phone-in talk shows, as mobilizers. For various reasons, clearly distinguishing between facilitating and mobilizing influences is not easy in survey-based research, yet the following analysis should still give us some insights into the issues involved.

Third, the current study treats common citizens as constituting a potentially important mobilizing agency. Citizens are not always passive consumers of information and opinions from the mass media. On the contrary, they often transmit the information and opinions to people within their social networks. In other words, interpersonal communication is also an important channel for the flow of information and influence, and when opportunities for political participation arrive, the "opinion leaders" in a social network are likely to call upon others to participate. In fact, such interpersonal persuasion can be particularly effective owing to the directness of the persuasion (often one-to-one and face-to-face) and the trust existing within interpersonal social networks.

Certainly, an individual's likelihood to join a specific rally is also dependent upon his or her social and political attitudes. To make the analysis more complete, this study also examines three types of social and political attitudes. First, protest participation may be driven by general participatory dispositions; that is, attitudes which tend to generate higher levels of participation in many kinds of political activities (e.g., interests in politics). Second, each individual rally would address a set of specific issues. The 2003 July 1 demonstration, for example, addressed the issue of national security legislation, while the 2004 July 1 demonstration dealt mainly with democratic reform. Specific issue opinions, therefore, are likely to have substantial explanatory influence on citizens' participation in specific rallies. Finally, citizens' participation in rallies may also be driven simply by a general sense of dissatisfaction. In the past few years, Hong Kong citizens have been deeply dissatisfied with government performance as well as the society's economic situation. In fact, for the three large-scale rallies under study, both general political and economic dissatisfaction are likely to have played an important role in driving citizens to march on the streets.

Survey method and analytical approach

Data used in this chapter were derived from onsite surveys conducted during the three large-scale rallies in 2003 and 2004 and two population surveys. For the onsite surveys, there was no way to obtain a comprehensive sampling frame. The best we could do was to design a method that would approach a probability sampling method.[1] In the July 1 demonstration in 2003, data were collected when the demonstrators gathered at Victoria Park. The space in which the demonstrators gathered was partitioned into nine areas (with a 3×3 grid system). Ten pairs of interviewers were scattered around the areas, with two pairs in the central area. Interviewers were instructed to move along a round trip, whereby they sampled one cluster of six respondents (aged 15 or above) every ten minutes. This design strives to spread the selection of respondents over space and time and to minimize biases introduced by interviewers' arbitrary decisions. In order to catch people who might join the demonstrations *en route*, we deployed the interviewing teams along the marching route shortly after the marching started. They were instructed to interview the person who came closest to them one minute after an interview. All respondents filled out the questionnaire by themselves. The procedure resulted in 1,154 completed interviews with a response rate of 87.2 percent. The sampling method for the two other demonstrations followed basically the same logic.[2] The 2004 January 1 onsite survey generated 788 completed interviews and a response rate of 83.8 percent, while the 2004 July 1 survey generated 610 completed interviews and a response rate of 85.0 percent.

Due to time concern, in all three surveys, a long and a short questionnaire were prepared. Therefore, some questions were answered by only about half of the whole sample. For convenience of analysis, we examined only the long questionnaire sample in the 2003 July 1 survey ($N = 597$). However, due to the small total sample sizes in the other two, we analyzed both the long and short questionnaire samples together. In any case, the valid number of answers involved in each analysis is given in the statistical tables below.

The two population surveys were conducted in March and September, 2004 respectively.[3] In both surveys, the computer-assisted telephone interviewing system was used with trained interviewers conducting the interviews. The target population is all Hong Kong Cantonese-speaking residents aged between 18 and 70 in the March survey (and aged between 15 and 70 in the September survey). The sampling procedure involved randomly selecting numbers from telephone directories, with additional procedures used to include non-listed numbers and to select a particular respondent from a household. For the March survey, a total of 983 interviews were completed, yielding a response rate of 51.5 percent. For the September survey, a total of 800 interviews were completed with a response rate of 69.3 percent.[4]

The three onsite surveys are important for the analysis of the role of mobilizing agencies in the formation of the three rallies. Besides demographics, the participants' connections with social groups, connections with people in their own social network, media use, and perceived influence of mobilizing agencies are analyzed. Next, data from the population surveys are used to present a multivariate analysis of the predictors of people's participation in the two July 1 demonstrations, with special attention paid to the set of mobilizing agencies and attitudinal variables discussed in the previous paragraphs.

Data analysis and results

Characteristics of the demonstrators

Table 1.1 provides the demographic profiles of the demonstrators in the three large-scale rallies. All five demographic variables register a statistically significant relationship with the "rally" variable in cross-tabulation analyses; that is, the demographic profiles of the demonstrators in the three rallies do differ. However, such statistically significant differences are less important than the substantive similarities. As Table 1.1 shows, in all three rallies, about 60 percent to 70 percent of the participants were male. There was also a significant presence of young people in the rallies, especially in the July 1 demonstration in 2003.

The rally participants are generally highly educated and belong to the middle class.[5] In the three rallies, between 55 percent and 59 percent of the participants hold a college or university degree. When asked to state whether their families belong to "upper class," "middle class," or "lower class," between 62 percent

Table 1.1 Demographics of participants in the three major rallies

	July 1 rally 2003 *(%)*	*January 1 rally* 2004 *(%)*	*July 1 rally* 2004 *(%)*
Sex[a]			
Male	60.1	67.2	65.4
Education[a]			
College educated	55.1	55.5	58.1
Middle school	43.1	39.6	38.3
Age[a]			
15–29	44.1	23.0	35.0
30–49	48.4	58.8	49.4
Occupation[a]			
Professional or semi-professional	40.6	41.1	30.7
Service/clerk	17.7	18.9	29.5
Class[a]			
Upper class	62.9	70.7	65.7
Middle class	2.2	1.6	2.5

Note
a Significant relationships ($p \ll 0.05$) with "rally" as a variable in a cross-tabulation analysis (with the Chi-square test).

and 71 percent of the participants regarded themselves as belonging to the middle class. Regarding occupation, about 40 percent of the participants in the 2003 July 1 demonstration and in the 2004 January 1 demonstration are professionals or semi-professionals, while the corresponding proportion in the 2004 July 1 rally is about 30 percent.

The fact that the demonstrators tend to be educated middle-class professionals has two implications in relation to the roles of different mobilizing agencies. First, we can expect educated and middle-class people to engage more actively in various kinds of mediated communication. Because of their levels of education, they are likely to pay more attention to the news media. Because of their higher levels of income, they are also more likely to have access to the internet. Therefore, they are more likely to have received information about the rallies from various media channels. But at the same time, these people are not likely to be blind followers of social activists' or media's calls to action. Even though they may have taken media information and activists' opinions into account, they were much more likely to be active interpreters than passive receivers of information and persuasive messages.[6]

Table 1.2 supports the expectation that the demonstrators use various kinds of media to larger extents when compared to the Hong Kong population as a whole. Again, the distributions of the various media use variables differ across the three rallies, yet the substantive similarities are more important than the statistical differences. Using data from population surveys, Table 1.2 shows that, while only about half of the Hong Kong population would read a newspaper on a daily basis, about 64 percent to 72 percent of the demonstrators in the rallies read a newspaper every day. The same applies to television news watching: the proportions of demonstrators watching television news every day are larger than the corresponding population figure.[7]

At the same time, demonstrators are more likely than citizens in general to have access to the internet. Even more remarkably, a significant part of the demonstrators' internet use is related to public affairs. In the 2003 July 1 rally, for example, 37.4 percent of participants with online access (that is, about 32 percent of all participants) reported that they share information about public affairs with others on the internet frequently. At the same time, about 30 percent of all demonstrators in the same rally reported sharing opinions about public affairs online frequently. About 29 percent of all participants in the rally even reported having shared information about the July 1 rally itself frequently.[8]

Regarding specific media outlets, Table 1.2 shows a substantial difference between the distribution of readers of different newspapers in the three rallies on the one hand, and the distribution of readers of different newspapers in the Hong Kong population as a whole on the other. While the *Oriental Daily* is the most popular newspaper in Hong Kong, and the September population survey has found that 35.0 percent of respondents were primarily readers of the paper, only about 10 percent to 23 percent of demonstrators in the three rallies were readers of the *Oriental Daily*. Instead, about half of the demonstrators in each of the three rallies were primarily readers of the *Apple Daily*, while about 15 percent to

Table 1.2 Communication behavior and social connections of the demonstrators

	July 1 rally 2003 (%)	January 1 rally 2004 (%)	July 1 rally 2004 (%)	Population (%)
Read newspaper daily[a,c]	64.7	69.9	71.9	51.1
Watch TV news daily[a,c]	72.5	83.1	76.2	69.5
Meet friends frequently[a]	71.7	49.9	–	46.4
Online[a]	85.5	75.9	79.5	62.5
Frequently use the internet[b]				
Chat room[a]	18.2	9.9	–	–
General discussion[a]	30.3	11.0	–	–
Connection[a]	44.2	32.3	–	–
Share information[a]	37.4	31.9	–	–
Share opinions[a]	35.3	26.6	–	–
Share rally information[a]	34.2	26.4	–	–
Most frequently read newspaper[a,c]				
Apple Daily	49.5	51.4	52.1	32.7
Oriental	22.4	12.8	10.3	35.0
Ming Pao	15.7	19.1	19.8	10.0

Notes
a Significant relationships ($p \ll 0.05$) with "rally" as a variable in a cross-tabulation analysis (with the Chi-square test).
b Questions about internet use and access are based on the long questionnaire which was answered by only about half of the sample.
c The population figures for newspaper reading and television viewing are derived from a population survey conducted in September, 2001 by the Institute for Asia-Pacific Studies. Other population figures are derived from the September population survey employed in this chapter.

20 percent were readers of *Ming Pao*. These figures seem to support the Chinese government's accusation of *Apple Daily* being a mobilizer in the rallies. We will return to this issue later in the discussion section.

Table 1.2 also shows that the rally participants have close connections with their friends and relatives. When asked whether they would agree with the statement "I have frequent gatherings with my friends and relatives," 71.7 percent of the participants in the 2003 July 1 demonstration expressed agreement. The figure dropped substantially to 49.9 percent in the 2004 January 1 demonstration, but it is still somewhat higher than the figure of 46.4 percent derived from the September population survey.

As discussed earlier, the current study treats citizens themselves as constituting a mobilizing agency in the rallies. People can encourage their acquaintances to participate with them. The onsite surveys strongly suggest that it was the case in all three rallies. Besides the findings in Table 1.2, Table 1.3 shows that most demonstrators did not participate alone in the three rallies. It is especially true in the two July 1 demonstrations, in which only 7.5 percent and 17.2 percent of the participants joined the protests alone. Instead, participants tended to join the protests together with their family members or friends.

Table 1.3 Demonstrators' group participation and companions in rally

	July 1 rally 2003 (%)	January 1 rally 2004 (%)	July 1 rally 2004 (%)
Members of groups[a]	27.0	23.4	18.2
Participate in group activities[a]			
Frequently	18.2	34.3	37.3
Very frequently	11.5	12.4	12.7
Rally companions			
No companion[a]	7.5	25.5	17.2
Spouse[a]	16.1	21.7	9.0
Family[a]	29.0	27.8	27.4
Boyfriend/girlfriend	8.5	6.0	7.7
Friends	42.4	21.3	40.8
Schoolmates[a]	8.0	1.5	5.1
Colleagues[a]	6.2	1.3	4.3
Groups[a]	4.2	1.8	3.8
Sectors	0.7	0.6	0.5

Note

a Significant relationships ($p \ll 0.05$) with "rally" as a variable in a cross-tabulation analysis (with the Chi-square test).

Last but not least, very few participants joined the three rallies together with the social or political groups to which they belonged, nor did many participants join the rallies together with the "social sector" to which they belonged. This suggests that social and political groups had very limited mobilizing power in the three rallies. Another finding suggesting the same point is that most participants in the three rallies did not belong to any social or political groups, and among the participants who did belong to certain social groups, many did not participate in the groups' activities frequently. Based on the figures in Table 1.3, the percentage of demonstrators in the 2003 July 1 rally who belonged to certain groups *and* participated in the groups' activities frequently is only about 8 percent. The corresponding figures for the other two demonstrations are 11 percent and 9 percent respectively.

Perceived influence of mobilizing agencies

In the three onsite surveys, respondents were asked to evaluate how important the calls to action issued by various people and groups are to their decision to participate in the rallies. The survey items cover all three types of mobilizing agencies. Table 1.4 summarizes the results.

When the three rallies are compared, we see that all the percentages declined from the 2003 July 1 demonstration to the 2004 July 1 demonstration. It shows that various mobilizing agencies were much more important in the 2003 July 1 demonstration than in the demonstration one year later. This is not hard to

Table 1.4 Importance of calls to actions issued by various agents

	July 1 rally 2003 (%)	January 1 rally 2004 (%)	July 1 rally 2004 (%)
Importance of calls from			
Newspaper report[a]	69.2	51.0	35.0
Radio news[a]	66.7	52.2	32.3
Television news[a]	63.9	47.6	34.2
Radio phone-in programs[a]	68.7	58.8	33.8
Internet (including email)[a]	59.6	39.6	23.5
Family[a]	56.5	45.3	24.7
Friend, schoolmate, colleague[a]	69.3	52.9	39.1
Public figures[a]	49.7	45.5	24.6
Political parties[a]	47.9	40.5	22.8
Groups[a]	45.4	30.4	19.0

Note
a Significant relationships ($p \ll 0.05$) with "rally" as a variable in a cross-tabulation analysis (with the Chi-square test).

understand. The 2003 July 1 demonstration was a historic event. It was the largest public rally following the handover, and the second largest rally in the history of Hong Kong. It is reasonable to expect that a larger range of mobilizing forces was at play in the formation of such a historic rally.

The 2004 July 1 demonstration, on the other hand, was more or less the "sequel" of the demonstration one year earlier. This may be shown by a number of findings. First, 80.8 percent of respondents in the 2004 July 1 onsite survey reported having participated in the July 1 rally one year earlier. Second, when asked whether their participation in the demonstration was for the purpose of "sharing the experience of participation," 78.8 percent of the respondents reported positively. Third, when asked about when they decided to participate in the 2004 July 1 demonstration, 55.6 percent of respondents selected the answering category "after last year's July 1 demonstration." What these findings suggest is that the experience of participating in the 2003 July 1 rally itself may have been one of the most important factors driving citizens to participate in the July 1 rally again.

Despite the difference among the three rallies, when perceived levels of influence of the mobilizing agencies are compared with each other within each rally, we can actually see that the three surveys shared a consistent pattern. Mass media and friends were regarded as the most influential agencies in all three cases, followed by family members and communication via the internet. Relatively speaking, the calls from public figures, political parties, and social and political groups were not perceived as particularly important. This is consistent with the findings in Tables 1.2 and 1.3. Interpersonal network and mass media were the two more important sources of influence in the three demonstrations. Social and political groups, on the other hand, were not major mobilizers.

Predictors of participation in the 2003 July 1 demonstration

We now turn to the analysis with the population survey data. First, in the March 2004 survey, we asked whether respondents had participated in the 2003 July 1 demonstration. We therefore conducted a logistic regression analysis on the factors associated with participation. Following our discussions and the analysis in the previous sections, we included six communication variables in the analysis. They are: (1) newspaper reading (time per day), (2) television news watching (time per day), (3) whether a respondent is a reader of the *Apple Daily* (*Apple Daily* reader = 1, others = 0), (4) whether a respondent is a reader of *Ming Pao* (*Ming Pao* reader = 1, others = 0), (5) connection with social or political groups (answer to a five-point Likert-scaled statement on whether respondents have close connections with social or political groups), and (6) connection with friends and relatives (average of answers to two five-point Likert-scaled questions on how frequently they have gatherings with friends and relatives).

The analysis also examines the impact of political and social attitudes on participation. Participatory disposition variables include concern with public affairs (answer to a five-point Likert-scaled statement on whether the respondents were concerned with the issue of legalizing soccer gambling in Hong Kong) and internal efficacy (average of answers to two five-point Likert-scaled statements). Specific issue opinions include respondents' opinion on national security legislation (level of support expressed with a five-point Likert scale) and opinion on democratization (level of support for direct elections of chief executive in 2007 expressed with a five-point Likert scale). General (dis)satisfaction included respondents' evaluation of the performance of the Hong Kong and Chinese government (both measured with a 0 to 10 scale), as well as citizens' evaluation of the economic situation in Hong Kong (average of answers to two five-point Likert-scaled questions).

Four demographic were also controlled. At the same time, for the purpose of comparison, we also conducted regression analysis on respondents' participation in other protests and rallies, as well as their participation in voting in the 1998 or 2000 Legislative Council elections. The results are summarized in Table 1.5.

The goodness of fit of the regression models can be discerned with pseudo-R^2, which is analogous to R^2 in multiple regression analysis. Table 1.5 shows that the pseudo-R^2 value is 24.8 percent for participation in the 2003 July 1 protest, but only about 11 percent in the other two cases. This is not surprising, since the regression model includes issue attitudes – attitude toward national security legislation – specifically relevant to the July 1 protest.

Regarding individual independent variables, education emerges as the only demographic variable having a significant relationship with participation in the July 1 protest. More importantly, consistent with our earlier analysis, respondents' connection with social and political groups has no relationship at all with participation in the July 1 protest. Instead, group connection is significantly related to respondents' participation in other protests and rallies. It suggests that,

Table 1.5 Predictors of participation in the July 1, 2003 demonstration

Demographics	July 1, 2003 protest	Other protests	Voting
Sex	−0.28	−0.11	−0.20
Age	0.04	−0.00	0.26***
Education	0.24**	0.09	−0.01
Income	−0.01	0.02	0.05
Communication:			
Newspaper reading	−0.03	0.08	0.03
TV news	−0.00	0.07	0.05
Apple Daily reader	0.72**	0.20	−0.06
Ming Pao reader	0.92**	0.78*	−0.07
Group connection	0.14	0.31**	0.13
Social connection	0.07	0.23	0.20*
Participatory dispositions:			
Internal efficacy	0.14	0.27^	0.32**
Concern with public affairs	0.10	0.07	0.14
Specific issue opinions:			
National security law	−0.63***	−0.02	−0.22*
Support democracy	0.41***	0.20	0.12
General satisfaction:			
HK government performance	−0.27***	−0.18**	−0.06
Central government performance	−0.02	0.00	0.03
Societal economy	−0.00	−0.00	−0.07
Psuedo-R^2	24.8%	10.6%	11.3%
Chi-square	229.7***	72.9***	118.3***
N	814	814	780

Notes
Entries are unstandardized logistic regression coefficients.
***$p \ll 0.001$.
**$p \ll 0.01$.
*$p \ll 0.05$.
^$p \ll 0.06$.

where small-scale rallies and protests are concerned, being connected with particular social and political groups is indeed a significant predictor of participation. But the same does not apply to large-scale rallies such as the 2003 July 1 demonstration.

Different from the findings from the onsite surveys, there is no relationship between social connection and participation. Instead, a significant relationship exists between social connection and voting. Nevertheless, it should be noted that the current social connection variable is essentially measuring the density of citizens' social network (by asking them whether they contacted their friends and relatives frequently). Therefore, what the findings suggest is that mobilization of social capital is not dependent upon the density of the network. People are not more or less likely to call upon friends to participate simply because they meet more frequently. Other properties and characteristics of social networks may be more important in this respect.

Among the media use variables, only the two newspaper readership variables have statistically significant associations with participation in the 2003 July 1 protest. The fact that both *Apple Daily* and *Ming Pao* readers are more likely than other citizens to have participated in the July 1 protest calls into question the argument of specific media outlets as mobilizing agencies. As discussed earlier, the mass media are important providers of information and opinions to the general public. As long as media put public affairs at the top of their news agenda, they would unquestionably be the facilitators of people's opinion formation and political participation. Coupled with the phenomenon of selective exposure to media with viewpoints similar to those of oneself, it is understandable why the two papers' readers are more likely to have participated in the 2003 July 1 protest, as both papers have devoted large amounts of news space to cover the national security legislation debate and the prelude to the July 1 protest. However, if media outlets such as the *Apple Daily* were not only facilitators but also mobilizers, the relationship between participation in the protest and reading the *Apple Daily* should be much stronger than that between participation in the protest and reading *Ming Pao* (which has refrained from calling upon citizens to join the protest). Table 1.5 shows that this was not the case. Therefore, media impact on people's participation in the July 1, 2003 protest is better understood as facilitation through agenda-setting and information provision, instead of mobilization through direct persuasion.

Regarding political and social attitudes, Table 1.5 shows that participation in the July 1, 2003 protest was not explained by participatory dispositions at all. Concern with public affairs has no relationship with all three dependent variables. Internal efficacy, which has a significant relationship with voting and a marginally significant relationship with participation in other protests, registers no significant relationship with participation in the July 1, 2003 protest. On the other hand, participation in the July 1 protest was driven by issue-specific opinions – support for democratization and opposition to national security legislation – and a general dissatisfaction toward the Hong Kong government.

It is notable that there is no significant relationship between satisfaction with the Hong Kong economy and participation in the July 1 protest. However, this should not be taken as meaning that the economic situation is irrelevant. It should be noted that evaluation of the economic situation is significantly related to support for democracy (Pearson $r = -0.17$, $p \ll 0.001$) and evaluations of the Hong Kong and Chinese governments (Pearson $r = 0.30$ and 0.25 respectively, $p \ll 0.001$ in both cases). It is therefore possible that the economic situation could lead to declining support for the government and increasing support for democratization, which in turn would lead to participation in protest. This latter argument is actually supported by the data. When support for democracy and performances of the Chinese and Hong Kong governments are removed from the regression model, a significant relationship between evaluation of the Hong Kong economy and participation in the July 1 protest would appear (beta = -0.32, $p \ll 0.02$). In other words, satisfaction with government performance and support for democracy have mediated the relationship between economic evaluation and participation in the July 1 protest. More concretely, it means that dissatisfaction with the economic situation would translate into political activism when the economic problems are attributed to failure of the government and/or the political system.

Predictors of participation in the 2004 July 1 demonstration

To examine the predictors of participation in the 2004 July 1 demonstration, logistic regression analysis is conducted with the data derived from the September 2004 survey, which has included a question on whether citizens have participated in the 2004 July 1 demonstration. The regression model is basically the same as that shown in Table 1.5, with a number of minor adjustments. Concern with public affairs was measured in the September survey by a five-point Likert-scaled question on respondents' concern with public affairs in general. Support for democratization was measured by a five-point Likert-scaled question on respondents' support for "quicker democratization in Hong Kong," instead of support for direct election of the chief executive in 2007.[9] National security legislation was no longer an issue in the 2004 July 1 demonstration. In place of it, a variable on citizens' concern with press freedom is included (measured by respondents' agreement with the statement "There is less and less press freedom in Hong Kong," expressed with a five-point Likert scale). Finally, economic evaluation was not included in the September survey, so it was removed from the regression model. Again, besides participation in the July 1 protest, the regression model is also used to predict voting in the 2004 Legislative Council election for the purpose of comparison. The results are summarized in Table 1.6.

The explanatory power of the regression model, measured by pseudo-R^2, is 26.2 percent for participation in the July 1 protest in 2004 and 19.2 percent for voting in the 2004 Legislative Council elections. Similar to Table 1.5, Table 1.6 shows that there is no significant relationship between social and group connections and participation in the 2004 July 1 demonstration. There is also no relationship between social connection and voting in the 2004 LegCo election. Readers of the *Apple Daily* are more likely to have participated in the 2004 July 1 protest and voted in the 2004 LegCo election. However, there is no relationship between reading *Ming Pao* and participation in the two political activities. As pointed out earlier, this is a pattern of findings that would lend support to the argument that certain media outlets in Hong Kong, and the *Apple Daily* in particular, have served as mobilizing agencies in the formation of the large-scale rallies.

Regarding political attitudes, Table 1.6 shows that participation in the 2004 July 1 protest is not related to internal efficacy or concern with public affairs. Again, participation in the large-scale rally was associated only with specific issue opinions and a general dissatisfaction with the performance of the Hong Kong government.

Two other findings from Table 1.6 should be noted. First, different from the findings in Table 1.5 regarding voting in the 1998 and 2000 LegCo elections,

Table 1.6 Predictors of participation in the July 1, 2004 demonstration

Demographics	*July 1, 2004 protest*	*LegCo voting 2004*
Sex	−0.83**	0.26
Age	0.05	0.59***
Education	0.10	0.25***
Income	0.14^	0.01
Communication		
Newspaper reading	−0.02	0.08
TV news	−0.08	0.10
Apple Daily reader	0.65*	0.63**
Ming Pao reader	0.37	0.01
Group connection	0.04	0.09
Social connection	0.04	0.09
Participatory dispositions		
Internal efficacy	0.08	0.20*
Concern with public affairs	0.07	0.03
Specific issue opinions		
Less and less press freedom	0.20^	0.01
Support democracy	1.03***	0.27**
General satisfaction		
HK government performance	−0.22**	−0.10^
Central government performance	0.13	0.07
Psuedo-R^2	26.2%	19.2%
Chi-square	142.0***	198.4***
N	752	752

Notes
Entries are unstandardized logistic regression coefficients.
***$p \ll 0.001$.
**$p \ll 0.01$.
*$p \ll 0.05$.
^$p \ll 0.06$.

Table 1.6 shows that voting in the 2004 LegCo election was driven by a support for democratization and a general dissatisfaction with the performance of the Hong Kong government. This is highly suggestive of the so-called "July 1 effect" on Hong Kong citizens' political participation. At the very least, the meaning of the act of voting seems to have changed somewhat following the series of large-scale rallies in 2003 and 2004.

Second, Table 1.6 shows that there is no relationship between evaluation of the Chinese government's performance and participation in the 2004 July 1 protest. Despite the fact that the Chinese government has adopted a high-key approach in the debate on democratic reform in 2004, Hong Kong citizens seemed not to be ready to directly confront the Chinese government. In a bivariate analysis, it can be shown that participants in the 2004 July 1 rally did have more negative evaluations of the Chinese government (mean = 5.21 vs. 5.60, $p < 0.05$). But the association becomes insignificant once other variables are taken into account. Protesters in Hong Kong do not have negative feelings toward the Chinese government per se. It is only the Chinese government's handling of democratic reform in Hong Kong that has led to negative sentiments among supporters of democracy in the city.

Conclusion

In sum, the profiles of demonstrators vary significantly across the three huge rallies in terms of proportions. However, they share important similarities when compared with the population as a whole. It should be stressed that the large-scale rallies were participated in by people from all walks of life and from different social strata, but in terms of proportion a typical demonstrator in the three rallies may be characterized as follows: mainly male, college educated, young, semi-professional or professional, and belonging to the middle class. This social group is generally considered to constitute the very basis of contemporary Hong Kong. While it might be easier to pass over shouts from groups of lower social caliber, the collective voice of this important class can hardly be ignored. Their collective actions carry special weight because they are implemented in a rational, peaceful, and restrained manner which accords with the dictates of Hong Kong's political culture. They demonstrate the maturity of Hong Kong's political society and the readiness of the city to further democratization.

The results of both the onsite and population surveys demonstrate clearly that organizational affiliation plays an unimportant role in large-scale political mobilization in Hong Kong. Very few people took to the streets because they were members of social or political organizations. This is not to deny that there may be a few exceptions to the rule (e.g., the possible influence of the Catholic Bishop Joseph Zen on Catholics). This is also not to deny the necessity of having an organization making a rallying call. Indeed, for an openly scheduled event, it is essential to have an entity for making the call and providing the necessary coordination. The three demonstrations were, after all, organized by social and political groups. However, in this case, the rallying point did not originate from a strong organization. Indeed, the Human Rights Front, the organizer of the huge rallies, was hardly recognizable prior to (or even after) the rally held on July 1, 2003.

While organizational mobilization is weak in Hong Kong, what appears to be at work is the interaction between mass communication and interpersonal communication. The demonstrators in general did not join the rallies alone. As a rule, they participated with their family members, friends, and other acquaintances. Many acknowledged the importance of the calls to actions issued by their friends and family members. This fundamental importance of interpersonal networks in protest mobilization is shared by Western studies which have also found social network to be playing a critical role (Curtis and Zurcher 1974; Opp and Gern 1993).

Of equal importance to interpersonal communication is mass communication. Many participants learned about the issues through the media. There is a tendency for the audience to expose themselves to media sharing a common perspective. Lending support to this observation is the fact that the demonstrators chose to read in order of preference the *Apple Daily* and *Ming Pao* which are known for their heavy coverage of social issues pertaining to the protests in question. This does not necessarily mean that mass media serve as direct mobilizers. It is more often the case for mass media to report on the views of social leaders who support the cause of a given rally. What the demonstrators recognized as calls from the mass media to act, hence, might indeed be calls from leaders of social and political groups that were reported as news. Some audiences, especially those treated as opinion leaders in interpersonal networks, might pass on what they had learnt from the media to their acquaintances, thereby forming some kind of two-step flow of information which was conducive to participation.[10]

In some earlier studies, we have emphasized that the various large-scale protests in 2003 and 2004 were mainly the results of citizens' "self-mobilization" (Chan and Chung 2004; Chan *et al.* 2004b). The analysis and findings presented in the chapter, taken as a whole, illustrate this point again.

This helps explain why attempts to cast the demonstrations in a bad light were often met with a frown in public discourse. The protesters understood that they were not being manipulated by political elites on any side. They were acting together with their fellow citizens, hoping to bring about changes to the society and the polity. These rallies thus become part of the symbolic resources from which Hong Kong people can draw upon for the purpose of self-empowerment. In fact, in the July 1 demonstration in 2003, the onsite survey also asked whether participants believed that "the collective action of Hong Kong people can change the society." More than 65 percent of respondents gave an affirmative answer. The two population surveys also showed that Hong Kong people have particularly high levels of "collective efficacy" – a belief that the collective action of the public can be influential in the political arena. Such a feeling of collective efficacy is tied to citizens' support for democracy, political participation, and identification with Hong Kong (Lee 2006).

Nevertheless, this does not mean that the continual lack of mobilizing power on the part of social and political organizations is desirable for Hong Kong's political development. The success of specific protests may not rely on the mobilizing power of the organizers, but the success of a sustained democracy movement is unlikely unless social and political organizations in Hong Kong can strengthen their own material and symbolic resources. In fact, in the 2003 July 1 survey and 2004 January 1 survey, the respondents were also asked whether they agree with the statement "The democracy movement in Hong Kong lacks leadership." In both cases nearly 60 percent of respondents agreed, while less than 15 percent of respondents disagreed.

The findings in this study also highlight the importance of a free and responsible media in Hong Kong serving as a facilitator of the formation of public opinion. Behind their apparent political radicalism, media outlets such as the *Apple Daily* and several prominent radio talk shows in the past may have served an important function of generating more private and public political discussions among citizens (Lee 2002, 2007). From the perspective of media professionalism, providing vocal and outright support for specific political viewpoints may be regarded as problematic. But what the media unquestionably should do is to identify and report sensitive yet important political issues and views to sustain an ongoing process of public discourse.

The analysis of the population surveys also informs us about the relationship between protest participation and citizens' political attitudes. Most notably, during the heated debates over national security legislation, a widespread concern was whether people's dissatisfaction with the economy was related to the massive participation in the protests. Our analysis has found that the relationship between economic evaluation and participation in the July 1, 2003 rally is mediated by satisfaction with government performance and support for democracy. This indicates that negative economic evaluation may be turned into protest behavior when the economic problems are attributed to the failure of the government and/or the political system as a whole. In this chain of causes, what ultimately matters is whether or not people are satisfied with the government and the political system. It is therefore of imperative importance for the government to deliver to the public what is expected of an effective government. This is perhaps the most important way of preventing economic and social issues from translating into political problems.

Protests and demonstrations are the results of a confluence of macro-, meso-, and micro-level factors and processes (Chan and Lee 2005). This chapter has focused mainly on the micro-level factors contributing to the three large-scale demonstrations. Given the macro-level conditions of Hong Kong society and politics in the past few years, citizens were full of grievances, which became overwhelmingly the basis for individuals' protest participation. Through mass and interpersonal communications, grieving citizens were mobilized or mobilizing each other to participate in the protests. Nevertheless, the mobilization did not seem to reach beyond the group of citizens who were holding highly negative opinions toward the government. In other words, the protests may have had an impact on those who share the negative attitudes but not on those who harbor positive views on the government.

Having said this, this is not to deny that these huge rallies may have had significant impacts at the organizational and societal levels. Unlike many minor demonstrations which end up nowhere other than merely noted by the news media, these rallies appear to have had strong repercussions in the sociopolitical arena (Chan and Lee 2005). The rally on July 1, 2003, hailed as a Hong Kong-styled "people power," not only resulted in the postponement of the national security legislation but also the establishment of the importance of public opinion for governing Hong Kong. Both the central authorities and the SAR government have found that they can hardly ignore local public opinion. The sense of empowerment among the public has grown, as evidenced by the increasingly favorable reference to the notion of civil society in public discourse and rising aspirations for democracy in the population. Indeed, July 1 has become a symbolic resource from which groups and social leaders draw support in their fight for interests and rights. At the same time, the historical rallies have led Beijing to take a policy turn, moving from leaving Hong Kong to run its own affairs to heavy engagement, as testified by the active role it played in pacing democratic reform in the wake of the rallies. The resulting tension between the nation-state of China and the civil society of Hong Kong is expected to play a critical role in shaping the future development of this Special Administrative Region. How this tension and other societal change will in turn affect people's protest participation will be important questions for us to ponder in the years to come.

Acknowledgment

The work described in this paper was fully supported by a grant from the Research Grants Council of the Hong Kong Special Administrative Region (Project no. CUHK4136/04H). The authors would also like to thank Dr. Robert Chung for his help in gathering data for the three onsite surveys.

Notes

1 Admittedly, the sampling methods, despite being the best possible approach within the given circumstances, cannot guarantee the representativeness of the samples. This is a limitation of the onsite surveys that has to be kept in mind.
2 The methods are not detailed here due to space concerns. Information may be obtained from the authors.
3 The March survey was conducted by the Hong Kong Institute of Asia Pacific Studies at the Chinese University of Hong Kong, while the September survey was conducted by the Quality Evaluation Center at the City University of Hong Kong.
4 The March survey was conducted by the Hong Kong Institute of Asia Pacific Studies at the Chinese University of Hong Kong, while the September survey was conducted by the Quality Evaluation Center at the City University of Hong Kong.
5 For detailed studies of the middle class in Hong Kong, see for instance, Lui and Wong (2003), So and Kwitko (1990), Lee (2001), Lui (1997). The class status of the respondents is self-designated. While designation may lean toward leniency, cross-tabulating class status with education, income and occupation indicates that the middle-class respondents are indeed the more educated, better paid, and working in more skilled jobs.
6 The arguments in this paragraph follow the theory of mass opinion outlined by Zaller (1992).
7 The "population figures" here are actually sample estimates derived from surveys. Since survey research is likely to over-sample politically interested citizens, the real population figures about news media use are likely to be lower.
8 In another study devoted to the role of the internet in the July 1 demonstration in 2003, we argued that the medium has allowed Hong Kong citizens to mobilize their social capital for participating in the protest. See Chan et al. (2004a).
9 The operationalization of support for democratization here is different from the corresponding one in the March survey due to changes in political circumstances in Hong Kong. Therefore, caution should be taken when comparing the findings regarding support for democratization in Tables 1.5 and 1.6.
10 In some further analyses, we have found that this step-by-step process was most apparent in the January 1 demonstration in 2004 (Chan and Lee 2005).

References

Chan, J. M. 1992. "Mass media and socio-political formation in Hong Kong, 1942–1992." *Asian Journal of Communication* 2, no. 3: 106–129.

Chan, J. M. and F. L. F. Lee. 2005. "Mobilization and protest participation in post-handover Hong Kong: a study of three large-scale demonstrations." Occasional Paper. Hong Kong: Hong Kong Institute of Asian Pacific Affairs, the Chinese University of Hong Kong.

Chan, J. M. and F. L. F. Lee. 2007. "Media and public opinion in post-handover Hong Kong." In *Contemporary Hong Kong Politics*, ed. W. M. Lam *et al.* Hong Kong: Hong Kong University Press.

Chan, J. M., and P. S. N. Lee. 1992. "Communication indicators in Hong Kong: conceptual issues and findings." In *The Development of Social Indicators Research in Chinese Societies*, ed. S. K. Lau *et al.* Hong Kong: Institute of Asia-Pacific Studies. The Chinese University of Hong Kong.

Chan, J. M. and C. So. 2003. "The surrogate democracy function of the media: citizens' and journalists' evaluations of media performance." In *Indicators of Social Development: Hong Kong 2001*, ed. S. K. Lau, M. K. Lee, P. S. Wan, and S. L. Wong. Hong Kong: Hong Kong Institute of Asia-Pacific Studies, the Chinese University of Hong Kong.

Chan, J. M., R. T. Y. Chung, and F. L. F. Lee. 2004b, July 7 to July 9. "Series on July 1 demonstration survey." *Ming Pao.* Forum section.

Cheung, A. and K. Louie. 1991. "Social conflicts in Hong Kong, 1975–1986: trends and implications." Occasional Paper No. 3. Hong Kong: Hong Kong Institute of Asia-Pacific Studies, the Chinese University of Hong Kong.

Chiu, W. K. S. and T. L. Lui. 2000. *The Dynamics of Social Movement in Hong Kong.* Hong Kong: Hong Kong University Press.

Choy, I. C. K. 1999. "Political parties and political participation in Hong Kong." In *Political Participation in Hong Kong*, ed. J. Cheng. Hong Kong: City University of Hong Kong Press.

Curtis, R. and L. Zurcher. 1974. "Social movements: an analytical exploration of organizational forms." *Social Problems* 21, no. 3: 356–370.

DeGolyer, M. and J. L. Scott. 1996. "The myth of political apathy in Hong Kong." *The Annals of the American Academy of Political and Social Science* 547: 68–78.

Fung, A. Y. H. 1995. "Parties, media and public opinion: a study of media's legitimation of party politics in Hong Kong." *Asian Journal of Communication* 5: 18–46.

King, A Y. C. 1975. "Administrative absorption of politics in Hong Kong: emphasis on the grassroots level." *Asian Survey* 15, no. 5: 422–439.

Ku, A. S. 2001. "The public up against the state: narrative cracks and credibility crisis in post-colonial Hong Kong." *Theory, Culture and Society* 18, no. 1: 121–144.

Kuan, H. C. 1998. "Escape from politics: Hong Kong's predicament of political development?" *International Journal of Public Administration* 21, no. 10: 1423–1448.

Kuan, H. C. and S. K. Lau. 2000. "Political attitudes in a changing context." In *Social Development and Political Change in Hong Kong*, ed. S. K. Lau. Hong Kong: Chinese University Press.

Kuan, H. C. and S. K. Lau. 2002. "Cognitive mobilization and electoral support for the Democratic Party in Hong Kong," *Electoral Studies* 21, no. 4: 561–582.

Lam, W. M. 2004. *Understanding the Political Culture of Hong Kong.* New York: M. E. Sharpe.

Lau, S. K. 1982. *Society and Politics in Hong Kong.* Hong Kong: Chinese University Press.

Lau, S. K. 1994. "Public attitudes towards political leadership in Hong Kong." *Asian Survey* 34: 243–257.

Lau, S. K. 1998. "Democratization, poverty of political leaders, and political inefficacy in Hong Kong." Occasional Paper No. 72. Hong Kong: Hong Kong Institute of Asia-Pacific Studies.

Lau, S. K. 2000. "Democratization, poverty of political leaders, and political inefficacy in Hong Kong." In *Social Development and Political Change in Hong Kong*, ed. S. K. Lau. Hong Kong: Chinese University Press.

Lau, S. K. and H. C. Kuan. 1988. *The Ethos of the Hong Kong Chinese.* Hong Kong: Chinese University Press.

Lau, S. K. and H. C. Kuan. 1995. "The attentive spectators: political participation of the Hong Kong Chinese." *Journal of Northeast Asian Studies* 14: 3–24.

Lau, S. K. and P. S. Wan. 1997. "Social conflicts in Hong Kong 1987–1995," Occasional Paper No. 62. Hong Kong: Institute of Asia-Pacific Studies, The Chinese University of Hong Kong.

Lee, F. L. F. 2002. "Radio phone-in talk shows as politically significant infotainment in Hong Kong." *Harvard International Journal of Press/Politics* 7, no. 4: 57–79.

Lee, F. L. F. 2006. "Collective efficacy, support for democracy, and political participation in Hong Kong." *International Journal of Public Opinion Research* 18: 297–317.

Lee, F. L. F. 2007. "Talk radio listening and public opinion expression." Paper presented at the International Communication Association Annual Convention, New York, USA, May.

Lo, S. H. 1999. "Citizen participation, political culture and governability in Hong Kong: a critique of the psychocultural approach." In *Political Participation in Hong Kong*, ed. J. Cheng. Hong Kong: City University of Hong Kong Press.

Lui, T. L. 1997. "The Hong Kong New Middle Class on the Eve of 1997." In *The Other Hong Kong Report 1997*, ed. J. Cheng. Hong Kong: The Chinese University Press.

Lui, T. L. 1999. "Pressure group politics in Hong Kong." In *Political Participation in Hong Kong*, ed. J. Cheng. Hong Kong: City University of Hong Kong Press.

Lui, T. L. and S. W. K. Chiu. 2000a. "Introduction – changing political opportunities and the shaping of collective action: social movements in Hong Kong." In *The Dynamics of Social Movement in Hong Kong*, ed. S. W. K. Chiu and T. L. Lui. Hong Kong: Hong Kong University Press.

Lui, T. L. and S. W. K. Chiu, eds. 2000b. *The Dynamics of Social Movement in Hong Kong.* Hong Kong: Hong Kong University Press.

McAdam, D., J. D. McCarthy, and M. N. Zald. 1988. "Social movements." In *Handbook of Sociology*, ed. N. J. Smelser. Newbury Park, CA: Sage.

Opp, K. D. and C. Gern. 1993. "Dissident groups, personal networks, and spontaneous cooperation: the East German revolution of 1989." *American Sociological Review* 58: 659–680.

Snow, D. A. and R. D. Benford. 2002. "Master frames and cycles of protest." In *Frontiers in Social Movement Theory*, ed. A. D. Morris and C. McClurg Mueller. New Haven, CT: Yale University Press.

So, A. and L. Kwitko. 1990. "The new middle class and the democratic movement in Hong Kong." *Journal of Contemporary Asia* 20: 382–398.

Tse, P. W. S. 1997. "The impact of 1997 on political apathy in Hong Kong." *The Political Quarterly* 66: 210–220.

Wong, W. P. T. and T. L. Lui. 2000. "From one brand of politics to one brand of political culture." In *Social Development and Political Change in Hong Kong*, ed. Lau Siu-kai. Hong Kong: the Chinese University Press.

Zaller, J. 1992. *The Nature and Origin of Mass Opinion*. New York: Cambridge University Press.

Zuo, J. P. and R. D. Benford. 1995. "Mobilization processes and the 1989 Chinese Democracy Movement." *Sociological Quarterly* 36 no: 1: 131–156.

Chinese references

Chan, J. M. 2006. "Hong Kong style 'people power': the mobilization pattern of July 1 rally and reconfiguration of public opinion politics." In *Hong Kong Style Cultural Studies*, ed. C. H. Ng, E. Ma, and T. L. Lui. Hong Kong: Hong Kong University Press (Chinese).

Chan, J. M. and R. T. Y. Chung. 2004. "Who can mobilize five hundred thousands people to march." In *Reading July 1*, ed. J. M. Chan. Hong Kong: Ming Pao Publishing.

Chan, J. M., R. T. Y Chung, and F. L. F. Lee. 2004a. "Mobilizing social capital: internet's role in a historic rally in Hong Kong." Paper presented at the International Communication Association Annual Convention, New Orleans, USA, May 26–29.

Ku, A. S. 2002. "Culture, identity, and politics." In *Our Place, Our Time: A New Introduction to Hong Kong Society*, ed. K. C. Tse. Hong Kong: Oxford University Press, 2002: 343–375. (Chinese)

Lee M. K. 2001. "The class, crisis and conflict of post-handover Hong Kong." In *Social Transformation and Cultural Change in Chinese Societies*, ed. S. K. Lau. Hong Kong: Hong Kong Institute of Asia-Pacific Studies, 2001: 531–546. (Chinese)

Lui, T. L. 1989. "The politics of pressure groups and political participation." In *Hong Kong in Transition*, ed. J. Cheng, Hong Kong: Joint Publishing (Chinese).

Lui, T. L. 2002. "Thinking 'pre-97' and 'post-97' Hong Kong." In *Our Place, Our Time: A New Introduction to Hong Kong Society*, ed. K. C. Kwan. Hong Kong: Oxford University Press (Chinese).

Lui, T. L. and C. T. Wong. 2003. *Observing the Situation of Hong Kong Middle Class*. Hong Kong: Joint Publishing (Chinese).

2 Civil society's dual impetus

Mobilizations, representations and contestations over the July 1 march in 2003

Agnes Shuk-mei Ku

Introduction

On July 1, 2003, Hong Kong saw the staging of a spectacular street theater of "people power" with about 500,000 people alleged to be joining in a march to protest against the government. This episode, amidst a chain of mass mobilizations in 2002 to 2004, came to rejuvenate and reinvent a pro-democracy movement that had been in decline since the 1990s (Ku 2007). A sense of civic empowerment and solidarity was heightened in society giving rise to a self-congratulatory discourse of a rising civil society. For a while, the idea of civil society not only appeared to carry new meanings, hopes, and possibilities regarding state-society relations but also held the promise of a participatory form of citizenship practice from below. Subsequent developments nonetheless also showed a society that was increasingly fragmented along class and ideological lines. In the process of reconstructing the meaning of the event, competing representations arose over who the chief protagonist was. The aim of this chapter, however, is not to examine the socioeconomic composition of the participants in the demonstration. Rather, it seeks to bring to light how the event, as it unfolded in the process, was endowed with particular social and political meanings in the way they were represented, contested, and developed in the public sphere(s).

With a view to furthering the current discussion on civil society in Hong Kong, this chapter will start with a brief review of two divergent approaches to civil society in the literature. Drawing on the theoretical discussion, our analysis will demonstrate how the chain of mass mobilization in 2002 to 2004 was shaping up through a dual logic of "civil society against the state" and "civil society as a contested space." While the former was at work in the processes leading to the momentous event, the latter manifested itself as the public began to reconstruct the meanings of the event in its aftermath. Mainstream discourses saw a shift from an interpellation of the "people" to the "middle class" as the chief agent in the mobilization, which later triggered a counter-discourse of "grassroots community" by a multitude of small groups and radical activists within civil society. The contestation brings to light a question that is often glossed over in the public sphere: whose civil society is it? A deeper look at the processes of mobilization, representation, and contestation is crucial for a more profound understanding of the dynamics of civil society as well as state–civil society relations in Hong Kong.

Conceptualizing civil society: the dual impetus

In a most neutral sense, civil society denotes a realm of free association among citizens that falls outside the direct control of the state. Within civil society, people carve out different public spaces to engage in different forms of politics. In the literature on civil society, there have been two major competing theoretical traditions, namely liberalism and Marxism (as well as post-Marxism). Despite theoretical and ideological incompatibility, the two approaches may be taken as capturing two different facets of civil society which, accordingly, spell out two different kinds of political impetus in modern society: (1) struggle against state despotism, and (2) struggle over hegemonic power.

The liberal conception, which has become prevalent in modern thinking, expresses itself as an analytical distinction between public/state and private/-non-state/market. It serves both to explain a modern form of civil society and to justify the need for guarding against the state's despotic potential by fostering self-organization in society (Keane 1988). Within liberalism, Ku (2002) distinguishes between an oppositional thesis and a relational thesis of civil society. The former conceives state–civil society relations in antagonistic terms, a variant of which may be found in the rallying idea of "civil society against the state" that arose as a challenge to the ruling party in Eastern Europe and in Latin American in the late 1970s and the 1980s. Historically, an oppositional dichotomy between the state and civil society has been strategically necessary in democratic struggle against political autocracy.[1] Alternatively, in the context of a liberal-democratic state, the relational thesis sees civil society as being necessarily intertwined with the liberal state that can serve as a safeguard for itself against potential state despotism through legal and political institutions (Habermas [1962] 1991; Shils 1991).[2] In a nutshell, the liberal conception of civil society remains a sphere of political freedom whose relationships with the state may vary from relational-autonomous to oppositional.

The Hegelian–Marxist tradition, instead of embracing it as a realm of individual freedom, conceives civil society as being ridden with class inequalities and conflicts under modern capitalism. For Marx and Engels, the bourgeois civil society is the base of economic relations that operates under the capitalist logic of exploitation. Class inequality is the hallmark of such a sphere. The state serves as a necessary instrument for the bourgeois civil society through the legal institution of civil rights. As compared to the liberal tradition, the Marxist approach is more inclined to penetrate the hidden relations between the state and the economy and is hence critical of the hierarchical and conflictual nature of civil society under capitalism. However, confined within the Marxist problematic, the danger of state despotism against civil society, or a meaningful state–civil society distinction in the sense of "civil society against the state" remains non-existent (Ku 2002).

The liberal and the Marxist approaches to civil society each has its relative merits, but both risk reducing the multi-dimensional quality of the idea of civil society within its own framework. In our alternative approach, we seek to highlight the double character of civil society: it is *conceived* as a sphere of individual freedom vis-à-vis the state which is nonetheless embedded within diverse structures of social inequalities and conflicts. Yet, far from asserting a universalistic claim, two caveats are in order. First, the state and civil society consist in heterogeneous structures within themselves which often show multifold relations – for example, cooperative, confrontational, instrumental, or institutionally intertwined – rather than a simple dichotomy or integration between the two domains (Migdal 2001; Migdal *et al.* 1994). This brings us to our second point, which is that state–civil society conflicts/relations and internal conflicts within civil society are neither automatic nor necessary outcomes but are often mediated through an intricate interplay between culture and politics. Just as state legitimacy has to rest on a set of beliefs, traditions, and practices that is often open to dispute, the claim to civil society is also subject to contested representations about civic-ness, rights, freedom, order, agency, and so on. On this count, the Gramscian notion of hegemony would be quite useful. For Gramsci, civil society is the domain of cultural and ideological practices where consent is forged for the governance of the state (at the service of capital) through a host of hegemonic practices. The exercise of hegemony, rather than a simple one-way domination, often entails a process of continuous negotiation with the subaltern classes. This approach opens up different possibilities regarding the interplay among state power, hegemony, and resistance. In recent years, with the emergence of cultural studies, some scholars further incorporate the insights of semiotics and discourse analysis into a post-Gramscian framework to decipher a wide range of political, socioeconomic, and ideological relations.

Extending from the above discussion, this chapter proposes that civil society carries a dual political impetus as a sphere of voluntary association and political mobilization. First, it has an interest in defending itself against any despotic potential of the state (though such an interest is often compromised in some situations). Second, diverse interests will struggle for hegemonic or counter-hegemonic persuasion under particular socioeconomic, political, ideological, and cultural divisions. In Hong Kong, state–civil society relations have to be analysed against a power and hegemonic structure that is in part inherited from colonial times and in part subsumed under the "one country, two systems" framework after the handover. In the case under study, a "civil society against the state" impetus was at work in the dual sense of opposition against the SAR government (a quasi-local state) and opposition against the legislation of national security (Article 23 of the Basic Law). As we shall see, the anti-state impetus was effected through several interrelated processes: (1) a process of the cumulative weakening of the hegemonic authority of the SAR government through a series of crises, (2) an opposition discourse of democracy that laid the basis for a discourse of civil society, and (3) a mobilizational process in civil society that gathered momentum through a contingent process of theater-making of people power.[3] Moreover, as civil society was embedded within a structure of power relations, the event also opened up a critical moment for struggle over the claim to political agency and hegemonic order that was based on a set of class-related symbols and discourses.

From social activism to pro-democracy struggle – oppositional unity vis-à-vis the government and internal tensions within the movement

Hong Kong has had an authoritarian government structure that is skewed in favor of business and conservative interests. In other words, it is both undemo-cratic and class-based. Regarding state–civil society relations, on the one hand, the government's ruling strategy ensures that it remains on cordial terms with the traditional charity and welfare associations, business groups, and professional associations, which (especially the latter two) are interlocked with the power structure. On the other hand, outside the power bloc, protests, social movements, and other forms of mobilization by the grassroots community have posed a challenge against the reign of capitalism and authoritarianism. The late 1960s and the 1970s, in particular, were a period of burgeoning student activism and growing urban collective action. Given the closed and undemocratic polit-ical structure, these grassroots movement groups were bound to take a dissenting political position against the government through non-institutional actions (Lui and Chiu 1999). During the 1970s, while the common experience of exclusion from the political system helped nurture a united oppositional strategy of con-tentious action among the different movement groups, a class-based discourse of resource allocation and redistribution was prominent in the struggle.

During the 1980s and the 1990s, the decolonization process opened up new political opportunities for civil society. A pro-democracy movement emerged partly out of the pre-existing networks of social activism and partly under the leadership of some newly formed middle-class-led political groups. The opposi-tional claims began to shift from a primary concern about resource allocation to the questions of representative democracy and political rights (the opposition dis-course of democracy). The 1990s further saw the emergence of diverse agendas of human rights, anti-discrimination, identity, and community issues on a broader front of struggle that was tied to the pro-democracy cause. The agenda of demo-cracy brought the diverse groups together under a united banner against the authoritarian structure of the government. (Yet in retrospect, underneath the unify-ing anti-state position were divergent agendas that could cause tensions and splits within the camp, for example, between a *radical discourse of democracy for social justice* by the grassroots organizations and a *liberal discourse of democracy for freedom* by the middle-class groups, and also between those who desired a faster pace of democratization and those who preferred a more moderate approach to political reform.) Throughout the transitional period, the pro-democracy groups adopted a mixed strategy of opposition and cooperation under the reform initiative by the government. That is, they continued to undertake contentious actions while struggling for inclusion through electoral politics. During the 1990s, riding on the anti-Chinese government sentiments in society after 1989, the democrats succeeded in creeping further into the space of institutional politics with a landslide victory in the direct elections to the legislature, first in 1991 and then under Governor Patten's reformed structure in 1995 (Pepper 2002).

Yet, despite rising political consciousness in society, the mobilizational power of civil society for the democratic cause remained generally quite limited. Except for the events in 1989,[4] the movement was never very successful at mass mobilizations (Sing 2000). Apart from internal organizational problems of the movement and external constraints (Sing 2003), the hegemonic strategies by the government remained largely effective in containing popular discontents in society. A narrative of economic and governing success – with an effective administrative system put in place through the rule of law, a prospering economy, a stable order, and an efficient team of civil servants – was propagated to win popular consent to its rule as well as the existing power structure (Ku 2001a). During the 1990s, the movement appeared to lose steam as it became partially institutionalized with the introduction of electoral politics. Moreover, as the development of political reform was circumscribed by the Basic Law,[5] the democratic agenda seemed to become quite out of the question at least in the early post-handover years.

It was not until 2003 when another expansive theater of resistance was produced that the movement came to rejuvenate itself with new possibilities. What put into place this spectacular theater of resistance? Survey statistics show that the people were mobilized not only by formal organizational links (about 25 to 36 percent) but also through the mass media, the internet, and other kinds of informal connections among family members, friends, and acquaintances (Chan *et al.* 2004; Chan and Lee 2005). Among the protesters, medical professionals, lawyers, religious groups, journalists, artists, academics, teachers, university and secondary school students, workers, women's groups, homosexual groups, civil servants, political groups, and individual citizens held a variety of banners about Article 23, the SARS issue, workers' livelihood, gender equality, sexual rights, and so on. In other words, a civil society with heterogeneous interests and diverse associational forms and networking ties was mobilized into united action. These included not only the social movement groups and the dissenting parties that were conventionally on the opposition side, but also the more established professional associations (e.g., doctors and lawyers) that, being part of the hegemonic bloc with the government, rarely adopted any open contentious action. These included also a large number of people who did not fall neatly within the narrowly defined scope of activism and formal association. What this shows is that the ruling hegemony of the government was undermined to the extent that it could no longer contain widespread discontent in society at large, especially in the face of a growing opposition discourse of democracy in the public sphere.

Still, the question of timing cannot be overlooked, namely why didn't the mass demonstration take place earlier or later? After the handover, protests of various kinds were on the rise (So 2002), but the government remained adamant in responding to public sentiment. Feelings of discontent were piling up, until the final impetus came from what the local community perceived as a rather inapt and overacted performance of state power by the SAR government over the issue of national security. Prior to the extraordinary mobilizations in the summer of 2003, a resistance movement against the national security legislation was already gathering strength during the three-month consultation period in 2002. The resistance did not start as a movement for democracy but as a crusade against un-freedom and injustice, and it could have been set back in the face of counter-mobilizations from the pro-Beijing camp (Ku 2007). Yet, when it came to the momentous moments in July, 2003, a script of people power was evoked which in turn strengthened the pro-democracy cause. We argue that civil society was mobilized into collective action through an anti-state impetus via the inter-play among the challenge to hegemony, opposition discourses, and mobiliza-tional processes. At the same time, the events opened up a vast space of opportunities for different groups to construct and reconstruct the meanings of the event in the process of contesting or reasserting the hegemonic values and power structure in society.

Civil society against the state

The issue of Article 23 was indisputably the triggering point for the mass demonstration on July 1, 2003. Yet, although it was a planned event by the Civil Human Rights Front (CHRF), neither the size of the turnout nor the spectacular effect achieved was anticipated. Earlier on, during the consultation period in September through December in 2002, a resistance campaign was already underway through a host of activities on a smaller scale. On December 15, several days before the end of the consultation period, local resistance as well as international concern was escalating leading to tens of thousands of citizens marching in opposition to the proposed law under the initiative of CHRF. The turnouts made it the biggest demonstration since 1989. This began to evoke an emergent script of people resisting in unity and in peace for the cause of freedom as well as justice. Yet shortly after this, the pro-government groups formed into the Hong Kong Coalition for National Security Legislation,[6] which mobilized about 40,000 people to join in a rally in an outpouring of patriotism at Victoria Park on December 23. The counter-mobilization presented a political moment from within civil society that served to buttress state power while coun-tering the effects of the resistance movement. The SAR government, instead of conceding, reinforced its authoritarian position.[7] The movement could have lost steam with the setbacks, but it was finally able to mobilize the people to a higher level of resistance in the summer of 2003 through a strong impetus against the state. The following will first look at the political and cultural dynamics involved in the working of the anti-state impetus.

State power and hegemony under challenge

The anti-state impetus found its way to challenge the legitimacy of the SAR government in at least three ways, which built into a set of opposition discourses that in part drew on the hegemonic values and in part challenged them. In the first place, the SAR government showed itself to be taking the lead to undermine the rule of law that was believed to be a major pillar of the society's success. After the handover, the government became inclined to an ideology of law and order which stressed control over rights, political discretion over legal consistency, and state power over procedural justice, as shown in the right of abode saga in 1999 (Ku 2001b) and the Public Order Ordinance disputes in 2000 (Ku 2004). The post-handover years thus saw the legal professionals, especially the Bar Association, change their role from silent defender of the status quo to a most outspoken and unyielding fighter against the government. In the course of struggle, the rule of law was articulated with the ideas of democracy and rights into a growing discourse of civil society by an expanding opposition alliance.

In the second place, with a more immediate impact in society, the SAR government showed itself to be increasingly overbearing, which finally reached boiling point over Article 23 in 2003. At stake was the issue of civil liberty that was also considered to be the foundation of Hong Kong's success. The question of national security was very sensitive all along. For Beijing, it was an indisputable matter about nationalism and sovereignty. Yet, for the local democrats, depending on the details, the legislation could carry the danger of infringing upon the civil rights of the people (Ma 2005). This issue would seem to be the litmus test of the "one country, two systems" framework, which many Hong Kong people looked upon as a buffer against an interventionist state under Beijing. In the first few years of Tung's leadership, the SAR government adopted a wait-and-see attitude over the legislation of national security. On September 24, 2002, it finally released a consultative document on what was referred to as Article 23 of the Basic Law. Local and Beijing officials alike stressed the idea of constitutional duty.

During the three-month consultation period, the government launched a series of intensive public relations initiatives through pamphlets, the news media, legislative council hearings, and numerous open forums, persuading the public of the need for such legislation. However, to the pro-rights groups, the consultation launched by the government was just a fake show. Although the public showed much worry about the proposed laws undermining political freedom, the security chief (as well as other officials), as spokesperson of the government, displayed an uncompromising determination to complete the legislative process in July, 2003. Its refusal to concede to the strong public demand for publishing a White Paper on the details of the proposed law underscored a tinge of resolute authoritarianism that undermined the role of civil society in the political process. Moreover, the security chief, who stood at the forefront to act out the role of ferocious defender of law and order, cast herself increasingly as an unyielding and arrogant bureaucrat who finally turned the consultation into a theatre of anti-consultation (Ku 2007).

In the third place, the hegemonic narrative of governing success was demysti-fied through a number of crisis events to such an extent that the fragility of the authority of the government became nakedly exposed. Financial crisis and eco-nomic recession gave rise to increasing unemployment, declining wages, and negative asset, which caused social hardship among the middle-class and the working-class people alike. The mass demonstration on July 1 thus saw many people protesting against the government on such livelihood issues. Apart from such immediate class-based concerns about bread and butter, the government made serious policy blunders resulting in a series of political and health-related crises (Ku 2001a). Among others, the SARS crisis in March and April of 2003 was a critical intervening factor that added fuel to popular discontent against the government.

During the SARS crisis, the government's mishandling of the situation not only undermined its authority but also gave rise to open discord with the medical practitioners over the ethic of professional accountability (Ku and Hwang 2004). After the crisis, the Chief Executive further failed to institute mechanisms that could adequately assure government responsibility to the public. He initially ordered a government-led investigation to be led by the Secretary for Health, Wealth and Food Yeoh Eng-kiong. Lawmakers and health-care professionals nonetheless questioned the impartiality and credibility of the committee, and they also questioned the efficacy of a committee with no legal powers to summon witnesses or seize confidential documents. On this issue, the medical practitioners' claim to professionalism converged with the democratic discourse of public accountability, which put this group of socioeconomic elite on the opposition side of civil society. On July 1, 2003, the medical profession-als took part in the mass demonstration and decried the government for a lack of public accountability in the SARS issue. They were not alone in their demands but their collective participation in such contentious action on matters of general social concern was quite unprecedented in local history. This exemplified an instance of how some established socioeconomic elite, in asserting an estab-lished value of professionalism, articulated a public claim that converged with the opposition discourse of democracy.

Civil society in action: performing people power

While the weakening of the hegemonic power of the local state laid out the necessary conditions, it would need certain symbolic mechanisms and political processes to put into place an emergent script of people power in the process. These included, in the particular case under study, (1) subversion and parody of state power, (2) the circulation of an implicit message that size made power, and (3) creation of solidarity among the participants (Ku 2007). As it unfolded, the event achieved a more far-reaching significance of an empowered civil society embarking on a pro-democracy cause vis-à-vis the government.

To begin with, the date of July 1 itself carries symbolic significance broader than the scope of any specific issues, which could be another reason for the big turnout. It commemorates the return of Hong Kong to Chinese sovereignty, or the birth of the HKSAR. The government makes it a public holiday and officiates an annual handover celebration in the Convention and Exhibition Center in the presence of top political leaders from Beijing, senior local officials, and socio-economic elites from society. In 2003, people nevertheless subverted the political meaning of the holiday and turned the occasion into a people's theater by organizing protests and demonstrations on the day designed to honor the handover. As it evolved, the agenda was not confined to national security legislation but was widened to include a parallel theme of democracy: power to the people.

Toward July 1, 2003, as the government showed no signs of concessions, a spirit of solidarity and empowerment was being nurtured in the community in anticipation of and through the march. Political, social, religious, and professional groups and trade unions called on the public to join the march through radio phone-in programs, the press, and the internet. As the day of the march drew near, an implicit idea that "size is power" seemed to be circulating in society, and the projected size of the demonstration seemed to be growing day by day. Even the government and the pro-Beijing groups could sense the immensity of the mobilization. For example, the security chief said that people taking part in the huge July 1 rally would do so "as a kind of activity because it's a holiday." The chair of the DAB remarked that even if there were 100,000 or even 200,000 people, the legislation would go ahead because the people were misled. With such remarks, a sentiment seemed to be shared among the public that if the number exceeded 100,000 or 200,000, the power of the people could no longer be underestimated. That is, size made power. In a more sensational way, newspaper headlines made some highly emotive and rousing statements such as "Hong Kong people come united against Article 23. History will be made tomorrow" (*Apple Daily*, June 30, 2003).

Finally, on the day of the demonstration, the heat, the hours of waiting, and the sheer scale all contributed to a collective experience of catharsis in a spirit of endurance as well as power. The demonstration was organized by CHRF, which consists in a loose and decentralized structure of coalition without strong leadership. Under the broad theme of opposition against Article 23 as well as a subsidiary theme of power to the people, participants wrote their own scripts with various banners and slogans. Despite the absence of a single leadership, the demonstration was able to create a monumental moment of solidarity-in-resistance among the people through the setting, the props, the slogans, and the action. For example, the people, dressed mostly in black, captured the public imagination as the most powerful piece of theater of the people. Blackness, a colour designated by CHRF, symbolized strong feelings of rage and desolation; at the same time it connoted the meanings of will, determination, and resistance. During the march, the most prominent rallying or unifying symbols were the political leaders who embodied impotence, authoritarianism, and arrogance. The people showed their anger at what they perceived to be an inept government that had presided over a six-year decline of their fortunes since 1997. Puppets and cartoons bearing the images of Tung Chee-hwa and Regina Ip were a common sight; banners carrying calls for the Chief Executive to step down were waved. People shouted slogans such as "Oppose Article 23, power to the people," "Down with Tung Chee-hwa," "Down with Ip Lau Suk-yee," and "We march for freedom, not for fun." In a most eye-catching way, the popular newspaper *Apple Daily* provided a ready prop for many people with its cover and inside pages posting such words (as well as a big picture of the Chief Executive slapped with a cake on his face): "Article 23 doing harm to Hong Kong + 6 years of miserable days = We don't want Tung Chee Hwa." The occasion became a genuinely participatory political theater stirring up mass emotions. Collectively, the people demonstrated power through their action, and they parodied the government's power with their props and slogans. The march, as repeatedly shown in the mass media, became the most spectacular icon in and of the event. The people looked upon themselves as agents who collectively made history through the march.

Rejuvenation of the pro-democracy movement

The mass demonstration created a looming political crisis that instantly held the legitimacy of the government in suspense. The final concessions from the government were mediated through party politics,[8] which nonetheless signified a great victory for the people. Thus instead of coming to an end, the opposition force developed into a people's movement for democracy. The initial rallies and demonstrations did not start as a pro-democracy movement, but armed with a sense of victory, the movement organizers and the democrats turned up the opportunity to organize further rallies on July 9 and July 13 to demand universal suffrage to elect their chief executive and legislature respectively in 2007 and 2008. Through the chain of mass mobilizations, the pro-democracy movement was reinvented and rejuvenated within an empowered civil society.

The resistance nonetheless did not develop into a revolutionary moment to topple the government, but sought instead to make its way of influence through the interstices of institutional and extra-institutional politics (under the restraints of the Basic Law). Thus although the government conceded on the resignation of the two ministers, at that time it did not appear that the Chief Executive himself would step down with the strong support from Beijing. Nor did it look hopeful that Beijing favoured the idea of universal suffrage in 2007. During the subsequent demonstrations on July 9 and 13, speakers called on the people to register themselves as voters and looked to the hope of effecting changes via the upcoming elections for the legislature in September. People were also exploring new possibilities in electoral politics. The mass demonstrations in July had created new political stars who announced intentions to run in the upcoming LegCo elections in the following year. In November, the District Board elections saw the emergence of some new political forces from among the pro-democracy camp who beat down some of the long-serving DAB members.[9] On January 1, 2004, CHRF organized another demonstration to call for universal suffrage. From the organizer's point of view, the year 2004 was crucial because of the LegCo elections in September, which provided an opportune occasion to maximize the effects of the mass demonstrations through institutional politics. People participating in the New Year demonstration were not necessarily driven by the same goal, but in participating, they helped move the agenda forward.

Changing state–civil society relations

Regarding state–civil society relations, once again the local government, the central state, and the Hong Kong people were in a tug of war over the issue of political reform. For a time, the pro-democracy alliance successfully moved the issue of electoral reform to the center of public debate. However, the issue of universal suffrage touched on the nerve of Beijing. After more than six years of restrained performance of power, it finally turned to a more confrontational stance to counteract the demand for political reform. In a high-profile manner, it moved to undertake a constitutional interpretation of the Basic Law by the Standing Committee of the National People's Congress to close off the possibility of universal suffrage in 2007. There then came the propagandistic talks of patriotism in a succession of high-level political shows by the senior officials from Beijing. For many Hong Kong people, at stake were not only the issue of democracy but also the question of the rule of the law as well as political autonomy. Yet by neither retreating from the pro-democracy cause nor challenging the Chinese government head-on, the Hong Kong people appeared to be groping a way of resilient but non-confrontational resistance. In 2004, the second "First of July" demonstration took place under a broad and general appeal of "power to the people." In the face of Beijing's ferocious opposition, the rallying call for universal suffrage in 2007 and 2008 itself would mean a direct challenge against state power (Beijing). Yet, unlike the one in 2003, this second "First of July" march made little direct attack on individual government officials, while Beijing continued to remain an "absent" object of contention (which would seem weird to the Taiwanese counterparts). On the whole, it was less combative in spirit and carried fewer burning issues than the previous one, but it appeared to make a step forward in a sustained movement for local democracy.

Civil society as a contested space: competing discourses over political agency

The previous section focused on how civil society was mobilized into collective action through the working of the anti-state impetus. As we have seen, the different strings of opposition discourses that called into question the legitimacy of the government in part drew on the hegemonic values and in part challenged them. From a (post-)Gramscian perspective, the hegemonic values were associated or endowed with certain class-related and other political meanings in support of a structure of unequal power relations. Thus in the aftermath of the July 1 march, a vast space of cultural politics was opened up for different groups to construct and reconstruct the meanings of the event as they reasserted or contested the hegemonic values and power structure in society. Indeed, through the chain of mass demonstrations, not only was the pro-democracy movement recounted with greater strength and new possibilities vis-à-vis the local state. In a far broader and more significant sense, what emerged was also an expansive and participatory civil space opened up by the people in and through the collective actions. It is only in seeing the event in this light that we would be able to look more closely at the cross-purposes, differences, tensions, and diverse voices within the movement. This will bring us to the second impetus of civil society: civil society as a contested space within a structure of power and hegemonic relations.

In reconstructing the meaning of the event, disputes were raised within civil society over the question of political agency. Competing frames were forged over who the chief protagonist was under a generalized discourse of people power and a set of class-specific discourses. The crystallization of divergent discourses brought to light a deeper question about the relations between social inequalities, political conflicts, and cultural hegemony within civil society. On the one hand, the agency of the event was signified with reference to an inclusive category of "the people," which was consonant with the idea of "civil society against the state." It underlined a generalized usage of Hong Kong people as a collectivity and contained an everyday sense to mean ordinary people from all walks of life. The following quotations, for example, made no reference to social classes or specific social categories but highlighted instead families, children, or the people as a whole:

> This is definitely an historic moment, as it is the first time Hong Kong people have fought for their freedom and rights. It is a day to be proud of.
> (Tsoi Yiu-cheong of CHRF, *South China Morning Post*, July 2, 2003)

> The people of Hong Kong made history on Tuesday by showing they were willing to march for what they believe in and for demanding a future for their children. Many of the marchers took their families, including babies. They wanted to give their children a lesson in civic responsibility as they asserted the values that made Hong Kong what it is.
> (S. Tsang, *South China Morning Post*, July 5, 2005)

On the other hand, however, a competing discursive frame was forged when the public began to anchor its focus to identify the chief actors. This entailed the construction of a set of minute differentiating devices that classified the participants into different socioeconomic categories. Newspaper editors, political analysts and academics, as shown in the local press, mostly highlighted the agency and participation of the middle-class professionals in the mass demonstrations; that is, the representation of the movement was subsumed under a new "middle-class" discourse. The discourse was stitched together through a number of elements: (1) survey findings that showed that educated, middle-class people made up a significant proportion of the participants, (2) public discourse that transposed the event into one showing the leadership of the middle-class professionals as well as the virtuous quality of rationality characteristic of the middle class, and (3) public discourse that further extended the logic to stress the significance of the middle class as the pillar of effective governance in society.

The "middle-class" discourse

Survey findings by academics, polling agents, and the newspapers corroborated one another about the middle-class class composition of the participants in the mass rallies. The "middle-class" thus constructed was generally understood to be consisting of those who had attained a higher level of education, who were professionals, as well as those who subjectively identified themselves as such. As Chan and Lee (2005) cite from their own survey findings, the rally particip-ants were generally highly educated and belonged to the middle class. More than 50 percent of the participants held a college or university degree; about 40 percent were professionals or semi-professionals; more than 60 percent of the participants identified themselves with the middle class. In the press, similar findings were presented with cross-references to survey results by the acade-mics. For example, *Ming Pao*'s headline read "Half of the participants have post-secondary school qualifications," with elaborations of the details in the news report as follows:

> During the mass rally [on July 9], 457 participants were interviewed in a survey.... Most of the interviewees were intellectuals, with 50.8 percent of the participants having a college degree or above, and 30 percent are even professionals.... The survey results are quite close to the findings collated by the Chinese University and the University of Hong Kong during the big march on July 1.
>
> (July 10, 2004)

Within the middle-class category, intellectuals and professionals were singled out as playing a prominent role in the mobilizations. This was not only congru-ent with but also reinforced media representations that showed a small bunch of people in the prestigious professions of law and medicine taking the lead in the march. In this connection, a few prominent leaders from the legal profession were in the process of becoming new political stars for the public.

Apart from the question of class composition, the event was further associ-ated with the qualities and leadership of the middle class in public discourses. The following quotation by an academic in the press provides an example of how the composition issue was intermingled with the leadership question, which was further transposed into a discursive construction of the superior intellectual qualities of the middle-class professionals:

> What is unprecedented in this march [on July 1] was that professional associations including doctors, lawyers, accountants and even churches have become the leading actors in appealing to the people.... The author

believes that without their fervent appeal, there would not have been 500,000 people making their appearance.... Sociological studies in recent decades begin to reveal that the middle-class professional class have taken up a vital role in social change or the so-called new social movements. They are reputed to be very articulate, having a high capacity for conceptual thinking, and superb in creating effective political symbols in society.

(Kwan Sui-man, *Ming Pao*, July 4, 2003, translated by the author)

In other instances, as an extension of the class composition discourse, public critics focused not so much on the role of the professionals as on the quality of the participants that made the event possible. Not only did the scale of the event capture public discourse, the march on July 1 was also highly acclaimed to be showing the splendid and well-behaved qualities of the Hong Kong people that made it a symbol of pride in their collective memories. Despite the scorching heat of the sun and the size of the turnout, it was a peaceful and orderly procession from beginning to end. Among all the qualities shown, rationality, mildness, and law-abidingness were singled out, which, by a sleight of hand, were stretched to be associated with the middle-class ethos. The following quotation from an academic was a telling example:

The participants in the First of July march appeared to come mostly from the middle class, fully showing the virtues of mildness, rationality and law-abidingness of the middle-class in Hong Kong.... The local middle-class people all along had been politically apathetic, used to be self-reliant instead of expecting "free lunch" from the government.... The middle class have been an important pillar of social stability, but even they took to the street, and this showed that the legitimacy of the government has crumbled.

(Y. S. Cheng, *Ming Pao*, July 11, 2004, translated by the author)

Apparently, the middle-class discourse involved a logic of symbolic extension that enabled itself to stretch from the composition and quality discourses to finally arrive at a political agenda: the middle class being an important pillar of social stability and effective governance. This middle-class discourse began to gain wide currency both within the government and among the middle-class sector.[10]

A counter-discourse of "grassroots" identity

Among the activists, the "middle-class" discourse was much contested by the more grassroots organizations which felt that their voices and participation were slighted and silenced. Through their own publications and discussion (e.g., journals, newsletters, and web discussion), they deconstructed the mainstream discourse, crystallized a grassroots identity, and created a subaltern discourse in their own public spheres. A special issue of the journal published by Grassroots College in November, 2003 provided a most distinct emblem of the counter-discourse. The grassroots community did not dispute the role of the middle class in the mobilizations but challenged the middle-class discourse by pointing out some ungrounded assumptions in its reasoning. It stressed that the voices and participation of the grassroots community were overlooked and slighted, and concluded that "the people" instead of the middle class should be taken as the chief political agent in the demonstrations. This presents a milder version of a counter-discourse that foregrounded "the people" as a united collectivity.

Taking a step further, however, some began to configure a more uncompromising and distinctive grassroots identity in a stronger profile. The following is an example of a strong version of the counter-discourse from another source:

> To many labor and grassroots organizations, the "First of July" was definitely not a middle-class demonstration under the leadership of several reputed legal and political personages, and nor was it a pure "prodemocracy" movement without livelihood demands. It is instead a release of cumulative discontents by ordinary citizens over various democracy and livelihood issues. Labor and grassroots organizations participated in the "First of July" demonstrations twice and played an important role.... In the absence of an effective channelling mechanism, it would be naïve to believe that the gains from the demonstrations are directly transferable into the political account of the democratic camp.[11]

The quotation stressed the distinction between the "democracy-only" and the "democracy plus livelihood concerns" orientations and interpreted the mass demonstration in July, 2003 in terms of the latter. In this way, it countered the claim that it was a middle-class-led mobilization. It highlighted instead the role of the ordinary people as well as the grassroots organizations. From the author's point of view, the success of certain novice, non-party-affiliated candidates (such as "Long Hair") in the direct elections to the legislature in 2004 testified to the rising prominence of a more grassroots-oriented discourse from within the pro-democracy camp.

The emergent counter-discourse not only presented a new way of representation but also carried radical implications for the strategies and tactics used in subsequent mobilizations. For instance, it was decided that the grassroots organizations were to take the lead in the mobilization on January 1, 2004. On that day, riding on the success for the pro-democracy cause, CHRF organized another demonstration to call for universal suffrage. The event drew tens of thousands of people under the rallying slogans of "power to the people; better livelihood." Apart from the issue of universal suffrage, a wide range of social concerns was also voiced out including elderly welfare, labor, women's rights, sexual equality, outsourcing of government services and the merger of the two liver transplant centers in the procession, making the occasion another participatory theater with multiple agendas and voices from the people after the mass demonstration on July 1, 2003. (This, however, also laid the basis for some further tensions and splits within the camp and among the supporters when it came to the demonstration on July 1, 2005.[12])

Concluding remarks: rethinking civil society in Hong Kong

It is indisputable that the mass demonstration on July 1, 2003 has been among the most significant events in the political history of Hong Kong. Much of the prevailing discussion has focused on the causes for widespread discontent against the Tung government in society that finally led to the 500,000-strong demonstration. Such account is valid in its own terms but is insufficient in explaining the dynamics of civil society, both prior to the event and in the course of its unfolding. This chapter has sought to further the discussion by bringing to light two related facets of civil society: the working of an anti-state impetus in a non-democratic context, and also structural conflicts within a hierarchically ordered and politically divided civil society.

An impetus does not necessarily translate into a momentous political force. For example, as we have pointed out, the mobilizational power of civil society for the democratic cause had long remained limited since the 1980s. It was not until the mass demonstration in 2003 that the movement was rejuvenated with new possibilities, though it also gave rise to new tensions and conflicts within civil society. As this chapter has argued, a critical mechanism working through the two impetuses lies in the notion of hegemony. Hegemony, embodied within a structure of power relations, often expresses itself in the cultural realm of established and contested values, narratives, discourses, and representations in the process of political struggle. The anti-state impetus, as the case analysis shows, was mediated through a number of contingent processes including a cumulative weakening of the hegemonic authority of the government, a growing momentum of the opposition discourse within civil society, and a strong mobilizational process on the ground. In the course of the event, a civil society with heterogeneous interests and diverse associational forms and networking ties was mobilized into united action. These included not only the social movement groups and the dissenting parties conventionally from the opposition side, but also the more established professional associations that had always been part of the hegemonic power bloc. These included also a large number of ordinary men and women outside the traditional network of activism and secondary associations. This shows that the effectiveness of the ruling hegemony of the government had almost totally broken down, which constituted a necessary condition for the mass demonstration.

As it turned out, the mobilization succeeded in undermining the legitimacy of the government, bringing about the immediate downfall of two ministers (which was followed by the downfall of yet another minister later and finally the Chief Executive himself in March, 2005), halting the legislation of national security, and empowering the democratic struggle (to a certain extent) vis-à-vis the state. Yet, precisely because of the weakening of the authority of the government, which resulted in the high-profile participation of the well-established middle-class elites, the event also created a juncture for struggle within civil society over the hegemonic order around a set of class-related symbols and discourses.

With the benefit of hindsight, both impetuses had in fact been at work in society long before the march, and the event could be further tied back to the history of state–society relations. During the 1970s, the common experience of exclusion from the political system helped nurture a united oppositional strategy among the different movement groups. A class-based discourse of resource allocation and redistribution was prominent in the struggle. The oppositional claims began to shift to democracy and political rights in the 1980s, followed by the rise of diverse agendas of human rights, anti-discrimination, identity, and community issues on a broader front of struggle in the following decade. On the one hand, the agenda of democracy brought the diverse groups together under a united banner. On the other hand, underneath the unifying anti-state position were divergent agendas that could cause tensions and splits within the camp, for example, between a radical discourse of democracy by the grassroots organizations and a liberal discourse of democracy by the middle-class groups, and also between a generalized discourse of rationality by the middle-class elites and a marginalized discourse of social justice (including not only class issues but also various kinds of minority rights issues) within the grassroots community. This is what we witnessed in 2003.

The occurrence on July 1, 2003 was contingent upon a number of convergent conditions and processes, which may not repeat itself in the future. Still, it already generated a strong enough momentum for the relatively weak pro-democracy movement to rejuvenate itself through a chain of mobilizations until today. From the point of view of civil society, perhaps the challenge is to sustain the democratic struggle vis-à-vis the state yet without losing sight of the multiplicity of voices and claims in civil society. In pinning hopes only on the former, we may sacrifice the latter; in prioritizing multiplicity and differences, the loosely organized movement may easily disintegrate due to the lack of mutual trust and strong leadership. The movement appears to be at the crossroads. A more practical question is: how may we nurture a space *for* and *of* democracy that helps keep up a vigorous civil society on the one hand and channel it into effective political processes on the other? The movement must be able to strike a good balance between unity and differences, between participation and leadership, and between confrontation and strategic communication.

As for the government, it would be misleading to suggest that the old hegemonic framework has completely collapsed. On the contrary, as we have seen in the event, some people were charging the government with the failure to live up to certain established values and standards such as the rule of law, professionalism, accountability and good performance. Their relationships with the government remain ambivalent rather than strictly oppositional. On the part of the government, it is now seeking to re-establish its hegemonic authority on various fronts. However, it does so not by conceding to the democratic demands of the people but by enhancing its own administrative power and shifting public focus away from political issues. For example, Chief Executive Donald Tsang is trying to build up an image of strong leadership through greater public relations efforts, restructuring of the Executive Council, new social policy directives (e.g., environmental protection), and so on. Despite all its efforts, the government has yet to establish a way for effective negotiation and communication with the newly developed energies in civil society if it is not to fall back on the old set of governing practices. A tug of war is now taking place between the government and civil society over the question of political democracy. In the years to come, it remains to be seen how different hegemonic ideas may be articulated or de-articulated with the democratic discourse among various forces in the changing matrix of state–society relations (Ku 2001a). Within the framework of hegemony, a process-oriented approach that charts the course of conflicts as they unfold through a chain of episodes would enable us to study the dynamics of contention and mobilization and shed light on the affinities and fissures both between the state and civil society and within the latter. This has significant implications for a renewed understanding of civil society that draws on and yet goes beyond a simple dichotomy of the state versus civil society.

Notes

1 The "civil society against the state" framework could be a misnomer in certain ways. For instance, even though the Solidarity movement in Poland was poised as a battle of civil society against the state, and even though it was struggling for greater self-management against a dictatorial government, it was at the same time struggling for control of institutions that were all part of the state.

2 Within liberalism, a republican line of thinking about civil society focuses not so much on market relations as on civic participation, political associations, and social movement (Tocqueville 1900; Putnam 1993).

3 Most generally, the idea of performance bespeaks a distinctive understanding of political action as staged or dramaturgical practices involving an appeal to the audience. In contradistinction to ritual, which adheres closely to a conventionally prescribed format, theater delineates a form of performance that gives greater play to the creative powers of actors or scriptwriters (Esherick and Wasserstrom 1992).

4 In 1989, the demonstrations by more than one million people in support of the Chinese pro-democracy movement (or in condemnation of the Beijing government) over the Tiananmen Square Incident put on stage a powerful theater of participation among people from all walks of life that was never imaginable before. The mobilizations produced the effects of a spectacle that significantly enhanced the symbolic power of the democratic cause. Nevertheless, except for the immediate impact on electoral politics, the effects of the 1989 demonstrations on the local pro-democracy movement remained quite limited.

5 The Basic Law maintains an executive-led government with a slowly evolving legislature to be dominated at least until 2007 by a majority of indirectly elected representatives.

6 It included the Democratic Association for the Betterment of Hong Kong, the Liberal Party, the Hong Kong General Chamber of Commerce, the 310,000-member Federation of Trade Unions, as well as more than 300 pro-Beijing groups.

7 For instance, the security chief kept repeating that the public were being misled,

which aroused much criticism from the public. In January, 2003, the publication of *Compendium of Submissions* by the government generated a series of debates and protests against the distortion of public opinion. Despite strong opposition, the government was determined to table the proposals to the Legislative Council in February and to finish the legislation in July. The government made some token concessions but left the core issues unchanged. In June, the government made two more concessions ahead of the mass rally scheduled for July 1, but such efforts were to no avail.

8 For days, the government made no official response and appeared to be too impotent to govern until when the chair of the Liberal Party, James Tien, turned the tide against the government. The government then decided on July 7 to delay the legislation with an unspecified timetable.

9 For example, in Wanchai, a group of five candidates aligned into a new group called Civic Act-Up with such new agendas as community health, women, and ethnic minorities. They were all novices in electoral politics but three of the five candidates won the elections.

10 For instance, it was put down in the policy speeches of the Chief Executive in 2004 and 2005 that the government would create more channels for the middle-class people to participate in the public policy-making process. In this connection, the government formed a special forum on public affairs exclusively for the middle-class sector through a system of appointment. In 2004, a group of middle-class professionals jointly signed a public declaration to reassert a set of core values of Hong Kong in the direction of openness and fairness.

11 Ha Suk, "The 'First of July Effect' and Grassroots Movement," in the newsletter of Grassroots College, No. 145 (September, 2004), translated by the author.

12 The crux of the public debates concerned whether the object of struggle should be about democracy or democracy with livelihood concerns, and whether the homosexual groups, among other grassroots groups, should take the lead in the demonstration. From another angle, at stake was the meaning of democracy: a conventional conception of formal representative democracy, as opposed to a broader conception of inclusive and participatory democracy that aims to respect differences and minority rights on an equal footing.

References

Chan, Joseph M. and Francis L. F. Lee. 2005. *Mobilization and Protest Participation in Post-handover Hong Kong: A Study of Three Large-scale Demonstrations.* Hong Kong: Hong Kong Institute of Asian Pacific Affairs, the Chinese University of Hong Kong.

Chan, Joseph M., Francis L. F. Lee, and Robert Chung. 2004. "Internet Use, Social Capital, and Political Participation among Citizens and Activists: The Case of Hong Kong." Paper presented at the annual convention of the International Communication Association, New Orleans, May.

Esherick, Joseph W. and Jeffrey N. Wasserstrom. 1992. "Acting Out Democracy: Political Theatre in Modern China." In *Popular Protest and Political Culture in Modern China*, ed. Jeffrey N. Wasserstrom and Elizabeth J. Perry. Boulder, CO: Westview Press.

Habermas, Jurgen. [1962] 1991. *The Structural Transformation of the Public Sphere: An Inquiry into a Category of Bourgeois Society.* Cambridge, MA: MIT Press.

Keane, John. 1988. *Civil Society and the State*, edited by John Keane. London: Verso.

Ku, Agnes S. 2001a. "The 'Public' Up Against the State – Narrative Cracks and Credibility Crisis in Postcolonial Hong Kong." *Theory, Culture and Society* 18 (1): 121–144.

———. 2001b. "Hegemonic Construction, Negotiation and Displacement – Struggle over Right of Abode in Hong Kong." *International Journal of Cultural Studies* 4 (3): 259–278.

———. 2002. "Beyond the Paradoxical Conception of 'Civil Society without Citizenship'." *International Sociology* 17 (4): 551–570.

———. 2004. "Negotiating the Space of Civil Autonomy in Hong Kong – Power, Discourses and Dramaturgical Representations." *The China Quarterly* 179: 647–664.

———. 2007. "State Power, Political Theatre, and Reinvention of the Pro-democracy Movement in Hong Kong: The March on the First of July in 2003." Paper presented at the conference on Theatre/Performative Politics in Asia and Africa, organized by the School of Oriental and Asian Studies, London, May.

Ku, Agnes S. and Horng-luen Hwang. 2004. "The Making and Unmaking of Civic Solidarity – Comparing the Coping Responses of Civil Societies in Hong Kong and Taiwan during the SARS Crises." *Asian Perspective* 28 (1): 121–147.

Lui, Tai Lok and Kin Man Chan. 2001. "Between the Family and the Political Society – The Formation of Civil Society in Hong Kong." In *Political Theories in China*, ed. Jo Wai Chan and Man To Leung. Hong Kong: Oxford University Press (in Chinese).

Lui, Tai Lok and Stephen Chiu. 1999. "Social Movements and Public Discourse on Politics." In *Hong Kong's History: State and Society under Colonial Rule*, ed. Tak Wing Ngo. London: Routledge.

Ma, Ngok. 2005. "Civil Society in Self-defense: The Struggle against National Security Legislation in Hong Kong." *Journal of Contemporary China* 14 (August): 465–482.

Migdal, Joel S. 2001. *State in Society: Studying How States and Societies Transform and Constitute One Another*. New York: Cambridge University Press.

Migdal, Joel S., Atul Kohli, and Vivienne Shue, eds. 1994. *State Power and Social Forces: Domination and Transformation in the Third World*. New York: Cambridge University Press.

Pepper, Suzanne. 2002. "Hong Kong and the Reconstruction of China's Political Order." In *Crisis and Transformation in China's Hong Kong*, ed. Ming K. Chan and Alvin Y. So. Armonk: M.E. Sharpe, and Hong Kong: Hong Kong University Press.

Putnam, Robert. 1993. *Making Democracy Work – Civic Traditions in Modern Italy*. Princeton, NJ: Princeton University Press.

Shils, Edward. 1991. "The Virtue of Civil Society." *Government and Opposition* 26: 3–20.

Sing, Ming. 2000. "Mobilization for Political Change – The Pro-democracy Movement in Hong Kong (1980s-1994)." In *The Dynamics of Social Movement in Hong Kong*, ed. Stephen W. K. Chiu and Tai Lok Lui. Hong Kong: Hong Kong University Press.

———. 2003. "Governing Elites, External Events and Pro-democratic Opposition in Hong Kong (1986–2002)." *Government and Opposition* 38 (4): 456–478.

So, Alvin. 2002. "Social Protests, Legitimacy Crisis, and the Impetus Toward Soft Authoritarianism in the Hong Kong SAR." In *The First Tung Chee-hwa Administration – The First Five Years of the Hong Kong Special Administrative Region*, ed. Lau Siu-kai. Hong Kong: Chinese University of Hong Kong.

Tocqueville, Alexis de. 1900. *Democracy in America*. New York: Colonial Press.

3 Governance crisis and social mobilization of the Christian churches in Hong Kong

Shun-hing Chan

Introduction

One of the areas in the study of democratization is the relationship between Christianity and democracy. In sociological literature, researchers have argued that the Christian churches are a constructive force facilitating democratization. Many of these researchers have focused on the Protestant churches in the USA. In the early 1980s, researchers studied how the Christian churches helped the development of the civil rights movement,[1] and more recent studies have examined how the Christian churches, as faith-based organizations, provide resources for organizing social movements and developing democratization.[2]

Outside the USA, researchers have studied the relationship between the Catholic church and democratization in South America. Their views on the role of the church differ widely. Some researchers have argued that the doctrine of the church is consistent with the values of democracy,[3] while others hold that the church has its own interests and makes rational choices when facing political realities.[4] Rational choice is one explanatory model commonly used by researchers in the study of Christianity and democracy in other nations, such as Russia and South Africa.[5] In fact, each church in South America reacted differently according to the political situation, and the churches expressed different positions over different periods of time in the same country. Clergy and laity at different levels in the church hierarchy took different positions on political issues. Hence, the study of the Christian churches and democratization should take all these factors into consideration, and avoid making sweeping statements about whether Christianity is or is not favorable to democratization.

This chapter attempts to examine the relationship between Christianity and democracy in Hong Kong from 2001 to 2006, focusing particularly on the sociopolitical issues and the response of the Christian churches to the Hong Kong SAR government from 2003 to 2006. The research question of this chapter is: Why do some denominations and para-church organizations in Hong Kong express concern about and respond to sociopolitical issues, while others do not? Using Scott Mainwaring's theory on church and democracy as the conceptual framework, I examine how the institution of a church can facilitate or restrain its sociopolitical engagement. The subject of this study is the Catholic church, some leading Protestant denominations as well as para-church organizations in Hong Kong.

Theoretical framework

In the study of church and democracy, I find Scott Mainwaring's research on South America and the theory he proposed stimulating and useful. His research focus is on the relationship between institutional change in the Catholic church and democratization, with special focus on the factors contributing to institutional change, and how such change leads to democratization. The variables in his theory include broader social process, international churches, model of the church, grassroots movements, and institutional change. His discussions are summarized below.[6]

Broader social process can effect institutional change in the church. However, such institutional change is made possible only through a change of understanding of the model of the church. Generally, the church has its own doctrine and the mission to be achieved, and thus has its own organizational hierarchy and identity. Doctrine and mission will provide guidance for the church when it faces sociopolitical issues. When changes occur in society, the church will assess the social environment. In doing so, the church might learn new ways of thinking about society and its role within it. Such new understanding could lead to institutional change.

At the same time, the church can help shape political change. There are two possible ways the church is able to mobilize political forces to act. First, the church can speak to different social classes and change the ideologies of the elite and the masses. Second, religious practices and discourses can change the consciousness of the social classes. As such, Mainwaring argues that institutional churches are major political actors who have relative autonomy with respect to the class struggle.

International church organizations can effect local church institutions. According to Mainwaring, the Vatican can exercise control over the local churches by choosing the bishops who will be in charge of the dioceses in South America. For example, the Vatican can choose a liberal bishop to encourage the church's sociopolitical participation, or a conservative bishop to discourage the church's involvement in extreme or radical activities. National churches in South America could also affect each other. When the Brazilian church became strong in fighting for social justice, it strongly encouraged other national churches to become more progressive.

Grassroots movements and the model of the church have a kind of dialectical relationship. Grassroots movements refer to the collective action taken by grassroots agents including priests, nuns, and laity. As pointed out by Mainwaring, grassroots movements in South America produced a new understanding of the doctrine, new ideologies, and new pastoral practices. Such new thinking greatly affected the traditional model of the church. For example, grassroots movements led to the creation of Basic Christian Communities, a new form of organization and pastoral practice in the church. However, grassroots movements work under the hierarchy of the church and have not separated from it. These grassroots movements also often uphold popular religious practices and beliefs. Outside the institutional church, popular Catholicism retains some traditional values. These traditional values have affected the formation and ideologies of the grassroots movements.

Mainwaring provides a detailed analysis of the relationship between the model of the church and institutional change. He holds that the church as an institution has its own interests. In order to maintain unity and coherence, the church avoids extreme and radical change. Furthermore, the church seeks to preserve the organization and expand its influence. However, some churches may uphold that the struggle for justice is more important than organizational preservation and expansion. Thus, the values chosen by the church are a determining issue. The values determine the focus of interest and shape the institution. Thus, the doctrine and mission expressed by the institution reflect its values and interests and the hierarchy is designed to help the institution realize those objectives. Different churches have chosen different kind of values, which help shape different models of institution. When there is a change in understanding of doctrine and mission, such change could lead to institutional change. For example, the Second Vatican Council, held from 1962 to 1965, changed the self-understanding of the Catholic church, and greatly influenced the South American churches. Many churches were willing to sacrifice their interests and became involved in the struggle for social justice.

Mainwaring's analyses are heuristic in constructing a theoretical model to analyze the complex situation in Hong Kong. However, due to the differences in social contexts between South America and Hong Kong, I have modified his ideas (and see Figure 3.1) as follows:

X1 *Broader social processes* refer to the social environment and how it affects the government, social organizations, and individuals. The focus of this chapter is on how the social environment affects the sociopolitical involvement of churches and para-church organizations. For example, the government's policy-making and implementation may trigger opposition from churches and para-church organizations, and the churches and para-church organizations may mobilize Christians to express opposition to the policy. The social protests by Christians may induce the wider population to likewise oppose the policy, which could lead to a social movement advocating democratization.

X2 *International church organizations* refer to the Vatican and the World Council of Churches. The focus of this chapter is on how the doctrine and institutional structures of these international church organizations affects the sociopolitical engagement of the churches in Hong Kong.

X3 *Model of the church in sociopolitical engagement* refers to the effects of doctrine, institution, and leadership on the sociopolitical involvement of the churches and para-church organizations. Mainwaring has provided detailed

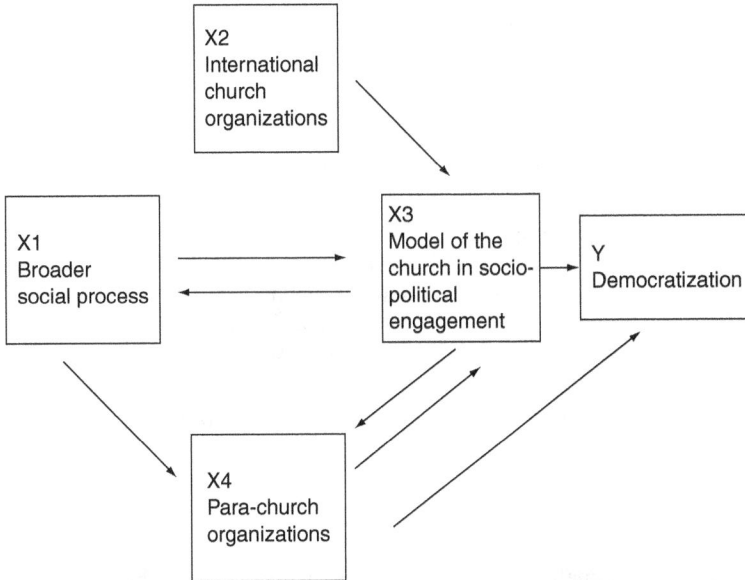

Figure 3.1 A revised model of Scott Mainwaring's theory on church and democracy.

discussions on various doctrines and institutional structures. I only borrow his ideas here. In this chapter, doctrines refer to the church's theology and mission, whereas institution refers to the church's organizational hierarchy. For example, the doctrines of the Anglican church are deeply influenced by the theology of William Temple, and the institution has adopted the model of episcopacy. However, the concept of "church leader" does not occupy a significant place in Mainwaring's discussion. I suggest that "church leader" should be given enough attention so as to examine its effect on the sociopolitical engagement of a church. This is particularly important in the case of Protestant churches. Generally speaking, Protestant church leaders in Hong Kong have the power to determine the degree of the sociopolitical involvement of the church.

X4 *Para-church organizations* refer to those Christian organizations advocating sociopolitical engagement. Some of these organizations are independent from the mainstream churches, whereas others are working within the organizational hierarchy of a church. An example of the former is the Hong Kong Christian Institute, and of the latter is the Justice and Peace Commission of the Hong Kong Catholic Diocese. A dialectical relationship exists between the church and the para-church organization. On the one hand, the doctrines of the para-church organizations come from the church, therefore both have a common denominator. On the other hand, the para-church organizations can be more progressive than the church, which often urges the latter to take part in and express a position on social issues.

Y   *Democratization* refers to the level of the church's sociopolitical engagement, which can help promote democratic reform.

Following the logic of the above theoretical model, this chapter seeks to answer the following questions: To what extent has post-1997 Hong Kong society been influenced by the sociopolitical engagement of the Christian churches? To what extent have international church organizations, such as the Vatican and the World Council of Churches, influenced the doctrine and mission of the Christian churches in Hong Kong? How do the different models of the Christian churches encourage or discourage sociopolitical invlovement? In what ways have the Christian churches and para-church organizations interacted with secular social movement organizations? Has such interaction facilitated or hampered democratic reform? To what extent have the tensions among the different Christian churches and para-church organizations affected social mobilization?

Data and method

This chapter is an analysis of field research. I collected data through direct participant observation and in-depth interviews. I also collected literature to supplement the information collected through field research. I am a member of the Protestant community in Hong Kong, and have been active in social issues. With this status I was able to observe how Christians understand and react to various social and political issues. The scope of this study covers 2001 to 2006, with special focus on the sociopolitical mobilization of the Christian churches and para-church organizations. During this period, I collected information on and attended the sociopolitical activities of the Christian churches, such as the Christian anti-Article 23 campaign, and the July 1 prayer meetings and march. On some occasions, I expressed my views to the media through the Hong Kong Christian Institute (HKCI), and added my name to the signature campaigns organized by the churches concerning the issues of democratic reform, human rights, and livelihood of the people.

In addition to participant observation, I conducted in-depth interviews with 12 Christians in order to understand how different denominations react to sociopolitical issues. The interviews, lasting from between 30 minutes to one hour 30 minutes, were conducted from July 12, 2006 to August 1, 2006. The interviews started with structured questions. New questions arose as the interviews progressed. The interviewees were Catholic and Protestant, including mainline and evangelical Protestants. Specifically, the Protestant interviewees, both clergy and laity, came from the Church of Christ in China (CCC), the Methodist church, the Anglican church and the Lutheran church. With the consent of some interviewees, I used their real names and quoted them because their positions were meaningful to the analysis of the issues. In other paragraphs, I have concealed the names of the interviewees.

Governance crisis and the response of the churches

From 1997 to 2006, the policies of the Hong Kong SAR government often triggered a critical reaction from the population. Many issues occurred between 2001 and 2003, including the introduction of legislation banning "evil" cults; an attempt to introduce tough national security legislation under Article 23 of the Basic Law, and the decision to deny universal suffrage for the election of the chief executive and all seats in the Legislative Council. On July 1, 2003, 500,000 people took to the streets to protest against the government's proposed Article 23 national security legislation. During the march, the crowds chanted "Down with Tung," expressing anger toward the government. In 2004, the theme of the July 1 march was "Return Power to the People," revealing the participants' continued discontent on the issue of governance. In 2005, Chief Executive Tung Chee-hwa stepped down and was succeeded by Donald Tsang Yam-kuen.

The Christian churches and para-church organizations in Hong Kong expressed concern about many sociopolitical matters by issuing public statements, holding press conferences, organizing talks and seminars, and taking part in rallies and marches. The Christians who tend to take part in social issues usually agree with many universal social values, and also tend to consider that such values have a religious foundation. Democratic reform, human rights, and the livelihood of the people are good examples.

Christians in Hong Kong generally support democracy, though some are more active in promoting it than others. Those Christians who support democratic reform mainly come from the mainline churches that are closely related to the ecumenical movement. They believe that the power of the government is from God, and the function of it is for the well-being of people. The democratic system can hold government responsible and can help realize the will of God. Therefore, Christians in Hong Kong can pray for the government and at the same time criticize it, attempting to influence the policies of government so as to safeguard social justice.

Christians also support the value of human rights. From 2003 to 2006, they criticized the government for violating the principle of human rights in many social issues. However, Christians' understanding of human rights stems from the doctrine of creation. This differs from a secular understanding of the foundations of human rights. The story of Genesis says that God created human beings and therefore they are all equal and have dignity by their very nature as God's creation. Christians defend human rights on the basis that human beings bear the image of God (*Imago Dei*).

The issue of the livelihood of people is another example showing the uniqueness of Christian values. These values sometimes differ from the values of other Hong Kong citizens. In the New Testament, Jesus declared that his mission was "to bring good news to the poor ... to proclaim liberty to the captives, and recovery of sight to the blind, to set free the oppressed" (Luke 4:18) For Christians in Hong Kong, Jesus set the example for sociopolitical engagement, and he called on his followers to care for the weak and the oppressed. On this basis, Christians choose to react against social injustice in defense of the poor and therefore how well a government defends the poor and upholds justice can in part determine its legitimacy. When a government does not take the interests of the poor seriously in its policy-making, Christians will criticize it for favoring business and the rich at the expense of the poor. As such, the issue of the livelihood of the people is connected to good or bad governance of the Hong Kong SAR government.

Democratic reform

In 2003, Hong Kong citizens began to discuss the possibility of universal suffrage for the chief executive in 2007 and for the Legislative Council (LegCo) in 2008. Because the chief executive is elected by only 800 people who make up the Election Committee, and 30 seats of the 60-seat Legislative Council are elected through functional constituencies, the elections have been criticized as undemocratic.

Christian organizations have demanded democratic reform for many years. In December, 2003, six Christian organizations launched a signature campaign to call on Christians to demand universal suffrage. A total of 354 Christians and 12 Christian organizations publicly backed the campaign. The organizations included the HKCI, Student Christian Movement of Hong Kong (SCM), Christians for Hong Kong Society (CHKS), Fellowship of Evangelical Christians (FES), DCJP, and Hong Kong Catholic Commission for Labor Affairs (CCLA). In March, 2004, the HKCI issued another public statement strongly criticizing the National People's Congress's interpretation of the Basic Law regarding elections in the SAR.

In the same year, the Concern Group for Social Affairs of the CCC issued several public statements and submitted them to the government. In March, 2004, the Concern Group issued a public statement that made clear the church's support for universal suffrage for the election of the chief executive and LegCo. In April that year, the Concern Group criticized the Hong Kong government for asking the National People's Congress to interpret the Basic Law. The Ministerial Session of the Methodist church also issued two public statements in support of universal suffrage and criticizing the government's decision to ask the National People's Congress to interpret the Basic Law.

During 2002 and 2003, the Hong Kong government sought to introduce tougher national security legislation under Article 23 of the Basic Law. In June, 2003, a group of Christians opposed to Article 23 called on Christians in Hong Kong to support their position as laid out in a public statement entitled: "Opposing harsh legislation, building democratic institutions." The Christian organizations supporting the campaign included HKCI, SCM, CHKS, FES, DCJP, and CCLA.

On June, 20, clergy and laity from the Catholic church, the CCC, the Methodist church, HKCI, and so on held a press conference at which they called on Hong Kong citizens to participate in the July 1 march to oppose the introduction of Article 23.[7] On July 1, 2003, more than 8,000 Christians took part in a prayer meeting held prior to the march. Leaders from the Catholic and Protestant churches spoke at the meeting and prayed for the participants.[8] Since then, the prayer meeting has become a regular activity for Christians before the July 1 march every year.

According to the statistics announced by the Public Opinion Program of the University of Hong Kong, the number of participants in the July 1 march in 2003 ranged from 429,000 to 522,000.[9] In the survey, about 26.5 percent of respondents replied that the call from religious persons is "very important," and 17.5 percent replied "important" (see Table 3.1).

In June, 2004, seven Christian organizations issued a public statement entitled *Christian Manifesto on July 1*, calling on Christians to take part in the march that year. The theme of the march was "Return Power to the People." The organizations included DCJP, CCLA, Diocesan Youth Commission (DYC), HKCI, SCM, CHKS, and the Fellowship of Social Concern from the Sham Oi Church of the CCC (SOC).

According to the statistics announced by the Public Opinion Program of the University of Hong Kong, the number of participants in the 2004 July 1 march ranged from 180,000 to 210,000. In the survey, about 9.6 percent of the respondents said they were Catholic, and 21.1 percent said they were Protestant (see Table 3.2). The above statistics show that around 17,280 to 20,160 Catholics and 37,980 to 44,310 Protestants took part in the 2004 July 1 march.

In November, 2005, the Constitutional Development Task Force of the Hong Kong government released a Fifth Report to explain the government's position on democratic reform. On November 7, eight Christian organizations, including the Catholic church, CCC, the Methodist church and HKCI, held a press conference to reject the report. They urged the government to issue a new proposal with details of when universal suffrage for the election of the chief executive and LegCo would be introduced.[10] Seminars and prayer meetings for democratic reform were organized by Christian organizations, including the DCJP, Social

Table 3.1 Question 27 "The call from religious persons" in the July 1, 2003 march

	Actual number	*%*
Very unimportant	140	12.3
Unimportant	154	13.6
Neutral	289	25.4
Important	199	17.5
Very important	301	26.5
Don't know/not applicable	23	4.7
Total	1,136	100
No reply	18	

Source: Public Opinion Program, University of Hong Kong.

Table 3.2 Question D6 "Religion" in the July 1, 2004 march

	Actual number	%
Protestant	119	21
Catholic	54	10
Buddhist	25	4
Taoist	3	1
Atheist	6	1
No religion	349	62
Others	9	2
Total	565	100

Source: Public Opinion Program, University of Hong Kong.

Concern Group of St. Mary Church in Hung Hom, Committee for Social Justice and People's Livelihood of the Hong Kong Christian Council (HKCC), HKCI, SCM, and CHKS.

Human rights

In December, 2001, the SAR government refused to allow the mainland-born children of Hong Kong citizens to attend local schools while they were waiting to be granted right of abode. Bishop Joseph Zen Ze-kiun called on the government to grant these children the right to attend school, and sent letters to more than 300 Catholic kindergarten, primary, and secondary schools asking them to accept the children. Quoting from the *Convention of the Rights of Child*, six Christian organizations issued a public statement criticizing the government for depriving children of the right to receive education. The organizations included the DCJP, HKCI, SCM, CHKS, CCLA, and SOC. The Concern Group for Social Affairs of the CCC also issued a public statement in support of Bishop Zen.

That same year, the Hong Kong government introduced legislation to ban "evil" cults, to bring the SAR into line with a similar law introduced by the National People's Conference in Beijing. Twenty-one non-governmental organizations (NGOs) issued public statements opposing the legislation and stressing that the law would be harmful to religious freedom in Hong Kong. Among the organizations, ten were Catholic and six Protestant, including the DCJP, CCLA, Hong Kong Federation of Catholic Students (FCS), HKCI, SCM, CHKS, Hong Kong Women's Christian Council (HKWCC), and Hong Kong Christian Industrial Committee (CIC).

Again that year, the Court of Final Appeal ruled that the mainland-born children of Hong Kong citizens have right of abode in the SAR. Soon afterwards, the Hong Kong government sought to overturn the Court's ruling by asking the National People's Congress in Beijing to reinterpret the Basic Law on the issue. Twenty-one NGOs issued public statements in support of the mainland-born children's right to live in Hong Kong. The statements held that family union is a basic human right. Among the organizations, six were Catholic and seven Protestant, including the DCJP, DYC, FCS, HKCI, SCM, CHKS, and CIC.

In 2005, the Hong Kong government proposed introducing anti-discrimination legislation, which would have extended to banning discrimination toward homosexuals. Evangelical Protestants opposed the legislation while ecumenical Protestants supported it. The latter formed a Christian Concern Group for Anti-discrimination on Sexuality, and issued a public statement in the form of a prayer entitled "Love Without Fear" in July, 2005.

Livelihood of the people

In December, 2001, six Christian organizations issued a public statement opposing lowering, by 15 percent, the minimum wage of overseas domestic workers, as proposed by the Association of Employers of Overseas Domestic Workers. The organizations included the CIC, CCLA, DCJP, HKCI, and HKWCC.

In 2003, the Hong Kong government proposed cutting the Comprehensive Social Security Assistance Scheme by 11.1 percent in order to reduce its financial deficit. In March, 2003, 26 Christian organizations joined together to issue a public statement entitled: "Those who are without mercy will not obtain mercy." The title was taken from the biblical passage Romans 11:31. Among the organizations, 11 were Catholic and 15 were Protestant, including the DCJP, CCLA, Concern Group for Social Affairs of CCC, SOC, HKCI, SCM, CIC, HKWCC, Hong Kong Church Renewal Movement (CRM), and Mission to New Arrivals (MNA).

In April, 2005, 32 NGOs issued a public statement in response to the Hong Kong government's negotiations with the World Trade Organization on the issue of the liberalization of social services and trade. The statement criticized the Hong Kong government for placing public services in the bill of liberalization without proper consultation with local organizations, practitioners of social services, and the general public. Among the organizations, six were Christian groups, including the DCJP, CCLA, FCS, HKCI, SCM, and CIC.

In June, 2005, 24 NGOs and 104 individuals issued a public statement entitled: "An Illegal Worker is Still a Worker," supporting a judge of the District Court who ruled that the family of an illegal worker should be given compensation due to an accidental death. The government and some trade unions had proposed changing the law in order to prevent illegal workers from claiming compensation. Among the organizations, nine were Christian groups, including the CCLA, DCJP, Hong Kong Catholic Communications Office, St. Vincent's Church, HKCI, and HKWCC.

The Christian churches and social mobilization

As illustrated above, the Christian churches have been active in sociopolitical issues and have mobilized in response to government policy in Hong Kong.

However, different Christian churches have responded differently. In this section, I shall examine these differences and the reasons for it.

The Catholic church

Since the early 1980s, the Catholic church in Hong Kong has commented publicly on sociopolitical issues, and encouraged the clergy and laity to uphold social justice. Until 2002 the Catholic church was under the leadership of Cardinal Wu Cheng-chung. Cardinal Joseph Zen Ze-kiun succeeded Cardinal Wu that year. Cardinal Wu preferred to take a low-profile approach to sociopolitical issues and tended to use pastoral letters to express his views. This is common practice in the Catholic church. In 1999, Cardinal Wu issued a pastoral letter entitled *God is love* in support of the mainland children of Hong Kong citizens seeking right of abode in Hong Kong. In the letter he criticized the government for asking the National People's Congress in Beijing to reinterpret the Basic Law on the matter:

> The present question of the right of abode belongs within the competence of Hong Kong's autonomy. The SAR should itself give its own interpretation, but it has not done this. Asking for a reinterpretation from the Standing Committee of the NPC cannot help but damage the foundation of the autonomy of the SAR, shaking the foundations of the Hong Kong family, raise doubts in people's minds about the central government's promise of "one country, two systems with a high degree of autonomy" and undermine the confidence of the international community towards Hong Kong. Who can be sure how far-reaching the effects will be?[11]

It was unusual for a leader of the Hong Kong Catholic church to issue a pastoral letter commenting on sociopolitical issues and criticizing the government. The letter showed that Cardinal Wu was concerned about governance in Hong Kong and the policies of the government. Different in style and practice to his predecessor, Cardinal Zen has openly criticized the government on many occasions, and his views have been widely reported in the local newspapers. Since 2003, Cardinal Zen has taken part in prayer meetings organized before the annual July 1 pro-democracy march. In doing so, he has granted the march a moral legitimacy. Due to his critical stance toward the government on the issues of democratic reform, human rights, and livelihood of the people, he has become known as the "conscience of Hong Kong society."

The Catholic church's critical stance on sociopolitical issues in Hong Kong developed due to changes in the political and social environment and stemmed from the values promoted by Catholic social teaching. The teachings of the Second Vatican Council advocated that the Catholic laity and in some cases the institutional church should become more involved in social justice issues. On one occasion during a talk to university students on the sociopolitical role of the Catholic church in Hong Kong, Cardinal Zen explained that the position of the church on such issues was determined by Catholic social teaching.[12] Catholic social teaching may therefore be seen as being partly responsible for helping to mobilize Catholics to take part in social movements.

However, the leaders in the Catholic church are only part of the whole institution. In Hong Kong, most of the clergy take little interest in social issues and the majority of the laity are not involved in social movements.[13] Generally speaking, the clergy and laity are more concerned about spiritual and parish matters than social justice issues. Put simply, it appears that the leaders of the church are the ones attempting to mobilize the laity to become involved in social issues, while the majority of the clergy and laity lack motivation to become more active.

This being the case, how was the Catholic church able to mobilize large numbers of Catholics to take part in certain social movements, such as the July 1 march? The structure of the church and the role of its leaders is key. The church leaders openly express their views on social issues and through the media help to influence public opinion. Second, various organizations in the church work to mobilize the laity to become more socially active.

First, Cardinal Zen regularly comments on sociopolitical issues and the Hong Kong media often treat his comments as headline news. As a result, Cardinal Zen's comments often stir up public debate on sociopolitical issues. The heated sociopolitical environment effectively arouses the laity's attention and motivates them to take action. The weakness of this practice is that the Catholic laity can sometimes show little interest in matters that the cardinal has not spoken about.

Second, a few organizations within the Catholic church actively seek to educate and mobilize the laity, namely the DCJP, CCLA, DYC, and so on. One of the tasks for these organizations is to advocate the responsibility of Catholics to become involved in sociopolitical issues. This is done through seminars and workshops, as well as issuing public statements. Among these organizations, the DCJP is particularly noteworthy. After the Second Vatican Council, the Vatican urged the Catholic church around the world to form local DCJPs to assist the laity to become more engaged in society and to uphold justice. The Hong Kong DCJP was established in 1977, under the leadership of the local bishop, to advocate Catholic social responsibility. For example, the diocese issued a document named *Guidelines for Groups in Social Engagement* in 1999. The DCJP then went to each parish to help the clergy establish such groups and organize activities. In addition to this, many of the public statements representing the views of the Catholic church on social issues have been expressed through the DCJP.

The DCJP organizes social movements outside the parish and church forum. One example is the relationship between the DCJP and the Civil Human Rights Front (CHRF). The CHRF lacked both hard and human resources when it was established in September, 2002. The DCJP sent a staff member named Jackie Hung Ling-yu to assist the CHRF from the very beginning and two-thirds of her time was spent working for the CHRF. She was the vice-convener of the Article 23 Concern Group from 2002 to 2004, and the convener of the Concern Group for Democratic Development and People's Livelihood launched in 2004. She was named an Asian hero by the Asian version of *Time Magazine* in 2004 after the anti-Article 23 campaign organized by the CHRF in 2003 drew some 500,000 people on to the streets of Hong Kong. This showed how the institution of the church was willing to collaborate with secular social movement organizations to mobilize Hong Kong citizens to respond to government policy.

The Protestant mainline churches and para-church organizations

The many denominations in the Protestant churches in Hong Kong may be divided into two categories, namely mainline and the evangelical. The mainline denominations are those churches, such as the Anglicans and Lutherans, that accept the Catholic faith and take part in the ecumenical movement. The evangelical denominations are those churches, such as the Baptist and Christian Alliance churches, for which evangelism is paramount. In this section, I shall examine the mainline churches and their response to government policy. Afterwards I will examine the role of the evangelical churches.

The mainline churches focused on here include the Anglican, Lutheran, Methodist, and the CCC. The mainline churches are sometimes also called the ecumenical churches due to their involvement in the ecumenical movement, which advocates Christian social responsibility. Nevertheless, some churches are more active than others.

The Church of Christ in China

From 2001 to 2006, the Hong Kong Council of the CCC actively addressed sociopolitical issues, including democratic reform, human rights, and the livelihood of the people. Most of the public statements were printed in the church's official publication *Hui-sheng* (Convergent Voices), and submitted to the government. Generally, the statements would be reported by the Hong Kong Protestant newspaper *Christian Times*, and read by individual Protestants of all denominations and organizations. For example, the Concern Group for Social Affairs of the Theological and Ministerial Department of the church issued its public statement regarding democratization in *Hui-sheng* in April, 2004. Entitled "The Question of Principle regarding Institutional Development suggested by the Institutional Development Task Force of the Hong Kong SAR Government," the statement expressed the church's position in support of democratic reform:

> Based on the Christian doctrine, we believe that human beings bear the image of God and thus should enjoy equal rights from the time they are born. This logic extends to the equal rights of Hong Kong citizens to elect their chief executive and Legislative Councilors of the Hong Kong SAR government.... We strongly demand universal suffrage should be used in the election for chief executive in 2007 and the Legislative Council in 2008.[14]

In addition, the CCC publicly expressed its views on important sociopolitical matters. Below are two examples. Together with the Catholic church and other Protestant denominations, the CCC openly supported the anti-Article 23 campaign in June, 2003 and called on Hong Kong citizens to join the July 1 march.[15] In November, 2005, the CCC joined with the Catholic and Protestant churches again to publicly express its rejection of the Fifth Report released by the Constitutional Development Task Force of the Hong Kong government.[16]

The reasons why the CCC took an active role on sociopolitical issues was due to the problems it saw being caused by poor government policies, and due to flexibility in the institution of the CCC itself. From 2001 to 2005, the CCC regularly issued public statements in response to government policies and activities. In my interview with Reverend Wong Chun-ting, convener of the Concern Group for Social Affairs, he said the following:

> The government's policies in the era of chief executive Tung Chee-hwa made people angry. Many issues emerged and people felt an urgent need to respond to them. But [the present chief executive] Donald Tsang Yam-kuen is very clever. There have been fewer controversies and people appear less interested in responding to government policies.[17]

The remarks made by Reverend Wong show that the social environment was one factor that affected how the church responded. However, the social environment cannot fully explain why the CCC was able to organize such a swift response on sociopolitical issues. The institution of the church is key here.

Both the doctrine of the CCC and the organization of the church appear to favor sociopolitical engagement. The doctrine of the CCC mainly stems from Congregationalism and Presbyterianism, and the church identified itself with the ecumenical movement. The majority of the clergy in the CCC are trained in the Chung Chi Divinity School of the Chinese University of Hong Kong, and the theology of the Divinity School has been consistent with the ecumenical movement. This explains why the clergy of the CCC felt a strong sense of responsibility to criticize the government when they were faced with a policy they believed was wrong.

The organization of the CCC also makes social activism possible. An organization in the CCC, the Concern Group for Social Affairs, is responsible for analyzing social issues, drafting public statements, and suggesting courses of action to the church. The group has seven members, both clergy and laity. Since 2001, Reverend Wong Chun-ting has been the convener of the group. The group is under the Theological and Ministerial Department, which is made up of all the church's clergy, and is responsible for approving the drafts of statements written and action suggested by the group. Finally, the General Secretary of the CCC has the duty to examine the statements or actions approved by the Department and to provide or deny his endorsement. If the proposed statement or action goes through the above procedure smoothly, it will be adopted by the church as its official position on a sociopolitical issue.

Reverend Eric So Shing-yit, the General Secretary of the CCC, made the following comment on the mechanism:

> The organizational hierarchy of the CCC allows those who are not leader the chance to act. The group can speak out if the leader does not do so. More importantly, the leader cannot extinguish the voice of the group.[18]

Reverend So's comment not only explains why the CCC is able to realize the mission of social justice, but also why some denominations keep silent on social issues.

How many people the church has to call on is also important in determining the extent to which a church can become socially engaged. The members and convener of the Concern Group for Social Affairs are all volunteers. Reverend Wong has been convener of the group since 2001 but his chief duty has been as a minister of the church. He has to use his spare time to work with the Concern Group for Social Affairs. This working model affects the church's sociopolitical engagement in two ways: first, if the convener and members of the group are heavily involved in their other church duties they have less time to work with the group. Second, the commitment of the convener and members determines the level of activism. The stronger the social commitment they have, the more effective and persistent the group will be.

The Methodist church

The Methodist church in Hong Kong is one of the most sociopolitically active Protestant denominations. For example, the Methodist church joined the two press conferences with the CCC mentioned above. In 2003, Reverend Ralph Lee Ting-sun, the former President of the Methodist church, took part in the prayer meetings before the July 1 marches, standing alongside Cardinal Joseph Zen Ze-kiun. In the 2003 July 1 March, the Methodist church in Wan Chai was opened to allow people taking part in the march to stop for a drink of water or to use its toilets.

The Methodist church has also supported the process of democratization in Hong Kong. The Ministerial Session in the Methodist church issued two public statements on April 1 and 9, 2004. In the first statement, published in the local newspaper *Ming Pao*, the church criticized the government for asking the National People's Congress to interpret the Basic Law on the issue of democratic reform:

> Hong Kong's economic and legal conditions and highly educated population are mature enough to support universal suffrage, as the level of democratic participation has already shown. The National People's Congress in Beijing should therefore seriously consider allowing universal suffrage in Hong Kong in 2007 and 2008.[19]

In the second statement the Ministerial Session urged Hong Kong citizens to express their views on democratic reform:

> In this very moment of institutional reform, we call for Hong Kong citizens to express their views and to take action. They should discuss it in their communities, and tell the Hong Kong SAR government what they think. In this way they are assisting the chief executive to fully understand their views on institutional reform, so that the chief executive can report it to the central government.[20]

It can be considered somewhat progressive for the Methodist denomination to openly support democratization and call for Hong Kong citizens to support it.

The social environment is a crucial factor affecting the sociopolitical involvement of the Methodist church. In 2001, the Methodist church published a document entitled *Stepping into the 21st Century*, expressing how the church understood the social environment in Hong Kong:

> Hong Kong citizens believe that the chief executive lacks experience in governance, that the government lacks authority, and that there are clear contradictions between the Hong Kong and central governments.... In such a political environment, political parties are not able to develop themselves, and Hong Kong's citizens are not satisfied with the performance of the government.[21]

In 2005, the Methodist church published another document entitled *Redirection in the Second Half of the First Decade of the 21st Century*, in which the church expressed its observations on social change from 2001 to 2005:

> It seems Hong Kong's political issues are always in dispute, weakening the governing authority of the SAR government. The two July 1 marches and the interpretations of the Basic Law prompted Hong Kong people to express their concern.... The SAR government asked the Standing Committee of the National People's Congress to interpret the Basic Law to suppress the opinion of Hong Kong's population. The government's design, however, made Hong Kong people unhappy with the current style of governance and question if the SAR government will hold on to the rule of law.[22]

In my interview with Reverend Lee Ting-sun he pointed out that the social environment is an important factor that has caused the Methodist church to express its concern over sociopolitical issues.

> After 1997, many social issues emerged, such as the demand for direct elections, the controversy over Article 23, and many issues concerning the livelihood of the people. The basic question in Hong Kong concerns governance. The chief executive in Hong Kong today is de facto appointed by the

central government because only a small group of 800 select citizens are allowed to elect him. This is far from democratic. And because Hong Kong citizens have no control over who will lead them, it is reasonable to say that the chief executive may not be able to effectively rule Hong Kong. This situation has caused discontent among Hong Kong citizens.... Why does the church have to speak out? The church should face the challenge and be true to its beliefs.[23]

The sociopolitical engagement of the Methodist church can be explained by how the church sees its role in Hong Kong society. The two documents above show that the church sees its role as that of a prophet, servant, priest, and teacher. Among these roles, the role of a prophet is important in motivating social activism. The second document explains the work of a prophet in the world:

As a prophet, our church should display concern for society. In view of the unjust and demoralizing forces in the political, economic, social and cultural spheres, as well as the oppressive, enslaving and damaging institutions, the church should spiritually maintain its discerning and analytical powers. At this juncture, our church should demonstrate specific and appropriate attention to social problems, like the sharp disparity of wealth, pornography, gambling, drug abuse and the reforms of medical service, education and social welfare systems, as well as freedom, democracy, and the development of human rights and the rule of law.[24]

The quotation in the document regarding the role of a prophet shows that the Methodist church's doctrine, teachings, and sense of mission are key motivators for sociopolitical engagement.

The organization of the Methodist church is also important in helping to explain why the church has become involved in social issues. In the organizational structure, the Ministerial Session and the Social Services Division are two units responsible for reacting to social issues. The clergy make up the Ministerial Session of which there is a subsection named the Concern Group for Institutional Reform. This group has the responsibility for responding to social issues, such as democracy, drafting public statements, and drawing up submissions to be sent to the government. The two public statements mentioned above were released to the public in the name of the Ministerial Session. These statements represent the official position of the Methodist church. In the Social Services Division, there is a Concern Group for Social Affairs responsible for advocating sociopolitical engagement among the laity. Established in 1990, the members of the group consist of clergy and laity.

The theology of the Methodist church is also a key factor. The Chung Chi Divinity School of the Chinese University of Hong Kong is the only seminary recognized by the church, and all the clergy receive their theological training there. This arrangement helps to connect the identity of the clergy with the ecumenical movement, and to build consensus among the clergy in the church.

In sum, the social environment, the doctrine, and mission of the church, as well as its organizational structure, help in making the Methodist church more sociopolitically engaged.

The Anglican church

Contrary to the CCC and the Methodist church, the Anglican and the Lutheran churches are less engaged in sociopolitical issues. Since 1997, the Anglican Church has reacted only occasionally to some issues. Continuing a tradition started when Hong Kong was a British colony, the Anglican Archbishop of Hong Kong, Peter Kwong Kwong-kit, releases a public message each Christmas. The message usually contains comprehensive but ambiguous comments on social problems. However, one issue on which the Anglican church has spoken openly since 2001 was the government's Education Bill. The Anglican church opposed the bill on the grounds that it would have a detrimental impact on church-run schools.[25] On the whole, the Anglican church as an institution has been silent on many controversial issues. On the other hand, many clergy in the church support greater sociopolitical engagement by the laity and clergy. However, the voices of individual priests have seldom converged to impact upon the official position of the church. The institutional structure of the church is partly the reason why the church has remained silent.

Highly influenced by the theology of William Temple, the doctrine, teachings, and mission of the Anglican church support the sociopolitical engagement of the church *de jure*. In Hong Kong, the Anglican church provides a wide variety of key educational and social services. However, the Anglican church docs not allow the church as an organization to become involved in sociopolitical issues. If a priest has a strong interest in a certain issue, he or she can express or act upon it as an individual. Two examples suffice to explain the situation. The first is the case of Reverend Fung Chi-wood. Reverend Fung is a renowned democrat in Hong Kong who engaged in the democratic movement in the 1980s and 1990s. He was only allowed to take part in the democratic movement as an individual, and could not speak for the church. The other example is the Anglican official publication *Echo*. *Echo* publishes progressive social and political articles written by individual priests, but it never expresses the church's official views on social or political issues, or makes public statements.

The organization of the Anglican church is another factor constraining the church's sociopolitical engagement. Following the tradition of episcopacy, the process of policy-making and implementation of the Anglican church is top-down. There is no platform in the Anglican institution to allow priests to express their sociopolitical views. The complex organizational structure makes it difficult for an individual to affect the church's official views from below. If a priest or member of the laity wants to make the church express a public statement, he or she has to introduce the motion first in a parish council. If the motion is supported, the proposal may be adopted in that parish, or it may be discussed further at a Diocesan Synod. If the motion is further supported, the proposal may be adopted by the Synod, or be discussed further at the Provincial Synod level. If the motion is again supported, it will become the official position of the Anglican church. Most clergy and laity, however, simply adhere to the official views of the church and choose to express their views as individuals if they differ from the organization. Few attempt to influence church policy through their parish councils.

Compared with the Church Christ of China and the Methodist church, the Anglican church lacks a mechanism to allow the clergy and laity to discuss sociopolitical issues and to act effectively. The institution is able to suppress any effort to mobilize church members to take part in sociopolitical movements.

The Lutheran churches

There are many groups making up the Lutheran church in Hong Kong. They are the Evangelical Lutheran church of Hong Kong, the Hong Kong Synod of the Chinese Rhenish church, the Hong Kong and Macau Lutheran church, the Hong Kong Synod of the Lutheran church, and the Hong Kong Tsung Tsim Mission.

Generally speaking, the above denominations have been passive in sociopolitical engagement, though the social consciousness of some churches is stronger than others. This is due to two reasons: first, most of the churches are facing organizational survival, which makes it difficult to engage in sociopolitical issues. Second, the institution and practice of some Lutheran groups are more evangelical than mainline, which means they are less supportive of the ecumenical movement. Consequently, some of the Lutheran churches joined campaigns on moral issues organized by evangelical Christians, rather than the campaigns on sociopolitical issues advocated by the mainline churches.

Para-church organizations of mainline Protestant churches

Many para-church organizations exist in the mainline churches camp, such as the HKCC, HKCI, HKWCC, and SCM. Among these organizations, the HKCI is highly mobilized and engaged in sociopolitical issues.

The HKCI was established by Reverend Kwok Nai-wang in 1988 to unite those "Christians who are concerned about Hong Kong society and to make a contribution to the churches and the future of Hong Kong."[26] One of the functions of the HKCI is "to be a sign of promoting human rights, democracy and justice."[27] The doctrine and mission of the HKCI derives from the ecumenical movement. The HKCI also joined the two press conferences with the CCC and the Methodist church mentioned above. The organizational structure of the HKCI is simple and small, with only seven full-time staff members. Nevertheless, its simple and small structure makes the HKCI flexible and effective enough to engage in sociopolitical issues, such as democratic reform, human rights, economic justice, education, the rights of women, and globalization.

One of the capacities of the HKCI is its ability to mobilize Christians and the general population to respond to sociopolitical issues. These organizations include those of the Catholic church (e.g., the DCJP, CCLA, FCS), mainline Protestant churches (e.g., the HKCC, CIC, HKWCC), evangelical Protestant churches (e.g., the CRM, FES, CHKS), and secular social movement organizations (e.g., the Civil Human Rights Front, Hong Kong Human Rights Monitor, Asian Human Rights Commission, Amnesty International Hong Kong, Hong Kong People's Alliance on Globalization, Hong Kong Federation of Trade Unions).[28]

The power of the mainline para-church organizations in social mobilization is shown in the relationship between the HKCI and the Civil Human Rights Front (CHRF). Established in 2002, the CHRF is an alliance formed by more than 50 non-governmental organizations, including those representing religious, cultural, women, labor, minority, homosexual, democratic, and human rights issues. The HKCI is one of the founding members of the CHRF. In 2002, while the HKCI and other organizations were discussing the Anti-discrimination Bill, they felt that the upcoming Article 23 Bill would seriously damage Hong Kong's human rights and the rule of law. They decided to form the CHRF to oppose the Article 23 Bill. In 2003, the July 1 march organized by the CHRF successfully mobilized more than 500,000 people to take to the streets to oppose the introduction of Article 23. The campaign was one factor that caused the government to put aside the legislation. Later, the CHRF established the Concern Group for Democratic Development and People's Livelihood, pressuring the government on issues of democratic reform and human rights.

The role of the HKCI in the CHRF is threefold: providing material resources, facilitating communication, and injecting ideas and values. Regarding the provision of material resources, the CHRF lacked funds to run the organization at the initial stage. The CHRF therefore held its meetings at the HKCI office. Furthermore, the HKCI and other organizations gave HK$10,000 respectively to the CHRF to cover administration costs. The DCJP also provided a staff member, Jackie Hung Ling-yu.

Rose Wu Lo-sai, General Secretary of the HKCI, was the convener of the CHRF from 2003 to 2005, elected by all CHRF members. Wu was elected due to her experience in organizing social movements and because of the trust placed on her as a member of a Protestant church. The members believed that Wu and the HKCI did not have any political ambitions behind organizing the CHRF. Wu believed the CHRF was a useful platform where different organizations could exchange views and work together.[29] During meetings, she often took the role of mediator to facilitate communication among CHRF members.

Regarding the injection of ideas and values, Wu and other CHRF members provided many ideas and principles to help shape the rules and structure of the CHRF. One of the ideas founding the CHRF was that of encouraging the participation of minority groups. Plurality and participation are considered fundamental. The ideas and values are shared among CHRF members. As a result, no member of any one political party or group can take over the CHRF. This has made the CHRF inclusive in character and accepting of those groups representing ethnic minorities and homosexuals. CHRF members also established a consensus on some principles that are different from other social movement organizations. One of these was that anyone who is a member of a political party cannot be the convener of the CHRF, and the convener holds office for one year and can be re-elected only once.

In some circumstances, Christian values were able to influence the decision-making of the CHRF. An example is the theme of the July 1 march in 2004. During the meeting, some members proposed using "Down with Tung" (the then SAR chief executive) as the theme of the political rally. The HKCI and DCJP held that the direction of the social movement should focus on democratic reform rather than on attacking individuals in the government. Their reasons for opposing an attack on the chief executive was that it violated fundamental Christian values. After fierce debate, the theme was declared "Return Power to the People." This example shows that tension in values existed between the Christian and secular organizations in the CHRF.

The social movement launched by the CHRF was unique and novel compared to the Hong Kong Alliance in Support of Patriotic Democratic Movements of China (SPDMC), which was dominated by pro-democracy political leaders, while the CHRF represented grassroots community and minority groups. First, it was arranged that the minority groups should walk at the front of the march. From 2004 to 2006, the grassroots groups leading the march represented women's issues, homosexuals, ethnic minorities, youth, and trade unions. In the June 4 march organized by the SPDMC, political parties usually took the lead, and the media tended to focus on a few leading pro-democracy figures. Second, the July 1 marches emphasized the values of plurality and inclusiveness. During the marches, the organizations that took part were allowed to create their own slogans and express their own demands. Street stations were set up along the route of the march by different organizations so that they could propagate their organization and raise funds. During the July 4 march, non-core members were only allowed to follow the leading pro-democracy groups and figures, and the slogans were restricted by the organizers.

The values and practices of the July 1 march organized by the CHRF have changed the culture of social movements in Hong Kong. Such changes include from political party-centered to minority-centered, from a restricted model to a pluralistic model, and from a monopolization of the leadership by a few elites to a system of alternating leadership. After the chief executive gives his annual Policy Address, it has become practice for the CHRF to release a publication entitled *Agenda from the People*. CHRF members from different organizations each take responsibility for writing up a chapter of the agenda. The idea of this practice is to allow different organizations to express their social and political demands in response to the Policy Address. In my interview with Wu, she stated the following:

> CHRF helps members understand that they should look not only at their own agendas and interests, but at the agenda of all and for the common

good. This is a way to learn mutual empowerment. That is the spirit of civil society.[30]

Para-church organizations of evangelical Protestant churches

The evangelical churches are equally important in social mobilization. Different to the mainline Protestant churches, evangelical churches focus heavily on moral issues,[31] with some exceptions relating to the livelihood of people.[32] After 1997, many evangelical churches with their like-minded para-church organizations, such as the Society for Truth and Light (STL), CRM, Industrial Evangelistic Fellowship, were outspoken on a number of moral issues, including soccer gambling, homosexuality, unemployment, and poverty. Some of issues were also supported by the mainline churches. However, the evangelical churches and organizations seldom expressed views or commented on issues relating to democratic reform and human rights.[33] As this chapter is concerned primarily with the relationship between Christianity and democratization, which is closely related to issues such as democratic reform and human rights, the moral focus of the evangelical churches is considered periphery.

It is noteworthy, however, that tensions existed between the evangelical and mainline churches and organizations on these moral issues. In some cases, as the mainline churches sought to mobilize social forces into pressuring the government, the evangelicals took action to express their views, which in some respects led to counter-mobilization. Below are two examples.

The first concerns a pro-democracy politician Cynthia Ho Sau-lan, who lost her seat in the Legislative Council election in 2004. During the election campaign, Rose Wu Lo-sai, as the convener of the CHRF, called on Hong Kong citizens to cast their votes with reference to four indicators: workers' rights, livelihood of the people, human rights, and universal suffrage. She also told the candidates that Hong Kong's citizens would like to be able to elect politicians who would defend the common good in society.[34] A day before the election, Wu called on Hong Kong's citizens to choose those candidates who support democracy, freedom, human rights, and the rule of law, so that they would monitor the government.[35]

At the same time, the STL called for Protestants to cast their votes based on the moral standards of the candidates. The organization published an extra entitled *Legislative Council Election on September 12: Christian Reflections*, listing those candidates who supported or violated the moral standards of the Christian doctrine, with particular emphasis on gambling and homosexual marriage.[36] The extra was soon reported by the *Christian Times*, a Protestant newspaper in Hong Kong.[37] Ho once expressed her support for homosexual marriage in the media. As a result she was defined as a candidate that did not support the moral standards of the Christian doctrine. Protestants were advised not to vote for her. The "Christian doctrine" in this context refers to the understanding and interpretation of the evangelical churches.

In the election, Ho lost her seat by only 800 votes. The election result triggered a debate in the Protestant community on whether the church should take responsibility for Cynthia Ho losing her seat.[38] On the website of the *Christian Times*, a reader named Wong Kai-chung made the following comments:

> If Hong Kong had an established democratic political system that did not fear outside interference, then Protestants would be able to choose not to cast their votes for those democratic candidates who violate the moral values of Christianity. But, during this critical time of democratic development in Hong Kong, Protestants need to consider seriously the consequences of not casting their votes for the pro-democracy candidates, and should consider that they risk losing freedom and basic rights if they do not. ... Every Protestant needs to think seriously about it, because the future of democracy in Hong Kong and freedom and rule of law, to a certain extent are in the hands of Protestants.[39]

There is no evidence so far to judge whether there is a correlation between the mobilization of the STL and Ho's defeat. Nevertheless, it is possible to make a preliminary judgment using fragments of data and information. Ko Tin-ming in his study of Protestant voting behavior finds that the rate of voting of Protestants is higher than average citizens.[40] According to a member of the clergy working in Ho's election district, his church members said that they did not vote for Ho because of the appeal made by the STL.[41] It is possible to construe that Ho's defeat was due to the absence of the Protestant vote. The case shows that the evangelical churches and related organizations have the mobilization power to affect the views and behavior of the Protestant laity. Conflict between the evangelical and mainline Protestants occurs because of their different values and choices of strategy.

The second case concerns the controversy surrounding allowing a pro-homosexual group to take the lead on the July 1 march in 2005. After the July 1 march in 2003, the members of the CHRF decided that it was not a good idea to allow political party figure-heads to take the lead during the July 1 marches. They thought it would turn the march into a political party-dominated event. The CHRF decided that minority groups should lead in the marches starting from 2004. In 2005, the CHRF decided to let pro-homosexual groups and women's groups walk at the front of the march. This decision triggered fierce opposition from the evangelical churches and related organizations. Choi Chi-sum, General Secretary of the STL, criticized the CHRF's decision and boycotted the July 1 march.[42] Likewise, the evangelical clergy made a similar appeal in the media calling on Protestants to boycott the march.[43] One member of the clergy stated that if there had been no such controversy surrounding the homosexual groups he would have encouraged his church members to take part in order to show Protestant support for the ideals of the march.[44] Later, some CHRF members were reported in the media as saying, "The arrangement of the CHRF shows a more profound and comprehensive perspective of democracy: democratic movement is an effort nurturing the attitude to respect the weak and minorities, rather than limiting it to election and democratic reform."[45]

How much did the appeal by the evangelical churches to boycott the march affect the number of participants on July 1? A survey conducted in 2005 finds that the number of participants in the July 1 march was approximately 20,000 people, of whom 16 percent were Protestants and 8 percent Catholics. In 2004, it was 21 percent Protestants and 10 percent Catholics. The figures drop slightly.[46] The comparison shows that the number of Protestants dropped 5 percent in 2005, amounting to 1,000 people.

The two cases show that mobilization and counter-mobilization occurred in the Protestant community and weakened its participation in the democratic movement due to the conflict in doctrine and mission between the evangelical and mainline churches.

Discussion

This chapter argues that social environment, international church organizations, the models of the churches and para-church organizations are four crucial factors affecting sociopolitical engagement of the churches in Hong Kong. More importantly, para-church organizations in both the Catholic church and the mainline Protestant churches, such as the DCJP and the HKCI, are important in the development of social movements and the building of civil society in Hong Kong.

A question we have not dealt with but which is highly relevant to this study is: Could the Christian churches and their social mobilization affect the governance of Hong Kong SAR government? Or, how does the government respond to the Christian churches' social mobilization? From the data I have collected, it is premature to answer these questions. However, some data do provide a preliminary answer. The think-tank of the Central Policy Unit in the government regularly contacts Christian organizations to collect their opinions. One such Christian organization is the HKCC. From 2002 to 2004, members of the Central Policy Unit held several meetings with Reverend Eric So Shing-yit, the former General Secretary of the HKCC. They exchanged views on certain sociopolitical policies. In 2005, Reverend So was invited to be a part-time member of the Central Policy Unit. In my interview with Reverend So Shing-yit, he commented:

> The Central Policy Unit defines the church as an organization that is not pro-government. When we discussed issues related to political problems, they were highly attentive. When we discussed issues relating to the livelihood of the people, they would explain to me what the government policy intends to do, and asked me my position and views. They were interested to know how the church understands the social situation.[47]

The above information reveals that the government will take into consideration what the Christian community thinks about its policies. It will consider seriously the reaction of the Christian community toward sociopolitical policy.

Scott Mainwaring's theory is useful in explaining the relationship between the Christian churches and democratization. The case of Hong Kong can provide insight into the theory, in particular the model of the church. Mainwaring holds that as an institution the church has its own interests. The church will do its best to preserve its organization and expand its influence. He considers that doctrine and mission largely determine the model of the church's action, or lack of it. The problem is, in my view, that when a church makes a decision on whether to act or not, it is a decision taken by the leaders. In other words, it is the people who interpret the doctrine and mission who determine the extent of the church's sociopolitical engagement. Mainwaring provides many insightful analyses on the institutional change of the Brazilian Catholic church, and he suggests that the conservative position of the church can be explained in terms of its tendency to maintain unity and coherence. However, when the church decides not to act, it is difficult to judge whether that decision was based on the doctrine and mission of the church, or was a rational choice in the face of a political reality. Whether a church's decision not to act stems from its intention to preserve its organization and expand its influence, and that the doctrine and mission were only used for justification, is still open to question. In this chapter, such a question may be applied to the Lutheran and evangelical churches. In this regard, the rational choice theory seems useful to supplement the weakness of Mainwaring's theory and to provide an alternative explanation.

Notes

1 McAdam, *Political Process and the Development of Black Insurgency.*
2 Wood, *Faith in Action.*
3 Adriance, "Base Communities and Rural Mobilization in Northern Brazil"; Cavendish, "Christian Base Communities and the Building of Democracy: Brazil and Chile," and Hewitt, "Myths and Realities of Liberation Theology: The Case of the Basic Christian Communities in Brazil."
4 Gaskill, "Rethinking Protestantism and Democratic Consolidation in Latin America," and Gill, *Rendering unto Caesar: The Catholic Church and the State in Latin America.*
5 Kuperus, "Resisting or Embracing Reform: South Africa's Democratic Transition and NGK–State Relations," and Stan and Turcescu, "The Romanian Orthodox Church and Post-communist Democratization."
6 Mainwaring, *The Catholic Church and Politics in Brazil, 1916–1985,* pp. 1–22.
7 *Apple Daily,* June 21, 2003, p. A-2.
8 *Ming Pao,* July 2, 2003, p. A-14.
9 So and Chan, "How to Calculate the Number of People in the July 1 March."
10 *Hong Kong Daily News,* November 8, 2005, p. A-6.
11 Cardinal John Wu Cheng-chung, *God is Love.* Pastoral Letter, 1999.
12 Cardinal Zen explained this point to the students in my class at Hong Kong Baptist University in 2006.
13 Li *et al.* "The Social Role of Catholics in Hong Kong Society," pp. 525–529.
14 *Hui Sheng* 560 (April, 2004), p. 3.
15 *Apple Daily,* June 21, 2003, p. A-2.
16 *Hong Kong Daily News,* November 8, 2005, p. A-6.
17 My interview with Reverend Wong Chun-ting, July 19, 2006.
18 My interview with Reverend Eric So Shing-yit, July 27, 2006.

19 Ministerial Session of the Methodist Church, Hong Kong, "Our Views on Institutional Development." *Ming Pao*, April 1, 2004.
20 Ministerial Session of the Methodist Church, Hong Kong, "Our Views on Institutional Development after the Interpretation of Basic Law." *Ming Pao*, April 9, 2004, p. A-16.
21 *Stepping into the 21st Century.*
22 *Redirection in the Second Half of the First Decade of the 21st Century.*
23 My interview with Reverend Ralph Lee Ting-sun, July 18, 2006.
24 *Redirection in the Second Half of the First Decade of the 21st Century.*
25 *Ming Pao*, May 24, 2004, p. A-16.
26 See "Objectives." *Annual Report 2004–2005.* Hong Kong: Hong Kong Christian Institute, 2005, p. 1.
27 Ibid.
28 See "Public Statements," webpage of the Hong Kong Christian Institute.
29 My interview with Rose Wu Lo-sai, July 21, 2006.
30 Ibid.
31 See the webpage of the Society for Truth and Light.
32 See the webpage of the Hong Kong Church Renewal Movement.
33 One exception is the issue of anti-discrimination legislation. Evangelical Protestants opposed the legislation extending banning discrimination toward homosexuals.
34 *Sing Pao Daily News*, August 26, 2004, p. A-6.
35 *Hong Kong Economic Journal*, September 11, 2004, p. 5.
36 *Legislative Council Election on September 12: Christian Reflections*, pp. 2–3.
36 Ibid.
37 *Christian Times*, no. 888 (September 5, 2004), p. 2.
38 *Christian Times*, no. 891 (September 26, 2004), p. 10.
39 Ibid.
40 Ko, *Christians and the 1995 Legislative Council Election*, p. 7.
41 The clergyman is a personal friend.
42 *Ming Pao*, June 18, 2005 p. B-20.
43 *Ming Pao*, June 25, 2005, p. A-13.
44 *Christian Times*, no. 930 (June 26, 2005), p. 1.
45 *Ming Pao*, June 24, 2005, p. A-32.
46 Chan *et al.* "Is the July 1 Campaign Lacking Focus?"
47 My interview with Reverend Eric So Shin-yit, August 1, 2006.

References

Publications

Adriance, Madeleine. "Base Communities and Rural Mobilization in Northern Brazil." *Sociology of Religion* 55, no. 2 (1994): 163–178.
Cavendish, James. "Christian Base Communities and the Building of Democracy: Brazil and Chile." *Sociology of Religion* 55, no. 2 (1994): 179–195.
Chan To-man, Ting-yiu Chung, and Lap-fung Lee, "Is the July 1 Campaign Lacking Focus?" (in Chinese). *Ming Pao*, July 15, 2005, p. B-12.
Chiu, Stephen Wing-kai and Tai-lok Lui, eds. *The Dynamics of Social Movement in Hong Kong.* Hong Kong: Hong Kong University Press, 2000.
Gaskill, Newton. "Rethinking Protestantism and Democratic Consolidation in Latin America." *Sociology of Religion* 58, no. 1 (1997): 69–91.
Gill, Anthony. *Rendering unto Caesar: The Catholic Church and the State in Latin America.* Chicago, IL: University of Chicago Press, 1998.

Hewitt, Warren. "Myths and Realities of Liberation Theology: The Case of the Basic Christian Communities in Brazil." In *The Politics of Latin American Liberation Theology: the Challenge to U.S. Public Policy*, ed. Richard Rubenstein and John Roth. Washington, DC: Washington Institute Press, 1995.

Ko, Tin-ming. *Christians and the 1995 Legislative Council Election* (in Chinese). Hong Kong: Department of Public and Social Administration, City University of Hong Kong, 1996.

——. *The Sacred and the Secular City: Political Participation of Protestant Ministers in Hong Kong during a Time of Change*. Aldershot: Ashgate, 2000.

Kuperus, Tracy. "Resisting or Embracing Reform: South Africa's Democratic Transition and NGK–State Relations." *Journal of Church and State* 38, no. 4 (1996): 841–873.

Legislative Council Election on September 12: Christian Reflections. Hong Kong: The Society for Truth and Light, September, 2004.

Leung, Beatrice and Shun-hing Chan. *Changing Church and State Relations in Hong Kong, 1950–2000*. Hong Kong: Hong Kong University Press, 2003.

Li Kit-man, Ka-hing Cheung, and Kun-sun Chan. "The Social Role of Catholics in Hong Kong Society." *Social Compass* 45, no. 4 (1998): 513–531.

Mainwaring, Scott. *The Catholic Church and Politics in Brazil, 1916–1985*. Stanford, CA: Stanford University Press, 1986.

McAdam, Doug. *Political Process and the Development of Black Insurgency, 1930–1970*. Chicago, IL: University of Chicago Press, 1982.

Redirection in the Second Half of the First Decade of the 21st Century. Hong Kong: The Methodist Church, Hong Kong, 2005. At www.methodist.org.hk/frame_2nd_5_years.html.

So, Clement Y. K. and So-kuen Chan. "How to Calculate the Number of People in the July 1 March" (in Chinese). Hong Kong: Public Opinion Program, University of Hong Kong, 2003. At hkupop.hku.hk.

Stan, Lavinia and Lucian Turcescu. "The Romanian Orthodox Church and Post-communist Democratization." *Europe-Asia Studies* 52, no. 8 (2000): 1467–1488.

Stepping into the 21st Century. Hong Kong: The Methodist Church, 2001. At www.methodist.org.hk/frame_5_years.html.

Wood, Richard. *Faith in Action: Religion, Race, and Democratic Organizing in America*. Chicago, IL: University of Chicago Press, 2002.

Wong Kai-chung, "We Cannot Strike a Balance Just for the Sake of It: A Reply to Dr. Kwan Kai-man" (in Chinese). *Christian Times* 892 (October 2, 2004), p. 11.

Webpages

Civil Human Rights Front. civilhrfront.org

Hong Kong Anglican Church (Episcopal). www1.hkskh.org

Hong Kong Christian Institute. www.hkci.org.hk

Hong Kong Church Renewal Movement. www.hkcrm.org.hk

Hong Kong Council of the Church in Christ in China. www.hkcccc.org

Justice and Peace Commission of the Hong Kong Catholic Diocese. www.hkjp.org

Methodist church, Hong Kong. www.methodist.org.hk

Public Opinion Program, University of Hong Kong. hkupop.hku.hk

Society for Truth and Light. www.truth-light.org.hk

4 Social cohesion and governance problems in the Tung Chee-hwa era

Elaine Chan and Joseph C. W. Chan

Introduction

Social cohesion is such a desirable phenomenon that scholars from different disciplines, most notably sociology,[1] psychology,[2] and most recently, political science, have made it a topic of investigation. Although each of these disciplines may have a slightly different emphasis, their concerns are more or less the same – the basis of an inclusive, stable, and integrated society. This chapter approaches social cohesion from the political science or policy perspective and examines the state of social cohesion as Chief Executive Tung Chee-hwa concluded his first term of office.

Social cohesion has been a concern for policy-makers since the last decade, probably as an upshot of some unwanted results of globalization and rapid economic development. These unwelcome processes include, among others, increasing inequality, exclusion, and instability, all of which could be quite unsettling for society. The Canadian government first introduced social cohesion into its official agenda in the 1990s to promote multiculturalism. Gradually this concept became incorporated into other policy areas as well. From the early 2000s, social cohesion has come to encompass processes like income distribution, employment, housing provision, access to healthcare and education, as well as political and civic participation.[3] International regimes are also concerned with promoting social cohesion. The Structural Funds and the EMPLOYMENT Initiative are examples of the European Union's effort to foster social cohesion by tackling unemployment, poverty, and exclusion from the information society.[4] The Council of Europe sees disenchantment with democratic politics as a serious threat to social cohesion. It established The European Committee for Social Cohesion in an effort to promote political and civic participation.[5]

Amidst an economic slump and widespread social discontent at the turn of the millennium, the Hong Kong Special Administrative Region government began to be anxious about social cohesion in the community. The anxiety was not without merit, as the popularity ratings of the chief executive and his officials, as well as confidence in the government in general had been plunging since the Tung administration's honeymoon period ended.[6] Coupled with a series of policy blunders, cases in which the rule of law and human rights were thought to have been threatened,[7] failure to advance democratization as well as partiality for big businesses, the Tung administration was deemed ineffectual in its policy administration, and was accused of compromising the autonomy of Hong Kong. The dissatisfaction was so pervasive and tremendous that an estimated half-a-million Hongkongers took to the streets on the fifth anniversary of Hong Kong's reunification with the PRC on July 1, 2003 to express their aggravation. The government of Hong Kong was not entirely unaware of the intensity of the frustration and had convened the Panel on Social Cohesion between 2002 and 2003 to look into potential ways to enhance social cohesion in Hong Kong. In addition, it established the Community Investment and Inclusion Fund in 2001 to encourage inclusion and cross-sectoral cooperation in an effort to cultivate harmony and cooperation between different sectors of society.

Despite the HKSAR government's apparent concern about social cohesion, there has not been an empirical study devoted to charting the state of social cohesion in Hong Kong. This chapter reports the findings of the first of such a study. It gives an account of the state and the sources of social cohesion in Hong Kong in the year 2003, an important year in the history of Hong Kong. Politically, the government was pushing for the passage of the national security bill required by Article 23 of the Basic Law. The bill met with massive resistance because under closer scrutiny, it was revealed that the proposed bill was subjecting the citizens of Hong Kong to what they perceived to be unnecessary restrictions on their rights and liberty. Socially, society had just conquered the SARS epidemic; but not without paying a price. The government had underestimated the severity of the attack when it broke out in spring. As it transpired that the government was uncertain about ways to contain the disease, public fear resulted despite the professionalism displayed by medical personnel. By the end of May when the epidemic was finally contained, 299 lives were lost. Economically Hong Kong was still suffering from one of the most severe economic slumps in recent years. Property prices plummeted, the unemployment rate surged to a record high of 8.8 percent between May and August, and Hong Kong entered a period of prolonged deflation.

Hong Kong in the year 2003 was a city of discontent. To measure social cohesion at this point provides a baseline for future comparison, and could give us some hints on the sources that promote or undermine social cohesion. In a nutshell, we argue that the cohesion among members of society is satisfactory, but that between society and the government is quite poor. Moreover, the government is regarded as the major source that undermines social cohesion, and our findings suggest three problematic areas: leadership, politics, and policies. Before venturing into the situation of social cohesion in Hong Kong, the definition of social cohesion as used in this chapter will be discussed.

Dimensions of social cohesion

Despite its popularity, social cohesion does not have a well-defined meaning.[8] There appears to be a consensus that social cohesion as a goal (i.e., to achieve a socially cohesive society) is desirable. However, what constitutes social cohesion seems to vary with scholars and policy researchers, leading a scholar to conclude that it is at best a quasi-concept.[9] In fact, it has been shown that there is confusion between social cohesion understood as an end-state in itself and means to achieve a desirable end-state.[10] Such conceptual confusion could only muddle investigation of the phenomenon itself. We argue that the definition should be confined to elements or constituents of the phenomenon, and leave out the conditions leading to or the outcomes as a consequence of social cohesion.

It is not hard to imagine social cohesion being looked upon as a societal goal, but to define it in terms of how such a goal could be achieved mixes up means and ends. For example, Berger-Schmitt regarded social cohesion as distinctly consisting of two societal goals: reduction of social ills such as regional disparities, inequalities, and social exclusion; and building social capital in terms of strengthening social interactions and networks, as well as increasing civic engagement.[11] It is possible that a society rich in social capital and which is relatively equal and inclusive should be socially cohesive. However, the process of achieving this desirable state may give rise to heated argument and even conflict. To define a certain goal by the means or the processes leading to it therefore confuses the essential constituents of a phenomenon with the achievement of such a phenomenon. After all, the ways and means to achieve a goal may not always be consistent with the end goal itself. To use an analogy, peace is sometimes achieved through bloody conflict, and one certainly would not define peace by bloody conflict. Unfortunately, there are ample examples of social cohesion being defined in a manner that confounds goals and means.[12]

That social cohesion often has policy implications has again inadvertently contributed to the perplexity of the definition of the concept. After reviewing the definition of social cohesion as used by Canada, France, the OECD, and the Club of Rome, Jenson came to the conclusion that "there is no single way of even defining it. Meanings depend on the problem being addressed and who is speaking."[13] A more recent work by Beauvais and Jenson found the situation to be more or less still lingering on. They concluded that there had been five sets of conception of social cohesion: as common values and a civic culture; as social order and social control; as social solidarity and reduction in wealth disparities; as social networks and social capital, and as attachment and identification with a place.[14] There is therefore not yet a commonly accepted and clear definition of social cohesion in the literature. The term is probably so flexible that it is possible "to allow the meanderings and necessities of political action from day to day."[15]

One of the first and foremost requirements in the study of social cohesion is to come up with a definition that is void of the above shortcomings. The definition that we propose to adopt contains only the essential constituents, and is close to ordinary usage. The definition is to focus only on the essential components, and to leave out the conditions that facilitate social cohesion, the means to achieve it as well as its desirable results. Moreover, as the term "social cohesion" is not uncommon in daily use, in order not to inject additional confusion into the term, whatever definition we adopt should not depart much from ordinary usage. With these points in mind, we propose to define social cohesion as:

> a state of affairs concerning both the vertical and the horizontal interactions among members of society as characterized by a set of attitudes and norms that includes trust, a sense of belonging and the willingness to participate and help, as well as their behavioral manifestations.

The horizontal dimension describes interactions among members of society while the vertical dimension describes interactions between members of society and the government. There are also the attitudinal and the behavioral dimensions. A cohesive society should not only feel, but also act in a cohesive way. Taking horizontal/vertical and attitudinal/behavioral dimensions into consideration gives rise to four possible scenarios, as depicted in Table 4.1.

Cells A and B depict the horizontal dimension of social cohesion (i.e., the feelings and interactions of members of society). Feelings such as the extent of general trust in society, the willingness to cooperate and trust individuals from different sectors and backgrounds, the willingness to help others, and the level of belonging are being gauged in Cell A. Cell B tries to capture the behavioral manifestation of the feelings expressed in Cell A. It summarizes the extent to which individuals actually engage in helping others, be it physical, financial, or emotional; and the degree of social involvement (e.g., membership in organizations, giving behavior, and volunteering).

Cells C and D represent the vertical dimension of social cohesion; they are concerned with feelings and interactions between the state and society. Cell C is mainly about trust in major political figures and confidence in various governmental institutions. Cell D reflects the extent to which society and the state are linked through certain activities. It measures how concerned society is with politics and individuals' voting behavior.

We believe that this definition of social cohesion is an improvement over other definitions for the following reasons. First, social cohesion is defined by its essential constituents only. Elements like trust, willingness to help and participate, sense of belonging, and their corresponding behaviors work to bind people together. It is quite plain that a suspicious society in which people care only

Table 4.1 A two-by-two framework of social cohesion

	Subjective component (individuals' attitudes)	*Objective component (behavioral manifestation)*
Horizontal dimension (cohesion in civil society)	A	B
Vertical dimension (state–society cohesion)	C	D

about themselves and no one else cannot be called a "cohesive" society. Moreover, whether equality, social mobility, inclusion, improved quality of life, and life chances would facilitate social cohesion or whether they are the outcomes of social cohesion would not matter because they are not essential constituents of social cohesion and are thus left out of the definition. Second, social cohesion is understood as a state of affairs, and not a process or a means. There are different ways to attain cohesion. It is entirely conceivable that a certain way is more effective than others at one time, but it may not be so at other times. Thus, measuring cohesion as a process has to assume that a certain process remains effective at all times, which may not be realistic. Third, the vertical dimension introduces the relationship between society and government into the concept of social cohesion. We believe that a society united only to oppose the government does not satisfy the definition of what one would normally understand as a cohesive society. Finally, our definition stays close to ordinary daily usage of the term "social cohesion".

Having defined the concept of social cohesion in such a way, the distinction between social cohesion and social capital should become quite clear. As Putnam puts it, "social capital refers to connections among individuals – social networks and the norms of reciprocity and trustworthiness that arise from them."[16] Social capital in this sense is quite close to the horizontal dimension of social cohesion; however, it does not deal with the vertical dimension. Curiously, the comprehensive social capital index devised by Putnam does include measures of engagement in public affairs such as voter turnout in presidential elections and participation rate in town or school meetings.[17] This inclusion appears to be rather peculiar, since it does not follow from the definition of social cohesion. In contrast, we accord the relationship between society and the state a high degree of significance in our theoretical formulation. Thus, it includes political confidence and political concern in addition to voting behavior.

In the next section, we will show how we operationalized the framework of social cohesion and present the survey data we gathered in an attempt to measure the state of social cohesion in Hong Kong.

The state of social cohesion in Hong Kong

A door-to-door territory-wide questionnaire survey was carried out between August and October, 2003 to collect data on the state of social cohesion in Hong Kong. One thousand and fifty-four respondents aged 18 and above were successfully interviewed in a two-stage stratified random sample of the entire territory, giving a response rate of 71 percent.[18] The questionnaire contained attitudinal and behavioral questions based on the two-by-two framework depicted in Table 4.1.

Dimension A – Horizontal/subjective dimension

To make interpretation easier, eight summary indexes were created, two for each of the four dimensions of social cohesion (Table 4.2).[19] Dimension A is about subjective horizontal cohesion, which describes feelings among members of society. The two indexes in this dimension were termed Reciprocity Index and Commitment Index. The Reciprocity Index includes respondents' assessment as to how trustful they are of other members of society, and how willing they are to cooperate and trust specific groups. In the questionnaire, these groups comprise individuals coming from lower social stratum, higher social stratum, of different political ideologies, as well as former CSSA recipients, new immigrants from the mainland, Europeans/Americans, Indians/Pakistanis, and homosexuals.

The Commitment Index is made up two broad categories. One concerns questions on respondents' willingness to help others. They involve forgoing some sort of self-interest for the benefit of others, like using one's spare time, paying higher taxes, and accepting a salary cut. The other category taps the respondents' sense of belonging to Hong Kong. They were asked to indicate how proud they were of being a Hongkonger, how much they called Hong Kong their home, and their professed sense of belonging to Hong Kong.

The mean score for the Reciprocity Index was 5.89, indicating that the respondents were trustful of fellow Hongkongers in general and they were willing to trust and cooperate with specific groups and people from different socioeconomic strata. The mean score for the Commitment Index was 6.68, showing that the respondents displayed a moderately high sense of belonging to Hong Kong. Speaking overall, the horizontal/subjective dimension of social cohesion is positive, which implies that attitudinally the respondents feel quite comfortable about fellow Hongkongers.

Dimension B – Horizontal/objective social cohesion

The two indexes constructed under Dimension B are the Helping Behavior Index and Social Involvement Index. While the Commitment Index (Dimension A) reflects how much the respondents say they are willing to help others, the Helping Behavior Index actually taps how much respondents proclaim to have actually engaged in helping out their friends and neighbors. In the survey, the respondents were asked to indicate how often they had helped their friends or neighbors financially, emotionally, or with domestic work in the past year.

The Social Involvement Index reveals the degree of the respondents' involvement in society. It is supposed to reflect how much individuals translate their purported commitment (as depicted in the Commitment Index) to actual behavior. Whereas the Helping Behavior Index refers more specifically to friends and neighbors, individuals whom the respondents are acquainted with, the Social Involvement Index summarizes respondents' engagement in unpaid work

Table 4.2 Social cohesion indexes

Dimension	Content	Mean score
Dimension A		
Reciprocity index	• General trust • Willingness to cooperate • Willingness to trust	5.89
Commitment index	• Sense of belonging • Willingness to forgo individual interests for the common good	6.68
Dimension B		
Helping behavior index	• Helping friends and neighbors with household work • Helping friends and neighbors financially • Helping friends and neighbors emotionally	3.54
Social involvement index	• Membership in organizations • Number of charities to which respondents have donated • Volunteering	2.00
Dimension C		
Confidence in political institutions index	• Confidence in the Chief Executive • Confidence in the Executive Council • Confidence in the Principal Official system • Confidence in senior civil servants • Confidence in directly elected LegCo members • Confidence in functionally elected LegCo members	4.96
Confidence in the administration of justice index	• Confidence in the judicial system • Confidence in the police • Confidence in the ICAC • Confidence in the Ombudsman	7.33
Dimension D		
Political concern index	• Watch/read news reports • Discussion of politics with friends • Watch current affairs programs on TV • Listen to news/current affairs phone-in programs	6.60
Political participation index	• Voting behavior in past LegCo elections • Voting behavior in past District Boards/ Council elections	6.02

directed to persons whom they may not know. It comprises the number of organizations to which the respondents belong, the number of times they volunteer, and the number of charities to which they donate.

As Table 4.2 shows, the mean scores of the two indexes in Dimension B are the lowest among the eight indexes. The mean score of the Helping Behavior

Index was 3.54 and that for the Social Involvement Index, 2.00. Both scores are well below the 5.5 mid-point, leading to the situation that whatever good feelings individuals may have about fellow Hongkongers, it has not been translated into action. Individuals may be a little more willing to help out persons whom they know, but the amount of these behaviors still fell short of building social cohesion. The degree of social involvement is even lower. There has not been a tradition of joining organizations or volunteering in Hong Kong; thus the low score is not entirely surprising. However, given the socioeconomic development of the city and the positive feeling the society generally has toward other members (as captured in Dimension A), Hongkongers should be encouraged to adopt a more active role in society.

Dimension C – Vertical/subjective social cohesion

As one cannot talk about social cohesion without also paying attention to the relationship between the government and society, Dimensions C and D are designed to measure this aspect of social cohesion. Dimension C specifically tries to determine how society feels about the government. Two indexes were subsumed under Dimension C: the Confidence in Political Institutions Index, and the Confidence in the Administration of Justice Index. The Confidence in Political Institutions Index summarizes the degree of confidence respondents have in various government institutions and personnel, including the chief executive, the Executive Council, the Principal Official System, senior civil servants, popularly elected legislative councilors, and functionally elected legislative councilors.

The Confidence in the Administration of Justice Index collects the extent to which respondents are confident about such institutions. These institutions include the judicial system, the police, the Independent Commission Against Corruption (ICAC), as well as the ombudsman. These institutions are distinct from those making up the Confidence in Political Institutions Index because, first they are not involved in the daily ruling of Hong Kong, and second, their operations are in fact autonomous from the government.

The mean scores of the two indexes in Dimension C are indeed very different. While the Confidence in Political Institutions Index was a mere 4.96, indicating that the respondents felt that the government was actually undermining social cohesion, that of the Confidence in the Administration of Justice Index was 7.33, showing a high degree of trust in these institutions. The Confidence in the Administration of Justice Index actually obtained the highest mean score among the eight indexes. It appears that despite casting blame on the government for undermining social cohesion, the respondents had distinguished these justice administration institutions from other government institutions and praised them for building social cohesion.

Dimension D – Vertical/objective social cohesion

The Political Concern Index and the Political Participation Index have been constructed to reflect the vertical/objective dimension of social cohesion. The first step in fostering a meaningful link between the government and society is for the latter to be concerned with and to seek information from the former. The first index constructed along this dimension of social cohesion is thus the Political Concern Index, which basically taps the extent to which political news and discussion figure in the respondents' daily lives. It sums up how frequently the respondents read news reports, and watch or listen to news and current affairs programs, as well as how regularly they discuss politics with friends.

The second index under the vertical/objective dimension of social cohesion is the Political Participation Index. This reveals how actively the respondents make their voice heard in the government through electing their own representatives. The index includes how regularly the respondents have voted in all past Legislative Council elections, and District Boards/Council elections.

Given that the respondents did not have much confidence in the government, as reflected in the Confidence in Political Institutions Index, it was possible that they could be alienated from conventional politics altogether. The two mean scores indicate otherwise. The mean score of the Political Concern Index was 6.60, and that of the Political Participation Index, 6.02. Instead of eschewing politics, both scores illustrate that society tried to foster its linkage with the government by paying attention to political affairs and going to the voting booths.

All in all, the state of social cohesion in Hong Kong is mixed. While subjectively, Hongkongers show goodwill toward fellow Hongkongers and are quite attached to the city of Hong Kong, they do not behave as enthusiastically as their feelings suggest. It is not too common for Hongkongers to actually help friends and neighbors, and the degrees of social involvement like joining organizations and volunteering are mortifying. The situation of vertical cohesion looks brighter. Low confidence in government institutions has not been accompanied by political alienation. Society is apparently still concerned about politics and active in its voting behavior. In addition, society seems to be very trustful of institutions that administer justice. Thus, although the respondents might be disappointed with the government, they were hopeful that social justice would still be maintained.

Before turning our attention to the sources of social cohesion, let us find out whether one's socioeconomic background has any effect on the four dimensions of social cohesion. As Table 4.3 indicates, many attitudes and behaviors are related to one's socioeconomic background. As far as horizontal social cohesion is concerned, younger and more educated respondents are more likely to reciprocate, to help friends and neighbors, and to be involved socially. They are, however, more skeptical of political institutions at the same time. Females tend to show higher social involvement, as well as commitment to Hong Kong. Higher income groups show higher social involvement too.

Table 4.3 Cohesion indexes and socioeconomic background

	Dimension A		Dimension B		Dimension C		Dimension D	
	Reciprocity index	Commitment index	Helping index	Social involvement	Trust in political institutions	Trust in justice	Political concern	Voting behavior
Age								
18–30	6.17	6.43	4.28	2.24	4.74	7.26	6.44	5.24
31–45	5.9	6.69	3.74	2.06	4.84	7.37	6.87	6.19
46–60	5.54	6.74	3.12	1.97	5.01	7.4	6.81	6.2
Above 60	5.43	7.04	2.42	1.49	5.97	7.58	5.96	6.42
F sig.	0.00**	0.00**	0.00**	0.00**	0.00**	0.36	0.00**	0.02*
Gender								
Male	5.93	6.53	3.43	1.86	4.85	7.48	6.72	6.36
Female	5.85	6.85	3.65	2.15	5.1	7.17	6.48	5.64
F sig.	0.1	0.00**	0.08	0.00**	0.03*	0.00**	0.04*	0.01**
Education								
Primary	5.42	6.76	2.67	1.59	5.47	7.38	5.85	6.2
Secondary	5.84	6.62	3.59	1.86	4.96	7.31	6.75	5.85
Matriculated and above	6.25	6.72	4.18	2.58	4.67	7.39	7.00	6.1
F sig.	0.00**	0.05*	0.00**	0.00**	0.00**	0.74	0.00**	0.54
Income								
Below $5,000	5.88	6.83	3.85	1.70	5.83	7.54	6.01	5.98
$5,001–10,000	5.85	6.33	3.45	1.79	4.81	7.23	6.48	5.96
$10,001–15,000	5.94	6.72	3.9	2.05	4.67	7.44	7.09	6.54
$15,001–20,000	6.07	6.8	4.19	2.22	4.71	7.31	7.47	6.15
Above $20,000	6.29	6.66	3.91	2.61	4.47	7.53	7.56	6.88
F sig.	0.1	0.06	0.07	0.00**	0.00**	0.47	0.00**	0.04*
Mean	5.89	6.68	3.54	2.00	4.96	7.33	6.60	6.02
Range	1–10	1–10	1–10	1–10	1–10	1–10	1–10	1–10

Notes

* Significant at 0.05 level; ** significant at 0.01 level.

Scores range from 1 to 10, scores below 5.5 indicate negative tendency toward cohesion, and vice versa for scores above 5.5.

Likewise, socioeconomic backgrounds play a significant role in vertical social cohesion. The younger, more educated, higher income groups show more concern in politics,[20] but less trust in political institutions. Male respondents have more confidence in justice administration institutions and they are also more likely to vote. Thus our data suggest that those who lost trust in government institutions were neither ignorant nor politically uninformed. To regain the trust of society involves much more than propaganda.

Sources of social cohesion

What kinds of forces are deemed to promote social cohesion and what undermines it is a major concern for many policy-makers. This aspect was addressed in the survey through a series of questions asking about the extent to which the respondents deemed certain social issues and conflicts between groups to be undermining social cohesion in Hong Kong. Table 4.4 presents the results and the breakdowns by respondents' demographic and socioeconomic backgrounds. Four issues were posed to the respondents, including unemployment, youth unemployment, negative equity, and polarization of rich and poor. All four issues were regarded as damaging to social cohesion. Unemployment in particular was the most serious among the four, receiving a score of 2.82, followed by negative equity (3.34), youth unemployment (3.41), and polarization of rich and poor (3.43).

Respondents were asked to indicate their views as to how much the conflict between a few selected groups was harming social cohesion. As Table 4.4 indicates, respondents believed that the conflict between the government and its citizenry was most damaging to social cohesion (3.55), followed by that between democratic camps and pro-China camps (3.94), then between employers and employees (4.12), taxpayers and welfare recipients (4.88), and finally, the police and protestors (5.37). It is interesting to observe that male respondents, who were younger, better educated, and receiving a higher income were more likely than their counterparts to see the negative effect of the conflict between the government and its citizenry on social cohesion. Younger and better educated respondents also tended to regard the conflict between taxpayers and welfare recipients to be more serious than did their counterparts.

Other than the issues and conflicts discussed above, we identified 14 groups or subjects whose work might have quite an extensive influence on the social and political terrain of Hong Kong. Respondents were asked to indicate how much these groups or subjects were increasing or harming social cohesion. As Table 4.5 shows, the four items related to the government were all perceived to be undermining social cohesion. The worst aspect pertains to the style of governance (4.59), then public policy (4.75), the chief executive (4.85), and his principal officials (4.90).

The respondents seemed to have developed an aversion to politics, since the two major political camps were both perceived to be harming social cohesion. The pro-China groups, which were widely regarded as ardent supporters of the

Table 4.4 Perceived effects of various socioeconomic issues and social conflicts on social cohesion and socioeconomic background

	Issues				Conflicts				
	Unemployment	Youth unemployment	Negative equity	Polarization of rich and poor	Government versus citizen	Capitalist versus labor	Pro-democracy versus Pro-China	Police versus protestors	Taxpayers versus CSSA recipients
Mean	2.82	3.41	3.34	3.43	3.55	4.12	3.94	5.37	4.88
(n)	(1,015)	(1,003)	(985)	(996)	(997)	(994)	(944)	(993)	(988)
Gender									
Male	2.73	3.49	3.37	3.47	3.41	4.10	3.86	5.52	5.00
Female	2.91	3.32	3.31	3.38	3.71	4.14	4.04	5.20	4.74
F sig.	0.132	0.227	0.626	0.504	0.014**	0.774	0.172	0.019**	0.086
Age									
18–30	2.87	3.55	3.22	3.47	3.33	4.21	4.07	5.36	4.83
31–45	2.74	3.37	3.31	3.29	3.46	3.95	3.95	5.52	4.83
46–60	2.81	3.25	3.29	3.46	3.63	4.07	3.66	5.06	4.61
60 and above	3.02	3.68	3.84	3.85	4.20	4.55	4.13	5.55	5.63
F sig.	0.481	0.256	0.045*	0.095	0.000**	0.019*	0.127	0.068	0.001**
Education									
Primary	3.15	3.72	3.62	3.57	3.97	4.28	3.91	5.37	5.13
Secondary	2.72	3.30	3.36	3.30	3.63	4.03	3.91	5.28	4.91
Matriculated and above	2.77	3.42	3.12	3.53	3.09	4.09	3.98	5.48	4.61
F sig.	0.017*	0.069	0.03*	0.195	0.000**	0.299	0.868	0.452	0.037*
Income									
Below $5,000	2.60	3.10	3.82	3.77	3.51	4.49	3.98	5.96	4.87
$5,001–10,000	2.63	3.53	3.22	3.02	3.58	4.06	3.71	5.11	4.58
$10,001–15,000	2.84	3.48	3.14	3.44	3.49	3.68	3.72	5.39	4.80
$15,001–20,000	2.83	3.53	3.30	3.54	3.33	4.05	4.00	5.16	4.47
Above $20,000	2.82	3.53	3.10	3.56	2.80	4.16	3.95	5.68	4.81
F sig.	0.792	0.789	0.309	0.082	0.009**	0.104	0.720	0.049*	0.741

Notes
*Significant at 0.05 level; **significant at 0.01 level.
Scores range from 1 to 10, scores below 5.5 indicate tendency toward harming social cohesion, scores above 5.5 indicate tendency in the direction of having no effect on social cohesion.

Table 4.5 Perceived effects of various forces on social cohesion and socioeconomic background

	Central government	Chief executive	Principal Officials	Public policy	Style of governance	Pro-democracy groups	Pro-China groups	Business tycoons/chambers	Labor union/leaders	Police	Mass media	Professional associations	Religious leaders	Academics
Mean	5.95	4.85	4.90	4.75	4.59	5.26	4.70	5.26	5.74	6.73	5.89	6.28	5.83	6.59
(n)	(973)	(988)	(956)	(965)	(963)	(928)	(910)	(941)	(925)	(976)	(985)	(911)	(933)	(965)
Gender														
Male	6.26	4.79	4.84	4.63	4.48	5.20	4.62	5.14	5.64	6.68	5.87	6.27	5.73	6.54
Female	5.59	4.92	4.98	4.88	4.71	5.32	4.79	5.41	5.86	6.80	5.92	6.29	5.95	6.46
F sig.	0.00**	0.37	0.33	0.08	0.10	0.36	0.22	0.03	0.06	0.30	0.69	0.88	0.07	0.35
Age														
18–30	5.46	4.38	4.40	4.51	4.27	5.47	4.49	5.19	5.78	6.29	5.60	6.26	5.89	6.45
31–45	5.81	4.64	4.78	4.51	4.37	5.31	4.58	5.09	5.75	6.74	5.95	6.37	5.92	6.68
46–60	6.25	5.05	5.09	4.95	4.81	5.05	4.82	5.33	5.59	6.92	6.00	6.16	5.83	6.57
Above 60	6.95	6.12	6.05	5.71	5.66	5.06	5.51	6.01	6.07	7.34	6.23	6.41	5.49	6.68
F sig.	0.00**	0.00**	0.00**	0.00**	0.00**	0.12	0.00**	0.00**	0.13	0.00**	0.02*	0.41	0.19	0.40
Education														
Primary	6.39	5.67	5.57	5.53	5.42	5.19	5.39	5.74	6.06	7.32	6.20	6.44	5.84	6.78
Secondary	5.89	4.75	4.85	4.71	4.56	5.32	4.61	5.19	5.71	6.67	5.95	6.17	5.85	6.57
Matriculated And above	5.69	4.43	4.53	4.29	4.08	5.21	4.38	5.06	5.61	6.44	5.60	6.37	5.83	6.51
F sig.	0.00**	0.00**	0.00**	0.00**	0.00**	0.67	0.00**	0.00**	0.02*	0.00**	0.00**	0.10	0.99	0.20
Income														
Below $5,000	6.31	5.21	5.36	5.18	5.10	5.16	4.80	5.60	6.18	7.18	6.10	6.31	5.92	6.80
$5,001–10,000	5.85	4.50	4.77	4.65	4.56	5.20	4.57	5.04	5.56	6.46	5.92	6.01	5.71	6.45
$10,001–15,000	6.11	4.97	4.82	4.45	4.49	5.13	4.58	5.00	5.59	6.77	5.87	6.33	6.03	6.77
$15,001–20,000	5.86	4.77	4.55	4.43	4.33	5.60	4.50	5.05	5.84	6.68	5.56	6.54	6.14	6.46
Above $20,000	5.82	3.86	4.19	3.89	3.62	5.38	4.11	4.81	5.53	6.40	5.78	6.58	6.03	6.60
F sig.	0.56	0.00**	0.01**	0.01**	0.00**	0.56	0.24	0.15	0.15	0.03*	0.66	0.03*	0.42	0.39

Notes
*Significant at 0.05 level; **significant at 0.01 level.
Scores range from 1 to 10, scores below 5.5 indicate tendency toward harming social cohesion, above 5.5 indicate tendency toward strengthening social cohesion.

Hong Kong government, received the second lowest score (4.70). The pro-democracy camps, whose purported main task was to hold the government in check, fared a little better despite still being seen negatively (5.26). In fact, it appears that to the respondents, pro-democracy groups were no more damaging or contributing to social cohesion as the business people; for both groups were awarded the same score (5.26).

Apart from the central government (5.95), all groups that were judged to be building vertical social cohesion were not, strictly speaking, related to politics. Among them were: the police (6.73), academics (6.59), professional associations (6.28), the mass media (5.89), religious leaders (5.83), and labor unions (5.74).

It is quite obvious from the data that the government was regarded as the chief culprit in undermining social cohesion. It was to the chief executive, his governance style, public policy, and officials that the blame of undercutting cohesion between society and government was attributed. Moreover, the feeling was more prevalent among the younger, better educated, and higher income cohorts. Usually the younger and better educated groups were more critical; they saw pro-China groups, big businesses, the police, and mass media as doing more harm to social cohesion than their counterparts. However, the respondents' social economic background did not appear to have affected their assessment of the impacts of professional associations, religious leaders, academics, and pro-democracy groups on social cohesion.

Social cohesion and governance problems: leadership, politics, and policies

Consistently, our data point to the failure of the HKSAR government as the main source that undermines social cohesion. The diagnosis of the trouble in vertical cohesion has been well confirmed by political events subsequent to our survey in 2003.[21] Three of the 14 principal officials in Chief Executive Tung Chee-hwa's ruling "cabinet" resigned in the year following the July 1, 2003 demonstration.[22] Two weeks after the demonstration, Regina Ip (Secretary for Security)[23] and Antony Leung (Financial Secretary)[24] offered their resignations; E. K. Yeoh (Secretary for Health, Welfare and Food)[25] followed suit a year later. Officially, all three resignations may or may not have been directly as a result of their below-par performance, but they certainly have to do with public pressure. The finale was undoubtedly the resignation of Chief Executive Tung Chee-hwa himself halfway through his second term in office in March, 2005.[26] To be sure, Tung's resignation should not be mistaken as a direct result of public pressure or people's power, for the mandate to appoint and remove the chief executive rests with the National People's Congress, not the citizens of Hong Kong. And Tung did stay in office despite declining public support and massive demonstrations.[27] However, losing public support to such a vast extent may have led the PRC leadership to have second thoughts with regard to Tung's suitability and ability to stay on as head of the Hong Kong government. The survey results regarding social cohesion point to several issues underlying the problem of governance:

leadership, politics, and policies. In this section, we will discuss what these issues amount to according to our survey, and seek to explain the possible sources and substances of these issues by drawing on events and other relevant analyses. In the final section, we will attempt to derive lessons for future governance from our discussion.

Leadership

The findings indicate that the respondents were most unhappy with the political leadership. To recapitulate, they held the chief executive, his governance style, his hand-picked principal officials, and his public policy responsible for undermining social cohesion. They also found conflicts between the government and its citizens to be most unsettling to cohesion in society, even more so than conflicts arising from one's social class and economic status, such as those between capitalists and labors as well as those between taxpayers and welfare recipients.

The style of governance was a major issue of discontent. Tung Chee-hwa might be a seasoned businessman, but he was an inexperienced politician. Born into a wealthy family, he had been shielded from the mass society. He was rather oblivious to the public nature of the role of chief executive. He did not appear to recognize the importance of political communication with society, or even with the legislators, which eventually did great damage to his political support.[28]

Tung had been quite inactive in the political scene; he was but an amateur to the administrative bureaucracy until shortly before the handover. It has been said that Tung ran Hong Kong like his own family business. One of the most telling examples was the announcement of the discontinuation of a housing policy. To alleviate hiking property prices, Tung pledged to build 85,000 public flats each year in his first policy address in October, 1997. However, Hong Kong was adversely hit by the Asian financial crisis after the announcement and housing prices fell substantially. Instead of publicly reviewing the need to amend the policy, Tung casually made reference in a television interview on June 30, 2000 that the government had already abandoned the policy.[29] In the following days it became apparent that officials responsible for public housing were as confused and bewildered by Tung's announcement as the general public. This episode revealed that either Tung had adopted a casual approach to policy-making, for it transpired that he had not even consulted the relevant officials, or there existed a serious communication gap between the leadership and government officials. Either way, the incident was alarming and caused widespread public outcry.

If Tung's internal communication with his administration needed much improvement, his communication with society would require no less effort. One of the more effective ways to strengthen the linkage between the government and society is for the government to be more transparent and more open to public views. In an era when citizens are fast becoming familiar with their civil and political rights and are in favor of having a democratic system, government officials should shed their old colonial mentalities and be ready to face the public. The Legislative Council is the body in which the public is most widely and officially represented,[30] and is therefore an important linkage between the government and society. It may be true that certain powers of the legislature are more restricted under the Basic Law than in the colonial era, but it is by no means powerless. To be sure, the power of bill initiation vis-à-vis private members' bills and bill amendments was curtailed after 1997. Nevertheless, members of the legislature are still effective in overseeing the government and in forcing it to reconsider and amend legislation.[31] To say that the legislature has become lame is an overstatement. Instead of seizing this venue to reach out to society through its elected representatives, Tung was only an infrequent visitor to the Legislative Council, and he seldom engaged in meaningful dialogue with legislators and politicians of different political persuasions. Surrounded by a circle of like minded individuals, Tung was further removed and continued to lose touch with society. As Tung had no popular mandate, he would have much to gain had he tried to legitimize his policy through the legislature. Thus, it was really unwise of Tung to alienate legislators and shun the legislature.

Politics

Our findings also indicate that political issues could be a potential source that undermines social cohesion. Democratization is one of the most prominent and arguably divisive political issues that has been on the public agenda since the 1980s. There is general consensus that democracy, understood in the form of universal suffrage in the selection of the chief executive and the Legislative Council, is the ultimate goal. However, there has been much controversy around the timetable to achieve this ultimate goal, with the public demanding a faster pace than the government was willing to concede. The disagreement became the principal conflict between pro-China and pro-democracy groups, and one that was regarded by the respondents of our survey to be more damaging to social cohesion than those between socioeconomic classes.

The call for a faster pace of democratization was loud and clear at the time of the survey: 70.7 percent of the respondents supported or strongly supported popular election of the chief executive sooner,[32] and 72.1 percent of popular elections of all the legislators.[33] Of course, the chance for popular election of the next chief executive in 2007 and all legislative councilors in 2008 is close to non-existent. The decision of the Standing Committee of the National People's Congress (NPCSC) on April 26, 2004 practically rejected universal suffrage in both cases.[34] Nonetheless, the prevailing demand for universal suffrage in both elections remains. Tung should have been fully aware that the issue of democratization would need to be dealt with when he first assumed office. He, however, tried to evade this potentially contentious issue by diverting society's political demand to focus on social and economic concerns. Ironically, the outcome of avoiding politics did not save him from uncharted waters, but instead immobilized policy implementation owing to weakened social and political support.[35]

Also along the political dimension, Tung was generally perceived to imperil the rule of law in Hong Kong. One of the most widely cited cases concerns the right of abode of children born to Hong Kong residents. Litigations began soon after Hong Kong rejoined the PRC, and eventually the Court of Final Appeal handed down its decision in favor of the abode seekers in January, 1999. The government assessed the social impacts of the decision and concluded that the decision had far greater potential ramifications in resources than society could handle. A few months later in May the government sought the interpretation of NPCSC. The legal community was particularly distressed, since it feared that the rule of law in Hong Kong would be compromised. This incident led to the first ever protest of the legal community on June 30, 1999 in which over 600 lawyers took part in a silent march. There was also the infamous case of Aw Sian, who was allegedly an old friend of Tung and a fellow member of the Chinese People's Political Consultative Conference. In March, 1998, the Independent Commission Against Corruption charged three senior executives of the English newspaper, the *Hong Kong Standard*, with fraud over the paper's circulation. Ms. Aw, despite being the owner of the newspaper, had, for some unexplained reasons, escaped prosecution altogether. This incident resulted in a no-confidence motion against the Secretary of Justice Ms. Elsie Leung, which she escaped by a 29 to 21 vote.

The rule of law is often considered a pillar contributing to Hong Kong's success, and the demand for universal suffrage has been gathering more and more momentum. Actions that might be perceived to weaken the rule of law, or inaction to avoid the issue of democratization, are both going against the social current and thereby undercutting social cohesion.

Public policy

Finally, our data suggest that Tung was faulted on his public policy. The respondents in our survey deemed public policy as undermining social cohesion in Hong Kong. They saw it as the second most harmful force (4.75 out of 10), only slightly ahead of pro-China groups which received the lowest score (4.70). If Tung had indeed avoided the potentially divisive issues of politics by concentrating on public policies,[36] our data show that he was far from successful.

No public policy[37] in Tung's reign has roused more extensive attention and rampant opposition than the proposed national security bill, also known as Article 23.[38] The attempt to push the bill through the legislature in 2003 shows how the government could, if it chose to, ignore public sentiment, overlook public leaders, manipulate public consultation, and be resolute despite enormous societal resistance. Public consultation of the proposed bill officially began in September, 2002 for three months. As the bill involved striking a very fine balance between individual rights and national interests, legislators of the democratic camp called for a more formal and vigorous scrutiny in the manner of a white bill so that it could be deliberated and debated in the Legislative Council. Despite repeated demands from a wide range of social sectors, the government rejected the suggestion; and refused to see the need for another round of public consultation. The Secretary for Security, Regina Ip, made it clear that the government intended to complete the legislation process of the bill by July, 2003. Amid heavy protests, the government gazetted the bill in mid-February, 2003 and went through the first reading in the legislature later that month. Meanwhile, the bill was still severely criticized. The public was apprehensive about the expansion of executive powers at the expense of individual rights and liberty. Debate continued to heat up and even became personal at times. It became so intense that Chief Justice Andrew Li, in his speech at the opening of the new legal year, called for vigilance on the rule of law, and said that debate on the formulation of new laws should be carried out "calmly, rationally and thoroughly."[39] Opposition to the proposed bill was so strong that it aroused international interest. The US Congress passed a resolution overwhelmingly urging the Hong Kong government to shelve the bill.[40]

In spite of all these strong societal oppositions, the government was still continuing with the legislation process. Finally, on July 1, 2003, a public holiday to celebrate the reunification of Hong Kong with the PRC, a reported 500,000 individuals took to the streets to protest the bill and express their frustration at the government. The sheer number of protesters, however, was not enough to change the mind of the government. It still had no intention of withdrawing the bill. Four days after the demonstration on July 5, Chief Executive Tung was still insisting that the bill would be submitted to the legislative council for second reading on July 9. The bill could have passed had it not been for the resignation of the Chair of the Liberal Party James Tien from the Executive Council on July 6. It was only then that the government realized it would not have enough votes to carry the bill and thus decided to delay the legislation.[41] On July 16, Tung accepted Secretary Ip's resignation. On August 4, the newly appointed Secretary for Security Ambrose Lee announced that there was no timetable for the legislation of Article 23.

The proposed national security bill was obviously highly contentious, because it was basically about individual rights and freedoms. For example, under the proposed bill, it is an offence to organize or support activities of a "proscribed" organization. The Secretary of Security can exercise the power of proscription by reference to Mainland's proscription mechanism. Hong Kong society therefore worried that the government would adopt the more stringent standards of the Mainland. The bill, when passed, would allow the government to tighten control of organizations banned or not welcome in the Mainland, such as Falungong, or the Hong Kong Alliance in Support of Patriotic Democratic Movement of China. The proposed bill would also expand the police's investigation power, including financial investigation, without the need to seek the Court's authorization. These measures would pose additional constraints to the rights and freedom currently enjoyed by society.

Hong Kong has always taken pride in being one of the freest societies in Asia, and perhaps the freest Chinese city in the world. Liberty has long become a much treasured societal value. The respondents in our survey saw liberty (8.31

out of 10), the rule of law (8.15), and democracy (7.61) as important shared values of the society of Hong Kong. Furthermore, a full 96.3 percent thought that the right to demonstrate should be guaranteed even if protest brings inconvenience to others. The proposed bill had far-reaching implications for these shared values. Tung should have anticipated vehement resistance before he and his government embarked on the daunting task of legislating a national security bill. Unfortunately, Tung did not seem to understand that the content of the bill rattled the nerves of society. Rather than showing his empathy and allowing more time for discussion, Tung turned his back on an anxious society and thus further frustrated an already irate populace.

The consequence of Tung's faults in the three areas – leadership, politics and policy – was reflected in the dwindling trust in him and his administration. When asked how much they had trusted various political institutions, the respondents awarded the lowest level of trust to Tung's hand-picked principal officials, followed by Tung himself, the Executive Council and senior civil servants. Indeed, according to survey data distrust of the government had been on the rise since the turnover: it rose from 9.5 percent just after the turnover in July, 1997 to peak in June, 2003 (42.8 percent). The trend has been reversed since then and in June, 2005, 28.9 percent were distrustful of the government.[42] Dissatisfaction with the overall performance of the government reflects a similar trend. It climbed from a low of 15.4 percent in July, 1997 to a high of 56.5 percent in December, 2004, and then gradually went down to 31.1 percent in June, 2005.[43]

Overall, the root of society's diminishing confidence in Tung was perhaps his insensitivity to the voice and demands of society. Society was displeased with his style of governance, and that could be an outcome of his overly ambitious public policy, and/or his paternalistic insistence on getting certain things done without much consideration for the feelings of society, the timing of the policy, as well as the scale of the matter. This insensitivity could also partially explain why there had not been much communication between Tung himself on one hand, and the legislature and politicians of different persuasions on the other. He was simply too eager to introduce the policies he believed would have benefited Hong Kong, and too confident to listen to other suggestions. By cocooning himself in a circle of like-minded individuals, he further isolated himself from the society he was supposed to lead and became more stubborn because alternative viewpoints did not reach him. In a time when society demands democracy, and its associated mechanisms such as accountability, openness, and transparency, it is indeed unwise to shut oneself off from the real world.

Implications for governance in the post-Tung era

Our survey results indicate that horizontal social cohesion is not very problematic in Hong Kong. While social engagement is still wanting, society in general is trustful of and willing to cooperate with various social sectors. It also has a respectable sense of belonging to Hong Kong. The biggest problem of social cohesion in Hong Kong, as it transpires, lies with the government, and the executive branch of the government in particular. Society has lost confidence in the government. It blamed the government for bringing about extensive social distress and lamented its inability to relieve society from misery. Most of the complaints were concerned with the leadership, politics, and policy, hence having great implications for governance.

Donald Tsang succeeded Tung Chee-hwa as chief executive in June, 2005. He made public his vision, governing philosophy, and policy blueprint when he announced his candidacy for chief executive.[44] As reflected in his election platform, Tsang seems to have decoded the governance problems of the Tung administration. Apart from building and maintaining a good relationship with the central government, improving the economy, and developing strong links with the international community, the remaining items on Tsang's governing philosophy appear to be attempts to right what Tung had been faulted for. They tackle what we grouped under the headings of leadership, policy, and politics in the previous section. With regard to leadership, Tsang pledged to "pursue excellence in governance," which meant that he would try to improve the efficiency and quality of governance, install consistency and clarity in public policy, work closer with the legislature, increase transparency, and extend consultative networks. With respect to policy, Tsang vowed to govern with "people-based" principles, to cultivate a sense of harmony, and to safeguard core values such as freedom, equality, and the rule of law, as well as to guard against corruption. As to politics, Tsang promised to encourage higher levels of political participation, and nurture political talents.

In a keynote speech delivered to the Election Committee on June 3, 2005, Donald Tsang said that if he were elected, he would strive to build a "prosperous, stable and harmonious"[45] Hong Kong. This pledge sees the addition of "harmony" to prosperity and stability, the two goals of almost all leaders of Hong Kong ever since it entered the political transition period in the 1980s. The title of his speech, "Strong Leadership, Harmony, and People Based Governance," gives us some clue as to how Tsang plans to achieve social harmony. It is through strong leaders designing policies that are not only beneficial, but are also acceptable to society. This is a significant point because it shows that Tsang recognizes the importance of communicating with society and rallying societal support. It appears that Tsang understands much better than his predecessor that social support is paramount to effective governance. If done properly, Tsang could regain the trust of the people, as many of them viewed the style of governance and public policy as undermining social cohesion in the Tung era.

To judge Tsang's administration now is still rather premature. However, Tsang should be reminded that paying heed to the people is the heart of people-based governance. It includes listening to the demands and attending to the needs of the people, as well as respecting and upholding their core values. As early as it is now to doubt Tsang's promises, there are uneasy signs that societal values are not rightfully defended. Tsang's decision to issue an executive order to allow for covert surveillance in lieu of proper legislation is said to have infringed the fundamental right to privacy. Moreover, he may have overstepped his power by taking away the jurisdiction of the Court to decide on the necessity and appropriateness of covert surveillance and vesting it in the law enforcement agencies.[46] Although Tsang defended his decision by emphasizing that the executive order was a temporary measure and would eventually be replaced by proper legislation, it sounded the alarm to both the local community and international society. They worry about rights and liberty being taken away, and they also worry that strong leadership could mean "no checks and fewer balances," as an editorial of an international newspaper suggested.[47]

There is also the issue of the pace of democratization in Hong Kong. Popular demands for universal suffrage in the elections of the chief executive and the Legislative Council have been persistent all through the Tung era. While Tsang promised to introduce progressive changes to the election mechanisms, he has yet to lay out a concrete timetable. This is an issue that Tsang has to handle skillfully. Although universal suffrage is an ultimate goal promised in the Basic Law, Hong Kong does not have total freedom to decide on the pace to achieve universal suffrage. The decision of the NPCSC indicated that general plans had already been worked out for the next chief executive and Legislative Council elections, which were much slower than most of society had hoped for. For as long as the demand for universal suffrage persists – and it is highly likely that it will – Tsang will be walking the tightrope of satisfying the people of Hong Kong while remaining faithful to the ruling and wishes of the NPCSC.

As we have pointed out earlier in this chapter, liberty, the rule of law, and democracy are regarded by the respondents as core values of Hong Kong. To successfully carry out people-based governance requires that Tsang is seen to seriously uphold these values in his decisions and public policy. An improved economy may ease social frustration somewhat and even lift social spirit. However, social cohesion will not be achieved if core societal values are confronted and trampled on time after time. It is hoped that Chief Executive Tsang has the wisdom to see that prosperity and stability is not to be attained in place of core societal values, and that he has the courage to carry out his aspirations that are so forcefully stated in his election platform.

Notes

1 See, for example, Berger, P. *The Limits of Social Cohesion: Conflict and Mediation in Pluralist Societies* (Boulder, CO: Westview Press, 1998); Gough, I. and Olofsson G. eds. *Capitalism and Social Cohesion: Essays on Exclusion and Integration* (Basingstoke: Macmillan, 1999).

2 See, for example, Bollen, K. A. and Hoyle, R. H. "Perceived Cohesion: a Conceptual and Empirical Explanation," *Social Forces* 6, no. 2, 2000; Friedkin, N. E. "Social Cohesion," *Annual Review of Sociology* 30 (2004): 409–425.

3 canada.justsice.gc.ca/en/ps/rs/rep/comsocohe.pdf.

4 Jeannotte, M. S. "Social Cohesion Around the World: An International Comparison of Definitions and Issues." Paper SRA-309 (Ottawa: Strategic Research and Analysis Directorate, Department of Canadian Heritage, 2000).

5 Battaini-Dragoni, G. and Dominioni, S. "The Council of Europe's Strategy for Social Cohesion." Paper presented at the Conference on Social Cohesion, organized by the

Faculty of Social Sciences, the University of Hong Kong, and the Hong Kong Council of Social Service, November 28–29, 2003.

6   Wong, T. K. Y. "The Changing Public Perception of the Chief Executive." In Lau, S. K., ed. *The First Tung Chee-hwa Administration: The First Five Years of the Hong Kong Special Administrative Region* (Hong Kong: The Chinese University Press, 2002).

7   Chan, J. "Civil Liberties, Rule of Law and Human Rights: The Hong Kong Special Administrative Region in Its First Four Years." In Lau, S. K., ed. *The First Tung Chee-hwa Administration: The First Five Years of the Hong Kong Special Administrative Region* (Hong Kong: The Chinese University Press, 2002).

8   Jenson, J. "Mapping Social Cohesion: The State of Canadian Research." Paper SRA-321 (Ottawa: Strategic Research and Analysis Directorate, Department of Canadian Heritage, 1998); Jeannotte, M. S. "Social Cohesion Around the World: an International Comparison of Definitions and Issues." Paper SRA-309 (Ottawa: Strategic Research and Analysis Directorate, Department of Canadian Heritage, 2000).

9   Bernard, P. "Social Cohesion: A Dialectical Critique of a Quasi-concept." Paper SRA-491 (Ottawa: Strategic Research and Analysis Directorate, Department of Canadian Heritage, 2000).

10 Chan, J., To, H. P., and Chan, E. "Reconsidering Social Cohesion: Developing a Definition and Analytical Framework for Policy Research," *Social Indicators Research* 75 (2006): 273–302.

11 Berger-Schmitt, R. "Social Cohesion as an Aspect of the Quality of Societies: Concept and Measurement." EuReporting Working Paper No. 14 (Mannheim: Centre for Survey Research and Methodology, 2000).

12 The Canadian Council on Social Development has devised a set of social cohesion indicators which include both "elements of socially cohesive activity" and "conditions favorable for inclusive social cohesion." Canadian Council on Social Development, "Social Cohesion in Canada: Possible Indicators Highlights." Paper SRA-542 (Ottawa: Strategic Research and Analysis Directorate, Department of Canadian Heritage, 2000); see also Duhaime, G., Searles, E., Usher, P., Myers, H., and Frechette, P. "Social Cohesion and Living Conditions in the Canadian Arctic: From Theory to Measurement." *Social Indicators Research* 66 (2004): 295–317.

13 Jenson, J. "Mapping Social Cohesion: The State of Canadian Research." Paper SRA-321 (Ottawa: Strategic Research and Analysis Directorate, Department of Canadian Heritage, 1998).

14 Beauvais, C. and Jenson, J. "Social Cohesion: Updating the State of Research." CPRN Discussion Paper No. F\22 (Ottawa: Canadian Policy Research Networks, 2002).

15 Bernard, P. "Social Cohesion: A Dialectical Critique of a Quasi-concept." Paper SRA-491 (Ottawa: Strategic Research and Analysis Directorate, Department of Canadian Heritage, 2000).

16 Putnam, R. D. *Bowling Alone: The Collapse and Revival of American Community* (New York: Simon & Schuster, 2000), p. 19.

17 Putnam, *Bowling Alone*, p. 291.

18 The survey was carried out by Policy 21 Ltd. of the University of Hong Kong.

19 The indexes were constructed in the following manner. First, a reliability test was carried out for the questions which were thought to belong to a certain dimension of social cohesion. Questions that substantially lowered the overall Cronbach's alpha were excluded from further analysis. An exploratory factor analysis (principal component analysis) was then carried out for the remaining questions. An index was constructed by summing up all the questions that the factor analysis grouped under one component. The scores of the index were then standardized to range between 1 and 10, with 5.5 being the mid-point. Scores above 5.5 indicate feeling or action in the direction of cohesion. For a more detailed discussion of the construction of the indexes and the state of social cohesion in Hong Kong, see Chan, J. and Chan, E.

"Charting the State of Social Cohesion in Hong Kong." *The China Quarterly* 187 (2006): 635–658.

20 This is with the exception of the youngest group (age 18–30), whose Political Concern Index score is lower than the two middle-aged groups (31–45, 46–60), but is still higher than the most seniorage group (above 60).

21 For an account of the events and dissatisfaction leading to the July 1, 2003 demonstration, see Cheng, J. Y. S. "Introduction: Causes and Implications of the July Protest Rally in Hong Kong"; Cheung, A. B. L. "The Hong Kong System under One Country Being Tested: Article 23, Governance Crisis and the Search for a New Hong Kong Identity," both in J. Y. S. Cheng, ed. *The July 1 Protest Rally: Interpreting a Historic Event* (Hong Kong: City University of Hong Kong Press, 2005).

22 For an evaluation of the Principal Officials Accountability System, see Cheung, Chor-yung. "The Principal Officials Accountability System: Not Taking Responsible Government Seriously?" In J. Y. S. Cheng, ed. *The July 1 Protest Rally*.

23 Regina Ip resigned for personal reasons rather than taking responsibility for the failure to enact the national security law and of creating massive societal dissatisfaction.

24 Antony Leung was the leading character of what was called the "car-gate" scandal. He was alleged to have purposively evaded a soon-to-be imposed Motor vehicles first registration tax by purchasing a new car about a month ahead of the imposition of the tax. It caused a large-scale public outcry when the incident was revealed in a local newspaper. The chief executive considered Leung's act inappropriate and that it had breached the Code for Principal Officials under the Principal Officials Accountability System. Although Leung offered to resign when the incident was made known in March, Tung still did not think that Leung's misconduct warranted removal from office. It was not until after the July 1 demonstration that Tung accepted Leung's resignation. For a chronology of the "car-gate" affair, see Governance Reform Group, SynergyNet, Hong Kong. *Hong Kong Deserves Better Governance: An Evaluation of Hong Kong's System of Governance and its Performance* (September, 2003).

25 E. K. Yeoh was the Secretary of Health, Wealth, and Food at the time of SARS. An investigation committee was set up by LegCo to examine the case in December, 2003. On July 5, 2004, the Investigation Committee released the Report of the Select Committee to Inquire into the Handling of the Severe Acute Respiratory Syndrome Outbreak by the Government and the Hospital Authority (see www.legco.gov.hk/yr03–04/english/sc/sc_sars/reports/sars_rpt.htm). Even though the Select Committee found Yeoh to have some inadequacies in handling SARS, it did not think that they were so serious as to call for his dismissal. Nevertheless, Yeoh resigned two days later on July 7. His resignation was said to have to do with the criticism heaped on him by the families of SARS victims and was therefore more emotionally driven than politically motivated. See Governance Reform Group, SynergyNet, Hong Kong. *Hong Kong Governance in Capacity Crisis* (September, 2004).

26 Bradsher, K. "Hong Kong Chief Resigns, Deputy will Assume Post." *New York Times Late Edition East Coast*, March 11, 2005, p. A3.

27 "Farewell, Mr. Tung: Democracy is the Answer to China's Dilemma in Hong Kong." *Financial Times* (USA 2nd edn), March 11, 2005, p. 12.

28 Lau, S. K. "The Rise and Decline of Political Support for the Hong Kong Special Administrative Region Government." In Sing, M., ed. *Hong Kong Government and Politics* (Hong Kong: Oxford University Press, 2003), pp. 387–406.

29 Ko, K. and Woo, R. "Muddled Policies Compounding Insecurities over Home Prices." *South China Morning Post*, July 3, 2000, p. 2. See also, "Officials Blind to Policy Damage." *South China Morning Post*, July 3, 2000, p. 8.

30 At present, half of the legislature is made up of popularly elected councilors while the other half comprises functionally elected representatives.

31 Ma, N. "Executive–Legislative Relations: Assessing Legislative Influence in an

Executive-Dominant System." In Lau, S. K., ed. *The First Tung Chee-hwa Adminis-tration: The First Five Years of the Hong Kong Special Administrative Region* (Hong Kong: The Chinese University Press, 2002), pp. 349–371.

32 Popular election of the chief executive in 2007 was supported by over half of the respondents in various surveys; see hkupop.hku.hk, accessed July 15, 2005.

33 Popular election of the entire Legislative Council in 2008 was supported by over 60 percent of the respondents in various surveys; see hkupop.hku.hk, accessed July 15, 2005.

34 There are other restrictions as well. See Bradsher, K. "China Bars Universal Suffrage in Hong Kong." *International Herald Tribune*, April 27, 2004, p. 1.

35 Lau, S. K., "Tung Chee-hwa's Governing Strategy: The Shortfall in Politics," in Siu-kai Lau, ed. *The First Tung Chee-hwa Administration: The First Five Years of the Hong Kong Special Administrative Region* (Hong Kong: The Chinese University Press, 2002), pp. 1–39.

36 Lau, S. K., "Tung Chee-hwa's Governing Strategy."

37 Although the discussion here focuses on the Article 23 saga, it is by no means the only piece of public policy in the Tung era that aroused opposition. Tung had tried to introduce changes of various scales in many policy areas, most noticeably in housing, education, and health. However, almost all of them have met with resistance, and some were shelved before they were introduced. For an evaluation of these new pol-icies or attempted policies, see Lau, S. K., ed. *The First Tung Chee-hwa Administra-tion: The First Five Years of the Hong Kong Special Administrative Region* (Hong Kong: The Chinese University Press, 2002).

38 Article 23 of the Basic Law states:

> The Hong Kong Special Administrative Region shall enact laws on its own to prohibit any act of treason, secession, sedition, subversion against the Central People's Government, or theft of state secrets, to prohibit foreign political organi-zations or bodies from conducting political activities in the Region, and to pro-hibit political organizations or bodies of the Region from establishing ties with foreign political organizations or bodies.
>
> (*The Basic Law of the Hong Kong Special Administrative Region of the People's Republic of China*, April, 1990)

39 Shamdasani, R. and Chow, M. "Chief Justice Joins Article 23 Debate." *South China Morning Post*, January 14, 2003, p. 1.

40 Leung, A. "Withdraw the Laws, the US Congress Demands." *South China Morning Post*, June 28, 2003, p. 3.

41 Bradsher, K. "Hong Kong Delays Security Bill After Cabinet Member Quits." *New York Times Late Edition, East Coast*, July 7, 2003, p. A2; MacKay, A. "Hong Kong U-turn on Subversion Legislation." *Financial Times*, July 7, 2003, p. 1.

42 Figures quoted here come from data collected by the Public Opinion Program of the University of Hong Kong; see hkupop.hku.hk, accessed June 28, 2005.

43 hkupop.hku.hk, accessed June 28, 2005.

44 "Donald Tsang's Election Platform in Full," *South China Morning Post*, June 3, 2005, p. 4.

45 "Chief Executive Candidate Solicits Opinions from Hong Kong Election Committee," *BBC Monitoring Asia Pacific* (London: June 3, 2005), p. 1.

46 Shamdasani, R. "Lawyers Question Edict on Surveillance Chief Executive's Order Regulating Secret Monitoring by Police Could Make Things Worse, Barristers Argue." *South China Morning Post*, August 7, 2005, p. 2; see also, Cheung, J. "Bar Association Censures Chief Executive over Surveillance Order," *South China Morning Post*, August 9, 2005, p. 1.

47 "No Checks and Fewer Balances." *The Wall Street Journal Europe*, August 10, 2005, p. A.6.

References

Battaini-Dragoni, G. and Stefano D. "The Council of Europe's Strategy for Social Cohesion." Paper presented at the Conference on Social Cohesion, organized by the Faculty of Social Sciences, the University of Hong Kong, and the Hong Kong Council of Social Service, November 28 and 29, 2003.

BBC Monitoring Asia Pacific. "Chief Executive Candidate Solicits Opinions from Hong Kong Election Committee." *BBC Monitoring Asia Pacific*, June 3, 2005, p. 1.

Beauvais, C. and J. Jenson. "Social Cohesion: Updating the State of Research." CPRN Discussion Paper No. F\22. Ottawa: Canadian Policy Research Networks, 2002.

Berger, P. *The Limits of Social Cohesion: Conflict and Mediation in Pluralist Societies.* Boulder, CO: Westview Press, 1998.

Berger-Schmitt, R. "Social Cohesion as an Aspect of the Quality of Societies: Concept and Measurement." EuReporting Working Paper No. 14. Mannheim: Centre for Survey Research and Methodology, 2000.

Bernard, P. "Social Cohesion: A Dialectical Critique of a Quasi-concept." Paper SRA-491. Ottawa: Strategic Research and Analysis Directorate, Department of Canadian Heritage, 2000.

Bollen K. A. and R. H. Hoyle. "Perceived Cohesion: A Conceptual and Empirical Explanation." *Social Forces* 6, no. 2 (2000).

Bradsher, K. "China Bars Universal Suffrage in Hong Kong." *International Herald Tribune*, April 27, 2004, p. 1.

Bradsher, K. "Hong Kong Delays Security Bill After Cabinet Member Quits." *New York Times Late Edition* East Coast, July 7, 2003, p. A2.

Bradsher, K. "Hong Kong Chief Resigns, Deputy will Assume Post." *New York Times Late Edition East Coast.* March 11, 2005, p. A3.

Canadian Council on Social Development. "Social Cohesion in Canada: Possible Indicators Highlights." Paper SRA-542. Ottawa: Strategic Research and Analysis Directorate, Department of Canadian Heritage, 2000.

Chan, J. "Civil Liberties, Rule of Law and Human Rights: The Hong Kong Special Administrative Region in Its First Four Years." In *The First Tung Chee-hwa Administration: The First Five Years of the Hong Kong Special Administrative Region*, ed. Siu-kai Lau. Hong Kong: The Chinese University Press, 2002.

Chan J. and E. Chan. "Charting the State of Social Cohesion in Hong Kong." *The China Quarterly* 187 (2006): 635–658.

Chan, J., H. P. To, and E. Chan. "Reconsidering Social Cohesion: Developing a Definition and Analytical Framework for Policy Research." *Social Indicators Research* 75 (2006): 273–302.

Cheng, J. Y. S. "Introduction: Causes and Implications of the July Protest Rally in Hong Kong." In *The July 1 Protest Rally: Interpreting a Historic Event*, ed. J. Y. S. Cheng. Hong Kong: City University of Hong Kong Press, 2005.

Cheung, A. B. L. "The Hong Kong System under One Country Being Tested: Article 23." In *The July 1 Protest Rally: Interpreting a Historic Event*, ed. J. Y. S. Cheng. Hong Kong: City University of Hong Kong Press, 2005.

Cheung, C. Y. "The Principal Officials Accountability System: Not Taking Responsible Government Seriously?" In *The July 1 Protest Rally: Interpreting a Historic Event*, ed. J. Y. S. Cheng. Hong Kong: City University of Hong Kong Press, 2005.

Cheung, J. "Bar Association Censures Chief Executive over Surveillance Order." *South China Morning Post*, August 9, 2005, p. 1.

"Donald Tsang's Election Platform in Full." *South China Morning Post*, June 3, 2005, p. 4.

Duhaime, G., E. Searles, P. Usher, H. Myers, and P. Frechette. "Social Cohesion and Living Conditions in the Canadian Arctic: From Theory to Measurement." *Social Indicators Research* 66 (2004): 295–317.

Financial Times. "Farewell, Mr. Tung: Democracy is the Answer to China's Dilemma in Hong Kong." *Financial Times*, March 11, 2005, p. 12.

Friedkin, N. E. "Social Cohesion." *Annual Review of Sociology* 30 (2004): 409–425.

Gough, I. and G. Olofsson, eds. *Capitalism and Social Cohesion: Essays on Exclusion and Integration.* Basingstoke: Macmillan, 1999.

Governance Reform Group, SynergyNet, Hong Kong. *Hong Kong Deserves Better Governance: An Evaluation of Hong Kong's System of Governance and its Performance* (September, 2003).

Governance Reform Group, SynergyNet, Hong Kong. *Hong Kong Governance in Capacity Crisis* (September, 2004).

HKU Pop Site. hkupop.hku.hk (accessed July 5, 2005).

Jeannotte, M. S. "Social Cohesion Around the World: An International Comparison of Definitions and Issues." Paper SRA-309. Ottawa: Strategic Research and Analysis Directorate, Department of Canadian Heritage, 2000.

Jenson, J. "Mapping Social Cohesion: the State of Canadian Research." Paper SRA-321. Ottawa: Strategic Research and Analysis Directorate, Department of Canadian Heritage, 1998.

Ko, K. and R. Woo. "Muddled Policies Compounding Insecurities over Home Prices." *South China Morning Post.* July 3, 2000, p. 2.

Lau, S. K., ed. *The First Tung Chee-hwa Administration: The First Five Years of the Hong Kong Special Administrative Region.* Hong Kong: The Chinese University Press, 2002.

Lau, S. K., "Tung Chee-hwa's Governing Strategy: The Shortfall in Politics." In *The First Tung Chee-hwa Administration: The First Five Years of the Hong Kong Special Administrative Region*, ed. Siu-kai Lau. Hong Kong: The Chinese University Press, 2002.

Lau, S. K., "The Rise and Decline of Political Support for the Hong Kong Special Administrative Region Government." In *Hong Kong Government and Politics*, ed. Sing. M. Hong Kong: Oxford University Press, 2003.

Legislative Council. "Report of the Select Committee to Inquire into the Handling of the Severe Acute Respiratory Syndrome Outbreak by the Government and the Hospital Authority July, 2004." At www.legco.gov.hk/yr03–04/english/sc/sc_sars/reports/sars_rpt.htm. (accessed December 17, 2006).

Leung, A. "Withdraw the Laws, the US Congress Demands." *South China Morning Post*, June 28, 2003, p. 3.

Ma, N. "Executive–Legislative Relations: Assessing Legislative Influence in an Executive-Dominant System." In *The First Tung Chee-hwa Administration: The First Five Years of the Hong Kong Special Administrative Region*, ed. Siu-kai Lau. Hong Kong: The Chinese University Press, 2002.

MacKay, A. "Hong Kong U-turn on Subversion Legislation." *Financial Times*, July 7, 2003, p. 1.

"No Checks and Fewer Balances." *The Wall Street Journal Europe*, August 10, 2005, p. A.6.

Putnam, R. D. *Bowling Alone: The Collapse and Revival of American Community.* New York: Simon & Schuster, 2000.

Shamdasani, R. "Lawyers Question Edict on Surveillance: Chief Executive's Order Regulating Secret Monitoring by Police Could Make Things Worse, Barristers Argue." *South China Morning Post*, August 7, 2005, p. 2.

Shamdasani, R. and M. Chow. "Chief Justice Joins Article 23 Debate." *South China Morning Post*, January 14, 2003, p. 1.

The Basic Law of the Hong Kong Special Administrative Region of the People's Republic of China. April, 1990.

Wong, T. K. Y. "The Changing Public Perception of the Chief Executive." In *The First Tung Chee-hwa Administration: The First Five Years of the Hong Kong Special Administrative Region*, ed. Lau, S. K. Hong Kong: The Chinese University Press, 2002.

5 Hong Kong at the crossroads

Public pressure for democratic reform

Ming Sing

Pro-democracy rallies amid pressure for faster democratization

On July 1, 2003, over half a million Hong Kong people joined in a mass demonstration for greater democracy and against the proposed introduction of draconian anti-subversion laws.[1] This protest was the largest since 1989. The size of the participants, the huge variety of the social groups drawn in, and the enthusiastic demands they brought up eloquently testified to the pervasive public disenchantment with governmental performance, and their support for greater democracy. This protest compelled the Chinese government to proffer an assortment of economic packages to lift Hong Kong's economy.

Despite Beijing's economic carrots, and the succeeding recovery in the moribund property and stock market from the last quarter of 2003, the July 1, 2003 demonstration, plus the 200,000-strong pro-democracy protest on July 1, 2004, diverged sharply from the trifling participation in pro-democracy rallies between the 1980s and 1990s, the biggest of which saw only 5,000 marchers in 1987. More significantly, the record-breaking voter turnout for local elections held on November 23, 2003, and the ensuing landslide victory of the pro-democracy camp over the China-backed party, greatly worried Beijing as to the likely setback of pro-Beijing parties and its possible loss of domination over Hong Kong.[2] The mass demonstrations delivered a crystal-clear message to the Chinese government that notwithstanding some positive economic news, Hong Kong people have shown greater doggedness with their demand for democratic reform than what Beijing had assumed they would display.

More specifically, the mass protests testified to a withdrawal of public support for the non-democratic system and a strong support for greater democracy. Surveys on public attitudes toward universal suffrage in the past few years have shown a fairly persistent public demand for universal suffrage. A most noteworthy finding has been that, based on a representative survey conducted in early July, 2003, 75 percent of respondents were dissatisfied with the current governance system, suggesting that Hong Kong's political system, and not only its Chief Executive and Principal Officials, was undergoing a legitimacy crisis or severe paucity of public support.[3]

This chapter endeavors to first, explain briefly how and why the public bestowed political support upon the non-democratic political structure in Hong Kong from the 1970s to mid-1997. Second, it expounds how five major challenges have diluted the legitimacy; that is, public support for Hong Kong's non-democratic system following the handover. These challenges are expected to continue to undermine public support for the non-democratic system and keep up pressure for faster democratization of Hong Kong, at least in the medium term. Next, in the light of local and international data, this chapter will assess the urgency, preparedness, and usefulness of implementing democracy for Hong Kong. It will argue that comparatively speaking, Hong Kong has been long overdue for a transition to full democracy, and is very likely to enjoy a stable democracy should Beijing permit its establishment. In the light of international experiences, arguments are then made that the installation of democracy in Hong Kong will likely improve Hong Kong's governance and enable it to weather some major delegitimating challenges. Next, with the unexpected ascendancy to power of Donald Tsang, the new Chief Executive in Hong Kong in early 2005, the renewed mass mobilization for democracy in October, 2005 and the subsequent legislature's rejection of the Hong Kong government's blueprint of political reform will be investigated. Finally, the prospect of maintaining public pressure for democracy and improving the legitimacy of Hong Kong's non-democratic political system in face of the transfer of power to Donald Tsang, the new Chief Executive, will be examined.

Pre-handover Hong Kong legitimized authoritarianism

"Legitimacy" is an ambiguous concept that can mean public support for policies, leaders or political systems (Dahl 1984: 53–54; Habermas 1975; Lane 1984: 207–217; Lipset 1981; Pye in Verba *et al.* 1971: 136). The problem of legitimacy here pertains to the "general public's political support for the political system attitudinally" (O'Donnell and Schmitter 1986, 15). In the light of international experience, studying Hong Kong's legitimacy is pivotal to gauging its prospects of democratization. Comparatively speaking, for instance, in Latin America and Southern Europe, the problem of legitimation haunted authoritarian regimes and furnished both a general backdrop to, and a remote cause of, democratic transitions of those regimes (O'Donnell and Schmitter 1986). Similarly, in research on revolutions and political change of over ten Third World countries, popular perceptions of illegitimacy have been found to be a background cause for their revolutionary movements.[4]

The legitimation of a political system can be predicated on intrinsic values or on the performance of the system. It was rare that authoritarian or quasi-authoritarian regimes could legitimize their regimes by their own systemic characteristics, which included monopoly of power by bureaucratic elites or narrow parties, and the restrictions on popular elections for their governments. Those regimes must thus legitimize themselves by arguing for their relevance to attaining such goals as economic growth, socialism, communism, or other utopias.[5] When the regime apparently fails to accomplish its goals, their legitimacy can vanish very rapidly.[6] Lack of public support toward *policies* or political *leaders* of authoritarian countries may therefore accumulate. When the lack of support deepens beyond a certain threshold, it can trigger a basic removal of backing for the entire political structure, engendering a legitimation problem at a systemic level, and leading to pressure for democratization.[7]

Hong Kong, as a quasi-bureaucratic authoritarian system before the handover,[8] gained a moderate level of public support during the 1970s and 1997 by its capacity to satisfy public demands for three crucial legitimating bases: prosperity, stability, and civil liberties.

Hong Kong's miraculous economic track record in the past few decades before the handover bespeak clearly that that prosperity has been a goal splendidly attained. Between 1960 and 1982, Hong Kong achieved a staggering average growth rate of 7.0 percent per year, ranked fifth in the world.[9] Between 1980 and 1992, Hong Kong's average economic growth rate still rattled along at 6.7 percent per year. In 1995, Hong Kong's GDP per person gauged in parity purchasing power was the third highest globally.[10] In terms of civil liberties, under the shield of the British liberal tradition and the influence of robust student movements and pressure groups that appeared in the 1960s and 1970s, Hong Kong had already maintained the second highest level of civil liberties in Asia between the late 1970s to the late 1980s, before the democratic breakthroughs of some other East Asian societies (Sing 2004). As for political stability, the rare occurrence of only three major society-wide riots in Hong Kong since the 1950s also testifies to its magnificent achievement in that respect, particularly when considered comparatively with other developing countries. Consequently, as seen from Table 5.1, public support for the non-democratic political system was ranked moderate to strong between 1977 and 1997, but suffered a disastrous plunge in 2003.[11]

Since the handover of Hong Kong to China, its prosperity and civil liberties look increasingly shaky amid the following five major delegitimating challenges. Therefore, any attempt to ward off public demands for greater

Table 5.1 Levels of legitimacy for Hong Kong's non-democratic political system[12]

Year	%
1977	81.6
1985	74.5
1988	75
1990	59
1991	72
1992	56.3
1993	62.1
1995	63
1997	49.2
2003	25

Source: endnote 12.

democracy in Hong Kong in the medium and long run face greater resistance than in the pre-handover period.

Undermining the legitimacy of a non-democratic system

Endless economic restructuring

Late 1997 proved to be a monumental landmark for Hong Kong's economy. From that time onward, Hong Kong has suffered the most serious economic recession in a generation (Figure 5.1). The recession began to drag down not just the public support for government officials, but also gradually eroded the support for the entire political system.[13]

The Asian financial crisis, which broke out in Thailand in August, 1997, set off a landslide plummet in the value of Hong Kong's stock and property market in October, 1997 (Sing 2001). Between October, 1997 and September, 1998, many stocks have been curtailed by no less than 50 percent. Heavy tolls were also exacted in the property market, which had experienced a severe correction of average value of about 65 percent at its worst level since October, 1997. The overall economic growth rate, which was approaching 7 percent during the handover, dived to about minus 5 percent in September, 1998 (SCMP, October 4, 1998). Amid the bursting of the dotcom bubble and the September 11 terrorist attacks, the unanticipated and serious economic meltdown sent the unemployment rate skyrocketing to 8.7 percent in late 2003, an all-time high.

Despite the slight recovery in the economy, the unemployment rate still stood at 6.1 percent in February, 2005 (*Ming Pao Daily*, March 22, 2005). Furthermore, according to the World Economic Forum, Hong Kong has suffered a precipitous decline in economic competitiveness since 1999. Its competitiveness dropped precipitously from third place in 1999 to twenty-eighth in 2005 (Table 5.2).[14]

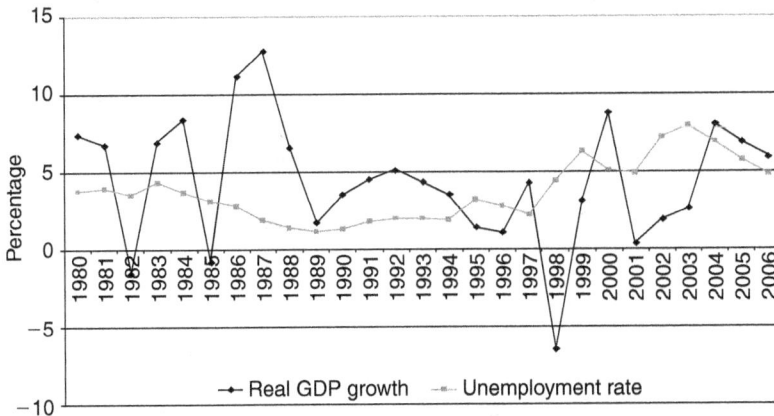

Figure 5.1 Economic performance in Hong Kong, 1980 to 2006 (source: World Economic Outlook Database 2007).

Table 5.2 Declining "Growth Competitiveness Index"

Year	Ranking (1 as the most competitive)
1999	3
2000	7
2001	13
2002	22
2003	24
2004	21
2005	28

Source: World Economic Forum at www.weforum.org/ (accessed on December 1, 2005).

To restore Hong Kong's competitiveness, the government has advocated economic restructuring toward a knowledge-based economy, which requires a drastic improvement in Hong Kong's education in both quality and quantity. Hong Kong's college enrolment, defined as those undertaking undergraduate degree studies, has for long lagged far behind those of Taiwan and South Korea.[15] The annual college enrolment rate for bachelor degrees for Hong Kong has been stagnant at 18 percent since the mid-1990s. In terms of quality, students at different levels have been subjected to incessant criticism by teachers and employers of a diversity of occupational sectors especially since the 1990s.[16] Without a drastic improvement in Hong Kong's education in both quality and quantity, successful economic restructuring for Hong Kong toward a competitive knowledge-based economy will be unattainable. The aforementioned education issue has overshadowed the chance of any successful completion of economic restructuring in the near term.

Although Mainland China's economic packages since late 2003 have contributed to a measure of economic rebound in Hong Kong, the economic effects of Closer Economic Partnership Arrangement (CEPA) have been recently criticized as limited, owing partly to the alleged inadequate coordination of the Hong Kong government[17] amid the dwindling consumption of tourists from the Mainland in 2005 vis-à-vis those of 2004. The huge difference in salaries between China and Hong Kong cast a big shadow over the adequacy of those packages in resolving the thorny issue of unemployment and economic restructuring.

The aforementioned features overshadow the chance of any successful completion of Hong Kong's successful transition to a knowledge-based economy, and thus economic restructuring in the short term. As long as economic restructuring remains unfinished, the prospect of fundamentally resolving Hong Kong's structural unemployment will remain unclear, and sustainable economic growth in the long run will also be in doubt. According to cross-national research, economic crises in authoritarian regimes will erode public support for non-elected political systems, and eventually inflame more powerful political movements to press for democratic reform (Gasioroworski 1995; Geddes 1999:

119; Haggard and Kaufman 1995; Przeworski *et al.* 2000). The economic gloom has greatly contributed to the withdrawal of public support for Hong Kong's non-democratic structure and enhanced its public pressure for democratization.

Severe social inequality

In addition to economic restructuring there has been a rising social inequality that has depleted the backing for Hong Kong's non-democratic system and caused additional public demands for democratization. As seen from Table 5.3, the Gini coefficient, a standard indicator measuring the level of inequality, rose from 0.43 in 1971, through 0.476 in 1991, to 0.525 in 2001 for Hong Kong.[18]

In 2001, Hong Kong's social inequality was not only worse than those of developed countries including Japan, Taiwan, and South Korea, but it was also more serious than less developed countries such as China, Thailand, Malaysia, and the Philippines. During that year, the poorest deciles in terms of income took up only 0.9 percent of the total income, while the uppermost deciles took up 41.2 percent. According to a United Nations' report published in 2003, in the early 2000s, out of 175 societies, the inequality in Hong Kong was ranked 132nd, when inequalities among societies are arranged in increasing order.[19] In addition, given that the fundamental cause of the intensification in income inequality has been Hong Kong's overall economic restructuring without the necessary backup of government-led economic and social policies (Zhao *et al.* 2004: 470), barring some unexpected major policy shifts, the severity in inequality has little prospect of subsiding soon. This is especially so, as Hong Kong will presumably be run by a government that continues to praise itself for allowing a large degree of economic freedom. The recent outcry over the privatization of public shopping arcades has been indicative of the breadth and depth of conflict that can arise from social inequality. Without fundamentally alleviating this inequality, those who are on the losing end will find themselves more amenable to pro-democracy mobilizations.

Table 5.3 Rising Gini coefficients in Hong Kong

Year	Gini coefficient
1971	0.43
1981	0.451
1991	0.476
1996	0.518
2001	0.525

Source: Wong (2000).

Intensifying cronyism

While there have been multiple reasons for the widening social inequality, one commonly perceived factor has been growing cronyism in post-handover Hong Kong, as manifest in oligopolistic competition in some sectors. The Hong Kong Consumer Council and some prominent local economists have contended that local oligopolies occupying the property sector, supermarkets, and container terminals, among other sectors, have dampened fair competition and undermined Hong Kong's economy. Although the European Union issued a report publicly blasting the lack of a level playing field in Hong Kong's economy in 2000, the Hong Kong government and major conglomerates have opposed introducing a "competition law," a law which has been implemented in over 100 developed and developing countries for securing fair competition.[20] The recent public accusations that certain senior officials had engaged in cronyism over the West Kowloon Cultural Development project and the Hung Hom Peninsula development have testified to the depth of sentiment among local people against cronyism.

Budget deficit and its effects on society

In addition, public discontent has deepened further by the cutting of public expenditure due to the rising budgetary deficit. Hong Kong's economic prospects have been dimmed by a rapid climb in its budgetary deficit. The deficit for the seven months to the end of October, 2003 rose to HK$81.1 billion ($10.4 billion), exceeding the government's target for the full year.[21] By the end of September, 2003, financial reserves had fallen to HK$250 billion. Nearly half of the reserve left by the British government has been used up to finance the deficit since the handover. Although the updated record up to March, 2005 showed an improvement in the financial deficit owing to the economic rebound, the government's continued reliance on the sale of land and the accompanying proceeds entail that Hong Kong is still faced with an uphill task of resolving the structural fiscal deficit.[22] The mounting deficit, which has been described as the "structural budget deficit" by the Hong Kong SAR government and local economists, has arisen as fiscal revenue grows slower than fiscal expenditure. In short, the problem is one of perennial overspending or of living beyond one's means.[23] The deficit has been due to the huge outlay for civil servants' wages and publicly subsidized bodies, the unsteady income from land sales, as well as the extremely narrow income tax base.[24] The narrow tax base is evidenced by the fact that 60 percent of Hong Kong wage earners do not need to pay any salary tax, and 90 percent of all salary tax revenues are provided by only 100,000 taxpayers; that is, 3 percent of the workforce (Lui 2006).

Constrained by its lack of public support, the post-handover government has not kept up its pressure on the civil service and employees of publicly subsidized bodies to reduce their wages, despite constant demands from various sectors to do so. Instead, the government has attempted to save money by drastically cutting expenses on social welfare and other policy arenas. These acts have heightened the tension between the government and those who have lost funding, including different actors as wide ranging as young teachers, doctors, social workers, older people, and welfare recipients. The slashing of funding has been accompanied by offering lower salary for new entrants than the existing staff for the aforementioned sectors. Such cutbacks and unequal pay for equal work have further eroded public support for the government.

On top of these economy-related elements, political factors have also played a pivotal role in the declining public support of the Hong Kong government and the mounting public support for democratization.

A deficient Principal Officials Accountability System

In the face of this unfinished economic restructuring, and the dismally low level of public support for the Chief Executive and the Hong Kong government, Tung established the so-called Principals Officials Accountability System (POAS) in mid-2002. Principal Officials, who are political appointees of the Chief Executive, became ministers with portfolios in various policy arenas. At the same time, the leaders of two pro-government parties have been co-opted into the cabinet-like Executive Council, where in Principal Officials decide on policies together with the Chief Executive. However, the lack of political experience of many Principal Officials, the dearth of cooperation among them, and the seeming absence of a common ideology, and the deficiency of adequate debates in the Executive Council[25] have contributed to a string of widely criticized blunders by Principal Officials. One noticeable blunder was the attempt to rush through the highly controversial Article 23. The act has been pervasively perceived as threatening freedom and has subsequently contributed to dampening the legitimacy of the political system. Other widely censured acts, including one Principal Official's handling of the merger of two local universities, the dismissal of staff of the Equality Opportunity Commission and handling of subsequent complaints, as well as the cheap sale of the Hunghom Peninsula housing development to a private developer, all speak volumes to the poor skills of individual Principal Officials, if not the problematic running of the Executive Council as well. It is also doubtful whether the problem can be resolved by appointing more officials at the administrative office grade as Principal Officials, given the increasingly limited pool of competent and experienced officials to draw from. The perceived resistance of the Chief Executive to demand those officials to be truly accountable, plus the growing tension between the executive and legislative branch since the handover, have largely undermined public support of the Hong Kong government and contributed to public support for democratic reform as evinced by the July 1 rally.

Furthermore, the rising centralization of power of the executive branch has further agitated pro-democracy forces to remain critical of the government, as the latter have found themselves increasingly deprived of any influence under an increasingly rigid government embedded within a soft-authoritarian system.

Challenged with the distressing economic restructuring, structural fiscal deficits, severe social inequality, widely perceived cronyism, and grave executive–legislative tensions, can greater democratic reform help allay the legitimacy problem confronted by the Hong Kong government?

Further democratic development for Hong Kong

Since 1974, a global wave of democratization has swept over different parts of the world. Between 1974 and 2004, the number of electoral democracies has rapidly increased from 41 in 1974 to 119 in 2004 (Figures 5.2 and 5.3).

This trend shows that democracy can better contribute to political stability, economic growth, reducing social inequality, and actualization of human rights than non-democracies:

1   Democracy promotes political stability: Based upon cross-national research, democracies have been found to be able to better promote political stability, affording more opportunities for political opposition and handover of power than non-democracies. For instance, between 1950 and 1990, though riots and demonstrations were more prevalent in democracies, they are much more destabilizing in dictatorships.[26] Because of the far greater opportunities for the public at large to use peaceful elections to replace unpopular leaders and parties under democracies than under dictatorships, most protests and demonstrations under democracies were not targeted at toppling the political system, as compared with the more violent anti-system demonstrations under dictatorships.

2   Democracy and economic growth: More recent cross-national research findings demonstrate increasing evidence that democracy does promote economic growth, especially in the long run (Feng 2003; Kurzman *et al.* 2002; Leblang 1997). A research study, which reviewed 31 cross-national studies, each covering a sample of 80 countries or more, found that 20 of them

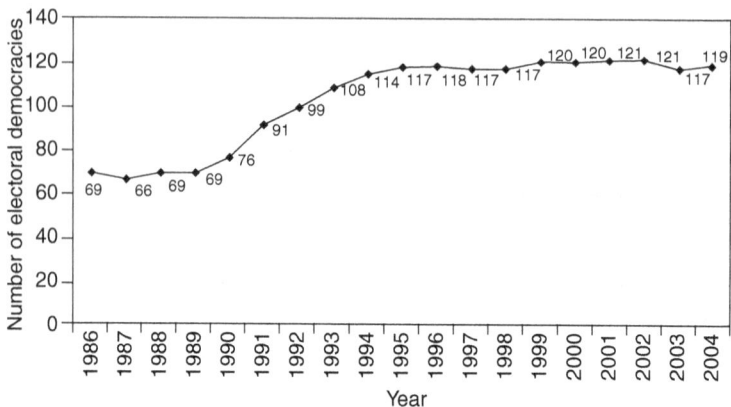

Figure 5.2 Global expansion of democracies since the late 1980s: number of electoral democracies (source: Freedom House (2005)).

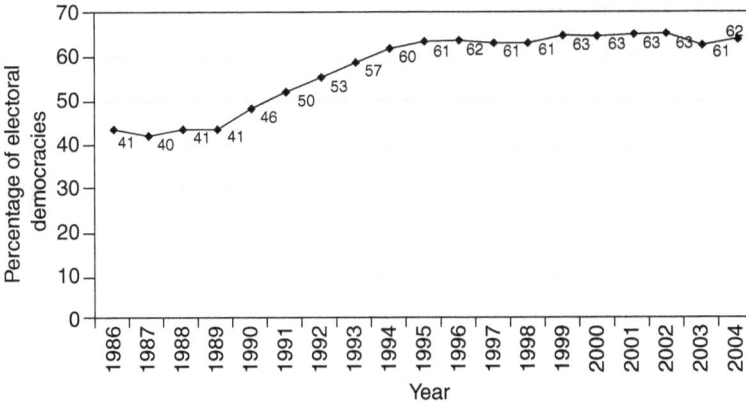

Figure 5.3 Global expansion of democracies since the late 1980s: percentage of electoral democracies (source: Freedom House (2005)).

supported the notion that democracy does promote economic growth, while only four disagreed (Kurzman *et al.* 2002). In addition, a recent work suggests that democracy does promote economic growth (Feng 2003). Based upon his study of 106 countries between 1975 and 1989, the author found that democracy did promote economic growth through strengthening political stability and "healthy changes" in replacing incompetent governing parties with competent ones. Overall, Feng found that an increase in one unit of democracy has the potential to raise the growth rate by about 5.6 percent per year. If an economy expands at 5.6 percent per year, it will approximately double in 12.72 years.

3   Democracy has also been found to be more capable of reducing social inequality, though it is not the only factor that matters.[27]

4   Democracy is the only system that respects contests for power and is in line with the "respect and promotion of all human rights – civil, cultural, economic, political and social."[28]

The above-mentioned benefits of democracy may directly ease the delegitimating effects posed by at least some, though not all, of the five major challenges. In the context of Hong Kong, installing democracy including free and fair elections will institutionalize a peaceful way to replace incapable or popular leaders through free and fair elections. The elections will also serve as an important self-correcting mechanism to replace problematic leaders and policies. Free and fair elections will furnish the procedural legitimacy for the new constitutional structure when the public discovers that the HKSAR government is no longer produced from a small circle of electors. In that context, the public is likely to offer at least a longer political honeymoon to an elected government than a non-elected one, enhancing it to launch necessary and bold measures to confront major challenges and implement policies for the long-term development of Hong Kong.

Bringing democracy to Hong Kong, especially if suitable political institutions are designed, will also provide more institutionalized channels to resolve societal conflicts in and between its legislature and Executive Council. Greater accountability is also expected owing to the rising political sensitivity to electoral pressure, reducing the worsening of political crises arising from political insensitivity and tactlessness. Last but not least, democratization in Hong Kong will greatly boost the development of political parties and the nurturing of effective political leadership.

Hong Kong's political culture is likely to sustain mass support for democracy

Moving further ahead with democratic development in Hong Kong many also help ward off political pressure by satisfying the persistently moderate to strong public demands for democratization that have unfolded since mid-2003. In the wake of mounting pressure from Beijing and economic recovery, how likely is it that the public will continue to shore up further democratic development?

In terms of the public backing for implementing democracy by 2008, based on four surveys with representative samples conducted between March, 2003 and January, 2004, between 70 percent and 80 percent of Hong Kong people have demonstrated consistent support. Faced with continuous attacks from Beijing since January, 2004, support for democracy among the public by 2008 still remained at 58.5 percent in early March, 2004.[29] The determination of Hong Kong people to have democracy by 2008 has been underlined by the fact that 43.6 percent of the public opined in March, 2004, amid the economic rebound, that they would probably or certainly rally for universal suffrage in the streets if election of the Chief Executive via universal suffrage cannot be achieved in 2007.[30] More recently, in a survey conducted in December, 2004, 56 percent of respondents in a representative sampled survey opted for direct elections for reforming the current 800-member Chief Executive Election Committee, and that should the direct election of the Chief Executive be implemented in 2007, 43.6 percent would welcome it while another 15 percent would accept it (DeGolyer 2005). Of no less importance, in at least two of the surveys already analyzed, is that support for democracy has been found across classes and age groups, testifying to a wide social base for it in Hong Kong.[31]

More significantly, findings from a survey conducted in June, 2003 testified that a culture of "post-materialist activism" and a lesser "respect for authority" rather than economic factors figured as the most powerful explanation for the mass support for universal suffrage among over a dozen possible explanatory factors. "-Post-materialistic activism" has been a cultural syndrome stressing the non-materialistic values of freedom, political participation by the public, and greater respect of public opinions in shaping important government decisions.[32] The importance of post-materialistic values in explaining mass support for universal suffrage has been underscored not just by cross-national research (Welzel and Inglehart 2001), but also by earlier research conducted in Hong Kong (Kuan and Lau 2002).

In addition, the value "respect for authority" has been found to be not just nega-tively correlated with but also the most powerful cause in explaining public support for universal suffrage in mid-2003. The negative correlation is not entirely surprising as a recent study of nine East Asian societies and four established Pacific Rim Western democracies confirm that all, except for Vietnam, their indi-vidual "respect for authority" has been negatively correlated with their own mass support for universal suffrage. Yet this study finds that in Hong Kong, only 11.1 percent regarded a general "respect for authority" as something good while 73.8 percent treated it as something bad. The former figure may suggest the erosion of economic development on traditional values including "respect for authority" (Inglehart 1999: 236–256).[33] What is most astounding is that the proportion of Hong Kong's population in subscribing to that traditional belief (11.1 percent) has been the second lowest among nine Asian and ten Western societies (Figure 5.4).[34] Another likely candidate that complements economic development in explaining Hong Kong's lower respect for authority has been the cumulated public frustration with the performance of the unresponsive post-handover authority.

Since culture seldom changes overnight, popular support for universal suffrage may be sustained in the short and medium run.[35] Furthermore, the calculation of the economic consequences of universal suffrage has been found to have exerted no effect on mass support for democracy attitudinally in June, 2003.[36] Thus, any attempt to suppress popular demand for universal suffrage via economic sweeteners alone may prove inadequate in the medium to long run.[37]

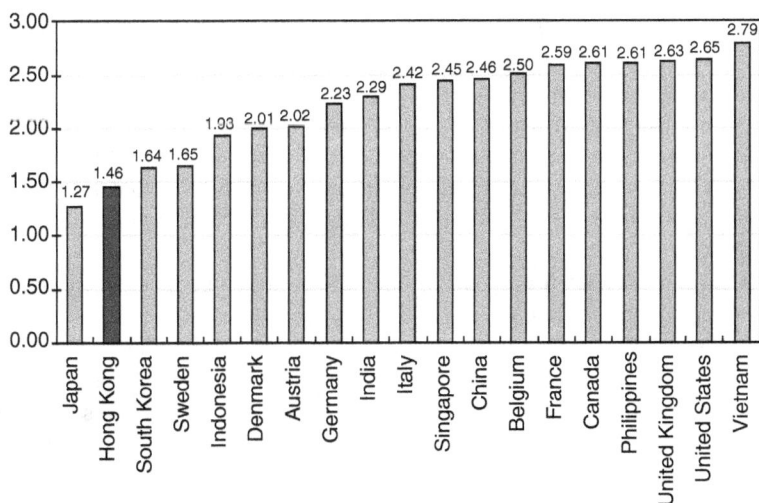

Figure 5.4 Comparing "respect for authority" among nine Asian and ten Western societies (source: 1999–2003 World Values Surveys and Survey on Political Attitudes and Democratic Development in Hong Kong, 2003).

Note
Respect for authority is a 1–3 point scale index; higher score suggests a greater level of respect.

Mass support for democracy may thus at least persist attitudinally, especially given that the post-handover Hong Kong government is likely to fail to overcome at least some of the aforementioned five major challenges.

Implications of fast-paced democratization for Hong Kong

Faster democratization may help prevent further political crises

Some may contend that the current economic rebound in Hong Kong has by itself adequately relieved the intense political pressure for democratic reform. Therefore, the argument goes, there is no urgency with democratization for Hong Kong in the face of the seeming subsidance of popular demand for greater democracy. They may add that comparative evidence has revealed that poor economic growth, especially when coupled with inter-elite rivalry and military defection, has accounted for landmark changes of authoritarian regimes in Latin America and Asia toward democratic regimes.[38]

However, many have argued it is precisely economic growth that triggers the expansion of the middle class, the flourishing of pro-democratic political culture, aggrandizement of pro-reform social forces in authoritarian regimes, and their final transitions toward democratic institutions (Huntington 1984, 1991). The swift economic growths of Taiwan and South Korea since the 1950s, and their ensuing democratic transitions since 1987, are cases in point. As both low and high rates of economic growth can trigger changes in authoritarian institutions, any view that asserts a simple relation between economic growth and institutional changes of authoritarian states is disproved by the data. In addition, comparatively speaking, Table 5.4 indicates that institutional transformations of authoritarian regimes can be engendered by non-economic causes. Overseas experience in the 1980s (Table 5.4) and beyond has clearly revealed that both economic and non-economic problems ranging from perceived cronyism, trespassing of freedoms, to severe inequality, and an ineffective government can raise public pressure for transitions to democracy (Bratton and Van de Walle 1997: 19–60; Huntington 1991; Linz and Stepan 1996; Shin 1994: 135–170; Sing 2004: 1–31).

As Hong Kong has been and will likely continue to be haunted by problems of economic restructuring, severe inequality, large executive–legislative tension, and occasional if not frequent policy blunders of the government, public pressure for democratization, amid a post-materialistic culture and a lower respect for authority, may escalate into mass mobilization. Hong Kong's prosperity, stability, and overall governance will be enhanced when these structurally induced issues are taken seriously and installation of democratic institutions is carried out as soon as possible, to head off a new cycle of political crises.

Is Hong Kong ready for a transition to full democracy?

Cross-national research highlights that the level of socioeconomic development has, for most of the time, been one of the most powerful determinants of the

Table 5.4 Both economic and non-economic factors trigger democratization

	Initial regime type (1980)	
	Democratic	Authoritarian
Regime change attributable in part to economic crisis	Turkey (1980)[a] Ghana Nigeria (1983)[b]	Argentina Bolivia Brazil Philippines Nigeria (1985)[b] Nigeria (1987)[b] Korea (1980)[c]
Regime endures or undergoes change not attributable to economic crisis	Costa Rica Colombia Jamaica Peru Venezuela Thailand Dominican Republic	Chile Mexico Korea (1987)[c] Taiwan Zaire Zambia Kenya Indonesia Turkey (1983)[a]

Source: Haggard and Kaufman (1992).

Notes
a Turkey had a military coup in 1980 that can be traced in part to deteriorating economic conditions. The military handed power back to a civilian government in 1983, but not because of worsening economic circumstances.
b Nigeria had a military coup in 1983 attributable in part to the poor performance and corruption of the civilian government. A second coup in 1985 may be attributed in part to the effects of declining oil prices. The initiation of a democratic opening in 1987 might also be traced to continuing dissatisfaction with the economy.
c Korea experienced a brief political opening in 1980 following the assassination of Park Chung Hee in 1979, but the military quickly returned to power in a coup in the same year. This coup may be interpreted in part as the result of poor economic conditions, exacerbated by the first oil shock. The transition to democracy, however, came during a period of strong growth later in the decade.

level of democracy (Barro 1999; Casper 2000: 1–19; Diamond 1992: 466; Geddes 1999: 118–119; Inglehart 1997, 1999; Welzel and Inglehart 2001, 2003). Higher socioeconomic development, it is argued, would induce an emancipative political culture propitious for democratization (Welzel and Inghelart 2001). The changes in political culture will allegedly trigger escalating support and opportunities for democratization (Huntington 1991: 69).

Huntington found that in 1976 while newly democratized countries in the new wave varied greatly in their level of economic development, it was the middle-income countries as defined by the World Bank that were most promising of transitioning to democracies.[39] Presence in the middle-income range, however, did not always ensure the existence of democracy (1984: 199–201). My analysis of recent data has given additional confirmation to this theory (Sing 2004).[40] From 1987 to 1999, all members of the "higher-income economies" as defined by the World Bank have been the most democratic regimes, except for Hong Kong, Singapore, plus such Middle-East oil-exporting countries as Brunei, Qatar, Kuwait, and the United Arab Emirates (Sing 2004). Furthermore, cross-tabulation of GNP per capita of 1998 and the level of democracy in 2000 also show that there is more or less a stepwise relation between the economic development and level of democracy (Sing 2004).[41]

Considering levels of economic development, Hong Kong has been in the transition zone for a long period. time after time the World Bank classified Hong Kong as a middle-income society from 1976 to 1982 (World Bank 1978, 1979: 126–127, 1980: 110–111, 1981: 134–135, 1982: 110–111, 1983: 148–149, 1984: 218–219), and as a "higher middle-income" society from 1982 to 1986 (World Bank 1985: 174–175, 1986: 180–181, 1987: 202–203, 1988: 222–223). Since 1987, Hong Kong has developed into a "higher income-economy" (World Bank 1989: 164–165, 1990: 178–198, 1991: 204–205). The probability of a "higher income-economy" being a full democracy is so high (Huntington 1984, 1991) that Hong Kong has been long overdue in its transition to a full democracy in comparison with most societies around the world.

Hong Kong is likely to achieve democratic stability

As shown in Table 5.5, after analyzing the longitudinal data of 32 countries that have adopted a presidential system at one time or another from 1950 to 2000, it has been found that when the GDP per capita of a society reaches beyond US$10,000, the probability of democratic breakdown is virtually zero when other variables are controlled at their mean value.[42] Given that Hong Kong's level of GDP per capita already stood at purchasing power parity of US$28,800 in 2003,[43] the probability of democratic breakdown in Hong Kong arising from inadequate socioeconomic development comes close to virtually zero.

Longitudinal research indicates that a greater openness to trade would also favor democratic stability. Greater optimism for survival of democracy in Hong Kong is thus further enhanced by Hong Kong's relatively high degree of openness to trade vis-à-vis many other societies in the world.[44]

The statistical test confirms that a higher level of economic development measured by GDP per capital favors democratic survival, which generates

Table 5.5 Thirty-two presidential regimes in the survey

Argentina	Dominican Republic	Malawi	Sierra Leone
Benin	Ecuador	Namibia	Switzerland
Bolivia	El Salvador	Nicaragua	Uganda
Brazil	Ghana	Nigeria	Ukraine
Chile	Guatemala	Panama	United States
Colombia	Guyana	Peru	Uruguay
Costa Rica	Honduras	Philippines	Venezuela
Cyprus	Korea South	Russia	Zambia

Total $N = 32$

positive implications for Hong Kong's democratic development for the subsample of presidential regimes (Table 5.5).

The Post-Tung era: conflict over democratic reform continues

In March, 2005, the widespread rumor of Tung's resignation was eventually confirmed. Beijing has proactively and skillfully captured an opportune moment to do away with a broadly ostracized leader. The Chief Secretary of the Hong Kong government, Donald Tsang, a veteran former civil servant, received Beijing's sanction for becoming the next chief executive for no less than two years during the remainder of Tung's second term in office. The unexpected resignation of Tung shows Beijing's leaders' intolerance of an incompetent and unpopular leader in Hong Kong. It also underlines Beijing's attempt to re-establish public support for the government by greater reliance on the leadership of a former senior civil servant. Finally, it highlights Beijing's determination to forestall pressures for democratization by replacing a less capable with a more able leader.

Ever since Donald Tsang became acting chief executive, his individual approval rating has hovered around 70 percent.[45] The perception that he has been more savvy and decisive than Tung coincides with the public's memory of him as a capable former financial secretary, and has earned him a consistently much higher level of "personal" support since coming to power. During his honeymoon period as chief executive his high personal approval rating continued. This coincides with the popular perception that local parties are not competent enough to govern Hong Kong in the short term.[46]

Yet, Tsang's high personal rating has undergone a severe test after he divulged a reform package for democratizing Hong Kong. On April 26, 2004, the Standing Committee of the National People's Congress decided against using universal suffrage for Hong Kong's chief executive in 2007 and for all members of the legislature in 2008. The reform package also stipulated that the ratio between members returned by functional constituencies and members returned by geographical constituencies through direct elections, who respectively take up half of the seats, would remain intact.[47] In the context of the Standing Committee's decisions, officials in Hong Kong and Beijing carefully crafted a reform package and tried very hard to persuade the public and legislators to accept it. The package would enlarge the legislators from 60 to 70 in 2008, with the number of directly elected seats continuing to be half of the total. The proposal would also pass new powers to district council members, with 20 percent of them to be appointed by Donald Tsang, as revealed in the government's Fifth Report of the Constitutional Development.[48]

Yet, the package has failed to win the support of pro-democracy legislators, and prompted at least 100,000 people to take to the streets on December 4, 2005 to protest against Beijing's and Hong Kong authorities' rejection of committing to a timetable for implementing full democracy.[49] According to a poll conducted soon after the rally, 66 percent of the public agreed that there should be a clear timetable for implementing universal suffrage in Hong Kong.[50]

In the face of the mass demonstration and reluctance of pan-democratic legislators to accept the package, Donald Tsang and his team announced on December 12, 2005 that it would cut the number of district councilors appointed by Hong Kong's chief executive from 102 to 68 in 2008, and wipe out all appointed seats in 2016 at the latest.[51] Yet, the concessions have been deemed totally unacceptable to pro-democratic legislators, as they have failed to satisfy a widespread public demand for a timetable for universal suffrage. The strong backing for a timetable for universal suffrage and the unexpectedly large number of protesters at the December 4 rally confirmed again persistent public support for fast implementation of full democracy in Hong Kong, despite the Hong Kong and Chinese governments' attempts to dampen it and the recovery of the economy since late 2003.

Hong Kong at the democratic crossroads

On November 25, 2005, the Hong Kong government raised its growth forecast for the year to 7 percent following the faster expansion of its economy in the third quarter. There is no doubt that the influx of tourists from Mainland China, and other positive spillover benefits from China's record-breaking economic growth, have contributed to the rapid turnaround of Hong Kong's economy.[52] Yet, as the public support for greater democracy has been underpinned by a post-materialistic activism, which has contributed to mass rallies for faster implementation of democracy in Hong Kong despite strong opposition from the Mainland, the non-democratic system in Hong Kong is more likely than not to suffer challenges to its legitimacy. In the medium and long term, it is particularly doubtful that its non-democratic system can avert legitimation problems for the following reasons.

First, confronted with the unsettled economic restructuring, structural fiscal deficits, severe social inequality, widely perceived cronyism, and grave executive–legislative tensions, the recent departure of C.H. Tung does not signal the end of the low public support or legitimacy for Hong Kong's non-democratic system. These are expected to continue to undermine public support for a non-democratic system and keep up the pressure for faster democratization of Hong Kong at least in the medium term.

Second, as stability has been stressed in the two-year term of Donald Tsang, it will be difficult for him to replace all incompetent Principal Officials with capable ones, and to overhaul the entire Principal Officials Accountability System to the extent that a sounder policy-making process can be institutionalized within and outside the Executive Council. As a result, political blunders by the government will be repeated, thus overshadowing the prospect of Hong Kong's non-democratic system enjoying a moderate to high level of legitimacy as seen during the pre-handover period.

Third, despite the economic vibrancy of Mainland China, the bubble in its property sector, the potential difficulties to steer its overheated economy toward a soft landing, the increasing risks of a new wave of foreign restrictions on China's exports, among other unpredictable domestic and international factors, may cause disruption to China's economic growth. Given the growing economic dependence of Hong Kong on China since the handover, the risk for Hong Kong's economy has multiplied correspondingly.

Fourth, the unresolved structural fiscal deficit and the imperative to restore it to a balance by early 2009 have put much pressure on different Principal Officials to cut money spent in their respective policy arenas. The reduction in expenditures may trigger waves of protests of various scales among those who finally suffer from a smaller budget, and rebuild the public pressure for democratization.

In short, the recent departure of C.H. Tung is unlikely to signal the end of the legitimacy problem for the non-democratic government. The new chief executive, who will be indirectly elected by a mere 800-strong Election Committee, will deprive him of the sorely needed public support derived from a free and fair election. The paucity of legitimacy in the system may continue to make the government shy away from boldly confronting squarely short-term and long-term challenges confronting Hong Kong, including the aging population, pollution, medical finance, fair competition, social inequality, and the excessive remuneration for some overpaid civil servants and some employees in the publicly subsidized sectors. The latter issue will continue to foil the government's attempt to resolve the structural budget deficit, forcing the government to reduce its expenditures for various public policies in order to strike a balanced budget. The cutbacks may trigger wider state–society conflicts and forge a spirally downward cycle of declining public support for the Hong Kong government and the political system as a whole. The declining public support would then make it even more difficult to recruit appropriate persons to replace some existing Principal Officials, even though some of them are regarded as inexperienced or incompetent. Although the government led by Donald Tsang may show improved performance in terms of decisiveness and soundness in policy-making vis-à-vis that of Tung's era, as long as some of the aforementioned five major challenges remain unresolved, mass mobilizations for democratization may mount again in the medium and long run.

Epilogue

Although post-materialism has been a cultural element that underpins the local public support for democracy, the sustained economic rebound in Hong Kong since mid-2003 (Figure 5.1), the sharp decline in the unemployment rate from 8.7 percent of 2003 to a new low of 3.6 percent in December, 2007[53] (i.e., near a ten-year low), and the accompanying improvement in living standards, has drained off the pressure for speedy democratization. Besides, the succession of Tung by Donald Tsang, a veteran former civil servant who has been widely applauded as more capable and prudent in policy-making and implementation, has nipped an important bud for speedy democratization in the minds of the Hong Kong people. In addition, Beijing's sustained rejection of democratization in Hong Kong has also contributed to a gradual erosion of public support for rapid democratization. Against this context, the public support for implementation of universal suffrage dropped from 80 percent in 2004 to slightly more than 50 percent in 2007 and for 2012 respectively.[54] In addition, the much publicized electoral contest between the veteran former civil servant Donald Tsang and pan-democratic leader Alan Leong exposed the pragmatism of Hong Kong people in the sense that the public support for the former versus the latter was in the ratio of 64.5 percent to 21.6 percent.[55] More unexpectedly, the pan-democrats have suffered a dramatic defeat in the local elections (i.e., in contests of seats for district councils). The pan-democrats have suffered a catastrophic defeat during the election by winning less than half of the contested seats during the election.[56]

That said, it should be noted that despite the aforementioned extremely remarkable economic recovery, and Beijing's outright rejection of implementing universal suffrage in 2012, a majority of Hong Kong people still demanded the implementation of universal suffrage for electing both the chief executive and legislature in 2012. Besides, despite the all-out support of Beijing for Regina Ip in her contest for a seat of legislature left vacant by a deceased member, Anson Chan, a democrat and former veteran civil servant, won in the fiercely fought election in November, 2007. Equally noticeably, in early December, 2007, when Donald Tsang unveiled his "Report on Public Consultation on Green Paper on Constitutional Development," he alleged that while a majority of Hong Kong people supported having universal suffrage in 2012, the chances of using universal suffrage to produce CE in 2017 is higher. His contradictory statement and lukewarm altitude toward speedy democratization in Hong Kong, side by side with Beijing's stiff resistance to holding universal suffrage in 2012, have triggered a precipitous decline in public support for the Hong Kong Special Administrative Region government by over 10 percent within weeks after the release of the report.[57] In short, in spite of the sustained and robust economic recovery, steadfast support for speedy democratization continues to be demonstrated by the Hong Kong people. In view of Beijing's overt rejection of implementation of full democracy in Hong Kong by 2020, the mobilizations and bargaining for and against democratization will persist for a long period ahead, to be reinforced when the economy turns sour.

Acknowledgment

Part of this chapter is funded by a grant from the Research Grant Council Grant of the Hong Kong Special Administrative Region (Project no. CityU 1498/05H).

Notes

1 Democracy may be defined as a system of government fulfilling three conditions: (1) Political competition: meaningful and extensive competition among individuals and organized groups (especially political parties) for political leadership roles, conducted regularly and peacefully. (2) Political participation: a highly inclusive level of political participation in the selection of leaders and policies through regular and fair elections, such that no major (adult) social group is excluded. (3) Civil and political liberties: freedom of expression, freedom of press, freedom to form and join organizations – sufficient to ensure the integrity of political competition and participation (Diamond *et al.* 1988).

2 The Democratic Party of Hong Kong has scored a record-breaking winning rate of close to 80 percent and won 92 seats amid the backdrop of a sharply rising voter

turnout rate from to 33.82 percent to 44.06 percent (*Ming Pao*, November 24, 2003). The 1.07 million voters who cast their votes represented a record of 44 percent of eligible voters, compared with a 36 percent turnout in the last election held in 1999. The Beijing-backed Democratic Alliance for Betterment of Hong Kong (DAB) won only 62 seats, a sharp decrease from 83 scored during the same election of 1999 (*Asian Wall Street Journal*, November 25, 2003).

3 See an unpublished draft by Sing, M. *A Draft for a Representative Sampled Survey on Public Attitudes towards Democracy*, July, 2003.

4 Schutz, R., O. Slater, B. M. Schutz, and S. R. Dorr (eds) *Global Transformation and the Third World* (Lynne Rienner, Boulder, CO: 1993), p. 247.

5 Diamond, L. "Beyond Authoritarianism and Totalitarianism: Strategies for Democratization." In R. Brad ed. *The New Democracies: Global Change and U.S. Policy*, London: MIT Press, 1990, p. 235; O'Donnell, G. A., P. C. Schmitter, and L. Whitehead eds *Transitions from Authoritarian Rule: Prospects for Democracy, Part III* (London: Johns Hopkins University Press, 1986).

6 See Linz, J. J. "Transitions to Democracy: A Comparative Perspective." A research paper prepared for the International Political Science Association Roundtable in Tokyo, March 29–April 1, 1982, pp. 15, 18.

7 Diamond, L. "Introduction: Persistence, Erosion, Breakdown, and Renewal." In Diamond, L., J. J. Linz, and S. M. Lipset eds *Volume 3: Democracy in Developing Countries: Asia*, Boulder, CO: Lynne Rienner, 1989). See also Easton, D. *A Systems Analysis of Political Life* (New York: John Wiley & Sons, 1965), pp. 153–340.

8 The system has been distinguished by a powerful bureaucracy which ruled by co-option of local unofficial elites, especially the bourgeoisie, together with political consultation at grassroots level. The bureaucracy has been committed to low levels of social and economic interventions and allowing a high level of civil liberties (M. Sing 2004).

9 World Bank. *World Development Report* (New York: Oxford University Press, 1984), p. 218; Deyo, F. C. *Beneath the Miracle: Labor Subordination in the New Asian Industrialism* (Berkeley, CA: University of California Press, 1989), p. 26.

10 See various issues of *Asiaweek*, 1995.

11 See Sing 2004.

12 When asked whether the local general public supported its political institutions, surveys conducted in 1977, 1985, and 1988 unveiled that 81.6 percent, 74.5 percent, and 75 percent, respectively, answered affirmatively. They have conferred a moderate to high level of legitimacy on the benign soft-authoritarian institutions since the 1970s. Stepping into the 1990s, despite a slight decline in those levels of support, moderate degrees of public support for the soft-authoritarian system may still be discerned. The corresponding figures for 1990, 1991, 1992, 1993,1995 and 1997 were respectively 59 percent, 72 percent, 56.3 percent, 62.1 percent, 63 percent, and 49.2 percent. The wordings for the questions were more or less the same, where the respondents were asked whether they agreed that "Hong Kong's political system, though imperfect, was still the best under existent circumstances." For data prior to the 1990s, see Lau, Siu-kai. *Society and Politics in Hong Kong* (Hong Kong: The Chinese University Press, 1982); Lau. *Indicators of Social Development: Hong Kong 1990* (Hong Kong: Chinese University Press, 1992), p. 132. Regarding data for the 1990s, see Lau, Siu-kai Lau and Hsin-chi Kuan. "Public Attitudes toward Political Authorities and Colonial Legitimacy in Hong Kong," *The Journal of Commonwealth and Comparative Politics* 33, no. 1 (1995): p. 81; and Lau. "Democratization, Poverty of Political Leaders and Political Inefficiency in Hong Kong." Occasional Paper (Hong Kong: Hong Kong Institute of Asia-Pacific Studies, Chinese University of Hong Kong, 1998); Lau. "The Rise and Decline of Political Support for the Hong Kong Special Administrative Region Government," *Government and Opposition*, 2000. Although the components of the political system have changed over time, it

may be argued that the basic features of the soft-authoritarian system have remained largely intact. For the figure for 2003, see Sing 2003.

13 The five major problems mentioned here have been in part discussed earlier in Sing, M. "The Legitimacy Problem and Democratic Reform in Hong Kong," *Journal of Contemporary China* 15, no. 48 (August, 2006): 517–532.

14 www.weforum.org/ (accessed December 1, 2005).

15 See World Bank at devdata.worldbank.org/edstats/cd5.asp.

16 For those criticisms, see *Ming Pao*, August 28, 2003, December 18, 2004, and *Oriental News*, November 4, 2002, March 7, 2004, directed from a personnel manager of Jardines Company and some well-known business leaders. Many of those employers preferred to employ graduates from overseas rather than local universities for high-quality reasons. Although students in Hong Kong have been ranked highly in scores for mathematics and the sciences in a survey of 41 societies of educational achievement called PISA, a local expert comments that there was little statistical difference among the top countries in maths and science. In addition, it has been found that Hong Kong slipped from seventh to tenth place in reading among 41 societies, though it was still above the OECD average (*South China Morning Post*, December 11, 2004).

17 The limited implementation of the CEPA has been criticized by an executive councilor and the CEO of the Hong Kong General Chamber of Commerce (*Ming Pao*, March 22, 2005).

18 Panel on Welfare Service (Hong Kong Legislature, November 12, 2001).

19 See World Bank. *World Development Indicators 2003*. CD-ROM. Washington, DC. It should be noted that owing to the fact that "the underlying household surveys differ in method and in the type of data collected, the distribution data are not strictly comparable across countries." In addition, "the Gini index measures inequality over the entire distribution of income or consumption. A value of 0 represents perfect equality, and a value of 100 perfect inequality."

20 See Ho and Chan 2003: 70.

21 See asia.news.yahoo.com/031130/3/18olv.html (accessed December 1, 2003); see also Reuters – Hong Kong (November 29, 2003).

22 See the budget for 2004 to 2005 on www.budget.gov.hk/. The same message has been emphasized by an international rating agency Flitch, who warned of an unsettled outlook for future land sale proceeds and other revenue-related items (*South China Morning Post*, May 5, 2005). See also Lui 2006.

23 See Wong, Y. C. R., "Hong Kong's Fiscal Issues, 2001," www.tdctrade.com/econforum/hkcer/hkcer010301.htm.

24 Both the HKSAR government and local leading economists have argued that the budget deficit in Hong Kong tends to be a repetitive one.

25 For the inadequate debates of the executive councilors, see the comments by the Chair of DAB (*Hong Kong Economic Journal*, April 14, 2005).

26 See United Nations. *Human Development Report* (Washington, DC, 2002).

27 See Rodrik, D. "Institutions for High Quality Growth: What They Are and How to Acquire Them." *Studies in Comparative International Development* 35, no. 3 (2000): 3–31; United Nations. *Human Development Report*, 2002.

28 United Nations. *Human Development Report* 2002.

29 See the poll conducted by the Chinese University of Hong Kong between March 1 and 8 (*Ming Pao*, March 24, 2004).

30 See the poll conducted by the Chinese University of Hong Kong between March 1 and 8, 2004 (*Ming Pao*, March 24, 2004).

31 See Sing 2003.

32 See Sing 2005a. Post-materialism Index. This index is generated from respondents' first and second choice of what the aims of a country should be for the next ten years as the most important. The goals are "maintaining order in Hong Kong," "giving Hong Kong people more say in important government decisions," "fighting against deflation," and "protecting

freedom of speech." The first and third goals are the measures of materialism, and the second and fourth goals are of post-materialism. If both materialist items are given a higher priority the score will be 1, or if both post-materialist items are given high priority the score will be 3. The score will be equal to 2 if one materialist and one post-materialist item are chosen. Noticeably, while inflation is used in the WVS survey, deflation has replaced inflation in the question to take account of Hong Kong's current economic situation.

Indicator of sign petition: "have you ever done singing a petition. If never, and given you have an opportunity, whether you might do it or would never do it, where '1' is never, '2' is might do, and '3' is have done (Sing 2005)."

33 The argument can be reinforced by survey data from as early as 1992, which showed that 56.8 percent of the public did not favor a government with paramount and unchallenged authority, and that 54 percent versus 25.3 percent of respondents regarded institutions as more important than good political leaders for the good governance of Hong Kong (Ho and Leung 1995: 229–258). These data may hint that the erosion of authority as impelled by long-term economic development may have begun much earlier than the start of the millennium.

34 What is staggering is that even when compared with such advanced economies as Canada, France, the United Kingdom, and the USA, the level of general "respect for authority" in Hong Kong is much lower. Given the higher level and longer history of economic development of those advanced Western economies vis-à-vis that of Hong Kong, it is unlikely that economic development can exhaustively explain the relatively lower level of "respect for authority" in Hong Kong.

35 See Sing 2005a.

36 Ibid.

37 Ibid.

38 Scholars studying communist regimes have also found that their economic failures have contributed to the erosion of their political public support (Pei 1994: 16).

39 Of the 31 countries democratized or strongly liberalized between 1974 and 1989, 27 were in the middle-income range. In addition, half of the new wave countries had per capita GNP of between $1,000 and $3,000 in 1976 (Huntington 1991: 62). Huntington's conclusion has been confirmed in a recent comparative survey using different indicators. In 1986, Lipset and Turner correlated the GNP per capita of 1982 as recorded by the World Bank with the combined index of civil and political freedom published by Freedom House (Gastil 1985: 4–6). The correlation between GNP per capita and levels of freedom was appreciably high. All upper-income industrial nations were classified as "free." The proportion of countries with "partly free" political systems also rises significantly from category to category as levels of national income increase (Lipset and Turner 1986: 11).

40 Sing 2004.

41 "Democracy" has been operationalized as those regimes that have their combined scores of civil liberties and political rights equal to or less than four (Diamond 1992). Diamond conceptualized those regimes with combined scores of no more than two as "liberal democracies," and those of between three and four as competitive, pluralist, partially institutionalized democracies (Diamond 1992).

42 See Sing 2005b.

43 See www.cia.gov/cia/publications/factbook/geos/hk.html (accessed April 1, 2005).

44 See Sing 2005b. The fact that the "rule-of-law" in Hong Kong has been kept as one of the best in Asia will also help consolidate its democracy.

45 See hkupop.hku.hk/.

46 There has been an above-average level of rejection of parties in Hong Kong when compared with other 30-plus societies (see Sing 2004).

47 See www.cab.gov.hk/cd/eng/report5/ (accessed January 14, 2006).

48 See www.cab.gov.hk/cd/eng/report5/ (accessed January 14, 2006).

49 See Leo F. Goodstadt, "Hong Kong's Long March to Democracy." *Far East Economic Review* (January/February, 2006).

50 The poll was conducted by the Chinese University of Hong Kong between December 5 and 7, 2005, which had a sample size of 924 respondents. See *Ming Pao*, December 10, 2005.
51 See *Financial Times*, December 13, 2005.
52 See *Financial Times*, November 26, 2005.
53 *South China Morning Post*, December 19, 2007.
54 See hkupop.hku.hk/ (accessed January 20, 2007).
55 *Ming Pao*, March, 20, 2007.
56 *Ming Pao* March 20, 2007, p. A03.
57 See hkupop.hku.hk/ (accessed January 20, 2007).

References

Barro, R. "Determinants of Democracy." *Journal of Political Economy* 107, no. 6 (December, 1999): 158–183.

Bratton, M. and N. Van de Walle. *Democratic Experiments in Africa: Regime Transitions in Comparative Perspective*. Cambridge: Cambridge University Press, 1997.

Casper, G. "Explaining the Installation and Survival of Democracy." Paper for 96th American Political Science Association Meeting at Washington, DC, August 31–September 3, 2000.

Dahl, R. A. *Modern Political Analysis* (4th edn). Englewood Cliffs, NJ: Prentice-Hall, 1984.

De Golyer, M. "Hong Kong Constitution Reform: What do the People Want?" A Public Opinion Survey Commissioned by Civic Exchange. Hong Kong, December, 2005.

Diamond, L. "Economic Development and Democracy Reconsidered." *American Behavioral Scientist* 35 (1992): 450–499.

Diamond, L. *Developing Democracy: Toward Consolidation*. Baltimore, MD: Johns Hopkins University Press, 1999.

Diamond, L., Juan J. Linz, and S. M. Lipset. *Democracy in Developing Countries: Africa*. Boulder: Lynne Rienner Publishers, 1988.

Feng, Y. *Democracy, Governance, and Economic Performance: Theory and Evidence*. Cambridge, MA: MIT Press, 2003.

Gasiorowski, M. J. "Economic Crisis and Political Regime Change: An Event History Analysis." *American Political Science Review* 89, no. 4 (December, 1994): 882–897.

Geddes, B. "What Do We Know About Democratization After Twenty Years?" *Annual Review of Political Science* 2 (1999): 115–144.

Habermas, J. *Legitimation Crisis*. Boston, MA: Beacon Press, 1975.

Haggard, S. and R. Kaufman. *The Political Economy of Democratic Transitions*. Princeton, NJ: Princeton University Press, 1995.

Ho, K. and S. Leung. "Materialism and Political Attitude." In *Indicators of Social Development – Hong Kong*. Hong Kong: Chinese University Press, 1995.

Ho, S. and C. Chan. "In Search of a Competition Policy in a Competitive Economy: The Case of Hong Kong." *The Journal of Consumer Affairs* 37 (2003): 68–85.

Huntington, S. P. "Will More Countries Become Democratic?" *Political Science Quarterly* 99 (1984): 193–218.

Huntington, S. P. *The Third Wave: Democratization in the Late Twentieth Century*. Norman, OK: University of Oklahoma Press, 1991.

Inglehart, R. *Modernization and Postmodernization*. Princeton, NJ: Princeton University Press, 1997.

Inglehart, R. "Postmodernization Erodes Respect for Authority, but Increases Support for Democracy." In *Critical Citizens: Global Support for Democratic Governance*, ed. P. Norris. Oxford: Oxford University Press, 1999.

Inglehart, R. and C. Welzel. "Political Culture and Democracy: Analyzing Cross-Level Linkage." *Comparative Politics* 36, no. 1 (2003): 61–79.

Kuan, Hsin-Chi and Siu-Kai Lau. "Between Liberal Autocracy and Democracy: Democratic Legitimacy in Hong Kong." *Democratization* 9, no. 4 (2002): 58–76.

Kurzman, C., R. Werum, and R. E. Burkhart. "Democracy's Effect on Economic Growth: A Pooled Time-series Analysis, 1951–1980." *Studies in Comparative International Development* 37, no. 1 (2002): 3–33.

Lane, C. "Legitimacy and Power in the Soviet Union Through Socialist Ritual." *British Journal of Political Science* 14, no. 2 (1984): 207–217.

Leblang, D. A. "Political Democracy and Economic Growth: Pooled Cross-Sectional and Time-Series Evidence." *British Journal of Political Science* 27 (1997): 453–472.

Linz, J. J. and A. Stepan. *Problems of Democratic Transition and Consolidation: Southern Europe, South America, and Post-communist Europe.* Baltimore, MD: Johns Hopkins University Press, 1996.

Lipset, S. M. *Political Man: The Social Bases of Politics.* Baltimore, MD: Johns Hopkins University Press, 1981.

Lipset, S. M. and F. C. Turner. "Economic Growth and Democratization: The Continuing Search for Theory." Paper presented at the Seminario Sobre Cultura Politica en Las Neuvas Democracias, Madrid, April, 1986.

Lui, F. T. "Some Views on the Hong Kong Economy." *Hong Kong Journal.* www.hkjournal.org/archive/2006_spring/lui.html (accessed December 1, 2006).

O'Donnell, G. A. and P. C. Schmitter. "Tentative Conclusions about Uncertain Democracies." In *Transitions from Authoritarian Rule: Prospects for Democracy, Part IV*, ed. G. A. O'Donnell, P. C. Schmitter, and L. Whitehead. London: Johns Hopkins University Press, 1986.

Pei, M. *From Reform to Revolution: The Demise of Communism in China and the Soviet Union.* Cambridge, MA: Harvard University Press, 1994.

Przeworski, A., M. E. Alvarez, J. A. Cheibub, and F. Limongi. *Democracy and Development: Political Institutions and Well-being in the World, 1950–1990.* Cambridge: Cambridge University Press, 2000.

Pye, L. W. "The Legitimacy Crisis." In *Crises and Sequences in Political Development*, ed. S. Verba *et al.* Princeton, NJ: Princeton University Press, 1971.

Shin, D. C. "On the Third Wave of Democratization: A Synthesis and Evaluation of Recent Theory and Research." *World Politics* 47 (October, 1994): 135–170.

Sing, M. "The Problem of Legitimacy For the Post-handover Hong Kong Government." *International Journal of Public Administration* 24, no. 9 (2001): 847–867.

Sing, M. *Hong Kong's Tortuous Democratization: A Comparative Analysis.* New York: RoutledgeCurzon, 2004a.

Sing, M. "Origins of Anti-partyism in Hong Kong." *East Asia: An International Quarterly.* Piscataway, NJ: Transaction Publishers, 2004b.

Sing, M. "Public Support for Democracy in Hong Kong." *Democratization* 12, no. 2 (2005a): 244–261.

Sing, M. "Executive–Legislative Relations and Democratic Survival: Lessons from Comparative Studies." *Hong Kong Law Journal*, Special Issue, Constitutional Review and Democratic Development: The Way Forward" (2005b).

Welzel, C. and R. Inglehart. "Human Development and the 'Explosion' of Democracy: Variations of Regime Change across 60 Societies." Unpublished Conference Paper Presented at Berlin, April, 2001.

Zhao, Xiaobin, Li Zhang and Tak O Kelvin Sit. "Income Inequalities under Economic Restructuring in Hong Kong." *Asian Survey* 44, no. 3 (May/June, 2004): 442–473.

6 The days after the end of the Asian miracle

The budget crisis of Hong Kong

Wilson Wong

Introduction

Problems in budgeting often cannot be completely understood without the appreciation of the political constraints and institutional context of the budgeting system.[1] At the same time, changes in human systems are complicated and hard to accomplish not only owing to technical complexity but also due to resistance from different stakeholders and actors induced by the incentive structure super-imposed by the institutional setting.[2] From these perspectives, to gain a more comprehensive view of the budget problem of a government and the reasons behind the difficulties of resolving it, it will be more appropriate to view it as a problem embedded in a bigger structural and institutional context. The budget problem of Hong Kong presents such a scenario.

When the sovereignty of Hong Kong was transferred from Britain to China in 1997, its economic fate also changed. The Asian Financial Crisis of 1997 brought a disastrous effect to its economy. Hong Kong, which was once part of the East Asian economic miracle, suddenly became a declining city with major economic troubles. Its fiscal system, which is ingeniously designed to take full advantage of an economic boom to minimize tax burden and maximize political stability, is poorly equipped for sustaining such a structural change in the economy and its transition, and the economic crisis has quickly transformed itself into a severe budget crisis.[3]

The persistence and complexity of Hong Kong's fiscal problem cannot be fully explained by the lack of technically sound fiscal options. The crux of the Hong Kong case is that its budget problem is closely related to the constraints of its new institutional setting brought about by the transfer of its sovereignty to China. The existing institutional setting of governance, particularly the lack of legitimacy of the political system in Hong Kong, does not equip its policy-makers with sufficient capacities and incentives to resolve the budget crisis with the needed fiscal reform. It leads Hong Kong to a slow and difficult process in its attempt to address its worsening budget problem. Since 2004, due partly to the active effort from Beijing to stabilize the political situation through boosting its economy, the budget problem has been temporarily alleviated. However, this has made Hong Kong's economy and budget more dependent on the political considerations of Beijing and the economic situation in China. Unless the economic recovery can be built on more solid ground contributed by a successful economic restructuring, it is expected that the same kind of budget crisis and institutional constraints described in this chapter will re-emerge and persist in the near future.

This chapter examines the budget problem of Hong Kong from both fiscal and institutional perspectives. It is an in-depth case study of the budget problem of Hong Kong and also an application of an institutional framework of analysis in diagnosing the problem. It is organized into four major sections. First, it traces the forming of the traditional fiscal principles of Hong Kong in the colonial era and explains how they are related to its special political and economic context. Second, it examines the fiscal structure of Hong Kong to explain how it is deliberately designed to take full advantage of the economic bloom but is very vulnerable in face of economic downturn and structural change in the economy. After that, it reviews the impact of the Asian financial crisis on Hong Kong and discusses the possible fiscal reform packages. Finally, it relates the budget crisis to the institutional setting of its governance to explain how it has been attributed to the slow pace and difficult process of fiscal reform in Hong Kong.

Economic miracle and traditional fiscal principles

Hong Kong was considered as an Asian economic miracle because it could support a large population, with a high international standard of living, when it had very little natural resources to rely on. Its impressive economic success could be seen and measured by one of the major economic indicators, its GDP per capita, which has caught up and even surpassed that of the Britain, its colonial sovereign state.[4]

The prudent fiscal principles of the government played a critical role in the economic miracle of Hong Kong, and the unique economic and political position of Hong Kong during the colonial period provided an institutional context that facilitated the adoption and maintenance of these principles.[5] Before its handover, Hong Kong was often described as "the borrowed place, the borrowed time." As a colonial regime, the British Hong Kong government governed Hong Kong without long-term perspective and vision. It was partly because part of Hong Kong was leased from the Chinese government for 99 years and needed to be returned to China in 1997. More importantly, the Chinese government never officially recognized any "unequal treaty" signed between the British and the Imperial China regime on Hong Kong and threatened to take back Hong Kong even before 1997 so that the time horizon of the British in governing Hong Kong was always shorter than the 99 years. The governing plans of Hong Kong under British rule were often developed through the combination of a short-term perspective and a series of incremental but somehow coordinated reactions to significant economic and social events.[6]

When this governing mentality was translated into fiscal management, two major principles emerged. On the expenditure side, since the British had no long-term planning in Hong Kong, they had a strong incentive to maintain a low level of expenditure to avoid any "over-investment" in the colony. On the revenue side, the government wanted to maintain a low level of revenue, which also meant a low level of taxation. These were derived from both political and economic necessities. As a foreign power, the British did not want to provoke negative sentiments in Hong Kong by imposing a heavy tax burden on its subjects. Economically, due to the lack of natural resources in Hong Kong, it was necessary for the government to keep a low level of taxation to attract investment.

Table 6.1 Overview of public finance in Hong Kong

Year[a]	Public expenditure as real GDP (%)	Growth in real GDP (%)	Growth in public expenditure[d] (%)	Growth in social expenditure[c] (%)
1982	18.5	2.7	10.4	0.4
1983	18.2	5.7	3.6	2.5
1984	15.6	10	−2.5	4.7
1985	16	0.4	2.7	3.0
1986	15.3	10.8	2.6	9.2
1987	14	13	3.5	1.9
1988	14.2	8	7.8	1.7
1989	15.6	2.6	10.8	7.7
1990	16.3	3.4	2.3	8.9
1991	16.2	5.1	3.3	4.1
1992	15.8	6.3	3.7	3.1
1993	17.3	6.1	15.2	14.5
1994	16.4	5.4	−2.2	5.9
1995	17.8	3.9	6.2	12.7
1996	17.7	4.5	2.9	9.1
1997	**17.7**	**5**	**4.2**	**9.0**
1998	21.2	−5.3	8	19.1
1999	22	3	0.6	13.4
2000	20.3	10.2	−0.4	9.5
2001	20.7	0.5	2.6	−4.2
2002	20.9	1.9	0.1	−3.0
2003	22.2	3.2	1.7	3.8
2004	19.9	8.6	−3.5	−5.2
2005	17.7	7.5	−4.1	−2.5
2006[b]	16.7	6.8	−0.3	−0.3

Source: *Hong Kong Yearbook* (various years), Treasury Bureau and Censis and Statistics Department, Hong Kong SAR Government.

Notes
a Fiscal year starts on April 1 and ends on March 31 in Hong Kong. Data in the table are labeled with the beginning year of the fiscal year (e.g., fiscal year 2000/2001 is labeled as 2000).
b Data for 2006 are estimates which are subject to revision by the government.
c "Social expenditure" is defined as expenditure on the following items: housing, education, health and social welfare.
d Expenditure of public corporations, statutory organizations, and organizations in which the government only has an equity position, such as the railway corporations and the Airport Authority in Hong Kong, is not included in public expenditure. Expenditure by institutions in the private or quasi-private sector is included to the extent of their subventions.

When the government really had to spend, much of its spending was concentrated on items of high economic return and promotion of social and economic development which included public health and education.[7] At the same time, cautious efforts were made by the government to avoid becoming a "welfare state," which would bring long-term and significant financial burdens.[8] The message the colonial government conveyed to the citizens was that enhancement of one's living standard was a responsibility of the individual, not of the state.[9]

Under these fiscal principles, Hong Kong was a big supporter of the "small government" ideology. Table 6.1 shows the overview of public finance in Hong Kong. By international standards, Hong Kong has a very small public sector.[10] From the early 1980s up until 1997, public expenditure as percentage of real GDP stayed in the range between 14 percent and 18 percent. The government also maintained a good record of exercising a high level of discipline in its budget. For the eight-year period between 1990 and 1997 shown in Table 6.2, the government always ended up with a surplus, apart from 1995. Even for 1995, the amount of deficit was negligible: only 1.7 percent of the public expenditure. On the other hand, the surplus generated each year could be very substantial. In 1997, the surplus was as much as 45 percent of government expenditure.

The surplus in each year was put into a fiscal reserve. The amount of the fiscal reserve throughout the years is also shown in Table 6.2. The accumulation of a large fiscal reserve was the outcome of both fiscal prudence and strong economic growth. The reserve served the functions of both a revenue source through investment and a "rainy day fund."[11]

The fiscal structure

A fiscal structure consists of both a revenue component and an expenditure component. Despite its prudent fiscal management, there are three major problems in the revenue system of Hong Kong: lack of transparency, inequity, and instability. Many of the taxes in Hong Kong are disguised as non-tax revenues, especially as revenue generating from direct exchange for goods and services. Second, the tax burden is heavily concentrated on the middle class. Third, the revenue system is built for the era of economic boom, making it vulnerable during economic downturn and economic change. This latter problem is one of the leading causes of the most recent budget crisis of Hong Kong in 1998 to 2003.

Lack of transparency

Table 6.3 shows the major revenue sources of Hong Kong. The two most important tax revenue sources in Hong Kong are profits tax and salaries tax. Altogether, they produce about 30 percent to 40 percent of the total revenue. However, a key feature of the revenue system of Hong Kong is that a very large part of its revenue comes from non-tax sources. These include land premium (i.e., revenue from land sales), investment income (mainly from investment of

Table 6.2 Fiscal conditions of Hong Kong: 1990 to 2006

Year[a]	Total government expenditure in millions of US$	Total government revenue in millions of US$	Surplus (deficit)		Fiscal reserve	
			In millions of US$	As % of total expenditure	In millions of US$	As months of total expenditure
1990	10,969	11,477	509	4.6	9,305	10.2
1991	11,819	14,705	2,886	24.4	9,813	10.0
1992	14,530	17,348	2,818	19.4	12,699	10.5
1993	18,902	21,359	2,457	13.0	15,517	9.9
1994	21,046	22,436	1,390	6.6	17,974	10.2
1995	23,482	23,083	(399)	–1.7	19,364	9.9
1996	23,421	26,713	3,292	14.1	18,965	9.7
1997[d]	**24,918**	**36,055**	**11,137**	**44.7**	**47,523**	**22.9**
1998	30,687	27,707	(2,980)	–9.7	58,659	22.9
1999	28,595	29,871	1,276	4.5	55,680	23.4
2000	29,858	28,854	(1,004)	–3.4	56,956	22.9
2001	30,627	22,508	(8,119)	–26.5	55,164	21.6
2002	30,664	22,755	(7,909)	–25.8	39,923	15.6
2003	31,181	26,582	(4,599)	–14.8	35,300	13.6
2004	31,151	33,551	2,400	7.7	36,833	14.2
2005	29,881	31,671	1,790	6.0	39,829	16.0
2006[b]	29,871	36,933	7,062	23.6	46,891	18.8

Source: Appendix, "Total Government Revenue and Expenditure and Summary of Financial Position" in *Hong Kong Yearbook* (various years); Appendix of the Budget Speech (various years) of the Financial Secretary, HKSAR government.

Notes

a Fiscal year starts on April 1 and ends on March 31 in Hong Kong. Data in the table are labeled with the beginning year of the fiscal year (e.g., fiscal year 2000/2001 is labeled as 2000).

b Data for 2006 are estimates which are subject to revision by the government.

c The Hong Kong dollar has been pegged to the US dollar at the fixed exchange rate of US$1 = HK$7.8 since October, 1983.

d The amount of fiscal reserve is measured on the first day of the fiscal year, i.e., April 1. At the end of each fiscal year, the surplus (deficit) is added to (deducted from) the fiscal year, plus (minus) the gain (loss) from the investment activities of the fiscal reserve. In 1997, the fiscal reserve received US$25,265.64 million from the trustees of the Land Fund of the former Hong Kong government.

Table 6.3 Revenue sources of Hong Kong (as percentage of total revenue): 1991 to 2002

Year[a]	Tax revenue					Non-tax revenue				Total non-tax revenue (%)[c]	Total housing-stock revenue (%)[d]
	Profits tax	Salaries tax	Stamp duties	Betting duty	Duties	Land premium	Investment income	Fees and charges	Other capital revenue[b]		
1991	22	15.2	8.3	6.2	6	7.8	2.6	6.3	5	35.8	24[e]
1992	23.8	14.9	9.9	5.8	5.3	6.6	1.3	5.9	5.3	34	23
1993	23.9	13.5	10.8	6	4.3	11.1	2	5.2	5	36	29
1994	27.1	13.5	7.3	5.3	4.3	10.9	2.8	5.5	5	37	26
1995	25.9	14.6	6.2	6.1	4.4	10.8	3.3	5.5	5.4	37	26
1996	24	13.8	9.8	5.9	4	12.9	2.7	5.2	5.1	36.1	31
1997	**19.7**	**10.7**	**10.3**	**4.8**	**3**	**22.6**	**5.3**	**4**	**4.7**	**46.5**	**43**
1998	20.9	11.6	4.7	5.7	3.6	8.9	14.6	4.9	9.3	48.8	38
1999	16.2	10.6	5.2	5.1	3.2	14.9	15.8	4.7	9.9	55	46
2000	19.1	11.7	4.9	5.6	3.2	13.1	8.7	4.9	10.8	47	38
2001	25.6	16.4	5.1	6.5	4	4.9	0	6.3	8	32	18
2002	22	14	4	6	4	6	15	7	6	40	31

Source: Table 12 in the Final Report to the Financial Secretary by the Task Force on Review of Public Finances.

Notes

a Fiscal year starts on April 1 and ends on March 31 in Hong Kong. Data in the table are labeled with the beginning year of the fiscal year (e.g., fiscal year 2000/2001 is labeled as 2000).

b Other capital revenue include rental income, income from selling government properties (other than land), and selling of stocks of public corporations owned by the government.

c Total non-tax revenue includes utilities, fees and charges, other non-tax revenue, investment income, land premium, and other capital income. Some of these revenue sources are not shown.

d Housing-stock revenue is defined as revenue generated from the following sources: stamp duties, investment income, capital revenue (land premium and other capital revenue).

e Numbers in each row do not add up to 100% as minor revenue sources are not included.

the fiscal reserve), fees and charges, and other capital income. For the period between 1991 and 2002, non-tax revenue sources contributed at least 32 percent of the total revenue in each year. It peaked in 1999 when more than half (55 percent) of the revenue of Hong Kong was coming from non-tax revenue sources.

It is often argued that a major advantage of depending on non-tax revenue sources is that the government can make revenue without taxing its people. However, in Hong Kong, this argument is not consistent with the fact. First of all, in Hong Kong, most government services are provided under very substantial subsidization by tax dollars. It is simply a myth that the Hong Kong government can make a large amount of revenue by selling and providing more services without taxing its people. Second and importantly, land premium itself is a land tax in disguise and much of the tax burden is borne by the middle class. Tax is defined as a compulsory payment from citizens to government, backed up by the government's coercive power, which is not for direct exchange of goods and services.[12] The government monopolizes the land market by owning all land in Hong Kong. The government can make so much revenue through land sales because it deliberately controls its supply with its power to set up a "high land price" policy. What the land developers are paying is much more than the true value of the land, as decided by competitive market forces, in the absence of the visible hand of the government.

Inequity

Most of the tax incidence of the land tax is shifted from the land developers to the middle class. The middle class is not qualified for public housing programs which are means-tested and targeted at the lower income groups. Land developers, as owners of capital, have other options of investment for their capital. But for the buyers of private housing, most of them middle-class people, they have nowhere to go to avoid the tax incidence unless they move out of Hong Kong.[13] The disguise of the land tax and other forms of taxes creates a lack of transparency in the tax system that can give people the illusion that they are not being taxed.

The middle class is the major financier in the public finance system in Hong Kong, taking up a heavy burden of funding many major public programs benefiting the lower income groups.[14] The land tax is only one of the several major taxes in Hong Kong that targets specifically the middle class.[15] The structures of salaries and profit taxes also make them unfavorable to the middle class. With the provision of a generous tax allowance by the government, most of the low income class does not have to pay any salaries tax. On the other hand, the rich can often legally avoid or reduce their salaries and profits taxes by manipulating the loopholes in the tax system.[16]

There are good political reasons for the design of such an inequitable system. By protecting the rich from being taxed heavily, it is preserving the low-tax business environment in Hong Kong as well as protecting the business interests which have huge political clout. The lower income group pays little tax but enjoys high-quality services because the government wants to keep them pacified. There were major riots in Hong Kong in the late 1960s which posed an unprecedented threat to the British governance of Hong Kong. After the riots were suppressed, the government concluded that improving communication with the public and providing better social services were critical to the continuation of its governance. But this fiscal arrangement had the undesirable side-effect of producing unsaturated demand for more public services from the lower income groups which would gradually drain the public purse. In contrast, the middle class is often taken as a stabilizing force in society who can afford to pay without strong protest. In addition, Hong Kong has been experiencing strong economic growth for decades. As the economic pie keeps getting bigger and members of the middle class continue to experience improvement in their economic lives, the unfairness of its tax system often goes undisputed and even unnoticed.

Instability

Heavy dependency on non-tax revenue, or more precisely the housing-stock revenue, makes the revenue system vulnerable and sensitive to economic downturn and instability. In the last column of Table 6.3, it may be seen that a very large proportion of revenue is actually built solely on the performance of the stock and housing markets. In 1999, the total housing-stock revenue as a percentage of total revenue reached its peak at 46 percent. In 2001, the percentage of total housing-stock revenue dropped to the level of 18 percent after the housing and stock markets collapsed.

Heavy state intervention in provision of services

Table 6.4 shows the breakdown of public expenditure by function. In 2006, education was the largest expenditure item of the government, followed by social welfare and health respectively. The figure of total social expenditure (housing, education, health and social welfare) continued to increase throughout most of the period, particularly from the early to the late 1990s. It jumped from 45.7 percent in 1991 to 57.79 percent in 1999. During the same period, expenditure on welfare increased from 6.4 percent to 10.3 percent.

It is important to note that the increase in share of total social expenditure does not start exactly in the period of economic downturn of the Asian financial crisis but in the pre-1997 era. Besides, on the eve of the handover, there was still heavy intervention in the sectors of education, health, and housing, with heavy subsidization by tax dollars even though Hong Kong had become a developed and mature economy.[17] Although the size of Hong Kong is still much smaller than many European countries, this trend of increasing social expenditure is what the British colonial government anxiously and purposefully tried to avoid in much of its governance period of Hong Kong.

One of the suggested reasons for the failure of the state to retreat is that the

Table 6.4 Public expenditure by function in Hong Kong (in terms of percentage of total public expenditure)

Year[a]	Education (%)	Health (%)	Housing (%)	Social welfare (%)	Security (%)	Environment (%)	Total social expenditure[c] (%)
1991	17.4	10.3	11.6	6.4	13.5	2.5	45.70
1992	17.5	11.1	10.5	6.4	13.2	2.5	45.40
1993	16.4	11.9	10.7	5.9	11.2	2.0	44.91
1994	17.4	11.7	11.9	6.6	11.4	2.7	47.56
1995	17.6	12.7	10.0	7.4	11.4	2.9	47.64
1996	18.0	11.9	11.5	8.5	11.5	3.0	49.85
1997	**20.0**	**11.9**	**10.5**	**9.3**	**10.1**	**3.0**	**51.70**
1998	18.2	11.8	14.6	9.9	9.4	5.0	54.47
1999	18.7	11.8	17.0	10.3	9.6	4.6	57.79
2000	19.2	12.3	15.9	10.5	10.0	4.2	57.93
2001	19.3	12.5	12.2	11.3	10.3	4.2	55.12
2002	20.7	12.6	9.1	12.3	10.3	4.3	54.70
2003	20.8	12.6	9.3	12.5	11.2	4.0	55.20
2004	21.0	12.2	7.4	12.9	9.9	4.0	53.50
2005	22.0	13.0	6.3	13.6	11.1	4.7	54.90
2006[b]	21.6	13.0	6.0	14.0	10.4	4.2	54.60

Source: Appendix, "Public Expenditure by Function" in the *Hong Kong Yearbook* (various years), Hong Kong SAR government.

Notes
a Fiscal year starts on April 1 and ends on March 31 in Hong Kong. Data in the table are labeled with the beginning year of the fiscal year (e.g., fiscal year 2000/2001 is labeled as 2000).
b Data for 2006 are estimates which are subject to revision by the government.
c Social expenditure is defined as expenditure on the following items: housing, education, health, and social welfare.

British Hong Kong government would like to ensure political stability in the transitional years and create a British legacy in Hong Kong by increased social spending. Moreover, the British and the Chinese had heated debates and severe confrontations on the pace of democratization in Hong Kong since the Tiananmen incident of 1989. It was difficult for the departing British government to concentrate on scaling back the state while having such a major dispute with China. The scaling back of the state, including cutbacks of services and subsidization, would make the government unpopular at a time when support from the Hong Kong people was critical for its negotiations with China. As the political environment changed, the British government adapted to the new environment by departing from some of its well-treasured fiscal principles.

End of the miracle

Structurally, there has been little change to the overall fiscal system of Hong Kong in the past two decades. Since its fiscal system remains unchanged, changes in the economic and political environments become the major variables in analyzing the budget problem faced by Hong Kong as well as the recent economic recovery. On the economic side, major changes include the Asian financial crisis and the lagged restructuring problem in its economy. On the political front, key variables include the new institutional context and governance system imposed on Hong Kong after its transfer of sovereignty, and the generous economic offers by Beijing, which are significantly affected by political considerations to stabilize Hong Kong's social and political conditions after the massive July 1 demonstrations in 2002 and 2003.

Negative impacts of Asian financial crisis

Until the recent economic recovery in 2004, Hong Kong was badly hit by the Asian financial crisis. The extent of the economic problem suffered by Hong Kong may be seen from the economic indicators shown in Tables 6.5 and 6.6. Table 6.5 shows that Hong Kong had been performing badly since 1998 in its general economic indicators. Its GDP shifted from high growth, to slow and even negative growth. Deflation, not inflation, became one of the economic problems troubling Hong Kong. These indicators showed that the Hong Kong economy was continually weakening. The unemployment rate was going up at a

Table 6.5 General economic conditions of Hong Kong: 1993 to 2006

Year[a]	Change in real GDP (%)	Change in consumer price index (%)	Change in GDP deflator (%)	Unemployment rate (%)
1993	6.1	8.8	8.5	2.0
1994	5.4	8.8	6.9	1.9
1995	3.9	9.1	2.5	3.2
1996	4.5	6.3	5.9	2.8
1997	5.0	5.8	5.8	2.2
1998	−5.3	2.8	0.4	4.7
1999	3.0	−4.0	−5.4	6.2
2000	10.2	−3.8	−5.6	4.9
2001	0.5	−1.6	−1.8	5.1
2002	1.9	−3.0	−3.5	7.3
2003	3.2	−2.6	−6.4	7.9
2004	8.6	−0.4	−3.5	6.8
2005	7.5	1.0	−0.1	5.6
2006[b]	6.8	2.0	−0.1	4.8

Source: Censis and Statistics Department, the Hong Kong SAR government, and *Annual Report* (various years), Hong Kong Monetary Authority.

Notes
a Fiscal year starts on April 1 and ends on March 31 in Hong Kong. Data in the table are labeled with the beginning year of the fiscal year (e.g., fiscal year 2000/2001 is labeled as 2000).
b Data for 2006 are estimates which are subject to revision by the government.

Table 6.6 Prices of housing market and stock market in Hong Kong: 1993 to 2006

Year[a]	Housing Price Index (1999 = 100)[c]				Rental Index (1999 = 100)[c]				Stocks	
	Private domestic	% change	Private office	% change	Private domestic	% change	Private office	% change	Hang Seng Index (HIS)[d]	% change
1993	93	n.a.	164.6	n.a.	97.4	n.a.	149.9	n.a.	11,888	n.a.
1994	114	22.58	230.3	39.91	118.1	21.25	181.8	21.28	8,191	-31.10
1995	107.3	-5.88	194.6	-15.50	120.7	2.20	178.6	-1.76	10,073	22.98
1996	116.9	8.95	188.4	-3.19	119	-1.41	152.3	-14.73	13,451.5	33.54
1997	163.1	39.52	213.1	13.11	134.5	13.03	156.8	2.95	10,723	-20.28
1998	117.1	-28.20	134.5	-36.88	112.6	-16.28	135.9	-13.33	10,049	-6.29
1999	100	-14.60	100	-25.65	100	-11.19	100	-26.42	16,962	68.79
2000	89.6	-10.40	89.9	-10.10	98.1	-1.90	98.5	-1.50	15,096	-11.00
2001	78.7	-12.17	78.7	-12.46	95.4	-2.75	101	2.54	11,397	-24.50
2002	69.9	-11.18	68.5	-12.96	83.4	-12.58	85.6	-15.25	9,321	-18.22
2003	61.6	-11.87	62.5	-8.76	73.6	-11.75	74.6	-12.85	12,576	34.92
2004	78	26.62	99.3	58.88	77.7	5.57	78.1	4.69	14,230	13.15
2005	92	17.95	133	33.94	86.5	11.33	96.4	23.43	14,876	4.54
2006[b]	92.6	0.65	139	4.51	91.6	5.90	117	21.37	19,965	34.21

Source: Information on Hang Seng Index (HIS) is taken from the *Annual Report* (various years), Hong Kong Monetary Authority; information on housing indices is taken from the *Hong Kong Property Review* (various years), Rating and Evaluation Department, HKSAR government.

Notes

a Fiscal year starts on April 1 and ends on March 31 in Hong Kong. Data in the table are labeled with the beginning year of the fiscal year (e.g., fiscal year 2000/20001 is labeled as 2000).

b Data for 2006 are estimates which are subject to revision by the government.

c Both the Price Index and Rental Index combine all classes of properties in their calculations. The indices are produced by the Rating and Evaluation Department of the Hong Kong SAR government.

d Hang Seng Index (HIS) is the major index of the stock market in Hong Kong. It is a composite of 33 major listed companies of Hong Kong. The HIS shown in the table is the closing figure on the last transaction day of the year.

very rapid rate and reached a record high, jumping from 2.2 percent in 1997 to 7.9 percent in 2003. Although the unemployment rate fell to 4.8 percent in 2006 as the economy started to recover under the active boosting efforts by Beijing, including the most visible one of opening Hong Kong up for mainland tourists from many parts of the country, this was still a big departure from the norm of "full employment" in Hong Kong in the pre-1997 era.

The economic bubbles in the housing and stock markets of Hong Kong formed in the 1990s burst in the Asian financial crisis. In Table 6.6, we can see that the housing and stock markets were undergoing substantial downward adjustment after the crisis. In the housing market, for example, the price index of private domestic housing dropped from 163.1 in 1997 to 61.6 in 2003, representing a total accumulated loss of 62 percent. During the Asian financial crisis, in the stock market, the Hang Seng Index (HIS) of the Hong Kong exchange market dropped more than 50 percent in total, from its peak of 18,320 points as of March, 2000 to around 9,000 points in 2002.

Since the revenue sources of Hong Kong were highly dependent on both the housing and stock markets, the collapse of these two markets created major problems for Hong Kong's fiscal health. As seen in Table 6.2, the Hong Kong government had a budget deficit for all years during the period of 1998 to 2003 apart from 1999. Because of the unprecedented severity of the budget problem, it has been perceived as a major crisis by both the government and the people in Hong Kong. This sense of crisis is also generated from an increasing realization that the underlying problem of the deficit is structural, not cyclical. The record of continued large deficits is closely related to the structural problems in its economy and fiscal structure. Admittedly, some relief has been felt by the public in face of the improved economic situation since 2004. However, as a considerable extent of the recovery may be attributed to Beijing's active efforts in boosting Hong Kong's economy, and the belief of the Hong Kong people in the long-term commitment of Beijing in continuing to do so, without proper economic restructuring and corresponding fiscal reform, the current situation may not be sustainable once there is a shift in Beijing's politically inclined economic policies or simply a change in public confidence.

A dual crisis: economic and fiscal

The economic downturn experienced by Hong Kong during the post-handover period of 1998 to 2003 clearly highlights two major problems for Hong Kong: the structural problem in its economy and its unbalanced fiscal structure. When the Asian financial crisis prompted economic hardship for Hong Kong, it was not the major reason why Hong Kong is experiencing such prolonged economic difficulties, as many other affected countries had a faster recovery than Hong Kong. Even before the financial crisis, Hong Kong had been facing problems in transforming its economy from a labor-intensive and low-technology economy to a more capital-intensive and high-technology economy. Since the 1980s, many of the labor-intensive industries moved to Mainland China to take advantage of its cheap inputs of production, particularly labor and land. The industrial and production bases of Hong Kong were being "hollowed out."[18] When most of the old industries are gone, the new industries have yet to develop to take their place. Many of the major projects targeted at reindustrializing Hong Kong for the new economy turned out to be no more than public relations campaigns or real estate development projects packaged with a new cover such as the controversial Cyberport project.

Industries in Hong Kong have lagged behind in upgrading its production technology.[19] Instead of upgrading its technology, most of the industries have simply moved their production base north across the border to China. Although the Hong Kong economy may be stimulated in the short run by some fiscal and monetary measures, rebuilding its economic base on competitive industries is the long-term and effective solution to its structural economic problem.

The economic downturn exposed the weaknesses of the fiscal system in Hong Kong as well. A common problem in the economic structure of Hong Kong and its fiscal system is their over-dependence on the housing and stock markets, which are designed more for their policy-driven and short-term factors, even market speculation, rather than on solid economic ground. In economics, a boom in the real estate market should be taken as the outcome of economic growth rather than the engine of economic growth. An economy structure enabling Hong Kong to compete successfully in the global marketplace is still what is ultimately needed to maintain good fiscal health, as what the fiscal system does is often no more than abstract resources from society to meet public needs. Before the completion of economic transition, fiscal reform that is more institutional in nature and extensive in scale is needed to address the structural problems of the budget for preventing the emergence of another major budget crisis.

Options for fiscal reform

There are many feasible options, which are not necessarily mutually exclusive, for long-term institutional fiscal reform. Like any sensible fiscal reform, it can focus on the revenue side, the expenditure side, or both. Given the fact that there are some major taxes that are not adopted in Hong Kong and the extremely high level of subsidization of public services, which are often not means-tested to target specifically the needy groups, there is plenty of room for maneuver in broadening the tax base and improving the inequity in the fiscal system in Hong Kong. For instance, the general sales tax, though regressive in nature, is widely used in advanced industrialized countries worldwide except Hong Kong, and can be considered for broadening the tax base to address some of the structural problems of the budget system. According to an IMF report of 2001, on average, general sales tax contributes 20.5 percent of the total tax revenue in OECD and major Asian countries.[20] Another major tax that may be considered seriously for adoption in Hong Kong is the capital gains tax. Although Hong Kong imposes taxes on transactions in the stock and housing markets based on the amount of transaction, gains in the stock and housing markets are not taxed. It is often ironic, if not strange, that money made through investment is not regarded as income or profit under the current tax system. In addition, no global taxation is used in Hong Kong. This means that profits of local firms and salaries of Hong Kong citizens obtained outside Hong Kong are not taxable. This arrangement has created many loopholes for tax evasion through some "creative" accounting methods, particularly for corporations and rich individuals. Since capital gains tax and global taxation are usually more progressive in nature, these two new revenue sources could raise more revenue as well as making the Hong Kong tax system more equitable.

Other feasible options may be found in changing the structure and rate of current taxes. The tax rate of Hong Kong profits tax is low compared with many other countries in the world as well as within the region.[21] Another option of increasing revenue is to lower the tax allowance of salaries tax in Hong Kong. Its significance is more than the additional revenue it could raise. As most of the working population in Hong Kong pay no taxes but enjoy good public services, having them pay some taxes could enhance their sense of fiscal responsibility and increase their incentive to hold the government accountable for its expenditure.

Because of their subsidized nature, public programs may be viewed as both targets for increasing revenue or reducing expenditure, depending on whether subsidization is reduced by raising user fees or services are cut back. For example, in the health service, the government has a market share of 94 percent and a subsidization rate of 97 percent of the true cost. The level of government subsidization and scope of state intervention in these services are often so extreme that it is difficult to adequately justify them through the economic arguments of public goods and externalities. Increasing the fee of government services to make it closer to the true cost is useful not only for raising revenue but also for avoiding wastage of valuable resources and abuse of services. Alternatively, an option the government has in reducing expenditure without affecting the subsidization rate is to create a better targeting system through the introduction of means-testing or other screening procedures. This ensures that the limited resources are allocated to the most needy groups.

As pay in the public sector usually reacts slower to change in market wages, there is often a gap between private market pay and civil service pay.[22] Adjusting the salaries of the civil service becomes one of the possible options in reducing public expenditure in Hong Kong. However, the government faces both constitutional and political limits on how much civil service pay can be cut. According to Article 100 of the Basic Law, the pay of the civil service cannot be lower than that of the transfer of sovereignty in 1997. As a weak government with low public support, it often finds itself faced with enormous resistance from the civil service unions while enjoying limited social support.

In July, 2002, the decision of a moderate civil service pay cut through legislation triggered an unexpected large-scale demonstration of 30,000 civil servants and their supporters. Faced with such strong opposition within and outside the government, and even though the legislation was finally passed since the government could secure enough votes in the Legislative Council under its undemocratic composition, it decided to adopt a more soft-handed and compromising approach. In February, 2003, the government reached a settlement with the civil service unions that the civil service pay would be reduced to the cash level of 1997, a cut of about 6 percent. Nevertheless, the total estimated saving was only about US$897 million per year, roughly 10 percent of the estimated deficit for 2002 to 2003. Even with the urgency of the budget crisis at that time, the pay reduction had to be divided into three phases over a period of three years. It was a so-called "0–3–3" package in which the civil service pay was frozen in 2002, and then reduced by 3 percent in 2003 and finally another 3 percent in 2004.

This demonstrates that a civil service pay cut is a politically costly option and a very slow process which has limited fiscal impact. It becomes increasingly clear that, without critically re-examining and redefining the role of the public sector and a more comprehensive reform of the fiscal system, a pay cut for the civil service alone will not be sufficient to provide a real and long-term solution to the budget problem faced by Hong Kong. The case of a civil service pay cut and the reaction of the civil service groups and society as a whole to the incident also point out the relevancy of the institutional context of the budget crisis in which the government often lacks sufficient legitimacy under the existing political situation to push forward many fiscally sound reform packages.

Institutional context of the budget crisis

When the economic problems and the unbalanced fiscal structure explain the emergence of the budget crisis in Hong Kong, problems and dilemmas in the institutional situation under which budget decisions are made help explain the persistence of the budget problem, and the slow, unsatisfactory pace of reform. The current institutional situation of its governance system does not equip the policy-makers with sufficient capacities and incentives to adopt and implement the much needed reform of the fiscal system.

Low legitimacy under a undemocratic system

To understand the institutional constraints on the budget reform, one would have to be introduced to the structure and context of governance in Hong Kong. Hong Kong was a British colony for more than 150 years before its sovereignty was returned from Britain to China in 1997. Because of the social and economic differences between Hong Kong and China, it was decided by the Chinese and British governments that many of the national policies of China were not suitable for the circumstances of Hong Kong. Consequently, the "One Country, Two Systems" principle was adopted in Hong Kong for its reunification with China. Under this principle, China would not exercise direct control over Hong Kong and a Special Administrative Region (SAR) would be set up in Hong Kong. As a SAR, Hong Kong would enjoy high autonomy in many of its internal affairs and China would be mainly responsible for the defense and foreign affairs of Hong Kong only. It was also promised that the systems and ways of life in Hong Kong would remain unchanged for 50 years. A mini-constitution, the Basic Law, was drafted and adopted to safeguard the rights of Hong Kong people, the authorities, and the autonomy of its new government under the "One Country, Two Systems" principle.

When Britain and China signed the Joint Declaration on agreeing the transfer of the sovereignty of Hong Kong, however, what the Chinese government had in mind was to transfer the whole power base and structure of the British over Hong Kong into its own hands, with little leakage of power and authority from government to society in the process.[23] In other words, Hong Kong would turn from a British colony to a "colony" of the Chinese government. However, democratic reforms had been introduced by the British during the transitional years and Hong Kong enjoyed some of the elements of a democratic system including freedom of speech, a free press, and an independent judiciary system during most of the British colonial governance. As a compromise, in designing the governance system of post-1997 Hong Kong, China would like to freeze the democratization of Hong Kong and keep it as a "partial democracy" or "bird caged democracy," in which the general public has a role to play in the formal policy-making process but the pro-China elite retains the decisive influence.[24]

In drafting the Basic Law, the Chinese government created a lop sided political system which allotted a substantial proportion of governmental power to the rich and business elite while limiting the influence of the general public.[25] An executive-led government was set up for Hong Kong under the Basic Law. Most of the constitutional power was concentrated in the executive branch, and more precisely in the hands of the chief executive. The Chinese government decided to choose the "rule of business tycoons" model and made their choice of chief executive from among major business tycoons in Hong Kong.

While the chief executive is a powerful political figure in Hong Kong, there is no direct mechanism to hold him accountable to the public as he is not elected directly by them, which has a significant negative impact on the low level of legitimacy of the government. He is basically handpicked by China, though he has to go through the formality of being elected by an election committee, which is dominated by the pro-Beijing rich and business elite. With the support of Chinese leaders, Tung Chee-Hwa, a shipping tycoon in Hong Kong, was "elected" for both the first term (1997–2002) and the second term (2002–2007) of chief executive in Hong Kong. However, he has recently stepped down with his own resignation in March, 2005, a move which is believed to be closely related to pressures exerted on him both by Beijing and the Hong Kong people due to the deepening governance crisis in Hong Kong. Donald Tsang, the Chief Secretary of Administration under Tung, became the new chief executive under the support of China, though he can only serve the remaining term of two years left by Tung, not the full five-year term as stated in the Basic Law for a chief executive.

There is no strong checking system on the chief executive from other branches. The Legislative Council is not a powerful independent institution in Hong Kong, though it is the only major political institution in Hong Kong that has a democratic element to its composition. Even so, only half of the 60 seats in the Legislative Council are directly elected by geographical constituencies. Under the current political system, the chief executive possesses the power to dissolve the Legislative Council and ask for its re-election.[26] Another major example of the weak power of the Legislative Council is that it cannot propose many of its own legislations without the approval of the chief executive. Article 74 of the Basic Law states that:

> Bills which do not relate to public expenditure or political structure or the operation of the government may be introduced individually or jointly by members of the Council. The written consent of the Chief Executive shall be required before bills relating to government policies are introduced.

In reality, it is impossible to find any meaningful bill which is not related to public expenditure or political structure or the operation of the government. What Article 74 of the Basic Law does is to take away the power of the Legislative Council in legislation initiation that may pose a strong challenge to the authority of the chief executive. At the same time, a special voting method, namely a split voting system between the directly elected members and functional consistency members, has been established in the Council to enhance the chance of bills proposed by the chief executive being passed.[27]

Inherent bias in a business-and-rich elite-dominated system

By understanding the structure and context of governance in Hong Kong, it is not hard to realize that the formal post-1997 political order in Hong Kong is dominated by the business-and-rich elite, with the concerns and interests of the middle and lower classes underrepresented in the system. While the business interest also exercised a strong influence in Hong Kong before 1997, it was often mediated and checked by both the Governor and the permanent bureaucracy in Hong Kong. The Governor, sent by Britain and who was often a British civil servant, played a critical role in aggregating, articulating, and balancing the different and competing interests in Hong Kong.

A direct consequence of creating a business-and-rich elite-dominated system is removing the incentive of the policy-makers in making fiscal decisions on a fair basis for the sake of the public interest. Instead, it has injected incentives of viewing any fiscal decision from the perspective of protecting the clientele and patrons. A logical deduction from this governance system is that the fiscal system can only be reformed with new revenue sources imposed on the middle and lower classes and the expenditure on them being cut to help balance the budget. At the same time, the interests of the business elite and the super- rich will be protected in the fiscal reform.

Part of this predication seems to be correct so far. The interest of the business elite and the rich is generally unharmed or even enhanced. A government commissioned report on fiscal reform recommended that because of the potential damage to the "economic competitiveness" of Hong Kong, no global taxation, capital gains tax, or major increase of profit tax should be considered.[28] Instead, the report recommended the introduction of a general sales tax. A general sales tax is a regressive tax harming a majority of the population but, from a political standpoint, it has the advantage of spreading the cost over the entire population to reduce the incentive of any specific individuals and groups to be mobilized to strongly oppose the tax. A formal consultation on the introduction of a general sales tax to Hong Kong was started by the government in July, 2006, though the government had previously openly stated that no general sales would be imposed in the near future.[29] Henry Tang, the Financial Secretary, a political appointee under the accountability system for Principal Officials and a rich businessman himself, also abolished the estate duty in his 2005 to 2006 Budget Speech. Although he argued that such an abolishment would attract more outside investment to Hong Kong, like the proposal of a general sales tax, it was widely perceived as a move to benefit the rich and shift more tax burden to the middle and lower classes.

However, relatively few significant reform proposals on cutting expenditure and raising revenue have been accomplished so far. Although there has been a decrease in the housing expenditure over the past few years, to a large extent, this decrease is owing to the decrease in housing and land prices following the collapse of the housing market. Even if incentives and intentions do exit, what is holding the government back from adopting many of the feasible options of fiscal reform is the lack of sufficient political legitimacy. The government is not confident that it can overcome the political opposition it will encounter in implementing the reform without seriously disrupting social stability in Hong Kong. An outcome of designing the governance institutions in Hong Kong without referring to its social, economic, and political realities is the creation of a mismatched hybrid system in which the chief executive has strong constitutional power, including budgeting authorities, but is not necessarily well equipped with the actual capacity to command and actualize such power.[30]

Tung, the Chief Executive of Hong Kong until March, 2005, has low political legitimacy.[31] Legitimacy, which may be defined as consent of the governed, comes from two major sources: performance and procedure.[32] The low political legitimacy of Tung is related to both the institutional design of the governance system and his poor governing performance over the past six years. Because the chief executive is not directly elected, he enjoys very little procedural legitimacy. On the performance side, Tung is not regarded as a capable leader.[33] He is heavily criticized not only for his performance in managing the economy but also for his handling of many major political incidents including issues on human rights, conflict of interest, rule of law, and the autonomy of Hong Kong.

Implementing fiscal reform in Hong Kong in an age of a shrinking economy will unavoidably involve the redistribution of interest in society which resembles a zero-sum game, at least in the short run. Hard choices have to be made on which group has to suffer by paying more taxes or enjoying fewer public services when their economic conditions are not improving or even deteriorating. A highly legitimate government will be more successful in achieving such interest redistribution in the restructuring of the economy and the fiscal system. It is not only the case that it will be more effective in offsetting the opposition of interest groups that may represent only the partial interest in society. It is also the case that different groups will place more confidence in such a government that a sacrifice of its interest in the transitional process will finally be compensated after restructuring is complete. In other words, the government in charge of fiscal reform should never be perceived as a guardian or protector of the interest of only one particular class, group, or sector in society, but unfortunately the current governance system prevents such an impartial government from being constituted.

With such a weak legitimacy and limited political capital, the chief executive is reluctant and also powerless to push significant fiscal reforms forward. Deadlocks have been reached in fiscal reform and also other policy reforms in Hong Kong.[34] Without such legitimacy, even with an executive-led constitutional design, the HKSAR government still often functions in a setting with "many veto players" in a de facto sense for fiscal reform. According to the "veto player theory" in the public finance literature, countries with many veto players will have difficulty altering their budget structures.[35] Veto players are defined as "any player, institutional or partisan, who can block the adoption of a policy." Hong Kong does not have many veto players in the budget reform in a formal and constitutional sense, as its constitution is designed deliberately to limit the representation of the general public and shut out the voices of many major groups in society in order to concentrate most power in the hands of the chief executive. Nevertheless, with an active civil society and Hong Kong being a free society, many "veto players" exist outside the formal political system which can mount enormous pressures on the government through various means including public demonstrations and court cases, so as to block its policies.

Weak constitutionalism and unenforceable budget rules

One more hindering institutional factor in the post-1997 governance context is the undermining of the integrity and independence of the constitutional and legal system in Hong Kong. This has weakened the capacity of the government to adopt formal and legal means to achieve better fiscal discipline. One illustrative example of this problem may be seen in the interpretation of Article 106 in the Basic Law. To ensure that Hong Kong can continue to maintain its fiscal discipline after 1997, the Chinese government added an article in the Basic Law to require a balanced budget and constrain the growth of public expenditure.

Article 106 of the Basic Law stated:

> The Hong Kong Special Administrative Region shall follow the principle of keeping expenditure within the limits of revenues in drawing up its budget,

and strive to achieve a fiscal balance, avoid deficits and keep the budget commensurate with the growth rate of its gross domestic product.

Ironically, this article is never enforced. It is understood that it is not easy to enforce any constitutional requirement on a balanced budget.[36] However, the post-1997 institutional situation in Hong Kong makes it even harder to have such a constitutional constraint on the fiscal behavior of the government.

First of all, the ultimate authority of interpreting the Basic Law rests in the Standing Committee of the National People's Congress (NPC), the authority that passes the Basic Law. However, a more major flaw in the enforcement mechanism of the Basic Law comes from the fact that there is no independence of judiciary or any separation of powers in China. In the political system of China, all branches of government are subject to the NPC and eventually to the Chinese Communist Party. Therefore, whenever necessary, any law can be interpreted to fit the political circumstances as desired by the government. Since the handover, the Basic Law has been reinterpreted three times by the standing committee of the NPC on the right of abode issue in 1999, denial of universal suffrage of the LegCo and the Chief Executive in their elections for the years 2007 and 2008 respectively in 2004, and the term limit of the chief executive by-election in 2005. With the implicit approval of Chinese officials, the Hong Kong government has interpreted Article 106 very "flexibly" so that the balanced budget and limited growth of public expenditure stated in the Article are only long-term fiscal goals that do not have to be met every year.[37] Essentially, it has ignored this constitutional requirement. This institutional weakness compromises the ability of the government in using a formal, legal, and apolitical budget process to enforce fiscal discipline. It further questions the effectiveness of the Basic Law as a constitutional document in defining and limiting the power of the government.[38]

Conclusion

The major underlying thesis of this chapter is that a budget problem is often embedded in an institutional context. Following this thesis, this chapter conducts an in-depth case study to analyze the recent budget crisis of Hong Kong. When Hong Kong has many problems in its fiscal structure, the root of the problem extends beyond the fiscal system itself, leading Hong Kong to a situation in which there are technical solutions available but institutional factors have delayed and blocked many of its reform efforts.

The institutional setting of the post-1997 Hong Kong situation impedes fiscal reform in at least three major ways. First and most importantly, the fragile legitimacy of the government has severely weakened its ability to initiate major fiscal reforms which will inevitably have significant implications for the interest distribution in society. This has made many fiscal options political difficult to implement and easier to veto. Second, the design of its governance system, particularly its composition, has taken away the incentive of the policy-makers in adopting impartial and balanced fiscal options that will benefit society as a whole. Instead, if any fiscal change is possible, the business-and-rich elite-dominated system has a strong inherent bias to tilt many proposed changes in favor of their own interest. Third, weak constitutionalism in the post-1997 political order of Hong Kong has reduced the effectiveness of using constitutional and apolitical measures to enforce fiscal discipline. These institutional obstacles make reforming the fiscal system a difficult and slow process in Hong Kong.

Since the July 1 demonstration in July, 2003, it is obvious that the Chinese government has made significant efforts in attempting to improve the economic conditions of Hong Kong as well as the fiscal conditions of the government. On the political front, the unpopular Chief Executive Tung was replaced by Donald Tsang, a former civil servant and an extremely popular political figure in Hong Kong. Apparently, the Chinese government hopes that Tsang can to some extent enhance the legitimacy of the HKSAR government. However, as explained in the analysis, Hong Kong needs not just a new chief executive but a change in its institutions and systems to make its desirable fiscal reform possible.

The experience of institutional problems hindering budget and economic reforms is not unique to Hong Kong. Many previous countries of the Asian miracle face similar situations. It also appears that the most critical determinants of successful fiscal reform are the actual structure of institutional design under which incentives of key budget actors are shaped and the process in which leaders, policy entrepreneurs, and different groups in society can participate in framing their interests and redefining their goals.[39]

Concluding from their study of how democratic countries manage to achieve fiscal prudence, Posner and Gordon wrote:

> To some extent, the design of budget processes in these nations has played a critical role in encouraging fiscal discipline. But even more importantly, these nations demonstrate that ideas matter and that the ability to sustain fiscal discipline is related to the ability of decision makers to reframe the budget debate in terms of broader national goals.[40]

In the context of Hong Kong, these contributing factors of fiscal discipline as identified by Posner and Gordon in their study – a good budget process, an open and democratic setting for communicating ideas, political leadership, and policy entrepreneurship – are all undermined to various extents by the institutional setting of post-1997 Hong Kong. In lifting the institutional constraints on fiscal reform in Hong Kong, one of the positive and feasible scenarios will be introducing governance reforms along these multiple dimensions. While these institutional changes do not guarantee success of fiscal reform, it can at least provide the structures and the processes, many of which are currently absent in the Hong Kong system, that are important and necessary for facilitating the desired fiscal reform.

Acknowledgment

The research project of this chapter is partially funded by the Direct Grant of the Faculty of Social Science (Ref. No.: 2020611), the Chinese University of Hong Kong. The author would also like to thank Susana Soo for providing excellent research assistance and the anonymous reviewers for their useful comments.

Notes

1 Christopher Reddick, "Testing Rival Decision-making Theories on Budget Output: Theories and Comparative Evidence," *Public Budgeting and Finance* 22, no. 3 (fall 2002): 1–25; Irene Rubin, *The Politics of Public Budgeting* (4th edn) (New York: Chatham House, 2000), 24–31; Jeffrey Straussman, "Ideals and Reality in the Evolution of Fiscal Reform in Central and Eastern Europe," *Public Budgeting and Finance* 16, no. 2 (summer 1996): 79–95.
2 Douglass North, *Institutions, Institutional Change and Economic Performance* (New York: Cambridge University Press, 1990), 3–10.
3 Yun-Wing Sung, "Hong Kong Economy in Crisis," in *The First Tung Chee-hwa Administration*, ed. Siu-kai Lau (Hong Kong: The Chinese University Press, 2002).
4 In 1998, the figures of GDP per capita for Hong Kong and Britain were US$20,763 and US$20,314 respectively. Hong Kong was ranked No. 23 in the world while Britain was ranked No. 26. See the Comparative International Statistics section in U.S. Census Bureau, *Statistical Abstract of the United States* (Washington, DC, 2000).
5 Michael Enright, Edith Scott, and David Dodwell, *The Hong Kong Advantage* (Hong Kong: Oxford University Press, 1997), 29–51; Norman Miners, *The Government and Politics of Hong Kong* (5th edn) (Hong Kong: Oxford University Press, 1998), 43–49.
6 Siu-Kai Lau, *Society and Politics in Hong Kong* (Hong Kong: The Chinese University Press, 1982), 25–48. One of these social events was the riots in the late 1960s and the sudden influx of refugees into Hong Kong from mainland China in the 1970s. To resolve these problems, Governor MacLahose started massive and progressive housing, health, and education programs that marked the beginning of a more active state intervention in society.
7 Kui-Wai Li, *The Hong Kong Economy: Recovery and Restructuring* (Singapore: McGraw-Hill, 2006), 137; see also World Bank, *East Asian Miracle: Economic Growth and Public Policy* (Washington, DC: Oxford University Press, 1993), ch. 5, for a discussion of the growth strategies of the Asian miracle countries.
8 In 1980, only 4.6 percent of the government budget was spent on social welfare. In addition, for the entire period of British governance, there was no social security program to protect the economic lives of people on retirement. It was not until 1998 that the new Hong Kong SAR government introduced a mandatory provident fund (MPF) program for the retirement benefits of Hong Kong people.
9 Lau, *Society and Politics in Hong Kong*, 17–23.
10 In 2005, public expenditure as apercentage of real GDP for the United States is 36.6 percent. For two Asian countries, Japan and South Korea, the figures are 36.9 percent and 28.1 percent respectively. This number is as high as 50 percent or more for some European countries: France (54.4 percent), Denmark (53 percent), Sweden (56.4 percent). See U.S. Census Bureau, *Statistical Abstract of the United States* (Washington, DC, 2007).
11 As of November, 2007, the amount of foreign currency reserve held by Hong Kong is US$150.4 billion (this includes the Exchange Fund, another reserve for stabilizing the exchange rate of the Hong Kong dollar). It is ranked No. 9 in the world.
12 See John Mikesell, *Fiscal Administration: Analysis and Applications for the Public Sector* (6th edn) (Belmont, CA: Wadsworth, 2002), ch. 7.

13 See Harvey Rosen, *Public Finance* (6th edn) (New York: McGraw-Hill/Irwin, 2002), ch. 12, for a discussion of the concept of tax incidence.
14 In theory, the middle class can still enjoy many of the public programs they help finance except public housing (since releasing this will lead to the collapse of the land tax system) as most of the programs are not means-tested. However, many middle-class people would prefer the private market for their services such as education and healthcare.
15 Other examples of taxes that mainly target the middle class include the special sales taxes on luxury items and vehicles. Tax rates on vehicles can be more than 60 percent of the value of the vehicle.
16 There is no capital gains tax in Hong Kong. Therefore, one legal way of manipulating the tax system to lower one's taxes is to have the company give one's salaries and income in shares. Another legal way of manipulating the system is to have the salaries paid in the form of company residences, cars, and other fringe benefits. Many of these can be written off as business expenses or receive favorable tax treatments. For a good introduction to the tax system in Hong Kong, see David Flux and David Smith, *Hong Kong Taxation: Laws and Practice 2002–2003.* (Hong Kong: The Chinese University Press, 2002).
17 Anthony B. L. Cheung, "New Interventionism in the Making: Interpreting State Interventions in Hong Kong after the Change of Sovereignty," *Journal of Contemporary China* 9, no. 24 (July, 2000): 291–308; Eliza Wing-Yee Lee, "The Political Economy of Public Sector Reform in Hong Kong: The Case of a Colonial-Development State," *International Review of Administrative Sciences* 64, no. 4 (1998): 625–641.
18 Manufacturing has lost its significance in Hong Kong in terms of both GDP and employment. In 2000, it only accounted for 7 percent of employment and 5.9 percent of GDP in Hong Kong. While the data show that service and finance sectors have became major components of GDP and employment in Hong Kong, part of the growth in these sectors is driven by the economic bubble in the housing and stock market.
19 Stephen Chiu, K. C. Ho and Tai-Lok Lui, *City-states in the Global Economy: Industrial Restructuring in Hong Kong and Singapore* (Boulder, CO: Westview Press, 1997), 51.
20 In 1998, for the OECD countries, the average amount of revenue contributed by a general sales tax was 14.4 percent. The Asian countries included in the IMF study are China, Indonesia, Malaysia, Philippines, Singapore, and Thailand. The general sales tax contributed on average 24.5 percent of the total tax revenue for these Asian countries. The highest number comes from China in which a general sales tax contributed 62.3 percent of the total tax revenue in 1998. See Howell Zee, *et al.*, *Hong Kong SAR: Policy and Administrative Issues in Introducing a Good and Services Tax* (Washington, DC: Fiscal Affairs Department, International Monetary Fund, 2001).
21 For example, the corporate tax rate in Canada is about 45 percent. For Singapore, the closest competitor of Hong Kong, the corporate tax rate is about 23 percent. See KPMG, *Tax Base Study for the Hong Kong Government Advisory Committee on New Broad-based Taxes* (Australia: KPMG, 2001). Given the many exemptions and deductions and the absence of capital gains tax, the effective tax rates in Hong Kong can be substantially lower than the nominal tax rate of 15 percent to 16 percent.
22 Anthony Cheung, "Civil Service Pay Reform in Hong Kong: Principles, Politics and Paradoxes," in *Public Service Reform in East Asia*, ed. Anthony Cheung (Hong Kong: The Chinese University Press, 2005).
23 Shiu-Hing Lo, *Governing Hong Kong: Legitimacy, Communication and Political Decay* (New York: Nova, 2001).
24 Siu-Kai Lau and Hsin-Chi Kuan, "Partial Democratization, 'Foundation Moment' and Political Parties in Hong Kong," *The China Quarterly* 163, no. 1 (September, 2000): 705–720.

25 Yash Ghai, *Hong Kong's New Constitutional Order: The Resumption of Chinese Sovereignty and the Basic Law* (2nd edn) (Hong Kong: Hong Kong University Press, 1999), 288–300.
26 See Article 50 of the Basic Law.
27 Legislative bills proposed by the government can be passed by the Legislature with a simple majority of the Council. However, legislative bills proposed by the Legislative Council itself have to be voted by separating the votes into two groups: the group of council members elected by direct election and election committee, and the group of council members elected by functional constituencies. The bill has to be passed by the majority of both groups in order to be passed by the Legislative Council. Many of these members coming from the functional constituencies have similar business interests and backgrounds to the constituency of the chief executive.
28 See Hong Kong Advisory Committee on New Broad-based Taxes, *Final Report to the Financial Secretary* (Hong Kong, 2002). There are still debates on the degree of linkage between taxes and economic development in cross-country studies. See Joel Slemrod and Jon Bakija, *Taxing Ourselves: A Citizen's Guide to the Great Debate over Tax Reform* (2nd edn) (Cambridge, MA: MIT Press, 2001), ch. 6.
29 Hong Kong SAR Government, *Broadening the Tax Base, Ensuring Our Future Prosperity: What's the Best Options for Hong Kong – A Consultation Document* (Hong Kong: HKSAR government, July, 2006).
30 From the experience of former communist countries, an authoritarian budgeting system works well only when all the authorities, administrative capacity, expertise, and other resources are centralized. This set of requirements does not match the actual setting and context of Hong Kong. See Stanley Vanagunas, "Problems of Budgeting during 'Great Transformation'," *Public Budgeting and Finance* 15, no. 1 (spring 1995): 84–95; and Straussman (1996) for discussion on the budgeting system of former authoritarian regimes in Eastern Europe and problems that may occur in mismatching the budgeting system and budgeting environment.
31 Siu-Kai Lau, "Tung Chee-hwa's Governing Strategy: The Shortfall in Politics," in *The First Tung Chee-hwa Administration*, ed. Siu-kai Lau (Hong Kong: The Chinese University Press, 2002).
32 Samuel Huntington, *The Third Wave: Democratization in the Late Twentieth Century* (Norman: University of Oklahoma Press, 1991), 48–50.
33 Wilson Wong, "The Second Term of Chief Executive Tung Chee-hwa," in *Brookings Northeast Asia Survey 2002–2003*, ed. Richard Bush and Catharin Dalpino (Washington, DC, 2003).
34 Lau 2002.
35 George Tsebelis and Eric Chang, "Veto Players and the Structure of Budgets in Advanced Industrialized Countries," *European Journal of Political Research* 43: (2004): 449–476.
36 See James Saturno and Richard Forgette, "The Balanced Budget Amendment: How Would It Be Enforced?," *Public Budgeting and Finance* 18, no. 1 (spring 1998): 33–53; and Daniel Mullins and Philip Joyce, "Tax and Expenditure Limitations and State and Local Fiscal Structure: An Empirical Assessment," *Public Budgeting and Finance* 16, no. 1 (spring 1996): 75–101. In general, difficulties in enforcing constitutional requirements on a balanced budget include deciding which budget to be balanced: the proposed budget or the actual budget; and the legal issue of who is going to be held legally responsible for the deficit: the government officials or the politicians.
37 Budget Speech of the Finance Secretary (HKSAR government 1999–2000).
38 Yash Ghai, "Litigating the Basic Law: Jurisdiction, Interpretation and Procedure," in *Hong Kong's Constitutional Debate: Conflict over Interpretation*, ed. Johnness, H. L. Fu and Yash Ghai (Hong Kong: Hong Kong University Press, 2000). In another case, known as the "right of abode" case in 1999, under the request of the chief executive,

the Standing Committee of the NPC "reinterpreted" the Basic Law to overturn the decision of the Court of Final Appeal in Hong Kong.

39 Stephan Haggard, *The Political Economy of the Asian Financial Crisis* (Washington, DC: Institute for International Economics, 2000).

40 Paul Posner and Bryon Gordon, "Can Democratic Government Save? Experiences of Countries with Budget Surpluses." *Public Budgeting and Finance* 21, no. 2 (summer 2001): 1.

References

Cheung, Anthony B. L. "New Interventionism in the Making: Interpreting State Interventions in Hong Kong after the Change of Sovereignty," *Journal of Contemporary China* 9, no. 24 (July, 2000): 291–308.

Cheung, Anthony. "Civil Service Pay Reform in Hong Kong: Principles, Politics and Paradoxes," in *Public Service Reform in East Asia*, ed. Anthony Cheung. Hong Kong: The Chinese University Press, 2005.

Enright, Michael, Edith Scott, and David Dodwell. *The Hong Kong Advantage.* Hong Kong: Oxford University Press, 1997, pp. 29–51.

Flux, David and David Smith. *Hong Kong Taxation: Laws and Practice 2002–2003.* Hong Kong: The Chinese University Press, 2002.

Ghai, Yash. *Hong Kong's New Constitutional Order: The Resumption of Chinese Sovereignty and the Basic Law* (2nd edn). Hong Kong: Hong Kong University Press, 1999, pp. 288–300.

Ghai, Yash. "Litigating the Basic Law: Jurisdiction, Interpretation and Procedure," in *Hong Kong's Constitutional Debate: Conflict over Interpretation*, ed. Johnness H. L. Fu and Yash Ghai. Hong Kong: Hong Kong University Press, 2000.

Haggard, Stephan. *The Political Economy of the Asian Financial Crisis.* Washington, DC: Institute for International Economics, 2000.

Ho, Stephen Chiu K. C. and Lui, Tai-Lok. *City-states in the Global Economy: Industrial Restructuring in Hong Kong and Singapore.* Boulder, CO: Westview Press, 1997, p. 51.

Hong Kong Advisory Committee on New Broad-based Taxes. *Final Report to the Financial Secretary.* Hong Kong, 2002.

Huntington, Samuel. *The Third Wave: Democratization in the Late Twentieth Century.* Norman, OK: University of Oklahoma Press, 1991, pp. 48–50.

KPMG. *Tax Base Study for the Hong Kong Government Advisory Committee on New Broad-based Taxes.* Australia: KPMG, 2001.

Lau, Siu-Kai. *Society and Politics in Hong Kong.* Hong Kong: The Chinese University Press, 1982, pp. 17–23, 25–48.

Lau, Siu-Kai. "Tung Chee-hwa's Governing Strategy: The Shortfall in Politics," in *The First Tung Chee-hwa Administration*, ed. Siu-kai Lau. Hong Kong: The Chinese University Press, 2002.

Lau, Siu-Kai and Hsin-Chi Kuan. "Partial Democratization, 'Foundation Moment' and Political Parties in Hong Kong," *The China Quarterly* 163, no. 1 (September, 2000): 705–720.

Lee, Eliza Wing-Yee. "The Political Economy of Public Sector Reform in Hong Kong: The Case of a Colonial-development State." *International Review of Administrative Sciences* 64, no. 4 (1998): 625–641.

Lo, Shiu-Hing. *Governing Hong Kong: Legitimacy, Communication and Political Decay.* New York: Nova, 2001.

Mikesell, John. *Fiscal Administration: Analysis and Applications for the Public Sector.* (6th edn). Belmont, CA: Wadsworth, 2002, ch. 7.

Miners, Norman. *The Government and Politics of Hong Kong* (5th edn). Hong Kong: Oxford University Press, 1998, pp. 14–29, 43–49.

Mullins, Daniel and Philip Joyce. "Tax and Expenditure Limitations and State and Local Fiscal Structure: An Empirical Assessment," *Public Budgeting and Finance* 16, no. 1 (spring 1996): 75–101.

North, Douglass. *Institutions, Institutional Change and Economic Performance.* New York: Cambridge University Press, 1990. pp. 3–10.

Posner, Paul and Bryon Gordon. "Can Democratic Government Save? Experiences of Countries with Budget Surpluses." *Public Budgeting and Finance* 21, no. 2 (summer 2001): 1–28.

Reddick, Christopher. "Testing Rival Decision-making Theories on Budget Output: Theories and Comparative Evidence," *Public Budgeting and Finance* 22, no. 3 (fall 2002): 1–25.

Rosen, Harvey. *Public Finance* (6th edn). New York: McGraw-Hill/Irwin, 2002, ch. 12.

Rubin, Irene. *The Politics of Public Budgeting* (4th edn). New York: Chatham House, 2000, pp. 24–31.

Saturno, James and Richard Forgette. "The Balanced Budget Amendment: How Would It Be Enforced?," *Public Budgeting and Finance* 18, no. 1 (spring 1998): 33–53.

Slemrod, Joel and Jon Bakija. *Taxing Ourselves: A Citizen's Guide to the Great Debate over Tax Reform* (2nd edn). Cambridge, MA: MIT Press, 2001, ch. 6.

Straussman, Jeffrey. "Ideals and Reality in the Evolution of Fiscal Reform in Central and Eastern Europe," *Public Budgeting and Finance* 16, no. 2 (summer 1996): 79–95.

Sung, Yun-Wing. "Hong Kong Economy in Crisis," in *The First Tung Chee-hwa Administration*, ed. Siu-kai Lau. Hong Kong: The Chinese University Press, 2002.

Stanley, Vanagunas. "Problems of Budgeting during 'Great Transformation'." *Public Budgeting and Finance* 15, no. 1 (spring 1995): 84–95.

Tsebelis, George and Eric Chang. "Veto Players and the Structure of Budgets in Advanced Industrialized Countries," *European Journal of Political Research* 43: (2004): 449–476.

World Bank. *East Asian Miracle: Economic Growth and Public Policy.* Washington, DC: Oxford University Press, 1993.

Wong, Wilson. "The Second Term of Chief Executive Tung Chee-hwa," in *Brookings Northeast Asia Survey 2002–2003*, ed. Richard Bush and Catharin Dalpino. Washington, DC, 2003.

Zee, Howell, *et al. Hong Kong SAR: Policy and Administrative Issues in Introducing a Good and Services Tax.* Washington, DC: Fiscal Affairs Department, International Monetary Fund, 2001.

7 Social mobilization, blame avoidance, and welfare restructuring in Hong Kong

Eliza W.Y. Lee

Introduction

In the past three decades, many states, both Western and non-Western, have undergone major restructuring in their social programs in response to factors such as economic globalization and socioeconomic change. Although the pressures faced are similar, the method and degree of restructuring differ widely among countries. This difference is said to have been caused by various institutional and historical factors (Pierson 2001a). As far as the characteristics of political regimes are concerned, studies have found that governments of Western liberal democracies are more constrained than authoritarian states in making radical cutbacks in social spending, as the pressure of electoral politics prompts "blame avoidance" strategies on the part of politicians. At the same time, studies have also revealed that authoritarian states with a high level of socioeconomic development will be more constrained in cutting back on social spending than less developed states. This chapter seeks to examine the characteristics of Hong Kong's welfare restructuring, and the relevance of social mobilization by societal actors and "blame avoidance" from political actors in affecting the dynamics of restructuring.

Hong Kong is sometimes described as a liberal autocracy (Zakaria 1997). It remained a British colony until it was returned to Chinese rule in 1997 as a Special Administrative Region (The Hong Kong Special Administrative Region, or the HKSAR) under the concept of "one country, two systems." Since the 1980s, partial democracy has been introduced in the sense that a portion of the seats of the legislature are returned by universal suffrage. The government, including the chief executive, remains non-elected. Civil liberties have been fairly well protected, especially since the latter days of colonial rule (from around the 1970s). It is thus worth exploring how a city-state that is non-liberal democratic, with a high level of socioeconomic development and a robust civil society, has been handling the fiscal pressure on the welfare regime and popular pressure for maintaining if not increasing welfare spending.

The politics of welfare restructuring in Western welfare states

Since the 1970s, Western welfare states have been generally confronted with financial austerity, and such a situation is often attributed to economic globalization and socioeconomic change. While economic globalization has pressurized states to adopt "market-friendly" policies such as low public expenditure and reduced tax rates (Mishra 1999; Rhodes 2001: 168–172), socioeconomic change including an aging population and changes in family structure have contributed to increasing demand for welfare programs. Added to the problem are high unemployment rates caused by stagnant economic growth and market fluctuations, which impose a further burden on social security programs (Pierson 2001a).

Despite these pressures, scholars dispute the logic that economic globalization and socioeconomic change will necessarily lead to the dismantling of the welfare state. Iversen (2001) contends that economic openness leads to labor market dislocation resulting in strong domestic demand for more state protection against economic fluctuation. Others point to the fact that economic openness has been the external condition of many welfare states, and does not necessarily mean that states will lose their autonomy in social policy. Indeed, while subjected to common pressure, states have not converged on the same mode of restructuring, because this is determined by a political rather than an economistic logic (Mkandawire 2001; Pierson 2001a). As Schwartz (2001) points out, we need to understand "the reasons actors transform economic pressures into policy choices and the specific causal mechanisms linking pressures, interests, policy preferences, and policy outcomes" to the restructuring of the welfare state (p. 30). Similarly, Pierson (2001b) regards policy reform as *"a political process, dependent on the mobilization of political resources sufficient to overcome organized opponents and other barriers to change"* (p. 411, my emphasis).

Pierson (1996) argues that the politics of welfare state expansion is qualitatively different from the politics of retrenchment. Historically, post-WWII welfare state expansion in western liberal democracies was mainly supported by labor unions and left wing political parties. It was generally a process of political credit claiming as it involved "the enactment of *popular* policies in a relatively undeveloped interest-group environment." The development of the welfare state, however, generated a totally different political dynamic, as social programs have given rise to the emergence of powerful interest groups. The politics of retrenchment thus entails imposing "tangible losses on concentrated groups of voters." The "negativity bias" of voters means that officials "must withstand the scrutiny of both voters and well-entrenched networks of interest groups" in their pursuit of unpopular policies. Any attempt at cutback is thus an exercise in blame avoidance. In public policy literature, blame avoidance denotes the tendency of politicians to avoid policies that will impose substantial loss on a concentrated group of voters in their constituency, even if they are "good" policies that might bring about real benefit to other voters, since the voters who have suffered loss will punish the politicians by voting them out of office (Weaver 1986). Weaver (1986) notes that policy-makers respond to potential blame-generating pressures by either attempting to prevent a blame-generating situation from arising in the first place, or by deflecting blame on to others, or at least attempt to diffuse it broadly. Such blame-avoiding strategies include shifting the blame on to others (finding a scapegoat), limiting the agenda, redefining the issue, and so on. Hood (2002) further categorizes blame-avoiding strategies into three types: presentational strategies, which entail selecting arguments to minimize or avoid blame; policy strategies, for which policy positions are selected to minimize blame; and agency strategies, which minimize blame through the selection of institutional arrangements.

In sum, welfare restructuring may be seen as a political process, in which one major dynamic is constituted by the ability of society to mobilize opposition and the ability of the state to avoid blame.

Welfare restructuring in non-Western states

In terms of welfare restructuring in non-Western states, the study by Brown and Hunter (1999) has shown that authoritarian regimes are more likely to cut back on social spending than democratic regimes in the face of economic downturn, as authoritarian rulers do not have to be concerned about short-term popularity or constraints on human rights. On the other hand, authoritarian states with a high GDP and a well-developed middle class and civil society may find it hard to repress popular demand, and may even need to appease social groups that are able to challenge them. Kaufman and Segura-Ubiergo (2001) show that autocratic regimes whose bases of power are linked to certain societal groups may tend to protect social programs which benefit that specific sector of the population (in this case, spending on social security).

Historically, the establishment of welfare programs in Asian late industrializers was part of a project to spur economic expansion. Social programs were established and expanded in order to complement the needs of economic development. The founding of a welfare system was thus state-led rather than due to pressure of labor unions or left-wing parties in a setting of competitive politics. The Asian welfare model typically entails relatively low levels of welfare spending; an ideological rejection of welfare as a citizen's right; an emphasis on self-help and reliance on the family; and the use of social programs as a policy instrument for state-building and economic development (Goodman *et al.* 1998).

The underdevelopment of welfare programs had been partially compensated by a relatively young population, sustained economic growth, and rising wages in real terms. In recent years, however, socioeconomic development has brought about an aging population, the decline of the traditional family, and rising expectations, all of which necessitate higher levels of state provision of welfare. At the same time, economic globalization pressurizes states to adopt market-friendly policies in order to maintain their economic competitiveness, making it more difficult for states to increase social spending. Thus Asian NICs are faced with internal pressure to enter a new phase of *welfare expansion* while the external economic conditions impose a pressure toward *welfare retrenchment*. Faced with these challenges, among the four Asian NICs, some distinct patterns of policy response have emerged which reflect the differences in political regimes and their state of political development. In South Korea and Taiwan, democratization and electoral politics have brought social rights to the public agenda, compelling these states to adopt progressive reforms in favor of more inclusive social security systems (Lee 1999; Tsai 2001). Singapore and Hong Kong, on the other hand, remain authoritarian states without much progress toward inclusive social policy reform. Singapore has largely restructured its social programs through multiple strategies of consolidation, expansion, recalibration, and retrenchment in line with its political and developmental objectives. The restructuring in Hong Kong is characterized by cutbacks in expenditure, leading to the retrenchment of the residual welfare state that has been established since the 1970s (Lee 2006). These Asian cases show that, confronted with the challenge of economic globalization and socioeconomic change, states have made different policy choices regarding the development of their welfare systems. Currently, a body of literature is emerging in an attempt to capture the characteristics of adjustment of the Asian welfare model and the politics of social policy development.

Among the various factors that can affect social policy development, the significance of social mobilization has been receiving more scholarly attention. In particular, Kwon (2002, 2005) has adopted the concept of advocacy coalitions to study the politics of healthcare reform in Korea (Kwon 2002) and comparative social policy reform in Korea and Taiwan (2005), paying particular attention to the collaboration between political actors across the state and non-state institutions. Wong's (2004) comparative study of healthcare politics in Taiwan and South Korea represents a major contribution to the study of the relationship between democratization and welfare. His work sheds light on, among other things, the importance of coalition-building and policy learning on the part of societal actors in effecting welfare policy change. Hsiao's (2001) study of the social welfare movement in Taiwan has also shown how the structure of civil society and the linkages of important social actors may have a direct impact on social policy development.

In the case of Hong Kong, as mentioned, its liberal autocratic system is characterized by the simultaneous presence of civil liberties and the absence of popular elections as a way of choosing the government.[1] This institutional arrangement logically leads to several results. First, the absence of popular elections as a mechanism for choosing the government means that the state is not strongly compelled to be responsive to popular demands when making public policy. On the other hand, the presence of civil liberties means that citizens can make demands on the state through robust interest group activities and social mobilization by various civil society groups.

The implication of these institutional characteristics on social policy development is that, while the liberal autocratic state has a strong tendency to limit the growth of collective consumption in social policy, avenues are available for societal actors to demand such growth. Social programs have also generated their own beneficiaries who will naturally protest against any cutback in benefits. Given the fact that a liberal autocracy lacks both the mandate conferred by popular elections and the option of suppressing political dissent, the basis of legitimacy of the state is tied to its policy performance, and societal mobilization will have a destabilization effect on the political regime. The result is a tendency toward blame avoidance in its policy decisions, a trend we have witnessed in recent years.[2]

In what follows, we shall examine the mode of welfare restructuring that Hong Kong has undergone in the postcolonial years, and look at how social mobilization and blame avoidance have dynamically shaped the outcome of such restructuring.

Characteristics of the welfare system in Hong Kong and the mode of welfare restructuring

Hong Kong as a residual welfare state

Like other Asian NICs, Hong Kong has been openly "anti-welfare" in the sense that it rejects a high level of social spending and does not wish to recognize welfare as a set of social rights. Instead, the ideology of self-reliance is heavily promoted. Priority is given to creating a favorable environment for economic development, including minimal labor protection and favorable tax rates for private corporations.

Compared with other Asian NICs, Hong Kong's social policy approach is distinguished by a relatively higher level of state financing, and a high reliance on nonprofit organizations (NPOs) in provision especially in the areas of education and social services. These special features are closely related to the history of the development of its social programs. During the colonial era up until the 1960s, state financing and provision of social programs was minimal. In the 1970s, after two major social riots which demonstrated deep social discontent with the colonial government, the latter greatly expanded social provision in the areas of education, healthcare, social assistance and services, and public housing. This "big bang" phase of welfare development (Tang 1998) represented a belated response on the part of the colonial state to the political discontent with the colonial government. Due to the limited capacity of the state, NPOs that were previously engaged in voluntary service were heavily utilized in social provision (Lee 2005a). Despite the expansion in state financing and provision of the welfare system, however, it remains largely "residual" in nature. The social provision was largely financed by taxation, with little attempt at institutionalization through insurance systems. The level of service output was thus tied to the revenue of the government (Lee 2005b, 2005c).

While the welfare system was residual, it has definitely enhanced the legitimacy of the political regime in providing a standard of human service and welfare that was generous by Third World standards, and which has improved the livelihood of the people. The residual welfare state constituted a social pact and contributed toward "consensus capitalism." In this sense, the welfare expansion was historically a credit-claiming exercise for the authoritarian state.

Welfare restructuring in Hong Kong: the retrenchment of the residual welfare state

The financial viability of the residual welfare state was met with a severe challenge following the Asian financial crisis, as the budget deficit had snowballed to a record high of 65 billion dollars, or 5.2 percent of GDP, by 2002. The government decided that the budget deficit needed to be eliminated as soon as possible lest the territory be downgraded by international credit rating agencies. In the face of the huge budget shortfall, the government imposed budget cuts across all policy areas. In the budget speech delivered in 2002, the official policy was laid down to reduce public expenditure from 22 percent to 20 percent of GDP by 2007. Subsequently, a range of recommodification and cost containment measures has either been adopted or proposed across the various social programs. In sum, in the face of economic globalization and socioeconomic change, Hong Kong has taken a largely budget-driven approach in welfare restructuring and this has resulted in the retrenchment of the residual welfare state (Lee 2006).

It suffices to highlight the major retrenchment measures in Hong Kong's social programs. In education, under-enrolled schools have been shut down despite strong societal demand to make use of the lowering birth rate to implement small-class teaching; and substantial budget cuts have been imposed on universities, including the withdrawal of public funding to associate degree and taught Masters programs. The salaries of university staff have been delinked from the civil service pay scale, thus allowing universities to cut salaries and fringe benefits of their staff. Private schools and Direct Subsidy Schools (DSS) are encouraged, both of which entail letting users pay higher fees for better quality education. In social welfare, there has been an increase in the number of CSSA cases in recent years, especially since the Asian financial crisis. The government has reduced the amount of subsidies, and imposed more stringent eligibility criteria such as a seven-year residency requirement. The budget for social services is also capped through new funding schemes for nonprofit organizations, namely the Lump Sum Grant System (LSGS), which give social service agencies more autonomy in determining staff salaries and other uses of the annual grant. Critics see the new funding system as a way to put a ceiling on if not to cutback on social service spending.

In 2002, the government, allegedly under pressure from real estate developers, finally announced the permanent cessation of the Home Ownership Scheme (HOS), thus forcing low-income families to buy apartments from the private market. The scheme for selling rental public housing to tenants was also suspended. The supply of public housing is capped at a three-year waiting period. A more stringent residency requirement is imposed so as to limit the eligibility of new migrants (mostly from mainland China) for rented public housing. In public health, the long-term sustainability of the public healthcare system is under strain as a result of the aging population and the rising cost of healthcare. The government has issued a few consultancy reports, all pointing to the need for new schemes of healthcare financing. There is, however, a lack of public support for or consensus on fundamental change to the status quo. Lacking political support, the government has not been able to pursue any reform plan. Meanwhile, budget cuts have been imposed on the Hospital Authority, forcing it to adopt measures such as salary cuts, hiring freezes, and more user charges (Lee 2005b, 2005c, 2006).

Social mobilization, blame avoidance, and welfare restructuring

As expected, the cutback on social programs is naturally unpopular and has aroused societal opposition. The question is to what extent such social discontent has been translated into political pressure and whether such pressure has effectively limited the state in attempting such cutbacks. In Hong Kong, the political system consists of an unelected executive, a partially popularly elected legislature, and a number of partially elected District Councils with no real executive power. As these competitive elections do not function as a means of selecting the government, the elections are not effective mechanisms for sanctioning the state from imposing unpopular policies from the top down. Electoral politics are, however, not totally insignificant in placing blame on the government. Especially, veto points do exist in the political institution that may restrain governmental actions. At the same time, under a system in which civil liberties are fairly well protected, robust interest group activities are allowed to proliferate which may exert significant pressure on the state. The effect of such pressures can be augmented by the critical views of the mass media, which plays a crucial role in shaping public opinion. On the other hand, studies have shown that even though collective actions are common in Hong Kong, they seldom take place as highly institutionalized activities. Unconventional forms of political participation such as mass rallies and demonstrations are the mainstay, while most of the population does not hold membership in organizations (Lau and Kuan 1995). In social policy, for most services, the well-organized groups are the public service professionals rather than the majority of the recipients of the services. This characteristic means that popular pressure is not forceful enough to effect great concession from the state, while the state is able to employ blame-avoidance strategies to shift the blame and marginalize the demands of organized interests.

The dominance of public service professionals as the major organized interests is evident in public health, education, and social services. In public health, the budget cut has put the Hospital Authority in a situation of acute financial austerity, and both medical staff and patients have suffered from the negative consequences. The worsening of the working environment has aroused protest actions from medical professionals. In education, the retrenchment in funding has affected various parties, including teachers, school principals, university heads, students, and parents. Among them, the teachers' unions are the most organized, while university student associations and heads of schools and universities have also stated their opposition and some have staged protest actions.

In social services, the government-funded NPOs that are responsible for delivering 90 percent of the service have suffered from budget cuts that have led to reductions in staff numbers, salary cuts, and the replacement of senior staff with those more junior as a means of reducing expenditure. The cutback has aroused protest action from social workers. Despite being confronted with these protests against the worsening employment conditions and work environment, and compromised professional standards and delivery of service, the government has so far been able to push through most of the reforms. The employment of blame-avoidance tactics is evident in several aspects. The first is the employment of policy strategies. The major cutback in spending has occurred in the form of salary cuts and the freeze in staff numbers, making the human service professionals the groups that are most directly hit by the cutback. Responding to their organized protests, the state has employed tactful representational strategies to marginalize these complaints as a selfish defense of parochial interests that stand against the interests of the public. Officials have framed the issue as one of appropriate use of taxpayers' resources. In addition, given one major characteristic of social provision in Hong Kong is that the service providers are predominantly either nonprofit organizations (as in the case of education and social service) or public corporations that operate at arm's length from the government, the autonomy in financial and personnel management "enjoyed" by these institutions makes it relatively easy for the state to impose financial cutbacks without the more rigid constraints of the civil service regulations (which would have been in force had the service provider been the government itself).[3] Thus, the state has agencies' strategies available to hand, enabling them to shift the blame through altering institutional arrangements.

Conversely, the impact of the cutback is either more indirectly felt by the users of the service or imposed upon users that are disempowered. In the case of education and public health, it is true that both the middle and working class are affected by the retrenchment. However, under the current welfare regime, the services provided are typically at a basic level that can barely satisfy the needs of the middle class. The middle class has been driven to exit the state system and opt to buy better quality service from the private market. A situation of cutback in social provision will likely further drive the middle-class users that are used to self-help to turn to market alternatives. This explains why the middle-class users who are most likely to make demands for good-quality education and health are not strongly protesting against the retrenchment in service. Where the lower class users are affected, they have limited means to defend their interests. In the case of reducing the amount of means-tested social assistance (the Comprehensive Social Security Assistance Scheme (CSSA)), NGOs and activists have mobilized recipients to protest against the cuts in benefits, citing the hardship of poor people in conditions of recession and economic restructuring. The government countered by stepping up propaganda, citing cases of fraud and figures proving that the amount had been overly generous, while associating CSSA recipients with new migrants and able-bodied adults who had low incentive to find jobs. Such a tactic of stigmatization marginalizes the voice of the social assistance recipients, and renders their political demand illegitimate to the larger populace.

In certain areas in social policy where the interests are highly organized among the users of the provision, these organized interests are able to significantly influence the policy approach of the state. For instance, in social security, to cope with the economic downturn, the business community demanded that contributions to the Mandatory Provident Fund (MPF) be temporarily suspended in order to lower business costs. The proposal aroused strong protests from labor groups and was never endorsed. Traditionally, private labor unions have always been marginalized if not rendered powerless under the current labor regime, in which there is no legal right to collective bargaining or to strike. Neither is there a corporatist arrangement of any kind for labor to exert influence on policies affecting their welfare and livelihood. The degree of unionization of the working population in the private sector is rather low (Chiu and Levin 2000, p. 97). Nonetheless, the major private labor unions still have over 200,000 members altogether, and in recent years an increasing level of labor union activism can be detected in actions such as forging strategic alliances with political parties, coalition formation among unions of different ideological stances in pushing for labor rights, and temporary alliances with community groups in protest movements. In elections, unions are a major source of support of pro-grassroot candidates with a social democratic stance. The labor unions also have designated seats in the functional constituency sector. Thus, in matters that affect the collective benefits of labor, the activism of labor unions can exert a powerful influence on public policy.

Another illustration of the power of highly organized interests is public housing. Given the massive stakeholdership the benefit entailed, housing has been a highly political area of collective consumption. In the 1970s and 1980s, many social movements and grassroots activism against the colonial government were directed toward public housing (Ho 2000), and over the years, the availability of subsidized rental housing has become a de facto political entitlement to the tenants. Pressure groups such as the People's Council on Public Housing Policy (PCPHP) have been able to link up various neighborhood associations and local concern groups (Ho 2000, p. 194). At the same time, as the largest owner of land, the government has been counting on a high land price policy as a means of ensuring that the selling of land is a major source of public revenue, and such land policy has been associated with the continuous rise in the price of real estate up until the onset of the Asian financial crisis. Over the years, such housing and land policy has created multiple political interests. While the middle- and lower-class citizens have come to expect the government to take care of their housing needs, real estate tycoons and the property-owning class are interested in the maintenance of a booming real estate market. As such, the housing and land policy is characterized by multiple and conflicting organized interests that the state feels pressured to satisfy. The government is politically constrained by the interests of the property-owning class and real estate developers who want to maintain the price of real estate, and also by the need to continue satisfying the sense of entitlement of the working class through subsidized housing. As a result, amidst financial austerity and the international trend toward the privatization of public housing, the government still maintains a large public housing project.

Electoral politics cut in where sectoral interests collaborate with political parties. Political parties in Hong Kong currently play only a limited role in shaping social policy reform, as their political role remains one of either opposionists or pro-government members in the legislature. Elected legislature, especially those from the democratic camp or those representing grassroots interests, will often oppose government cutback policies through making open criticisms or organizing collective action (such as demonstrations and rallies) in order to delegitimize the policies. Thus, the elected oppositionists are blame creators for the unelected government. Aside from popularly elected members, half of the Legislative Council is currently returned by functional constituencies, which elect representatives from selected sectors that are awarded one or more seats. These functional constituencies lean heavily toward pro-business and pro-establishment forces, although sectors such as education, health, social services, and labor occupy a minority of seats. These functional constituency representatives may then bring the voice of their sectors into the legislature. On some occasions, these sectors may successfully utilize the institutional "veto points" offered by the legislature. For instance, in the case of budget cuts in university funding, the strong protest actions of university students and the opposition of university presidents caused the Finance Committee of the Legislative Council to threaten to vote down the government's request for appropriation in education, thus forcing the government to make minor concessions in the level of the budget cut.

While the lack of highly organized interests among the general users of the services has led to ineffective challenges to cutbacks in social spending, the pluralism in interests prevents the state from enforcing major policy reform. The case of public health shows that the state has been unable to aggregate diverse societal interests and command public consensus so as to realize fundamental change in the mode of financing and provision of healthcare service. In this sense, financial cutback becomes the only viable choice in the face of the unsustainability of the present system.

The politics of welfare restructuring in Hong Kong: the neoliberal turn and interest pluralism in a liberal autocratic state

Confronted with the pressure of economic globalization and socioeconomic change, Hong Kong has adopted the strategy of retrenching its residual welfare state that was established in the 1970s. Contrary to local official discourse, such retrenchment is not the inevitable choice of an open economy confronted with economic and financial austerity. Rather, as studies show, welfare restructuring is often structured by politics. The major possible factor enabling cutbacks in social spending is the lack of pressure of competitive elections that is largely present in an electoral democracy. The absence of contested elections as a mechanism for choosing government means that elections cannot act as strong constraints on the state in pursuing unpopular reforms. On the other hand, as Weaver (1986) points out, and as substantiated by Brown and Hunter (1999), blame avoidance is relevant to liberal democracies as well as to authoritarian states. In an authoritarian state like Hong Kong, the basis of state legitimacy has been tied to policy performance, including public service quality and the achievement of economic growth. Despite the rhetoric of anti-welfarism and self-reliance, social programs have definitely generated their own beneficiaries and shaped social expectations, such that the withdrawal of benefits may generate public dissatisfaction and have a negative impact on state legitimacy. As a liberal autocracy with a mature civil society, Hong Kong cannot resort to strong repressive measures but would have to concede to popular sentiment in attempting any retrenchment measures. Thus the objective of blame avoidance for an authoritarian state is not to maximize its chance of re-election but to maintain its legitimacy to rule through maintaining public satisfaction at an acceptable level. Based on such observations, this chapter has sought to study whether social mobilization may have any relevance in constraining the state in its attempt to cut back on social spending.

The result shows that, in the case of Hong Kong, in order for interest group politics to make a significant impact on social policy, the interests must be highly organized, and the negative impact must also be concentrated such that a significant number of beneficiaries feel directly affected. The pattern of interest group formation and the structure of social programs are thus crucial to understanding the political limits of retrenchment, as they are related to the level of political pressure that are exerted on to the state and the strategy of blame avoidance that are available to the state. Where the recipients of the provision are highly organized and the negative impact of the retrenchment of the service is highly concentrated on the recipients, the state will be much more constrained in retrenching the service, as the cases of public housing and MPF show. Where the recipients are weakly organized, and market alternatives to that service are available to some members (especially the middle class), the pressure on the state will be much weaker. Where the organized interests are mainly confined to a relatively small or powerless sector, such as the human service professionals and the social assistance recipients, it is possible for the state to marginalize these sectoral interests through resorting to various strategies of blame avoidance, such as presentational, policy, and agency strategies.

As a whole, Hong Kong's situation seems to resemble that of welfare retrenchment in the liberal welfare states. Among Western liberal democracies, liberal welfare states such as Britain, New Zealand, and Australia have taken the most neoliberal turn in retrenching the welfare state. According to Pierson (2001a), the possibility of extensive cutbacks in these welfare states is related to the characteristics of the political and welfare regime. These states are characterized by the lack of strong linkage between the welfare system and the market economies; the inability of the systems "to pursue negotiated reform through systems of organized interest intermediation"; the weak attachment of the middle class to the system of public provision; the lack of power for labor to veto change; and the ability of political parties to win elections even without obtaining the majority vote under a strong two-party parliamentary system, allowing the government in power to pursue "electoral dictatorship." In Hong Kong, unlike other Asian NICs that are strong developmental states, there has been a weak linkage between social policy and political and developmental objectives. Rather, the public financial policy has been procyclical in nature (Tang 1994) and the level of social spending in Hong Kong has long been determined by the level of state revenue. Its interest group model resembles that of the pluralistic model rather than the corporatist model. The absence of systems of organized interest intermediation is coupled by the inability of political parties to aggregate political interests through the electoral process, making it possible for the authoritarian state to exploit the situation and adopt a "divide-and-rule" strategy among the different interests. The lack of attachment of the middle class to the welfare system is the natural result of a residual welfare state in which collective consumption is only provided at a minimal level. Unlike the situation of some Latin American states, the ruling position of the state in Hong Kong is not tied to the provision of social benefit of any single sector.

In sum, the absence of electoral democracy coupled with interest pluralism makes it possible for the authoritarian state to pursue neoliberal reform in its social policy. At the same time, this liberal autocratic state also lacks the legitimacy and the capacity to aggregate diverse social interests to come up with fundamental reforms in the existing welfare system, other than cutbacks, even though the system is found to be out of phase with the state of socioeconomic development. This is evident in the inability of the state to reform the public healthcare system despite a wide recognition that the current system is not financially sustainable, or to put forward proposals for large-scale reforms such as changing the taxation system in order to support the further institutionalization of the welfare state. In a way, when mobilizations by societal actors are met with blame-avoidance behavior from state actors, the result is the inability to carry out reform, and this might exacerbate the crisis of the residual welfare state as the present system is increasingly found to be unable to meet the challenges of economic globalization and socioeconomic change. Ultimately, the solution to such a problem lies in democratization.

Notes

1 The presence of civil liberties dates back to the era of British colonial rule. Upon China's resumption of sovereignty over Hong Kong, the Hong Kong Special Administrative Region was established under the principle of "one country, two systems." Through the Basic Law, the mini-constitution of the HKSAR, civil liberties, and the "capitalist ways of life" are largely preserved and guaranteed through constitutional provisions. At the same time, democracy is still largely restricted. For details see Hong Kong (1990).

2 This tendency seems to have started in the later years of Tung Chee-Hwa's (the first Chief Executive) leadership, when public dissatisfaction toward the government's policy performance led to a crisis in legitimacy.
3 The government had a hard time trying to cut the salaries of civil service personnel, especially because Article 100 of the Basic Law stipulated that the salaries and benefits of the civil servants of the HKSAR cannot be lower than that before 1997. The clause was originally put in by the drafters of the Basic Law in order to ensure stability during the political transition. It has now become a major obstacle for the government to cut down on public spending amidst economic recession and budgetary crisis.

References

Brown, D.S. and Hunter, W. 1999. "Democracy and Social Spending in Latin America, 1980–92," *American Political Science Review* 93 (4): 779–790.

Chiu, S.W.K. 1994. *The Politics of Laissez-faire: Hong Kong's Strategy of Industrialization in Historical Perspective*, Hong Kong Institute of Asia-Pacific Studies: Occasional Paper No. 40. Hong Kong: The Chinese University of Hong Kong.

Chiu, S.W.K. and D.A. Levin. 2000. "Contestatory Unionism: Trade Unions in the Private Sector." In *The Dynamics of Social Movement in Hong Kong*, ed. S.W.K. Chiu and T.L. Lui, 91–137. Hong Kong: University of Hong Kong Press.

Goodman, R., G. White, and Huck-ju Kwon (eds). 1998. *The East Asian Welfare Model: Welfare Orientalism and the State*. London: Routledge.

Ho, D.K.L. 2000. "The Rise and Fall of Community Mobilization: The Housing Movement in Hong Kong." In *The Dynamics of Social Movement in Hong Kong*, ed. S.W.K. Chiu and T.L. Liu, 185–208. Hong Kong: University of Hong Kong Press.

Hong Kong. 1990. *Basic Law of the Hong Kong Special Administrative Region of the People's Republic of China*. Hong Kong: Government Printer.

Hood, C. 2002. "The Risk Game and the Blame Game," *Government and Opposition* 37 (1): 5–37.

Hsiao, H.-H. 2001. "Taiwan's Social Welfare Movement since the 1980s." In *Understanding Modern Taiwan: Essays in Economics, Politics and Social Policy*, ed. Christian Aspalter, 169–204. Alderdot: Ashgate.

Iversen, T. 2001. "The Dynamics of Welfare State Expansion: Trade Openness, Deindustrialization, and Partisan Politics." In *The Politics of the Welfare State*, ed. Paul Pierson, 45–79. Cambridge, MA: Harvard University Press.

Kaufman, R.R. and A. Segura-Ubiergo. 2001. "Globalization, Domestic Politics, and Social Spending in Latin America: A Time Series Cross-section Analysis, 1973–97," *World Politics* 53 (July): 553–587.

Kwon, Huck-ju. 2002. "Advocacy Coalitions and the Politics of Welfare in Korea after the Economic Crisis," *Policy and Politics* 31: 69–83.

——. 2005. "Transforming the Developmental Welfare State in East Asia," *Development and Change* 36, 3: 477–497.

Lau, S.K. and Kuan, H.C. 1985. "The Attentive Spectators: Political Participation of the Hong Kong Chinese," *Journal of Northeast Asian Studies* 14 (1): 3–24.

Lee, E.W.Y. 2005a. "Nonprofit Development in Hong Kong: The Case of a Statist-corporatist Regime," *Voluntas* 16 (March): 51–68.

——. 2005b. "The Renegotiation of the Social Pact in Hong Kong: Economic Globalisation, Socio-economic Change, and Local Politics," *Journal of Social Policy* 34 (2): 293–310.

———. 2005c. *The Politics of Welfare Developmentalism in Hong Kong.* United Nations Research Institute for Social Development Programme Occasional Paper No. 21.

———. 2006. "Welfare Restructuring in Asian Newly Industrialized Countries: A Comparison of Hong Kong and Singapore," *Policy and Politic* 34 (3): 453–471.

Lee, H.K. 1999. "Globalization and the Emerging Welfare State – The Experience of South Korea," *International Journal of Social Welfare* 8: 31–37.

Mishra, R. 1999. *Globalization and the Welfare State.* Massachusetts: Edward Elgar.

Mkandawire, T. 2001. *Social Policy in a Development Context.* United Nations Research Institute for Social Development: Social Policy and Development Programme Paper No. 7.

Pierson, P. 1996. "The New Politics of the Welfare State," *World Politics* 48 (2): 143–179.

———. 2001a. "Coping with Permanent Austerity: Welfare State Restructuring in Affluent Democracies." In *The New Politics of the Welfare State*, ed. P. Pierson, 410–456. Oxford: Oxford University Press.

———. 2001b. "Post-industrial Pressures on the Mature Welfare States." In *The New Politics of the Welfare State*, ed. P. Pierson, 80–104. Oxford: Oxford University Press.

Rhodes, M. 2001. "The Political Economy of Social Pacts: 'Competitive Corporatism' and European Welfare Reform." In *The New Politics of the Welfare State*, ed. P. Pierson, 165–194. New York: Oxford University Press.

Schwartz, H. 2001. "Round Up the Usual Suspects! Globalization, Domestic Politics, and Welfare State Change." In *The New Politics of the Welfare State*, ed. P. Pierson, 17–44. New York: Oxford University Press.

Tang, K.-L. 1998. *Colonial State and Social Policy: Social Welfare Development in Hong Kong, 1842–1997.* Maryland: University Press of America, Inc.

Tang, S. H. 1994. "The Political Economy of Fiscal Policy in Hong Kong: A Historical Perspective." In *25 Years of Social and Economic Development in Hong Kong*, ed. B.K.P. Leung and T.Y.C. Wong, 602–631. Hong Kong: University of Hong Kong Press.

Tsai, M.C. 2001. "Dependency, the State and Class in the Neoliberal Transition of Taiwan," *Third World Quarterly* 22 (3): 359–379.

Weaver, R.K. 1986. "The Politics of Blame Avoidance," *Journal of Public Policy* 6 (4): 371–398.

Wong, J. 2004. *Healthy Democracies: Welfare Politics in Taiwan and South Korea.* Ithaca, NY: Cornell University Press.

Wong, Y.-C.R. 1998. *On Privatizing Public Housing.* Hong Kong: City University of Hong Kong Press.

Zakaria, F. 1997. "The Rise of Illiberal Democracy," *Foreign Affairs* 76 (6): 22–43.

8 The external challenge of Hong Kong's governance

Global responsibility for a world city

Lucy M. Cummings and James T.H. Tang

Introduction

Hong Kong's international personality has always been an important part of what makes it unique. This chapter argues that capitalizing on this asset by adopting a more visible and globally responsible external agenda will help address its governance challenges – in other words, Hong Kong should think globally in its efforts to improve governance locally.

In evaluating the external challenge to Hong Kong's governance and whether domestic governance could be improved with a globally responsible agenda, this study reviews Hong Kong's external relations performance and analyzes public attitudes toward global issues in Hong Kong based on an opinion survey conducted by this study.[1] Its findings indicate that a more visible and proactive globally responsible external relations agenda may advance governance in Hong Kong by (1) drawing local and international attention to the uniqueness of what the Hong Kong community has to offer the nation and the world, and (2) strengthening the confidence of Hong Kong people in their leaders. It also suggests that by accentuating Hong Kong's contribution to the nation and the world, a globally responsible agenda may help enhance social cohesion at home by helping to bridge class, political, and generational cleavages.

Hong Kong's leaders have been too timid in exercising the constitutional autonomy provided by the Basic Law to manage Hong Kong's external relations. Pro-actively and visibly participating in the global arena on issues not limited to commercial self-interest will help Hong Kong to maintain its distinctive international character and enhance its collective self-esteem.

Hong Kong's post-1997 external relations: the need to move beyond economics

Hong Kong's success and prosperity has always been closely related to its special international status and extensive global linkages.[2] The framers of Hong Kong's Basic Law understood this and so, since 1997, under the "One Country, Two Systems" framework (OCTS), Hong Kong's Basic Law has provided the constitutional basis for Hong Kong to conduct and manage its own "external affairs" while preserving the Central People's Government (CPG)'s control over Hong Kong's "foreign affairs."[3]

In practice, the CPG has accorded Hong Kong significant autonomy over the management of its own external affairs, limiting CPG involvement to areas of "high foreign policy," which traditionally includes issues such as international legal recognition, territorial claims, and areas related to international peace and security.[4] Examples of Hong Kong's latitude in managing its own external affairs may be seen in its separate role from the PRC as "Hong Kong, China"[5] in the World Trade Organization (WTO), the Asia Pacific Economic Conference (APEC), in international customs negotiations, in granting of refugee asylum, in visa abolition agreements, and as a member of 75 multilateral treaties of which the People's Republic of China (PRC) is not a party.[6] In these examples, as with many others, Hong Kong's authority for its external relations autonomy emanates from the CPG. As long as Hong Kong continues to demonstrate that its autonomy in conducting external relations serves the mutual interests of the Mainland and Hong Kong, the CPG will remain supportive of Hong Kong's external activities in accordance with the Basic Law.[7]

In this chapter, we will argue that Hong Kong's leaders have been too timid in exercising the constitutional autonomy provided by the Basic Law to manage Hong Kong's external relations. Both the C.H. Tung and Donald Tsang administrations have limited their focus to Hong Kong's value as a regional economic hub. The Tung administration, responding to recommendations made in 2000 by the Commission on Strategic Development, initiated an international "branding" campaign in 2001 in order to position Hong Kong internationally as "Asia's World City."[8] This global positioning strategy was "designed to highlight Hong Kong's existing strengths in areas such as financial services, trade, tourism, transport, communications, and as a regional hub for international business and a major city in China."[9] Tsang's administration has built upon this strategy and on previous groundwork conducted during Tung's administration, to further argue that Hong Kong's strengths should be considered alongside those of the Pan-Pear River Delta region (made up of nine southern Chinese provinces plus Hong Kong and Macau). In this vision, Hong Kong as "Asia's World City" is meant to provide the essential infrastructure (e.g., legal, financial, transport, and information technology) to develop this "huge regional economy in an area, with a current population of 460 million – equivalent to that of the European Union" – into a sophisticated, globally competitive engine of economic growth.[10]

Moreover, this external economic positioning strategy under both Tung and Tsang has been supported by an external relations infrastructure largely led by departments with economic functions and staffed by officials without proper training for broader external relations work or extensive overseas experiences. Very often Hong Kong's overseas Economic and Trade Offices (ETOs), the Hong Kong Trade Development Council, The Tourism Board, and business leaders provide the most visible international face for Hong Kong.

This chapter does not dispute the importance of global economic positioning, as the Tung and Tsang administrations have done, as a necessary first step in meeting Hong Kong's external relations challenges. However, an economic and commercial rationale alone is too narrow in addressing Hong Kong's external challenges. An international positioning strategy based on commercial aspects alone does nothing to distinguish Hong Kong from its major regional competitors, especially when Hong Kong has become part of China. In politics, identity is established through difference. Since Hong Kong's major regional competitors, including Singapore and Shanghai, have similar "World City" aspirations that focus on a similar combination of assets, the "Asia World City" strategy in its current form may not be able to project what is special about Hong Kong effectively.[11] Hong Kong's leadership is aware of this challenge. Donald Tsang's oft-repeated phrase during his fall 2005 overseas promotions trips, "Hong Kong will never be just another Chinese city." is an indication of his preoccupation with distinguishing Hong Kong in the eyes of the international community.[12] Given the increasing economic and social integration between Hong Kong and the Mainland, Hong Kong will have to continue to find ways to distinguish itself in order to remain worthy of the OCTS framework.

With economic and social integration between Hong Kong and the mainland becoming a foregone conclusion, what avenues does Hong Kong have at its disposal to maintain Hong Kong's distinctiveness? The global realm is a vital staging ground to assert the legitimacy of the Hong Kong Special Administrative Region's (HKSAR) political identity because Hong Kong's international status has always been an important part of its uniqueness. While other Chinese cities will inevitably become increasingly integrated with the global economy, no other Chinese city will likely be able to directly participate in the full range of international decision-making structures as readily as Hong Kong can. Capitalizing on Hong Kong's international personality by adopting a more visible and globally responsible external agenda will help strengthen local pride of place by demonstrating Hong Kong's important contribution to national and international stability and prosperity.

Moreover, by focusing not only on what it can take from the international arena, but also on what it can give back, Hong Kong will further distinguish itself in the eyes of its people and the world as a knowledgeable international player which wants to play a part in constructive solutions to the world's most pressing problems.[13] Pride of place does not only emanate from the level of per capita gross national product (GNP). A confidence that one's political community is contributing to the greater good, both nationally and internationally, can also help to strengthen community pride. Such pride will help enhance Hong Kong's legitimacy as a special place to live in the eyes of its residents. Proactively and visibly participating in the global arena on issues not limited to commercial self-interest will help Hong Kong to maintain its distinctive international character and enhance its collective self-esteem.

Global responsibility and governance: improved regime legitimacy

A globally responsible external relations agenda acknowledges that global inter-dependence makes issues in the global arena more relevant in Hong Kong resid-ents' lives than ever before. A currency crisis in one country may indirectly destabilize Hong Kong's own financial situation. A civil war in a neighboring country may lead to flows of refugees into Hong Kong. A globally responsible agenda also acknowledges that Hong Kong or even China can no longer act alone to protect its members from a growing number of transnational threats, including pollution, disease, transnational organized crime, large scale refugee flows, climate change, or international financial instability. Problems such as these require international cooperation and compromise to effect a change. While Hong Kong may not have the authority, power, or collective knowledge to unilaterally address the complexity of problems such as these, Hong Kong people have a vested self-interest in ensuring that their voice is heard and respected in the discussion of these issues at the regional and global level.

The Hong Kong community (like communities around the world) needs to see that "globalization" has not stripped its own government of its ability to protect Hong Kong citizens from the brutality of international political, finan-cial, and health contagions. In the transitional stage of Hong Kong's political existence, where reasonable disagreements exist about the type of governing structures that are best for Hong Kong, the HKSAR's international participation can be an important legitimizing factor for the Hong Kong government. Inter-national evaluations of Hong Kong's performance (including international organization or treaty body reports, bilateral reviews, or international NGO studies) are crucial resources, not only internationally but also domestically, for people to gage the Hong Kong government's effectiveness in a wide variety of areas.[14] By engaging more actively with international actors on issues of global responsibility, the Hong Kong government could widen its positive international exposure on these issues, which will reverberate down to the local community.

While national governments typically command higher degrees of authority in regulating against the excesses of globalization, people are recognizing that local governments have vital contributions to make in making people less vulnerable to the harshness of globalization. For Hong Kong in particular, people need to be convinced that their HKSAR leaders are making a difference in their lives in order to continue to support the OCTS framework.

Of course, Hong Kong's globally responsible external agenda must be in clear alignment with China's foreign policy strategy. Hong Kong is an insep-arable part of China and, in the area of foreign policy, China must have but one voice. Given that President Hu Jintao is already positioning China as a leader in the effort "to build a new just and reasonable eco-political order"[15] and given the CPG latitude afforded to Hong Kong as previously discussed, a more globally responsible external agenda for Hong Kong is consistent with the CPG's posi-tion. China's economic success since 1978 provides an amazing account of a poor country that has benefited and will continue to benefit from global eco-nomic integration generally and trade liberalization specifically.[16] Yet, as a developing country, it is also keenly aware of the obstacles that remain in continuing to raise living standards for its people. Its international strategy there-fore has to maintain a balance between continuing to support the current inter-national architecture while at the same time ensuring that this architecture is responsive to the needs of the developing world. A more pro-active and visibly globally responsible Hong Kong, conscious of the needs of those more vulner-able to the harshness of global integration, will thus serve the interests of the nation.

Canada is an example of a country that has pursued global responsibility as an important component of its foreign policy.[17] Canada's International Develop-ment Agency argues that the policy has helped to "establish Canada's reputation as a committed, constructive member of the international community – a reputa-tion that opens doors and gives Canada a stronger voice in world affairs."[18] While some critics doubt the impact of Canada's role in the world or may claim that Canada's action has not matched its rhetoric, Canada's globally responsible foreign policy has traditionally received strong domestic public support.[19] For example, three-quarters of respondents in an April, 2004 public opinion survey support Canada's continued role in international peacekeeping missions, regard-less of whether that mission was in Bosnia, Haiti, or Afghanistan.[20] Canada has used the policy to provide the government with much-needed legitimacy in the eyes of its own people. In this regard, it may serve as a model for Hong Kong's own external relations strategy.

Contrary to conventional wisdom which contends that Hong Kong people are concerned solely with domestic livelihood issues,[21] this study's survey data on public opinion toward Hong Kong's external relations and accounts of Hong Kong's global philanthropic activities[22] suggest that assumptions of Hong Kong's popular indifference toward global issues are not valid.[23] This study's survey found that not only do Hong Kong people believe that the SAR should continue to position itself as a world city, but they also believe that that role entails obligations to contribute to the greater global good.[24] Over 69 per cent of respondents felt that "Asia's World City" was an accurate description of Hong Kong's role in the world, and 88 per cent felt that if Hong Kong wanted to be seen as "Asia's World City" then it needed to contribute to the resolution of common regional problems.[25] Even putting aside Hong Kong's self-designated "World City" role, 69 percent of survey respondents believed that Hong Kong has a responsibility to try and help neighbors less fortunate than itself, such as Bangladesh or Laos.[26] Over 73 percent of our survey respondents agreed that making Hong Kong a neighbor that is more responsive and caring toward inter-national problems would make them prouder to live in Hong Kong.[27] Moreover, over 84 percent agreed that making Hong Kong a more globally responsible actor would increase Hong Kong's standing in the eyes of the rest of the world.[28] To test the validity of this sense of obligation, the study's survey also asked respondents whether they agreed with the notion that Hong Kong cannot afford to be concerned about its neighbors given its own serious social and economic problems. Only 39 per cent agreed.[29] These results suggest that there is strong practical and moral support among Hong Kong people for a more globally responsible agenda.

In addition to popular support, Hong Kong also has the constitutional and structural capacity to fulfill its role of what we would describe as "Asia's World City with a heart". Hong Kong has been granted a high degree of autonomy under the Basic Law in the area of external affairs. As a non-sovereign international actor, it has an unprecedented international presence. Beyond its high levels of economic integration with the global economy and extensive treaty obligations, Hong Kong's strong international orientation is illustrated in the government's participation (in 2000) in more than 1,300 international conferences (700 of these were limited to governments and 60 of them were as part of PRC delegations), and the presence of 104 foreign consulate and six international organizations (IFC, IMF, UNHCR, Bank for International Settlements, EU, and the World Bank) which have offices here. The Hong Kong community has a multicultural make-up and has a vibrant overseas diaspora, which serves as an international conduit for the city and its residents. In 2002, Hong Kong had over 14 million tourists visit. It has a sizable presence of international media (close to 100 foreign media organizations have offices in HK) as well as international humanitarian, educational, and environmental NGOs.

In short, while Hong Kong is not a sovereign international actor, it could use its special status as a non-sovereign international player to pursue a globally responsible external agenda that would serve governance at home. The next obvious question is: What would a globally responsible external relations agenda look like for Hong Kong? In identifying global responsibility as a key external challenge of Hong Kong's governance, the next section of this chapter will explore two potential themes, both of which fulfill three essential criteria for a globally responsible external affairs focus: each (1) demonstrates clear alignment with the Chinese national interest, (2) possesses high levels of salience for Hong Kong people, and (3) emanates from an area where Hong Kong's comparative status would enable Hong Kong to positively and concretely contribute to the region.

Global responsibility in practice: potential external relations agendas

While there are numerous potential focuses for a globally responsible Hong Kong, the two areas that fit the above three criteria and will be discussed as potential examples are the dialogue between free and fair trade and infectious disease prevention. Building upon Hong Kong's significant expertise in these areas not only highlights Hong Kong's commercial interests, but also places an equal emphasis on how Hong Kong is contributing to the alleviation of shared problems that threaten Hong Kong, China, and the world. By pro-actively and visibly demonstrating how Hong Kong "adds value" to these vital issues, Hong

Kong will gain the respect of the international community and increase the sense of pride associated with being a member of the Hong Kong community.

Free trade versus fair trade

Hong Kong can move beyond the commercially narrow version of trade promotion to become more active in facilitating the dialogue between free trade and a more globally responsible vision of "fair trade" as an important part of its external relations strategy.[30]

Hong Kong is positively positioned to aid in the resolution of the trade impasse that has emerged between rich and poor countries. According to Oxfam, World Trade Organization (WTO)-allowed agricultural subsidies and tariffs, which undermine successful agricultural production in much of the developing world, amount to about US$330 billion – exceeding the combined income of the 1.2 billion of the world's poorest people.[31] This situation is widely recognized to be one of the primary reasons why the current trading system is seen as unfair.[32] Yet, trade politics are contentious and pushing developed countries too quickly on changing their politically sensitive agricultural policies might jeopardize political support for the multilateral trading system in the developed world, which is already a bare majority.[33]

This is a highly divisive issue with much at stake. The WTO estimates that "cutting trade barriers in agriculture, manufacturing and services by one third would boost the world economy by $613 billion – equivalent to adding an economy the size of Canada to the world economy."[34] The failure of further multilateral trade liberalization might very well mean the sacrifice of these potential gains. Hong Kong could play a role in helping to resolve this global impasse given public support for this role and its already significant resources devoted to trade promotion and the support of the central government on this issue.

In 2004, Hong Kong's visible trade comprised 325 per cent of its GNP.[35] Hong Kong people recognize the relationship between free trade and Hong Kong's prosperity. According to this study's popular opinion survey results, 88 percent of respondents believed that the world becoming more connected through greater economic trade and communication has been good or very good for Hong Kong.[36] Over 74 percent of respondents rated international economic institutions, such as the WTO, World Bank, and IMF, as having either a positive or very positive influence on Hong Kong.[37] Interestingly, 64 percent of respondents also felt that "anti-globalization protesters" had either no influence or a negative influence on Hong Kong. Hong Kong people understand that the city has been a beneficiary of its high levels of global economic integration.[38]

This recognition, however, does not mean that Hong Kong people are blind to the inequities that characterize the global economic system. Seventy-two percent of this study's survey respondents rated the growing gap between rich and poor as a serious or very serious threat to the Asian region (as opposed to the over 40 percent of respondents who viewed weapons of mass destruction or terrorism as a serious threat to the region).[39] Moreover, the survey indicated that the majority of Hong Kong people would likely support Hong Kong playing a more pro-active role in trying to address this situation. Fifty-three percent of survey respondents, for example, would be willing to pay more taxes to the Hong Kong government to fund its greater efforts in encouraging fair trade.[40] Moreover, 92 percent strongly agreed or agreed that the CPG would support Hong Kong's efforts to play a more active international role in encouraging fair trade.[41]

Nor would Hong Kong be starting from scratch on this issue, since it has always had a distinguished international record on trade-related issues.[42] Most recently and notably, Hong Kong's Secretary for Commerce, Industry, and Technology John Tsang chaired the WTO's sixth ministerial conference (MC6) held in Hong Kong in December, 2005. Of course, Hong Kong's positive international trade reputation preceded the MC6. For example, Hong Kong was a founding member of the WTO, has been a Vice-Chair of APEC's Committee on Trade and Investment (CTI) since 1996, and is currently an observer on the Trade Committee and the Committee on Financial Markets of the Paris-based Organization for Economic Cooperation and Development (OECD).[43] This international commercial prominence has been supported by an experienced group of trade representatives, with the Bureau of Commerce, Industry, and Technology acting as the "conductor" orchestrating Hong Kong's official trade policy among multiple governmental and nongovernmental players and its 11 overseas ETOs.[44] Moreover, Hong Kong's civil servants have ably served in the WTO for many years. For example, Hong Kong's Tony Miller has been Chairman of the Council for Trade Related Aspects of Intellectual Property Rights (TRIPS), Joshua Law Chi-kwong was Chairman of the Committee on Budget, Finance, and Administration, Ivan Lee was Chairman of the Committee on Customs Valuation, and, most notably, Stuart Harbinson was Chairman of the WTO General Council.[45] Thus, it can be reasonably argued that "fair trade" is an area that may provide meaningful opportunities for Hong Kong in its effort to more pro-actively position itself as a responsible international player.

Moreover, promoting the dialogue between free and fair trade also serves Beijing's interests. As a developing country, China has a vested interest in ensuring that poorer nations have opportunities to participate fairly in the multilateral trading system. Notably, during the 2003 WTO Ministerial meetings in Cancun Mexico, "Beijing joined about 20 other developing countries – together representing more than half the world's population – in tabling a resolution on agriculture, calling on developed countries to substantially reduce agricultural subsidies."[46] China was openly supportive of Hong Kong's efforts to host the WTO MC6 and has collaborated closely with HKSAR Commerce Secretary Tsang in his efforts to push both developing and developed countries to compromise in order to achieve a successful conclusion to the Doha round of negotiations.[47] Moreover, China supported Hong Kong's leadership position in hosting the WTO's MC6 despite the fact that Hong Kong and China have different trading positions in many areas. For example, while Hong Kong advocates further market liberalization in the area of telecommunications (with Hong Kong telecoms wanting to expand overseas), Beijing's stance is more in line with its economic development and protected telecoms market.[48] Hong Kong's leadership efforts in the area of "fair trade" should secure the Central Government's support.

In fact, senior Hong Kong officials have attempted to address the delicate balance between free and fair trade. In a speech that discussed the relationship between trade and poverty delivered at an informal ministerial meeting in Zambia, Secretary Tsang discussed Hong Kong's own experience in remaining an open economy, arguing that the multilateral trading system provides the best defense "when you are a small economy and the big boys begin to bully you."[49] Tsang's efforts to reach out to multiple stakeholders (including rich countries, poor countries, NGOs, and businesses) in his role as Chairman of the WTO MC6 provides an important model for Hong Kong's globally responsible external agenda.

While Secretary Tsang's efforts represent an important step in the right direction, Hong Kong can be much more visible and pro-active in promoting Hong Kong's "global responsibility" in the area of trade. It could do this by investing more in promoting Hong Kong's role as a voice of compromise on this polarized issue. Moving beyond commercial circles to seek out public speaking opportunities in non-traditional settings, such as John Tsang's trip to Zambia, not simply Donald Tsang's London Trade Development Council audience, may be one such step. Providing broader and more in-depth training to Hong Kong's overseas representatives to enable them to participate in the wide variety of trading forums with the objective of establishing these representatives as global experts in the field is another potential avenue. More actively hunting down external relations opportunities to demonstrate that Hong Kong is not merely a "free rider" on multilateral trade issues, but is contributing to ensuring that the multilateral trading system is fair for all, is yet another step that could be taken.

The external–internal linkages of this important global issue were demonstrated when the local media questioned the wisdom of Hong Kong's decision to host the December, 2005 WTO conference. Critics argued that disruptions associated with the conference would negatively impact upon local retail outlets during the critical pre-Christmas shopping season.[50] These doubts were further exacerbated by the anti-WTO violent protests and the resources expended by the Hong Kong government to quell them.[51] When framed solely in terms of Hong Kong's commercial interests, these concerns accentuated the fact that the costs of hosting the WTO could be seen to outweigh the benefits for Hong Kong. Highlighting Hong Kong's contribution to the greater national and international good could have been an effective way to diffuse these inevitable pre- and post-conference frustrations.

In short, Hong Kong could work more actively to position itself as part of the vital "epistemic community" active on trade issues. Epistemic communities refer to the important role of knowledge brokers in today's global arena. The expertise and resources Hong Kong already possesses should allow the SAR to play a similar role as part of the international epistemic community in ensuring that the debate between free and fair trade receives the attention it deserves and generate respect and goodwill for the SAR in the developing world.

Infectious disease prevention

The Severe Acute Respiratory Syndrome (SARS) epidemic underscored Hong Kong's vulnerability, as a major economic and communications hub on the edge of Mainland China, to the global threat of infectious disease. The SARS epidemic also illustrated the crucial role that Hong Kong's effective and transparent crisis management of communicable disease threats originating in southern China will play in the world's ability to effectively combat any future disease pandemic. As such, Hong Kong also has the opportunity to distinguish itself as a vital international player in the realm of infectious disease prevention. The election of Dr. Margaret Chan, former Hong Kong Director of Health, as Director-General of the World Health Organization (WHO) in November, 2006 demonstrated not only her own personal qualities but also international recognition of Hong Kong's work in the area as well as the importance of the Central Government in securing international support for a Hong Kong person running for leadership position in a major UN agency.[52]

As with trade, Hong Kong brings considerable existing resources and expertise to bear on this issue. Hong Kong's low levels of infant mortality, high life-expectancy rates, and quality healthcare system are comparable, if not better, than those in any developed country.[53] In fact, the appointment of Dr. Margaret Chan in 2005 as WHO's Assistant Director-General responsible for its division on communicable disease already indirectly validated to the international community Hong Kong's valuable experience in battling the SARS epidemic.[54] In addition, the recent establishment of Hong Kong's Center for Health Protection (CHP) in response to calls by the post-SARS Expert Committee[55] and modeled after the US Center for Disease Control,[56] is expected to equip Hong Kong with a much more effective institutional mechanism to prevent and respond to the threat of infectious disease.[57] With international concern over the possibility of an H5N1 bird-flu pandemic reaching new heights, Hong Kong's important SARS and microbiology laboratory experience make its links with the WHO not only important to Hong Kong but to the international community.

Global prevention of infectious diseases is an area about which Hong Kong people care. Not only did survey respondents rate the threat that the spread of disease poses to Asia very highly (71 percent said it was a serious to very serious threat), but 71 percent of respondents said that they would be willing to pay more in taxes to the government to combat this threat.[58] Further, 91 percent of respondents believed that the Central Government in Beijing would support Hong Kong's more pro-active external strategy in the area of healthcare and disease prevention.[59] Looking at Hong Kong's pride in its healthcare system and its own struggles with growing public healthcare expenditures, it makes sense to assume that people would be supportive of government efforts to explore how to better position Hong Kong as a leader of the global epistemic community on effective provision of healthcare for all.[60]

Hong Kong's leading role in infectious disease prevention also serves Beijing's interests. With the spectrum of a worldwide avian flu pandemic looming, the world is looking toward China and its public health system to play a role in effectively curtailing the spread of H5N1 and other communicable diseases. Unfortunately China's "decentralized and fragmented"[61] healthcare system, notwithstanding its impressive accomplishments, is currently struggling with its own problems related to largely unregulated privatization which has been detrimental to the overall quality of and access to healthcare services, especially in rural areas.[62] Mindful of these problems, Chinese President Hu Jintao's vision for a "well-off" China by 2020 "has shifted from simply increasing GDP per head to achieving broader measures of wealth, such as enjoying good health."[63] In such a situation, efforts by Hong Kong to cooperate and collaborate with the CPG in order to strengthen the national public health responsiveness, especially in the area of infectious disease, would seem to be welcome. The decision of China's Ministry of Science and Technology to establish a State Key Laboratory of Emerging Infectious Disease at the University of Hong Kong's Faculty of Medicine (the first and only one in this field to be established outside the Mainland) is a strong indication of the CPG's intention to collaborate more effectively with Hong Kong in developing medical research infrastructure.[64]

In view of these factors, Hong Kong would be well served to take advantage of these assets and position itself as one of the world's leading players on infectious disease prevention. This would require Hong Kong's leaders to map out a strategy on how to effectively incorporate Hong Kong's private and nonprofit sector expertise on this issue into a coherent external affairs plan of action. It might also entail training its existing overseas representatives on local, regional, and global public health issues and Hong Kong's potential contribution to the global discussion. Finally, expanding Hong Kong's overseas team to include relevant non-economic experts in areas of public health and infectious disease might be an additional step to consider.

In short, these brief descriptions of how Hong Kong could position itself as a global leader of responsible deliberation in the areas of trade and infectious disease prevention are meant to demonstrate that advocacy of a globally responsible external affairs agenda can promote Hong Kong's existing strengths, China's international concerns, and Hong Kong people's wishes. By reforming its external relations agenda to focus on areas of Hong Kong's global responsibility, by seeking out other promotional opportunities, and by expanding the expertise of its overseas representatives, Hong Kong could have the opportunity to project itself as a globally responsible player which should serve to enhance its prestige to audiences at home and abroad.

Global responsibility and social cohesion: strengthening community bonds

Thus far this chapter has focused on how adopting a more visible, globally responsible external relations strategy for Hong Kong can improve its climate for governance by (1) increasing local pride in the uniqueness of what Hong Kong has to offer the nation and the world, and (2) strengthening the confidence of Hong Kong people in their leaders. We would like to conclude by suggesting that Hong Kong's climate of governance can also be improved by embracing a globally responsible external agenda that may strengthen the bonds among Hong Kong people themselves. In Hong Kong's case, a globally responsible agenda might be an important tool in helping to address social cleavages based on class, political identity, and generational differences.

Hong Kong has long grappled with the question of whether its relatively high levels of income inequality pose a threat to social cohesion and stability in Hong Kong.[65] While this chapter will not delve into this complex policy debate, it does suggest that a globally responsible external affairs agenda might help to enhance local social cohesion. For example, Hong Kong's involvement in constructing globally responsible solutions could signal to vulnerable segments of society that the government understands that not everyone is thriving as a result of global integration and that Hong Kong is not only striving to be part of the global solution but is trying to share the lessons learned around the world with those in need in Hong Kong. From a macro perspective, a global ethic of responsibility forces one to see "problems of the periphery as moral obligations to address" and therefore, local communities who engage at this level will be less likely to ignore their own community's peripheries.[66] From a micro perspective, when local stakeholders participate in global problem-solving, they have access to a global body of knowledge, technologies, and management skills from which to draw to solve local problems. Local stakeholders who are on the periphery of their societies, threatened with exclusion, can also utilize transnational networks and lobbying structures to further their own agenda at home.[67]

The potential for this positive cross-fertilization of ideas between the global and the local was seen in this study's survey results. When asked to rate the seriousness of various threats to the Asian region, over 72 percent of respondents felt that the growing gap between rich and poor was a serious to very serious threat to the region. In contrast, less than half agreed that weapons of mass destruction (41 percent) or terrorism (46 percent) represented a serious threat to the region.[68] Since this regional threat mirrors Hong Kong's own problem of growing inequality, it seems reasonable to assume that a more globally proactive Hong Kong, attentive to the regional threats such as these, might reap benefits for its own community by transferring lessons and experiences about how to enhance inclusivity and sustainability from the global level to the Hong Kong community itself.

Promoting a globally responsible external agenda can also act as normative glue for Hong Kong's OCTS political identity. The OCTS political balance is a highly sensitive issue for Hong Kong. If Hong Kong's leaders were to accentuate the "Two System" part of the Basic Law framework at the expense of its balance with the "One Country" side of the scale, then the cohesiveness between Hong Kong residents and the Chinese nation may be inadvertently jeopardized.[69] By the same token, if the "One Country" part of Hong Kong's identity becomes dominant, people may lose confidence in the relevance and legitimacy of Hong Kong's local government as "special" in the wider context of China.[70] Thus, maintaining a proper balance between local and national political allegiances seems crucial.

The task of developing a framework for inculcating a community identity, which combines a strong sense of national political identity (to assure that Hong Kong is a seamless and coherent part of the PRC) with local pride of place, needs to ensure that these identities are not in opposition, but complementary and mutually beneficial – working for the good of the nation and the SAR. A globally responsible external relations agenda for Hong Kong could be an important tool to achieve this balance. Hong Kong's special status with a high degree of autonomy in external affairs means that the SAR is in a unique position to help fulfill China's global moral obligations by pro-actively positioning Hong Kong on issues of global responsibility.

Hong Kong people, like most people, expect government leaders to set and operate within high moral standards for the community. Governments that do so operate from a base of principled authority that can serve as a legitimacy cushion if their material effectiveness declines. A globally responsible community identity for Hong Kong might thus also act as a local cohesive, providing a persuasive rationale for Hong Kong citizens to act in spite of individual differences in background, creed, and political beliefs for the good of the larger human community. These values, which support extending Hong Kong's radius of responsibility out to the global community, are also the same positive nationalist values that will help hold China together.[71]

Too often in politics, as Francis Fukuyama has noted, "group solidarity ... is purchased at the price of hostility towards our group members."[72] By paying closer attention to global responsibility, Hong Kong may not only help support local and national efforts toward the same goals, but may also cement its ties with the international community thereby helping to act as a hedge against the exclusive and ethnocentric tendencies that can be so destructive in purely nationalist constructions. Thus, a globally responsible external agenda could in essence provide an additional policy instrument to help Hong Kong maintain its healthy OCTS political balance.

Finally, a globally responsible external relations agenda could also appeal to the younger generation among the Hong Kong community. According to local studies,[73] values trends in Hong Kong seem to mimic those from other developed economies (using the World Values Survey as a basis of comparison[74]), where "after a long period of rising economic and physical security, one should find substantial differences between value priorities of older and younger groups."[75] In economically developed communities like Hong Kong, older generations tend to have more materialists values, "giving top priority to economic and physical security," while younger generations tend to adopt "post-materialist" values "with goals such as freedom, self-expression and quality of life."[76] Presumably, a Hong Kong collective identity that is shaped by its commitment to global sustainability would hold more appeal to this post-materialist generation, helping to keep them motivated and involved in making the city a better place for all.

While more research needs to be done to conclusively establish these link-ages between Hong Kong's external affairs and social cohesion at home, this study suggests that a stronger sense of global responsibility will help enhance social cohesion at home by providing a model of "responsible citizenship" for the local community. Social scientists have long noted, "cooperative norms [can] arise as a result of repeated community interaction."[77] When people see the benefits generated for Hong Kong as a result of actions conducive to good global citizenship, they would presumably be more likely to adapt the same standards at home. Conversely, how persuasive can a government be in calling on its own members to sacrifice for the good of the community, when the government itself is not willing to make any sacrifices for the good of the human community?

Conclusions

This chapter has attempted to demonstrate that a globally responsible Hong Kong can help address the external challenge of Hong Kong's governance problem. The chapter establishes that global responsibility enhances governance by (1) increasing local pride in the uniqueness of what the Hong Kong commun-ity has to offer the nation and the world, and by (2) strengthening the confidence of Hong Kong people in their leaders. In addition, it has also suggested that by accentuating Hong Kong's contribution to the nation and the world, a globally responsible agenda may help enhance social cohesion at home by helping to bridge class, political, and generational cleavages.

In promoting a broader external relations agenda, Hong Kong should focus its energies on those areas where it has relevant experience and expertise, such as in utilizing Hong Kong's weight in multilateral trade forums to encourage the dialogue between free and fair trade or by capitalizing on Hong Kong's experience in grappling with the causes and consequences of SARS to promote more in-depth regional cooperation on health issues. These are not only import-ant issues to the international community, but their high relevance to the Hong Kong domestic audience makes them highly salient in terms of local perception of regime legitimacy. Hong Kong people, having lived through the 1997 Asian financial crisis and the 2003 SARS epidemic, understand the potential heavy social costs for those communities who uncritically subscribe to the mantra of global economic integration.[78] A Hong Kong that does not pro-actively position itself to participate in potential solutions to mitigate against the brutality of glob-alization might be left behind on these important issues.

Of course, global responsibility is not the only avenue the SAR could pursue to strengthen political identity and sense of pride in its government as well as strengthen the bonds among the people, and in turn address part of its governance challenges. However, Hong Kong's aspiration to remain a special city within China with a separate international identity may depend on how successful the SAR can successfully engage its citizens and the world in a broad range of global issues that are impinging on the welfare of everyone on our planet.

Notes

1 "Hong Kong Global Citizenship Survey," a 1,000+-person telephone survey conducted by the University of Hong Kong's Social Science Research Center for the authors, December, 2004.
2 For an idea of how deeply integrated Hong Kong is with the global economy, one need only peruse Hong Kong's economic statistics. For example, Hong Kong is the second largest source of outward foreign direct investment (FDI) in Asia, the second largest FDI recipient in Asia, the world's eleventh largest trading economy, and the world's tenth largest exporter of commercial services; Hong Kong has the world's second highest per capita holding of foreign exchange reserves, the world's busiest airport for international cargoes, the world's second busiest container port, the second largest venture capital center in Asia, the second largest stock market in Asia (the ninth largest in the world), and the third largest foreign exchange market in Asia (the sixth in the world). Hong Kong Trade Development Council, www.tdctrade.com/main/economic.htm#highlights (accessed October 27, 2005).
3 The Basic Law of the Hong Kong Special Administrative Region of the People's Republic of China, Article 13, www.info.gov.hk/basic_law/fulltext/ (accessed November 5, 2005).
4 That said, the division between external affairs and foreign affairs is admittedly a fuzzy one, as elaborated on by Roda Mushkat in her *One Country, Two International Legal Personalities: The Case of Hong Kong* (Hong Kong: Hong Kong University Press, 1997). For further reading on Hong Kong's international status, see G.A. Postiglione and J.T.H. Tang, *Hong Kong's Reunion with China* (New York: M.E. Sharpe, 1997).
5 The Basic Law of the Hong Kong Special Administrative Region of the People's Republic of China, Articles 151, 152, 153, www.info.gov.hk/basic_law/fulltext/ (accessed November 5, 2005).
6 As of September 15, 2005, Hong Kong is party to 215 international multilateral treaties, 75 of which the PRC is not a member. HKSAR Department of Justice, www.legislation.gov.hk/interlaw.htm (accessed November 15, 2005).
7 By law, Hong Kong's external relations need to be conducted in close consultation with the CPG (BL Articles 150–157). Moreover, extensive off-the-record interviews conducted by the authors in 2002 with Hong Kong officials responsible for Hong Kong's external relations revealed that HKSAR officials at all levels of government felt they had a positive rapport and effective working relationship with their CPG counterparts.
8 *Hong Kong SAR: The First Five Years 1997–2002*, www.gov.hk/info/sar5/easia.htm (accessed November 5, 2005).
9 "Asia's World City" was also meant to be an "aspirational" objective, especially with regard to Hong Kong's development of an internationally competitive arts infrastructure. *Hong Kong SAR: The First Five Years 1997–2002*, www.gov.hk/info/sar5/easia.htm (accessed November 5, 2005).
10 HKSAR Chief Executive Donald Tsang (speech given at the Hong Kong Trade

Development Council Annual Dinner, London, UK, November 2, 2005) as cited in the Pan Pearl River Delta Cooperation Website, www.pprd.org.cn/hkenglish/speeches1/200511070002.htm (accessed December 2, 2005).

11 Shanghai and Singapore even share similar artistic aspirations. See, for example: Singapore's government website promotion to coincide with the 2006 World Bank and IMF Board of Governors annual meetings, www.singapore2006.org/sections/discover_sg/world_city.html (accessed November 13, 2005); Edward Leman, "Can Shanghai Compete as a Global City?," *The China Business Review*, September–October, 2002; Elaine Louie, "Shanghai Polishes Up Its Rough Edges," *New York Times*, November 14, 2002; and "Shanghai's Aim: A World City", Xinhua News Agency, November 3, 2002, www.china.org.cn/english/China/47773.htm (accessed November 15, 2005).

12 See, for example, HKSAR Chief Executive Donald Tsang's speeches given in Vancouver on October 24, 2005 (www.pprd.org.cn/hkenglish/speeches1/200510310013.htm), in New York on October 25, 2005 (sc.info.gov.hk/gb/www.info.gov.hk/gia/general/200510/26/P200510250267.htm) and in London on November 2, 2005 (www.pprd.org.cn/hkenglish/speeches1/200511070002.htm).

13 The UN Global Compact is one such vision of global responsibility, albeit largely targeted at the private sector. For example, at the January, 1999 World Economic Forum,

> United Nation Secretary-General Kofi Annan challenged business leaders to join [this] international initiative, [which] ... through the power of collective action, ... seeks to advance responsible corporate citizenship so that business can be part of the solution to the challenges of globalization. In this way, the private sector – in partnership with other social actors – can help realize ... a more sustainable and inclusive global economy.
>
> (UN Global Compact, www.unglobalcompact.org (accessed October 23, 2005))

14 See, for example, "United States Hong Kong Policy Act Report" (as of April 1, 2003, as required by Section 301 of the United States–Hong Kong Policy Act of 1992, 22 U.S.C. 5731 as amended) www.usconsulate.org.hk/ushk/pi/2003/040101.htm (accessed October 23, 2005); "Six Monthly Report on Hong Kong" (January–June, 2003, presented to the Parliament by the Secretary of State for Foreign and Commonwealth Affairs, July, 2003); HK Human Rights Commission, UN Committee on Economic, Social and Cultural Rights, "On the First Periodic Report in Respect of HKSAR of the PRC under Articles 2–16 of the ICESCR," January, 2001, www.locoa.net/news/reports/hong-human1.htm (accessed October 23, 2005).

15 For example, see speeches by Hu Jintao as both President and Vice-President of China. Chinese President Hu Jintao, "Working Together Towards a Common Future Through Win-Win Cooperation" (speech to the G8 summit in Gleneagles, Scotland, July 7, 2005); Chinese Vice-President Hu Jintao, "China and the World In the 21st Century" (speech to the French International Relations Institute (FIRI) in Paris, France, November 5, 2001).

16 See Nicholas Lardy's *Integrating China into the Global Economy* (Washington, DC: Brookings Institution Press, 2002) for more information about China's successful trade liberalization policies. See also his speech "Trade Liberalization and Its Role in Chinese Economic Growth" (speech delivered to the IMF conference "A Tale of Two Giants: India and China's Experience with Reform and Growth," New Delhi, India, November 14–15, 2003) for an interesting analysis of China and India's respective trade policy impacts on economic growth.

17 Canadian Foreign Minister Pierre Pettigrew, "Canada's International Personality" (speech given at the APEX Symposium, Ottawa, Canada, May 31, 2005), w01.international.gc.ca/minpub/Publication.asp?publication_id=382615&language=E (accessed November 15, 2005).

18 Canadian International Development Agency (CIDA) website, "Development at a Glance" and "CIDA and International Cooperation," June, 2000.
19 See Foreign Minister Pettigrew's speech for references to these critics. Pettigrew, May, 2005.
20 Canadian Institute of International Affairs (CIIA), Survey on Canadian Public Attitudes toward Foreign Policy, April, 2004, www.ciia.org/CIIA_summary.pdf (accessed November 10, 2005).
21 Walter Lippmann's *Public Opinion* (1922) is one of the classic works from which the notion of the low salience of foreign policy issues to domestic publics is typically taken. It should also be noted that some participants at a panel when an earlier version of this chapter was presented expressed the view that until the political issues of democratization are resolved, most people in Hong Kong would not pay attention to such external relations issues.
22 Chong Chan-yau, "Global Poverty and Hong Kong's Response," *HKDF Newsletter*, September 25, 2000, www.hkdf.org/newsletter (accessed November 5, 2005).
23 The increasing salience of global issues to domestic polities is not unique to Hong Kong. Risse-Kappen, for example, found that in the USA, Japan, Germany, and France,

> while only a minority can be regarded as politically active, large portions of the public seem regularly to follow news about foreign policy in the media. While domestic problems usually outweigh foreign and security issues in public salience, data reveal that substantial minorities consider foreign affairs among the most important problems facing their respective countries. On the average, 20–30 percent of the public [in these countries] indicate serious concern about foreign affairs.
> (Thomas Risse-Kappen, "Public Opinion, Domestic Structures, and Foreign Policy in Liberal Democracies," *World Politics* 43, no. 4 (July, 1991): 481)

24 "Hong Kong Global Citizenship Survey," December, 2004.
25 Ibid.
26 Ibid.
27 Ibid.
28 Ibid.
29 Ibid.
30 For an example of an analysis of the two different trade strategies and its policy relevance, see Daniel W. Drezner, *Free vs. Fair Trade: Council Report Presents Two Paths for U.S. Policy* (New York: Council on Foreign Relations Press, 2006).
31 "Making Trade Work for Development at MC6: What Hong Kong Can Do," Oxfam Hong Kong, June 14, 2005, www.maketradefair.org.hk (accessed September 2, 2005).
32 "The Future of Global Trade" (transcript of public discussion with WTO Director Pascal Lamy, Professor Jagdish N. Bhagwati, and journalist Paul Blustein, New York, March 10, 2005), Council on Foreign Relations www.cfr.org/publication/7940/future_of_global_trade.html (accessed September 2, 2005).
33 According to Pascal Lamy, domestic support for trade liberalization usually hovers around a bare majority. As he states, "the people who benefit from trade are many times ignorant of these benefits and hence silent, [while] the people who suffer from trade ... are much more visible and much more vocal." "The Future of Global Trade," March 10, 2005.
34 "10 Benefits of the WTO Trading System," World Trade Organization, www.wto.org/english/thewto_e/whatis_e/10ben_e/10b06_e.htm (accessed November 21, 2005).
35 *The Hong Kong Yearbook 2004*, www.info.gov.hk/yearbook/2004/en/03_02.htm (accessed November 17, 2005).

36 "Hong Kong Global Citizenship Survey," December, 2004.
37 Ibid.
38 Ibid.
39 Ibid.
40 Ibid.
41 Ibid.
42 This trade record has been spurred on by the fact that Hong Kong has always had and continues to have a highly externally oriented economy. For example,

> in 2004, the total value of visible trade (comprising re-exports, domestic exports and imports of goods) reached $4,127 billion, corresponding to 325 per cent of GDP. This was distinctly larger than the ratios of 171 per cent in 1984 and 233 per cent in 1994. If the value of exports and imports of services is also taken into account, the ratio is even greater, at 376 per cent in 2004, compared with 207 per cent in 1984 and 270 per cent in 1994.
> *(The Hong Kong Yearbook 2004*, www.info.gov.hk/yearbook/2004/en/03_02.htm
> (accessed November 17, 2005))

43 *The Hong Kong 2004 Yearbook*, www.info.gov.hk/yearbook/2004/en/05_07.htm (accessed November 17, 2005).
44 Key governmental and quasi-governmental players in Hong Kong's external commercial relations include: Hong Kong's Trade Development Council (TDC), Intellectual Property Department, Custom and Excise Department, Invest Hong Kong, Tourism Board, and the Hong Kong Monetary Authority.
45 C.K. Lau, "Committed To Making a Constructive Contribution," *South China Morning Post*, WTO Conference Supplement, December 13, 2005, p. 8.
46 Frank Ching, "Cancun and China's rising WTO Voice," *The Business Times On-line*, October 8, 2003, business-times.asia1.com.sg/sub/views/story/0,4574,96081,00.html (accessed November 12, 2005).
47 Chinese Minister of Commerce Bo Xilai (speech given during the mini-ministerial meeting co-hosted by Bo Xilai and HKSAR Commerce Secretary John Tsang, Dalian, China, October 12, 2005), PRC Ministry of Commerce, english.mofcom.gov.cn/column/print.shtml/newsrelease/significantnews/200507/20050700162326 (accessed December 15, 2005).
48 C.K. Lau, "Committed To Making a Constructive Contribution," December 13, 2005.
49 HKSAR Secretary of Commerce, Industry and Technology John Tsang, "Trade and Poverty" (speech delivered at the Panel Discussion on Trade and Poverty of the Informal Ministerial Meeting on Least Developed Countries, Zambia, June 27, 2005), www.info.gov.hk/gia/general/200506/28/06280224.htm (accessed August 23, 2005).
50 Raymond Ma, "Shops Fear Not So Merry Christmas," *South China Morning Post*, November 27, 2005, p. 6.
51 Media coverage of the demonstrations during the WTO's MC6 was extensive. One example may be found at "Curbside at the WTO" (curbside.jmsc.org/), a website set up by the University of Hong Kong's School of Journalism and Hong Kong's *Standard* newspaper to provide local real-time coverage of the MC6.
52 Frank Ching, "All Eyes on the Doctor," *South China Morning Post*, November 14, 2006.
53 "Hong Kong Just Behind Established Countries – Asia's New Centre for Biotechnology Development?" (Press Release, Faculty of Medicine, University of Hong Kong, February 25, 2003), provides information on Hong Kong's healthcare strengths.
54 Mary Ann Benitez, "Hope of Millions," *South China Morning Post*, November 23, 2005, p. A20.
55 "SARS in Hong Kong: From Experience to Action," Summary Report, SARS Expert Committee, www.sars-expertcom.gov.hk (accessed November 16, 2005).
56 Hong Kong's Centre for Health Protection's website is located at www.chp.gov.hk/.

57 While the CHP's effectiveness has yet to be tested, initial reports have been favorable. See, for example, Katherine Schlatter, "Hong Kong CHP Officially Open," *The Scientist*, October 27, 2004, www.the-scientist.com/news/20041027/02 (accessed November 21, 2005).

58 "Hong Kong Global Citizenship Survey," December, 2004.

59 Ibid.

60 See, for example, "Keeping up with a Graying Population," *HK Standard*, July 19, 2006, or Allen Nam's "Private Medical Cover on Rise," *South China Morning Post*, November 23, 2006.

61 Liu Yuanli, "China's Public Health-care System: Facing the Challenges," *Bulletin of the World Health Organization* 82, no. 7 (July, 2004).

62 Overviews of China's public health challenges may be found in: Liu Yuanli, "China's Public Health-care System: Facing the Challenges," *Bulletin of the World Health Organization* 82, no. 7 (July, 2004); David Blumenthal and William Hsiao, "Privatization and Its Discontents: The Evolving Chinese Health Care System," *The New England Journal of Medicine* 353, no. 11 (September 15, 2005); Therese Hesketh and Zhu Weixing, "Health in China: The Healthcare Market," *British Medical Journal* 314 (May 31, 1997); and "Special Report: Where are the Patients? China's Health Care," *The Economist* 372: 8389 (August 21, 2004).

63 "Special Report: Where are the Patients? China's Health Care," *The Economist*, 372: 8389 (August 21, 2004).

64 "Two State Key Laboratories Opened at HKU for Emerging Infectious Diseases and Brain and Cognitive Sciences," press release from the University of Hong Kong, October 4, 2005, www.hku.hk/press/news_detail_5196.html (accessed November 28, 2005).

65 Hong Kong's increasing Gini coefficient is an indication of its growing income disparity. See "Fact Sheet: Gini Coefficient," Research and Library Services Division, HKSAR Legislative Council Secretariat, FS07/04–05, December, 2004. See also HKSAR LegCo meeting Minutes from the Subcommittee to Study the Subject of Combating Poverty, LC Paper No. CB(2) 2532/04–05, June 23, 2005, www.legco.gov.hk/yr04–05/english/hc/sub_com/hs51/minutes/hs510623.pdf (accessed November 6, 2006).

66 Martha Nussbaum, "Patriotism and Cosmopolitanism," *Boston Review* 19, no. 5 (1994).

67 Social scientists might describe this reality as international involvement's impact on the "domestic distribution of power among social groups." Alastair Iain Johnston, "Treating International Institutions as Social Environments," *International Studies Quarterly* 45 (2001): 487.

68 "Hong Kong Global Citizenship Survey," December, 2004.

69 For discussions on the Hong Kong identity prior to 1997, see Hugh Baker, "Life in the Cities: The Emergence of Hong Kong Man," *The China Quarterly* 95 (1983): 469–479, and Siu-kai Lau and Hsin-chi Kuan, *The Ethos of the Hong Kong Chinese* (Hong Kong: Chinese University Press, 1988). A discussion on the changes post-1997 is available at www.usc.cuhk.edu.hk/wk_wzdetails.asp?id=1865. The most updated survey by the HKSAR's Committee for the Promotion of Civic Education in 2004 has demonstrated a rather balanced trend on identity issues. www.cpce.gov.hk/common/doc/keystatistics_c.doc.

70 It may also alienate important members of Hong Kong's non-Chinese local community.

71 See the discussions in Nussbaum, "Patriotism and Cosmopolitanism."

72 Francis Fukuyama, "Social Capital, Civil Society and Development," *Third World Quarterly* 22, no. 1 (2001): 8.

73 Ming Sing, "Public Support for Democracy in Hong Kong," *Democratization* 12, no. 2 (April, 2005).

74   The World Values Survey is a worldwide investigation of socio-cultural and polit-
      ical change. It is conducted by a network of social scientist at leading universities
      all around the world. The survey is performed on nationally representative
      samples in almost 80 societies on all six inhabited continents. A total of four
      waves have been carried since 1981 allowing accurate comparative analysis.
                                ("Background," World Values Survey, www.worldvaluessurvey.org/
                                                                        (accessed May 25, 2005))

75 Ronald Inglehart, "Globalization and Post-modern Values," *The Washington Quar-
    terly* 23, no. 1 (1999): 215–228.
76 Ibid.
77 Fukuyama, "Social Capital, Civil Society and Development," p. 16.
78 See, for example, Joseph E. Stiglitz, *Globalization and Its Discontents* (New York:
    W.W. Norton, 2002) or Dani Rodrik, "Trading in Illusions," *Foreign Policy* (March/
    April, 2002).

References

Baker, Hugh. "Life in the Cities: The Emergence of Hong Kong Man." *The China Quar-
    terly* 95 (1983): 469–479.
Blumenthal, David and William Hsiao. "Privatization and Its Discontents: The
    Evolving Chinese Health Care System," *The New England Journal of Medicine* 353
    (2005):11.
Chan, Hoiman. "Labyrinth of Hybridization: The Cultural Internationalization." In *Hong
    Kong's Reunion with China: The Global Dimensions*, ed. Gerard Postiglione and
    James T.H. Tang, pp. 169–199. Armonk: M.E. Sharpe, 1997.
Cheung, Peter T.Y. and James T.H. Tang. "The External Relations of China's
    Provinces." In *The Making of Chinese Foreign and Security Policy in the Era of
    Reform, 1978–2000*, ed. David M. Lampton, pp. 91–122. Stanford, CA: Stanford Uni-
    versity Press, 2001.
Chong, Chan-yau. "Global Poverty and Hong Kong's Response." *Hong Kong Demo-
    cratic Foundation Newsletter* (September 25, 2000). www.hkdf.org/newsletter*.
Connolly, William E. *Identity\Difference: Democratic Negotiations of Political Paradox*.
    Ithaca, NY: Cornell University Press, 1991.
Dittmer, Lowell and Samuel Kim. *China's Quest for National Identity*. Ithaca, NY:
    Cornell University Press, 1993.
Dower, Nigel. *An Introduction to Global Citizenship*. Edinburgh: Edinburgh University
    Press, 2003.
Drezner, Daniel W. *Free vs. Fair Trade: Council Report Presents Two Paths for U.S.
    Policy*. New York: Council on Foreign Relations Press, 2006.
Foyle, Douglas. "Public Opinion and Foreign Policy: Elite Beliefs as a Mediating Value,"
    International Studies Quarterly 41 (1997): 141–169.
Friedman, Thomas L. *The Lexus and the Olive Tree*. New York: Farrar, Straus, & Giroux,
    2000.
Fukuyama, Francis. "Social Capital and Development: The Coming Agenda," *SAIS
    Review* 22, no. 1 (2002): 23–37.
Fukuyama, Francis. "Social Capital, Civil Society and Development," *Third World Quar-
    terly* 22, no. 1 (2001): 7–20.
Ghai, Yash. *Hong Kong's New Constitutional Framework* (2nd edn). Hong Kong: Hong
    Kong University Press, 2001.

Giddens, Anthony. *Runaway World: How Globalization is Reshaping Our Lives.* New York: Routledge, 2000.

Goldstein, Judith and Robert Keohane, eds. *Ideas and Foreign Policy.* Ithaca, NY: Cornell University Press, 1993.

Harris, Lee. "The Cosmopolitan Illusion," *Policy Review* 118 (2003): 45–59.

Held, David, *et al. Global Transformations: Politics, Economics, and Culture.* Cambridge: Polity Press, 1999.

Hesketh, Therese and Weixing Zhu. "Health in China: The Healthcare Market," *British Medical Journal* 314 (1997): 1616.

Hill, Michael. "Citizenship and Social Closure: Predetermined and Post Modern Trajectories," *Asian Journal of Social Science* 31, no. 1 (2003): 72–85.

Hoffman, Stanley. *Duties Beyond Borders.* Syracuse, NY: Syracuse University Press, 1981.

Inglehart, Ronald. "Globalization and Post-modern Values," *The Washington Quarterly* 23, no. 1 (1999): 215–228.

Irwin, Douglas. *Free Trade Under Fire.* Princeton, NY: Princeton University Press, 2002.

Johnston, Alastair Iain. "Treating International Institutions as Social Environments," *International Studies Quarterly* 45 (2001): 487–515.

Klare, Michael T. "The New Geography of Conflict," *Foreign Affairs* 83, no. 3 (2001): 49–61.

Lardy, Nicholas. *Integrating China into the Global Economy.* Washington, DC: Brookings Institution Press, 2002.

Lau, Siu kai, "The Hong Kong Policy of the People's Republic of China, 1949–1997," *Journal of Contemporary China* 9, no. 23 (2000): 77–93.

Lau, Siu kai. *The First Tung Chee-hwa Administration: The First Five Years of the HKSAR.* Hong Kong: Chinese University Press, 2002.

Lau, Siu kai and Hsin-chi Kuan. *The Ethos of the Hong Kong Chinese.* Hong Kong: Chinese University Press, 1988.

Liu, Yuanli. "China's Public Health-care System: Facing the Challenges," *Bulletin of the World Health Organization* 82, no. 7 (2004): 532–538.

Lo, Sonny L.S. "Five Perspectives on Beijing's Policy Towards Hong Kong." In *Political Development in the HKSAR*, ed. Joseph Y.S. Cheng, pp. 41–59. Hong Kong: City University of Hong Kong, 2001.

Loh, Christine. "The China Polity: The Hong Kong Effect." In CLSA Asia-Pacific Markets – October, 2003 (November 3, 2003), www.civic-exchange.org/publications/2003/Chinapolity.pdf.

Luban, David. "Just War and Human Rights." In *International Ethics*, ed. Charles Beitz. Princeton, NJ: Princeton University Press, 1985a.

Luban, David. "The Romance of the Nation-state." In *International Ethics*, ed. Charles Beitz. Princeton, NJ: Princeton University Press, 1985b.

Madsen, Richard. "The Public Sphere, Civil Society, and Moral Community," *Modern China* 19, no. 2 (1993): 183–198.

Ming Sing. "Public Support for Democracy in Hong Kong," *Democratization* 12, no. 2 (2005): 244–261.

Mushkat, Roda. *One Country, Two International Legal Personalities: The Case of Hong Kong.* Hong Kong: Hong Kong University Press, 1997.

Nagel, T. "Moral Conflict and Political Legitimacy." In *Authority*, ed. Joseph Raz. Oxford: Basil Blackwell, 1990.

Neves, Miguel Santos. "The External Relations of the HKSAR." In *Hong Kong in Transition: The Handover Years*, ed. Robert Ash, *et al.* UK: University of Warwick Press, 2000.

Nussbaum, Martha. "Patriotism and Cosmopolitanism," *Boston Review* 19, no. 5 (1994): 3–34.

Overholt, William H. "Hong Kong: The Perils of Semi-democracy," *Journal of Democracy* 12, no. 4 (2001): 5–18.

Pepper, Suzanne. "Hong Kong and the Reconstruction of China's Political Order." In *Crisis and Transformation in China's Hong Kong*, ed. Ming Chan and Alvin So, pp. 20–66. New York: M.E. Sharpe, 2002.

Postiglione, G.A. and J.T.H. Tang. *Hong Kong's Reunion with China.* New York: M.E. Sharpe, 1997.

Risse-Kappen, Thomas. "Public Opinion, Domestic Structures, and Foreign Policy in Liberal Democracies," *World Politics* 43, no. 4 (1991): 479–512.

Rodrik, Dani. "Trading in Illusions," *Foreign Policy* 123 (2001): 54–62.

Rothschild, Joseph. "Observations on Political Legitimacy in Contemporary Europe," *Political Science Quarterly* 92, no. 3 (1977): 487–501.

Said, Edward W. "Nationalism, Human Rights, and Interpretation." In *Freedom and Interpretation: The Oxford Amnesty Lectures,1992*, ed. Barbara Johnson. New York: Basic Books, 1993.

Smith, Anthony D. "National Identity and the Idea of European Unity," *International Affairs* 68, no. 1 (1992): 55–76.

So, Alvin Y. *Hong Kong's Embattled Democracy.* Baltimore, MD: Johns Hopkins University Press, 1999.

Stiglitz, Joseph E. *Globalization and Its Discontents.* New York: W.W. Norton, 2002.

Taylor, Charles. "Why Democracy Needs Patriotism," *Boston Review* 15, no. 5 (1994): 119–121.

The Basic Law of the Hong Kong Special Administrative Region of the People's Republic of China. Hong Kong SAR Government Information Center. www.info.gov.hk (accessed October 10, 2005).

The Hong Kong 2004 Yearbook. Hong Kong SAR Government Information Center. www.info.gov.hk/yearbook/2004/en/05_07.htm (accessed November 17, 2005).

Walzer, Michael. "The Moral Standing of States: A Response to Four Critics." In *International Ethics*, ed. Charles Beitz. Princeton, NJ: Princeton University Press, 1985.

Wang Hongwing. "Hong Kong and Globalization." In *East Asia and Globalization*, ed. Samuel Kim. New York: Rowman & Littlefield, 2000.

Wendt, Alexander. "Collective Identity Formation and the International State," *American Political Science Review* 88, no. 2 (1994): 384–396.

World Values Study Group, "ICPSR Abstract," WORLD VALUES SURVEY, 1981–1984 AND 1990–1993 [computer file]. ICPSR version. Ann Arbor, MI: Institute for Social Research [producer], 1994. Ann Arbor, MI: Inter-university Consortium for Political and Social Research [distributor], 1994.

Zaller, John. *The Nature and Origins of Mass Opinion.* Cambridge: Cambridge University Press, 1992.

9 Electoral structures and public opinion in the 2004 Hong Kong legislative council elections

Michael E. DeGolyer

How the 2004 election became a referendum on reform

Significant steps occurred in Hong Kong's political development during and following the 2004 Legislative Council (LegCo) election campaign. Effectively, the Mainland's class approach to politics collapsed while the fractious democratic movement united, but largely outside rather than under the leadership of the Democratic Party (DP). Originally Beijing set up the Hong Kong Progressive Alliance (HKPA) for the rich, the Democratic Alliance for the Betterment of Hong Kong (DAB) for the middle class, the Federation of Trade Unions (FTU) for the working classes, and put what Mao called the "stinking ninth" category of intellectuals, academics, and assorted professionals into the New Century Forum (NCF). The FTU and DAB long campaigned together in what could be described as an alliance of workers and management while the HKPA practiced an elite form of closed-door deal-making politics in the Functional Constituencies (FC) and in the Election Committee (EC). The NCF generally functioned more as a think-tank than a party, but up until 2004 it had representatives in LegCo via the Mainland-dominated EC.

Constitutional reform was the immediate cause of the collapse and disappearance of the HKPA with half its 600 members joining the DAB, the relegation of the NCF to an advocacy and research role, and the effective split of the FTU from the DAB, as well as the rise of a pan-democratic movement more or less centered around new, non-formal party political groups. The reforms were long anticipated, but the realignment was triggered by the events of 2003. First, the reform process.

The Basic Law promulgated in April, 1990 contained provisions for a process following the return to Chinese sovereignty in July, 1997 toward, as it put it, the "ultimate goal" of universal suffrage election of all members of LegCo and of the CE. The supposition, until 2004, was that the Basic Law permitted Hong Kong on its own to change rules for electing the 2008 LegCo while the 2007 CE election would require permission from Beijing before substantial changes in the election by 800 designated voters in an EC could be made. The 2004 election saw the end of LegCo members chosen by the EC and the return, for the first time, of half its members by direct election from Geographic Constituencies

(GC). Half, as in the 2000 election, came from FCs which have far smaller electorates, restrictive qualification requirements, and which require corporate "designated voting" in many instances. The electoral reform process as planned from 1984 to 2004 is outlined in Table 9.1.

Hong Kong people in general and the democratic movement in particular had long expected and hoped that in 2008 all members of LegCo would be directly elected. There had also been growing support for implementing direct election of the CE in 2007. In March, 2004 the Standing Committee of the National Peoples Congress issued interpretations of the Basic Law which required that a report "on the actual situation" first be filed by the CE regarding Hong Kong's readiness for further democracy, and then the SC would stipulate the limits and the pace at which steps forward would be taken. The SC duly decided on April 26 that no change in the 50/50 division of geographic and functional constituencies would occur in 2008, nor would indirect election by an EC of the chief executive happen in 2007.

The democratic movement, which had grown considerably more organized and confident following the massive march of July 1, 2003 and its triumph in the November, 2003 District Council elections, decided on two strategies for the 2004 LegCo election.[1] The first would be to make the LegCo elections a referendum in effect by asking voters to vote for candidates who demanded full direct elections in 2007 for CE and 2008 for LegCo. The second strategy was to actively contest as many of the 30 Functional Constituency (FC) seats as possible. The second strategy turned out to be the most effective choice, and since the Standing Committee's April, 2004 decision also mandated continuation of the FCs into the foreseeable future, the features of these seats which comprise and will comprise half the seats of LegCo should be carefully examined. As part of the pan-democratic strategy for the 2004 LegCo elections, Civic Exchange initiated the first full-scale independent study of Hong Kong's almost unique FC electoral practices.[2] The next section refers to the main outlines of FC's effect on government, voting, and public opinion, and sets the structural context for the analysis of the dynamics and results of the 2004 LegCo campaign.

The structures and entrenchment of political and economic inequality

FCs have a determinative effect on policy-making in the Hong Kong SAR. Votes are taken according to a "two-house" voting rule that stipulates for amendments to motions or bills to pass, a majority of members from both the GCs and the FCs must assent. Since the government controls the introduction of legislation, this means any attempt to change its proposals without its consent triggers the requirement for what is in effect a double-majority vote. This means that 15 members of the GC or 15 members of the FC (half of either "house" in the current 30/30 division of LegCo) can veto a measure. It also means, in theory, a majority of 32 rather than 31 is the minimum majority to pass amendments or private members' bills in the 60-seat LegCo (16 votes from each

Table 9.1 Composition of Legislative Council: 1984 to 2004

Year of election	Ex-officio government members	Appointed	Elected functional constituency	Election committee	Directly elected	Total
1984	17	30				47
1985	11	22	12	12	**0**	57
1988	11	20	14	12	**0**	57
1991	4	18	21	0	**18**	60
1995	0	0	21 + 9 new large[a]	10	**20**	60
1996[b]	**Election of First Chief Executive by 400 appointed Election Committee members**					
1997–1998	Provisional LegCo by same committee					60
1998	0	0	30	10[a]	**20**	60
1998	0	0	30	6[a]	**24**	60
2002[b]	**Second Chief Executive election by 800-member Election Committee**		**200 ex-officio, 600 by Functional Constituency selection/election**			
2004[b]	0	0	30	0	**30**	60
2008[b]	**Election rules for LegCo to be set**					
2007[b]	**Election rules for Chief Executive to be set**					

Notes

a The Election Committee in 1995 was by all members of District Councils, to which appointments had been established. Corporate voting in Functional Constituencies had been abolished and the franchise expanded to nearly two million voters. This was reversed in 1998. In 2004, fewer than 200,000 registered in the FCs, including corporate voters.

b The April, 2004 Standing Committee interpretation limited reforms. See below.

30-seat "house") while the government's unmodified measures pass by a simple majority of 31 members. However, in reality, a bill might pass the GC half of the house unanimously and even be joined by 14 FC members, for a total vote of 44 of 60 votes (or nearly three out of four LegCo members) in favor, yet fail to pass due to just 15 FC members voting against. This means that passing amendments to a government bill are, in fact, more difficult than passing constitutional amendments. Amending the Basic Law requires 40 out of 60 votes, but in theory, up to 45 votes would be needed to pass amendments to a government bill. The government can rely on just 15 FC members to stymie any moves by the pro-democracy-dominated GC half to make what the Tung government considered legislative mischief. On the other hand, 15 GC members can halt any private-member-driven inroads from FC members. This situation has led to many frustrations over legislation, for legislators as well as for the government. These rules mean that control of the government which introduces bills is central to governance in Hong Kong. While nominally it appears that the government is equally able to pit directly elected minorities against FC minorities when it wishes, the reality is that control rests overwhelmingly in the hands of the 630 members of the CE Election Committee returned by FC voters, since the CE is the heart of the executive-led government of Hong Kong. The CE is elected by FCs; thus requirement for a super-majority of 45 out of 60 votes to amend a bill is in truth an empowerment of the FCs to frustrate nearly any and all amendments its interests dictate, whatever the desires and no matter how overwhelming the support from the three million GC electors and their 30 representatives. The Standing Committee perpetuated in its April 2004 intervention and reaffirmed in its December 2007 decision extending the existing legislative system until at least 2020 this system of the FC-dominated election of a CE dominated government. And it left in its place the 15-member veto of a LegCo super-majority.

In terms of democratic campaigning in these "small-circle' elections, barriers are equally steep. Eight of the 30 FCs are returned wholly by corporate voting. That is, registered bodies on a one-body, one-vote basis choose, by various means, a designated voter to cast their ballot. Some of these corporate voters have thousands of members while others may have the owner of a shelf company as the only real voter (there were a number of shelf companies with the minimum legal assets among the 15,119 corporate bodies registered to vote in 2000 and the 14,783 in 2004), yet each "body" has one vote to cast. The Transport FC is a case in point. In 2004 it had 182 corporate votes[3] and no individual registrants. The KCR and MTR had a vote apiece, as did scores of minor taxi and minibus companies and associations of drivers of firms in various areas of the SAR. Transport policy, not surprisingly, favors bus and taxi (road) over rail in nearly every single instance where there is a conflict, since there are far more votes among road interests than among rail interests.

The FCs provide a confluence of influence favoring certain broad policy and expenditure areas; for example, development via public works or public redevelopment via a bizarre system that actually made secondary mortgages nearly impossible to obtain on properties approaching 30 years of age. Purchasers of older properties had great difficulty obtaining a mortgage in a system regulated by the Monetary Authority's policy of forbidding such loans or undervaluing as capital assets loans on such properties.[4] This encourages owners to allow properties to deteriorate after 30 years in the hope of being bought out for redevelopment. However, as long as government can keep at least 15 of the FCs "sweet" on their policies (16 for "majority" votes), they keep control. Hence, however bizarre the policies or expenditures needed to secure their favor, government can count on controlling LegCo so long as a sufficient number of FCs are kept onside. As Table 9.2 shows, the government does not have to persuade that many voters or corporations to obtain the votes of 16 seats in LegCo it needs to pass or 15 to block a motion.

Due to uncontested seats, in 2000 only 1,728 votes were needed to return an ironclad 16-vote FC bloc. In 2004, the number of votes for the minimal 16 rose to 4,630, but contested seats among the 16 FCs dropped from seven to six.

Seldom have so few exercised so much power over so many, and almost wholly without scrutiny or accountability. Since most of these few votes are hidden among corporate bodies, and after voting disappear again into the corporate body, the corporate-vote elected LegCo FC representatives have no way to really tell what their "voters" actually think.[5] They must do simply whatever they think will please most members of the corporate bodies, and then hope for the best when the corporate vote gets cast. This is another factor behind the remarkable power of the depreciate, develop, and redevelop real estate voting bloc that dominates government policy on myriad issues. The same limited

Table 9.2 The sweet 16 FCs (pro-government supporters, actual votes)

	Functional constituency	*Votes in 2000*	*Votes in 2004*
1	Real estate and construction	357	0
2	Heung Yee Kuk	0[a]	0
3	Financial services	177	541
4	Textiles and garments	0	2,430
5	Sports, performing arts, culture	0	1,198
6	Industrial (first)	305	0
7	Industrial (second)	0	0
8	Agriculture and fisheries	0	0
9	Insurance	0	0
10	Transport	106	0
11	Labour (3 seats)	509	461
12	–	–	–
13	–	–	–
14	Commercial (first)	0	0
15	Import and export	0	0
16	Commercial (second)	0	0
Total		1,454	4,630

Note
a 0 indicates elected unopposed.

number and obscure identity of the FC voters make it nearly impossible for academics to study or reliably determine the sentiments of these very privileged, very powerful voters.

In contrast to the handful of votes which comprise the FC veto over the legislature, a veto bloc of 15 votes (or a passing "majority" bloc of 16) in the GCs is very difficult to assemble. Table 9.3 shows what could be called the "sour" 16 votes in the GC half of LegCo that generally voted together as a "pro-democracy" group against the government.[6] Prior to the 2004 election this group was a weak bloc of voters until a December, 2000 by-election on Hong Kong Island added Audrey Eu to the pro-democracy GC bloc, giving it 16 solid votes and one usually supportive vote in Andrew Wong. However, in contrast to the eight or nine naturally cooperative votes of the pro-development bloc in the FC half of LegCo which have only a relative handful of mostly corporate interests to appease, the GC bloc 16 have to satisfy the interests of hundreds of thousands to be elected. The election of 2004 gave the pan-democrats a secure majority of 18 in the GC half of LegCo for the first time, thus securing for the pan-democratic GCs a veto over FC amendments. Adding in the seven seats they secured in the FCs, the pan-democrats secured a 25-seat bloc that is able to deny

Table 9.3 The sour 16 GCs (based on actual votes cast)

Count	Constituency	Member 2000	Votes 2000	Member 2004	Votes 2004
1	HKI	Martin Lee	46,037[a]	Martin Lee	65,894[a]
2	HKI	Yeung Sum	46,037[a]	Yeung Sum	65,894[a]
3	HKI	Cyd Ho	25,988	Audrey Eu	73,844
4	KW	Frederick Fung	62,717	Fredrick Fung	46,649
5	KW	Lau Chin-shek	36,770[a]	Lau Chin-shek	43,460
6	KW	James To	36,770[a]	James To	60,536
7	KE	Szeto Wah	51,931[a]	Fred Li	56,409
8	KE	Fred Li	51,931[a]	Alan Leong	56,161
9	KE			Albert Cheng	73,424
10	NTW	Leung Yiu chung	59,348	Leung Yiu chung	59,033
11	NTW	Albert Chan	43,613	Albert Chan	36,278
12	NTW	Lee Chuek-yan	52,202	Lee Chuek-yan	45,725
13	NTW	Albert Ho	38,472	Albert Ho	62,342
14	NTW			Lee Wing-tat	62,500
15	NTE	Wong Sing chi	25,971	Leung Kwok-hung	60,925
16	NTE	Emily Lau	63,541	Emily Lau	56,277[a]
17	NTE	Andrew Cheng	49,242	Andrew Cheng	56,277[a]
18	NTE	Andrew Wong[c]	44,899	Ronnie Tong	56,277[a]
Total			735,470		1,037,935[b]

Notes

a Single tickets, number of votes equally divided among winning candidates.

b 890,637 votes would be required to make up the minimum number of GC votes required to form the minimum 16-seat GC veto bloc (removing the two highest voting candidates, Audrey Eu and Albert Cheng).

c Frequently but not always supported pro-democracy votes.

the government the 40 votes it must have for constitutional reforms which might minimize democratic progress. This bloc duly nixed proposed reforms in December, 2005. Table 9.3 lists votes cast in the 2000 and 2004 LegCo elections for pro-democracy legislators.[7]

Political lobbying by constituents, constituent service, and processes of accountability by subsequent votes (corporate votes may be cast by someone else in following elections) are nullified by the current system. The seven FC seats among the Sweet 16 contested in 2000 and the six seats contested in 2004 required so few votes as to pale into invisibility against GC votes. If a ratio in terms of actual votes cast of how many voters comprised a 16-seat FC veto were made against how many it took to do the same in the GCs, the 2000 ratio would be 506:1 and, in 2004, 192:1. With all GC seats heavily contested and most of the 16 FC "majority" bloc seats in LegCo not contested, even these highly uneven ratios cannot fully reveal the essential unfairness of the legislative system. Although not all FC franchises are tiny, all of the 30 have far fewer voters than any GC, a situation that continued in the 2004 election, as may be seen in Table 9.4, despite a rise in registered FC voters from 175,000 to nearly 200,000. Not surprisingly, the seats with the smallest electorates and/or those dominated by corporate votes are precisely those which pro-government candidates control. Nor is it surprising that those with larger electorates are most likely to fall to pro-democracy candidates or at least to be most closely contested.

The April, 2004 Standing Committee decision forced pro-democracy forces to rethink strategies which hitherto neglected all but the largest FCs. The insistence by FC LegCo members and voters in the EC which elected Tung Chee-hwa unopposed in 2002 to back his every misconceived move has been one of the major factors undercutting the legitimacy of the SAR system. But the system's fundamental unfairness and its entrenchment of gross inequality in terms of legislative representativeness and in power to protect voting groups' interests has been the fundamental factor causing a deterioration of support for the governance system. As Table 9.4 shows, disparity between the GC and FC voters is extreme, but so too is inequality among FC voters. (See Fairness Ratio columns below.) This inequality between FC and GC and within FCs has sparked constant disputes over influence and charges of government–business collusion, special ties with various tycoons, and unfair awards of lucrative developments such as Cyberport. The decision by the Standing Committee to perpetuate this grossly unfair structure cost even the Central People's Government (CPG) dearly in public esteem. The sentiments and attitudes tracked in following figures and tables must be put primarily within this overarching context of a system designed to implement and protect the unfair advantage of a very few over the very many. It forms the essential foundation of perception to which nearly all other attitudes react.

Table 9.4 Voters to LegCo representative, Functional Constituencies[a]

Functional Constituency	Registered in 2004 LegCo election[b]	Registered persons FC voters of total (%)	Registered corporate "voters"	Fairness ratio, GC to FC[c]	Fairness ratio, education FC to FC[d]
Education	77,696	42		1.4:1	1:1
Health services	35,442	19		3:1	2.2:1
Accountancy	17,500	9.5		6:1	4.4:1
Social welfare	10,405	5.6		11:1	7.5:1
Medical	9,356	5		12:1	8:1
Catering	7,353	4	433	14:1[f]	10:1[e]
Engineering	7,252	3.9		15:1	11:1
Architectural, survey, and planning	5,116	2.8		22:1	15:1
Legal	5,073	2.7		22:1	15:1
Information technology	4,309	2.3	262	24:1	17:1
Wholesale and retail	2,454	1.3	1,609	27:1	19:1
Commercial (second)	1,096	0.6	739	60:1	42:1
Import and export	618	0.3	767	79:1	56:1
District Council[g]	462	0.25		238:1[f]	168:1[f]
Real estate and construction	302	0.016	455	145:1	102:1
Heung Yee Kuk[g]	149	0.008		738:1[f]	521:1[f]
Textiles and garments	79	0.004	3,815	28:1	20:1
Sports, performing arts, culture	48	0.003	1,583	67:1	47:1
Financial services	46	0.003	598	171:1	121:1
Commercial (first)	0		1,077	102:1	72:1
Tourism	0		964	114:1	81:1
Industrial (first)	0		804	137:1	97:1
Industrial (second)	0		499	221:1	156:1
Transport	0		182	605:1	427:1
Labour (3 seats)	0		519[b]	636:1	449:1
Agriculture and fisheries	0		162	680:1	480:1
Insurance	0		161	684:1	480:1
Finance	0		154	715:1	505:1
Total	184,756	92.6	14,783		

Notes

a Ranked by number of individual voters.

b Actual votes per seat, 173.

c Using the New Territories East GC number of voters per LegCo seat, 110,084 as base. The actual fairness ratio is even higher due to FC voters also getting to vote in GCs.

d The education FC has the largest number of voters among the FCs.

e The 433 organizational votes range from one corporate voter for a ten-member taxi owner association to one voter for the MTRC with thousands of employees. The fairness ratio is, if overall corporate members are considered, far better, or, if different sized organizations are considered, far worse in terms of equality of voters. Given that one owner may control hundreds of corporate votes, the transparency and inequality of corporate/individual votes among the FCs is the most extreme, even more so than FC to GC.

f Ratios of voters, including corporate votes against the NT East GC base of 110,084 registrants per LegCo seat.

g Both District Council and Heung Yee Kuk are "elected" bodies.[13]

What was the election about? Trends in attitudes among the 2004 electorate

There is no need to elaborate on events here since the introduction of Article 23 legislation and the implementation of the Principle Officials Accountability System in 2002. Civic Exchange, the Hong Kong Transition Project and Synerg-yNet websites contain multiple reports about events which resulted in some of the largest demonstrations in Hong Kong's history, the resignations of three ministers and a member of Exco; the amendment, then withdrawal of Article 23 legislation; the defeat of many pro-government candidates in the 2003 District Council election; and the Standing Committee's unilateral intervention limiting electoral reforms. These events, despite improvement in economic indicators, affected sentiments toward life in Hong Kong during the election campaign (Figure 9.1).

The sharp drop in satisfaction between April, 2004, in a survey taken before the Standing Committee ruling, and May, after the ruling, indicates how Beijing's intervention impacted upon people's satisfaction with their lives in Hong Kong. Even with unemployment falling below 7 percent for the first time in nearly two years, satisfaction fell again in July, only recovering in early September as the time neared for voters to cast their ballots.[8] Dissatisfaction with the local government's performance peaked in December, 2003, after Tung insisted on packing the District Councils with over 100 pro-government appointees. Dissatisfaction remained as high in July, 2004 as it was in mid-June, 2003, shortly before over half a million marched and nearly brought down the CE and his government (Figure 9.2).

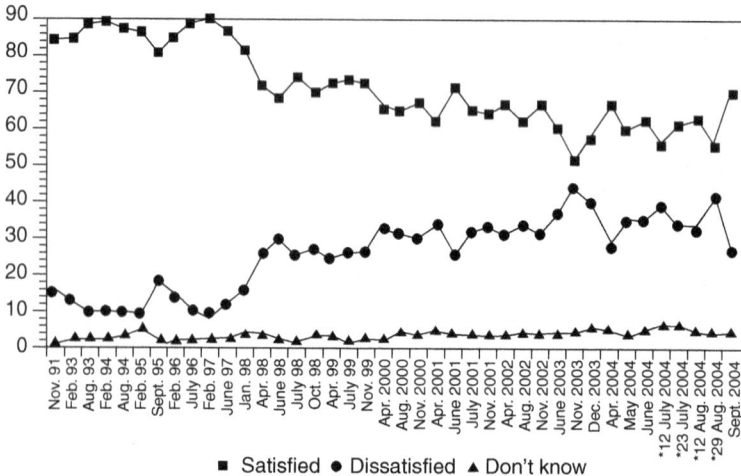

■ Satisfied ● Dissatisfied ▲ Don't know

Figure 9.1 Question: "Are you currently satisfied or dissatisfied with your life in Hong Kong?"

Note
*Of those who say they would definitely vote.

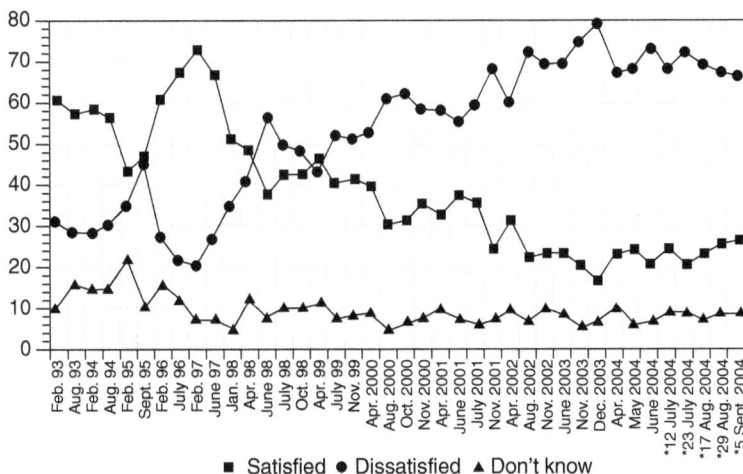

Figure 9.2 Question: "Are you currently satisfied or dissatisfied with the general performance of the Hong Kong government?"

Note
*Of those who say they would definitely vote.

While dissatisfaction with Tung's performance hit a peak in December, 2003 with his insistence on putting over 100 pro-government appointees on the District Councils, it recovered somewhat, only to return to that peak in June, 2004, before subsiding after he accepted the resignations of E.K.Yeoh and Leong Che-hung following the LegCo report on SARS (Figure 9.3).

Dissatisfaction with Tung seems clearly affected by how he handled relations with the Mainland. It appears that inviting Beijing to intervene in Hong Kong's affairs was primary among causes of public dissatisfaction. The peak of dissatisfaction with the Hong Kong government's dealings with the Mainland came in June and July, 2004 following the Standing Committee interpretation. Dissatisfaction had fallen sharply in November, 2003, when the SAR government appeared to accept the verdict of the people after the July march and their vote in the District Council Elections, and appeared to be defending Hong Kong people's rights to send the government and its supporters a message at the polls. The April decision sharply reversed that perception, and re-raised levels of dissatisfaction well into the summer. For most of the summer of 2004, during the LegCo campaign, Tung and his ministers adopted a very low profile. The strategy of hiding Tung away from sight and keeping from the media their greatest liability served to lower resentments by the time balloting took place in September (Figure 9.4).

The dramatic effect of Beijing's intervention in April may be seen in Figure 9.5. In November, 2003, barely two weeks before the District Council elections which saw its allies heavily defeated, Beijing's non-intervention in the run-up to those elections and its moderate response to the historic July, 2003 march of

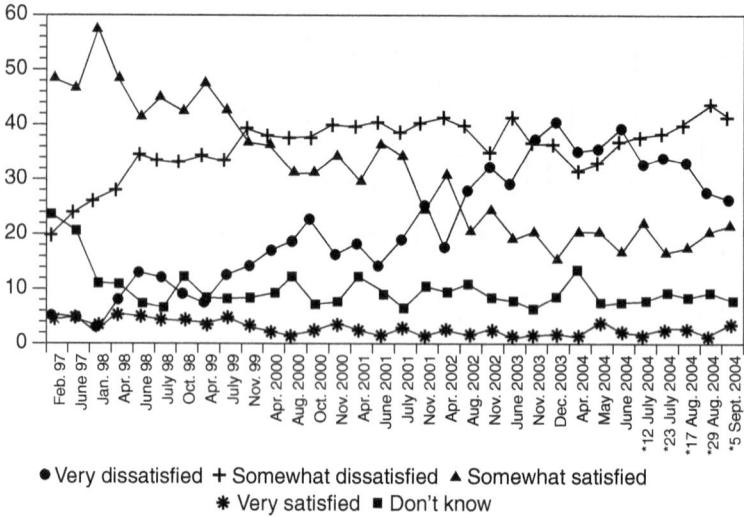

● Very dissatisfied + Somewhat dissatisfied ▲ Somewhat satisfied
✳ Very satisfied ■ Don't know

Figure 9.3 Question: "Are you satisfied or dissatisfied with the performance of C.E. Tung?"

Note
*Of those who say they would definitely vote.

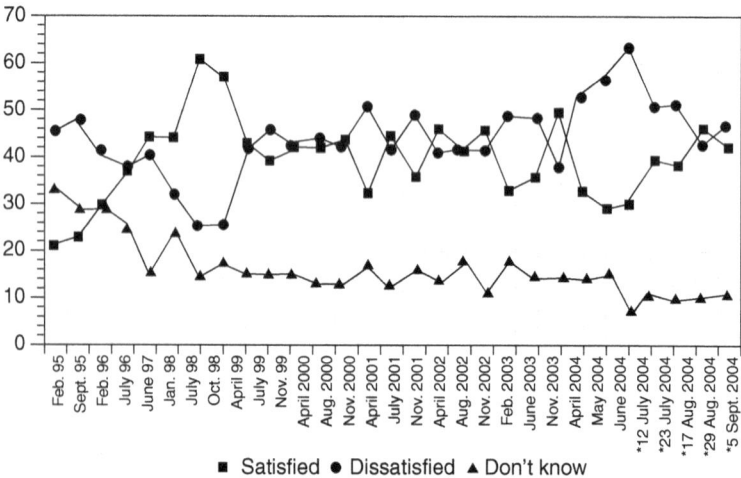

■ Satisfied ● Dissatisfied ▲ Don't know

Figure 9.4 Question: "Are you currently satisfied or dissatisfied with the performance of the Hong Kong government (SAR government) in dealing with the Mainland?"

Note
*Of those who say they would definitely vote.

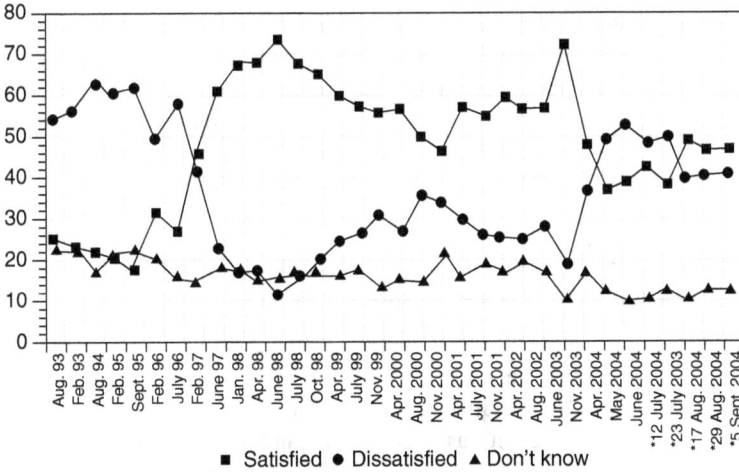

Figure 9.5 Question: "Are you currently satisfied or dissatisfied with the performance of the PRCG in dealing with Hong Kong affairs?"

Note
*Of those who say they would definitely vote.

over half a million had earned the Central Government its highest satisfaction ratings since July, 1998, when President Jiang Zemin and US President Clinton came to celebrate the first anniversary of the reunification of Hong Kong to the Mainland. Effectively, while the local government had extremely low ratings, the Central Government had offsetting high rates which gave it the political capital to buttress the deeply disdained Chief Executive. However, the controversial intrusion of the Standing Committee into the debate over constitutional reform triggered a massive fall in satisfaction with the performance of the Central Government in dealing with Hong Kong affairs. Levels of dissatisfaction with its performance exceeded levels of satisfaction for the first time since the 1997 handover. The April survey was concluded immediately before the April 26 announcement of the Standing Committee's ruling, the first intervention which asserted Beijing's power to set the rules and limits for constitutional reform even before launching consultations with Hong Kongers. The harsh rhetorical atmosphere created by its partisans had already cost it a great deal of the political capital it had accumulated in the previous six years. The Central Government, along with the local SAR government and its CE, entered the 2004 elections with high negative sentiments toward their performance, only recovering somewhat in the final weeks before balloting.

Despite these dramatic changes in satisfaction with the political management of Hong Kong–China relations, sentiment toward the economic integration of Hong Kong with the Mainland was quite different. It is perhaps ironic that the Central Government concluded that the cause of Hong Kong's intense disaffection in July, 2003 was mainly economic, not political, and subsequently embarked on a program of "concessions" to Hong Kong including personal visas instead of group visas for Mainland tourists and allowing them to take more money with them to spend in Hong Kong.[9] However, while economic worry in the shape of Hong Kong's future as a part of China dropped, political dissatisfaction rose. From this and other survey results related to economic worry discussed below, the correlation of concern about economic issues with relations with China affected the votes of very few (Figure 9.6).

What was the campaign about? A referendum on partial democracy and unequal representation

Having set the structural and attitudinal contexts of the 2004 election, the crucial question becomes: What did the voters themselves think they were voting upon? Was this election, as pan-democratic forces hoped and argued, a referendum on constitutional reform, or was it, as pro-Beijing and pro-government forces argued, more about who could deliver the economic goods and ensure good relations with Beijing so that the economy would improve? The following stems from a post-election survey conducted by the Hong Kong Transition Project during the last week of November, 2004, about five weeks after the LegCo election.[10] Table 9.5 sets the overall context of proportions supporting or opposing direct election of all LegCo seats, the key issue the pan-democrats chose as their primary campaign emphasis. The proportion in support, 62 percent (see Table 9.5), is almost exactly the same as the proportion of the votes which the pan-democrats took in the September election: 62.9 percent.

While 62 percent supported direct election of all seats, there were different views on when to implement this measure, with 43 percent for 2008, and 13

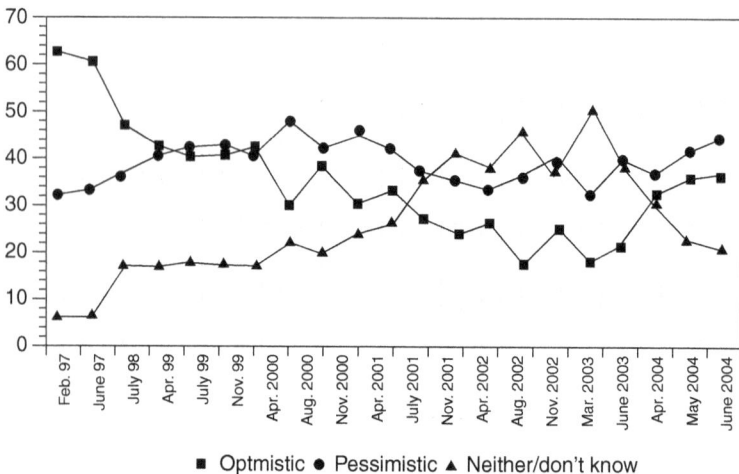

■ Optmistic ● Pessimistic ▲ Neither/don't know

Figure 9.6 Question: "How do you feel about 1997 and Hong Kong's reunion with China?"

Table 9.5 Question: "Do you support or oppose direct election of all Legco seats?" (percentage of column total)

	FC registered voter	GC registered voter	Unregistered	Total
Strongly support	24	22	10	19
Support	37	44	42	43
Oppose	18	15	15	15
Strongly oppose	7	5	4	5
DK	13	14	30	18
Total	100	100	100	100

Notes
Chi-square = 34.44 with 8 df $p \leq 0.0001$.

percent for 2012. About four in ten opted for later dates, had no views, or opposed direct elections.

Some 65 percent of those surveyed claimed they voted in September. Telephone surveys tend to over-sample the age and educational groups most likely to have voted, so it is possible that this percentage, which varies by about ten percentage points from the actual turnout of 55.63 percent, is accurate in terms of respondents' behavior. But it is more likely that some respondents who claim they voted are doing so on the basis of social norms which make it embarrassing to admit one did not vote. On the other hand, 24 percent of respondents (185 in number) indicated that they had not registered to vote, a proportion close to the 70 percent of eligible voters who are registered. Only 11 percent claimed they registered to vote but did not vote.

The call by the pan-democrats for the elections to be a referendum on direct elections had a motivating effect on both supporters and opponents, but particularly on supporters. While just 10 percent of non-voters strongly supported direct elections, 24 percent of voters strongly supported direct election of all LegCo seats. And while just 3 percent of non-voters strongly opposed, 6 percent of voters strongly opposed direct elections. In addition, the don't knows on the issue dropped from 28 percent of non-voters to just 12 percent of voters, indicating that interest in and stance on the issue raised turnout, explaining in part why the 2004 LegCo election set a new record not just in the highest percentage of registered voters to vote of 55.63 percent in GCs, 70.1 percent in FCs, but also in record numbers of registered voters, 3,207,227, and of voters, 1,784,406 in GCs and 192,374 registered in FCs and 134,852 FC voters, for a total of nearly two million votes cast. Total votes cast were 1,919,258, over twice the total votes cast in the last election under the British in 1995. There is no evidence that Hong Kong people are rejecting formal politics in voting terms; quite the contrary.

A majority of voters went to the polls either to support or oppose the election of a pro-democracy majority to LegCo. One in five voters opposed election of pro-democracy majority; 52 percent supported. However, in terms of overall public opinion, these voters represented 13 percent and 33 percent respectively.

About one-third, 35 percent of respondents but even more of the populace, had not registered or had not voted, and 18 percent who did register (28 percent of voters) said they did not know whether they supported or opposed. Clearly, democracy is an issue dividing the community, but in three ways, not just in two, between supporters and opponents and those not participating.

The survey asked voters how important various issues were in persuading them to vote for particular candidates. The independent variable (the columns) in each cross-tab is support for a democratic majority. The dependent variable (the row results) are their ratings of importance of each issue. The assumption in these cross-tabs is to test whether support or opposition to a democratic majority affects other reasons for supporting a candidate. For example, in Table 9.6(a) the candidate's effect on political stability – a codeword for Beijing supporters meaning support for Beijing's top priority for Hong Kong as its version of stability – shows a strong correlation with support or opposition to a democratic majority. Support for a democratic majority means instability for many

Table 9.6 Question: "In persuading you to vote for your candidate/name list of candidates, how important were the following?" (percentage of column total)

(a) They promote political stability

Importance[a]	Support[b]	Oppose	DK	Total
Very important	16	40	18	21
Somewhat important	41	40	41	41
Of little importance	23	5	22	19
No importance at all	18	13	13	15
Don't know	2	3	6	4
Total	100	100	100	100

Notes
Chi-square = 40.02 with 8 df $p \leq 0.0001$.
a i.e., they promote political stability.
b i.e., support election of pro-democracy majority.

(b) They have good relations with Beijing

Importance[a]	Support[b]	Oppose	DK	Total
Very important	7	36	12	14
Somewhat important	37	41	35	37
Of little importance	22	14	20	20
No importance at all	32	9	26	26
Don't know	1	1	6	3
Total	100	100	100	100

Notes
Chi-square = 72.32 with 8 df $p \leq 0.0001$.
a i.e., they have good relations with Beijing.
b i.e., support election of pro-democracy majority.

pro-Beijing supporters. Surely enough, of those who oppose election of a pro-democracy majority (20 percent of voters), 40 percent rate a candidate's promotion of political stability as very important, and 35 percent as of little or no importance. Only 16 percent of pro-democracy voters rated "political stability" as very important, while 41 percent rated it as of little or no importance. A similar pattern may be seen in Table 9.6(b) on candidates having good relations with Beijing.

Association of a candidate's or voter's support or opposition to a democratic majority with a candidate's ability to promote economic prosperity in Hong Kong is very weak. While 49 percent of democracy opponents consider a candidate's ability to promote economic prosperity very important, 41 percent of supporters feel the same, and overall, 89 percent of opponents versus a statistically identical 88 percent of supporters rate the issue very or somewhat important. But among democracy supporters, while 12 percent say it is of little or no importance to their vote (that is, they rank a candidate's stance on democracy or another issue as much more important than economics), only 7 percent of opponents say economic effect of a candidate does not matter. Now presumably, the 12 percent and 7 percent respectively of supporters and opponents of a pro-democracy majority are thus taking a principled or at least an ideological stance in which the one issue of a candidate's stance toward democratization determines their vote.

This presumption was tested with a question on support for full direct elections in 2007 to 2008. Three times as many supporters of electing a pro-democracy majority consider a candidate's support of full direct elections in 2007–08 very important as opponents of a pro-democracy majority. Oddly, the DAB kept in their party platform a pledge to seek full direct elections in 2007 to 2008, even after coming out in support of the Standing Committee's decision to postpone such a move. The party platform did not drop the pledge until much later. So supporters of the DAB could claim support for full direct election in 2007 to 2008, and opposition to the election of a pro-democracy majority (codeword for the pan-democrat candidates) was not necessarily contradictory. A majority of all voters, 54 percent, considered support for full direct election in 2007 to 2008 as very important in their decision on whether to support a candidate. Supporters of full direct elections sooner rather than later claim that this is the only way to ensure Hong Kong freedoms are fully protected. While democracy and support for freedoms in Hong Kong are associated by many if not most, Table 9.7 makes clear that the proportion of those who consider a candidate's ability to promote freedom of little or no importance is very small, just 18 percent of all voters, while 80 percent of all voters consider it very or somewhat important.

Political party affiliation is very or somewhat important to about one-third of voters, with more supporters of a democratic majority considering it very important than opponents. Of much more importance to voters, and even more so for pro-democracy majority supporters, is the ability or pledge of candidates to monitor the HKSAR government. Only 15 percent of the electorate considered this of little or no importance, and about one in five voters, with no

Table 9.7 Question: "How important is it to your vote that they can promote freedom in Hong Kong?" (percentage of column total)

Importance[a]	Support[b]	Oppose	DK	Total
Very important	46	25	22	35
Somewhat important	42	41	52	45
Of little importance	8	21	14	12
No importance at all	3	12	9	6
Don't know	–	2	4	2
Total	100	100	100	100

Notes
Chi-square = 49.15 with 8 df $p \le 0.0001$.
a i.e., they can promote freedom.
b i.e., support election of pro-democracy majority.

statistical difference between supporters and opponents of democracy, considered controlling social welfare expenditure very important. On the other hand, about one in four voters put reducing the gap between rich and poor as very important to their support for a candidate, with somewhat more pro-democratic majority supporters than opponents ranking this as very important. On the contrary, 18 percent of opponents to a pro-democracy majority considered this as not important at all while only 7 percent of pro-democracy majority supporters did so. There does seem to be some association of what might be termed economic resentments of the poor with support for direct elections (somewhat buttressing the notion among direct election opponents that if full direct elections were implemented the first votes would be to put up their taxes), but this does not seem to be the top priority of a majority of either supporters or opponents, or of voters as a whole. About as many consider it very important (26 percent) as consider it of little or no importance (23 percent). This is even more the case with a minimum wage, with 44 percent considering it of little or no importance while only 12 percent consider it very important.

If there is a class aspect to politics, it seems to have little association with the democracy movement. The next section tests the association of satisfaction with a party's performance with its stances, and also examines whether a party has a distinct group of income-based supporters or opponents; that is, whether certain income groups affiliate or disaffiliate with a party.

Political parties, issues versus incomes

Figure 9.7 sets out the responses of voters in the survey to the question whether they were satisfied or dissatisfied with a named party's performance.

In Table 9.8(a), (b), (c) and (d) the independent variable (columns) are rankings on importance of an issue in voting for a candidate. We examine only two issues, namely having good relations with Beijing and support for direct elections in 2007 to 2008, the two key issues dividing the pan-democrats from

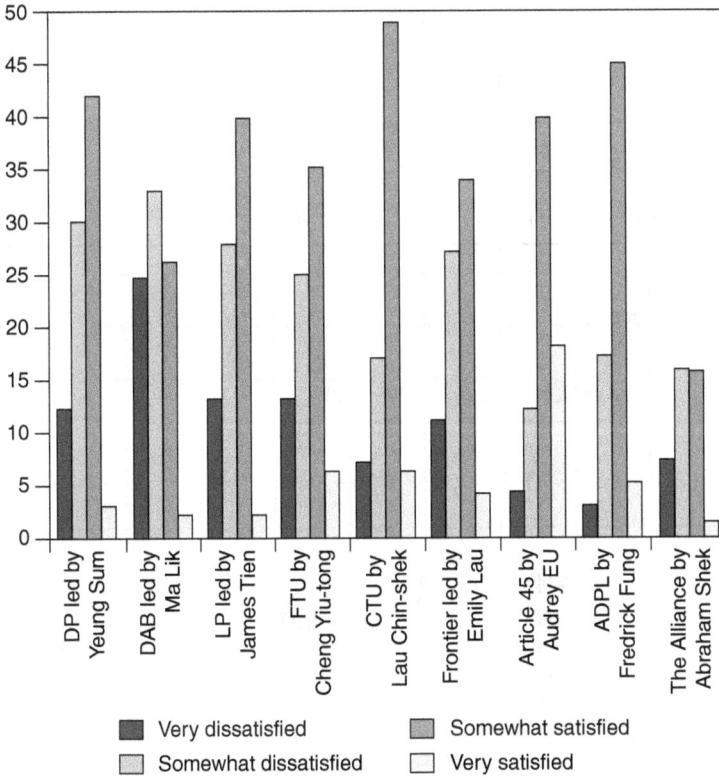

Figure 9.7 Satisfaction with performance of a political party (November, 2004).

Note
Don't know responses have been left out of the figure but retained by implication.

Table 9.8 Question: "In persuading you to vote for your candidate/name list of candidates, how important were the following by satisfaction with a party?" (percentage of column total)

(a) They have good relations with Beijing (DP)

	Very important[a]	Somewhat important	Of little importance	No importance at all	DK	Total
Dissatisfied[b]	66	49	44	38	57	48
Satisfied	34	51	56	62	43	52
Total	100	100	100	100	100	100

Notes
Chi-square = 12.98 with 4 df p = 0.0114.
a i.e., good relations with Beijing.
b i.e., satisfaction with Democratic Party.

(b) They have good relations with Beijing (DAB)

	Very important[a]	Somewhat important	Of little importance	No importance at all	DK	Total
Dissatisfied[b]	45	61	75	81	88	68
Satisfied	55	39	25	19	13	33
Total	100	100	100	100	100	100

Notes
Chi-square = 32.25 with 4 df $p \leq 0.0001$.
a i.e., good relations with Beijing.
b i.e., satisfaction with DAB.

(c) They support full direct election in 2007/2008 (DP)

	Very important[a]	Somewhat important	Of little importance	No importance at all	DK	Total
Dissatisfied[b]	29	32	57	79	53	48
Satisfied	71	68	43	21	47	52
Total	100	100	100	100	100	100

Notes
Chi-square = 71.10 with 4 df $p \leq 0.0001$.
a i.e., support full direct election in 2007/2008.
b i.e., satisfaction with Democratic Party.

(d) They support full direct election in 2007/2008 (DAB)

	Very important[a]	Somewhat important	Of little importance	No importance at all	DK	Total
Dissatisfied[b]	82	72	65	55	44	68
Satisfied	18	28	35	45	56	33
Total	100	100	100	100	100	100

Notes
Chi-square = 22.66 with 4 df $p = 0.0001$.
a i.e., support full direct election in 2007/2008.
b i.e., satisfaction with DAB.

pro-Beijing parties, and we focus in these tables on the two leading parties, the DAB and the Democratic Party. The dependent variable (rows) is satisfaction with party performance. Assumption: satisfaction with a party depends on their stance on the issue.[11]

All parties show strong to very strong association of its relationship with Beijing and satisfaction with its performance. Those considering good relations

Table 9.9 Question: "What is your approximate monthly family income?" (percentage of column total)

Group	Range	Count	%
1–2	None to under 5,000	57	7
3–4	5,000–14,999	150	19
5–6	15,000–24,999	150	19
7–8	25,000–34,999	99	13
9–10	35,000–49,999	71	9
11–12	50,000–69,999	55	7
13–15	70,000–90,000+	51	7
16	Refuse to answer	140	18

(a) Satisfaction with Democratic Party by income

	1–2	3–4	5–6	7–8	9–10	11–12	13–15	16	Total
Dissatisfied	69	46	40	47	59	60	53	55	50
Satisfied	31	54	61	53	41	40	47	46	50
Total	100	100	100	100	100	100	100	100	100

Notes
Chi-square = 17.02 with 7 df p = 0.0173.

(b) Satisfaction with DAB by income

	1–2	3–4	5–6	7–8	9–10	11–12	13–15	16	Total
Dissatisfied	53	52	66	68	75	66	78	64	64
Satisfied	47	48	34	32	25	34	22	36	36
Total	100	100	100	100	100	100	100	100	100

Notes
Chi-square = 17.52 with 7 df p = 0.0143.

not important tend overwhelmingly to be satisfied with pro-democracy parties, while those considering good relations with Beijing as very important tend to be just as satisfied with pro-Beijing parties and dissatisfied with pro-democracy parties. This association is tested further with Table 9.8(c) and (d), namely support for full direct election in 2007 to 2008.

Again, as in good relations with Beijing, the stance of the party toward direct elections in 2007 to 2008 clearly affected satisfaction or dissatisfaction with their performance. Table 9.9(a) and (b), tests satisfaction with the DAB and Democratic parties' performance on the basis of the income of respondents.

The poorest income groups seem more dissatisfied with the Democratic Party than with the DAB, and certainly more satisfied with the Liberal Party, the business or wealthy class party. However, the Liberal Party shows no association of satisfaction with income level at all, indicating that if there is class politics in Hong Kong, either they are out of it or rich business people are unaware of it.

The party most associated with demonstrations for direct elections and strident demands for the same, the Frontier Party, shows no association between income levels and satisfaction. Oddly, the party dominated by professionals and well-off academics, the Article 45 Concern Group (now the Civic Party), shows that higher income groups tend to be less satisfied with it while a party strongly associated with public housing tenants and poorer groups, the ADPL, shows its satisfaction levels as highest with the highest income groups. If there ever were class-based politics in Hong Kong, clearly, in the 2004 LegCo election, they were overwhelmed by the issue of direct election of the chief executive in 2007 and of all LegCo members in 2008. Some might assert that those who did not vote or did not register to vote did so out of class, being probably the disenfranchised poor, but all 773 survey respondents were asked about their satisfaction with a party's performance and about their incomes, not just voters. Thus the above results seem to show conclusively that Beijing's abandonment of class-based politics is based on a realistic assessment of Hong Kong's politics. The HKPA's merger with the DAB to form the Democratic Alliance for the Betterment and Progress of Hong Kong after the 2004 election, and the virtual disappearance of the NCF, is the structural reflection of this assessment. The pan-democratic strategy of making the election a virtual referendum on direct elections worked, as most voters seemingly did cast their votes accordingly. But while 62.9 percent of the 2004 GC voters voted for pan-democratic candidates, the pan-democrats took only 25 out of 60 LegCo seats due to the grossly unfair FC system. The FCs entrench narrow, interest-based and thus interest-dominated politics (not class politics per se) at the core of Hong Kong governance.[12] Those interests seem to have allied themselves into an ideological grouping – rather than class or income groupings – behind Beijing's determination to slow progress toward direct election. Once full direct elections arrive, perhaps class or income interests will assert themselves. Until then, Beijing sees in its most capitalist enclave not class warfare between rich and poor but ideological division between those demanding democracy and those who fear it.

Notes

1 See Chan and Lee (Chapter 1, this volume) as well as Ku (Chapter 2) and Chan (Chapter 3). In head-to-head competitions, DP candidates defeated DAB candidates 69 seats to 12. Cyd Ho defeated the DAB's Vice-Chair, Ip Kwok-him, in a race targeted specifically at the DAB's support of Tung Chee-hwa.
2 More details of the Civic Exchange FC study may be found on its website at www.civic-exchange.org and in Christine Loh and Alan Sargent, eds. *In Functional Constituencies: A Unique Feature of the Hong Kong Legislative Council* (Hong Kong: Hong Kong University Press, 2006).
3 Up from 153 in 2000 despite a severe economic downturn.
4 The policy was obscured by HKMA and bankers' mutual unwillingness to discuss the issue other than to deny it existed. The policy was finally changed in late 2004, after

the LegCo election. Older properties no older than 25 years may now warrant loans, but still at a discriminatory rate to new properties.

5 For example, the EC elected in 2000 had roughly 100 voting members who no longer qualified in their FCs as voters, due to retirement, job field change, or employer change, yet they retained the right to vote in the 2005 July 10 CE by-election.

6 It should be noted that the Democratic Party, the largest of the bloc, has voted with the government 90 percent of the time according to a study by Dr. Rowena Kwok of Hong Kong University.

7 The resignation of DAB member Cheng Kai-nam and the by-election of pro-democrat Audrey Eu by over 100,000 votes is not considered in the 2000 election results.

8 It is likely that satisfaction with life in Hong Kong rose as a result of people feeling that government and parties were listening to their demands, and that they would soon have a say about them. Satisfaction with life and a sense of helplessness and voice-lessness over events and policies affecting people seem to vary inversely.

9 The Tung government also took the step, reluctantly, of opening Lok Ma Chow, the smallest land crossing, 24 hours a day on January 26, 2003. Lo Wu, the main cross-ing, is still closed from midnight to 6:30 a.m., even though the Lok Ma Chow crossing is now having to be expanded to deal with the growing traffic.

10 A total of 773 respondents took part in the random sample survey.

11 The pan-democratic parties are the Democratic Party, Frontier, Confederation of Trade Unions, Article 45 Concern Group, and the Association for Democracy and Peoples Livelihood (ADPL). Pro-Beijing parties are the Democratic Alliance for the Betterment of Hong Kong (DAB), the Federation of Trade Unions, and the Liberal Party.

12 There is considerable evidence to show that most FC voters are more supportive of direct election of the CE and all LegCo members than other groups. See "Compara-tive Profiles of FC and GC Voters in the 2004 LegCo Election Campaign," in Chris-tine Loh and Alan Sargent, eds. *In Functional Constituencies: A Unique Feature of the Hong Kong Legislative Council* (Hong Kong: Hong Kong University Press, 2006), pp. 175–221.

13 However, the 18 District Councils are formed by universal suffrage voting for 400 members with a further 100 government members appointed. The Heung Yee Kuk is formed by village representatives elected by those living in indigenous New Territo-ries villages (once restricted to males with provable provenance to 1898 ancestors, franchise has been extended to permanent residents living in a NT village for at least four years). Villagers can thus vote for their Heung Yee Kuk representative indirectly for that FC, for their GC, and if in business or professional groups, for that FC as well.

14 May, June, July 12 survey results of registered voters indicating they plan to vote (other survey responses of all respondents) July 23, August 12, of those saying they definitely will vote.

15 Don't know responses have been left out of the figure but retained by implication.

10 An unexpected chapter two of Hong Kong's constitution

New players and new strategies

Benny Y.T. Tai

Introduction: constitutional game

In 2002, I published "Chapter One of Hong Kong's New Constitution: Constitutional Positioning and Repositioning" (Chapter 1).[1] In it, I had applied a game framework to analyze the constitutional development of the HKSAR in the first five years following the changeover.[2]

To illustrate the nature of a constitutional game further, it has several features. There must be more than one player in a constitutional game. The players can basically be identified within the constitutional structure. The various constitutional institutions in the constitutional system are the main players in the game.[3] However, a new player can join a constitutional game if it has a significant role to play in the game after some fundamental changes in the social and political context.

To distinguish a constitutional game from a purely political game, one must look at the rules. In a constitutional game, the constitution provides the rules, and all players accept to be bound by them when they join the game. However, in a political game, only power matters.[4] In a constitutional game, rules limit the moves of the players, since no free fight between the players is allowed as in a purely political game. The constitution defines the role, powers (their cards), and limitations of each player in the game. Like all games, players play to win. The definition of winning and the methods used to attain success may not be the same for each player in a constitutional game. These are also set by the constitution. The strategies of the players in a constitutional game are therefore constrained by the constitution.[5]

As rules are so important, their set-up in the game and their interpretation become the main battlefields in a constitutional game. Political bargaining and strategies are still needed, but the resolution of disputes is mainly done through a legal platform, which includes the chamber of the legislative body and the courtroom. If all players have almost equal strength in the game, equilibrium will be achieved through give-and-take interactions between the players on the legal platform. Ultimately, the moves of the players to win must be on the legal platform. Acts that will be accepted by other players as legitimate moves can only be acts that can, in the end, find authority from the rules and are recognized by the legal platform. Illegitimate moves by any player will be boycotted by the other players. Such a player may be excluded from the game or may be forced by other players to abandon its illegitimate move if it still wants to stay in the game. Equilibrium will be maintained through the operation of such a balancing mechanism. Players will try their best to exert influence through the legal platform. The characteristic of a legal platform is that it sets limits. These limits could be changed, but they must also conform to the predetermined rules on rule changing.

However, the limits set by the rules cannot be absolutely accurate, owing to the nature of language. There are times when language cannot indicate what the exact boundary is, and in most cases the rules in a constitutional game will leave room for the players to act. All players will try their best to justify their moves by reading the rules expansively to best fit their interests. All players will play according to their understanding of the constitutional provisions and strive to win the game. This applies to both the process of identifying their positions in the game and determining what legitimate moves they can make in the game.

Interaction between the players is the key to any game, including a constitutional game. A player must respond to the moves of other players and may need to refine its original winning strategy. In some cases it may even have to adopt a completely different strategy.

The understanding of the constitutional provisions by a player on its role, powers, and limitations may not be the same or may even be in conflict with how other players in the game see the same. As constitutional provisions could never be absolutely accurate, players must tolerate a certain degree of difference in their understanding of each others' role, powers, and limitations. As a result, there is always a varying degree of room for each player to fine tune its winning strategy.

One main reason for adopting a game framework to present the constitutional development of Hong Kong is to demystify the "sacredness" of the so-called "legal meaning" of constitutional text. In almost all the constitutional controversies in Hong Kong, disputes focused on the interpretation of certain provisions of the Basic Law. Many people believe that the key to the resolution of these disputes is to discover the "legal meaning" or the "right answer" of the relevant constitutional text by using the proper rule of interpretation to interpret the relevant constitutional provision. However, by adopting a game framework, one can see that there is no such "one" proper rule of interpretation or "one" right answer. Different legal meanings may come from the same rule of interpretation and different rules of interpretation arrive at the same legal meaning. In addition, constitutional interpretation does not just happen within the courtroom and is not monopolized by judges.

I hope to illustrate through this game framework that constitutional interpretation is not rule-based, but interpreter-based (or player-based in a constitutional game setting). In any constitutional controversy, the meaning of the constitutional text is derived from the rule of interpretation chosen by a specific player. However, a player will not arbitrarily choose a rule or an approach of interpretation and meaning for the text.[6] It is under internal and external constraints as determined by the context of the constitutional and political settings.

Each player will adopt a certain rule of interpretation and a particular meaning for the constitutional text that best fits the constitution based on the perspective of the player's position in the constitutional game, a position that each player believes to be its proper constitutional position. This is the internal constraint. The choice is limited by the specific constitutional position adopted by the player.

The language of the constitutional text is the first external constraint, as it would be very difficult for a player to justify an interpretation if the meaning adopted is a meaning that the language cannot bear. Another external constraint is the pressure generated from the interpretations by the other players who are also under their internal constraints. Depending on the relative powers and limitations in the constitutional game, a player may have to adjust even its rule of interpretation as a result of strategic interactions with the interpretations of other players. Constitutional interpretation is therefore part of a player's winning strategy in a constitutional game.

Chapter one

In the first chapter of Hong Kong's new constitution or the first round of the new constitutional game in the Hong Kong Special Administrative Region (HKSAR), all players, including the Beijing government, the First CE, the Legislative Council (LegCo), and the political parties represented in it, the Hong Kong Courts – especially the Court of Final Appeal (CFA) – and the civil service had to search for their initial position, a position which they understood to be their position so determined by the Basic Law of the HKSAR.

The most powerful player in Hong Kong's constitutional game is surely the Beijing government. It has reserved for itself enough power in the Basic Law to dominate the game including: the power to enact and amend the Basic Law; the power to conduct HKSAR's defense and foreign affairs; the power to review local legislation; the power to apply national laws to the HKSAR; and the power to interpret the Basic Law. However, the Beijing government did not need to use these powers actively to protect its interest in Hong Kong. The constitutional position taken by the Beijing government was an open-minded sovereign so as to give an impression to the outside world that Hong Kong, under "One Country Two Systems," is able to decide its own affairs.

The Beijing government could do so because it has another powerful constitutional tool. By keeping a close supervision on the selection process of the CE, the Beijing government could ensure a loyal CE would be selected. By further granting him vast powers under the Basic Law, the Beijing government could more or less assure that the HKSAR would be in safe and trusted hands.

The First CE, Tung Chee Hwa, selected under this constitutional arrangement, knew very well his role in the game as the political agent of the Beijing government. Although he was the leader of the HKSAR and should be accountable to the HKSAR, he was mainly accountable to the Beijing government. If there were to be any conflict between the interests of the HKSAR and Beijing governments, priority must be given to the Beijing government. He was extremely careful in handling this delicate balance between the Beijing government and the HKSAR. He adopted a strategy to avoid any possible conflict of interests between the Beijing government and the HKSAR by trying to predict what the Beijing government liked or disliked and then acted accordingly so as not to antagonize the Beijing government.

In Hong Kong's internal affairs, Tung was given a free hand but his policy orientation was not very consistent. At some points in time he tried to give the impression that he wanted to reform Hong Kong's systems, but on other occasions he emphasized more the maintenance of the existing systems. The problem is that it would be very difficult to maintain a balance if one wants to be a reformer and a conservative at the same time.

Under the original design, the CE would be assisted by the efficient and (believed to be) neutral civil service. Tung did appoint all the secretaries under the colonial rule to be the corresponding Principal Officials in the HKSAR government. However, some senior officials of the HKSAR government did not share the same view as Tung on how the HKSAR government should position itself under the new constitutional order. As Tung needed these senior officials in the government to implement his policies, tension within the HKSAR government could be foreseen.

The Basic Law has already assumed that the LegCo would not be a very influential player in the constitutional process. The design of the composition of the LegCo prevents a majority party from being formed. There are also strict limitations on members of the LegCo to initiate any policy change. As a result, the LegCo does not have a capacity to position itself in any significant way other than putting up some feeble opposition against the government. However, this same arrangement also makes it difficult for the HKSAR government to have any guarantee that its policies would be supported in the LegCo.

In this first chapter, the constitutional positions of all the players mentioned above would not be too difficult to ascertain. What was most uncertain immediately following the establishment of the HKSAR was the newly formed CFA. In its first constitutional case, *Ng Ka Ling* v. *Director of Immigration* [1999] 1 HKLRD 315, the CFA had positioned itself as the guardian of Hong Kong's high degree of autonomy, the guardian of Hong Kong's rule of law, and the guardian of human rights in Hong Kong.

However, the decisions of the CFA in this case encountered serious challenges from both the Beijing and HKSAR governments. Hong Kong courts' constitutional jurisdiction to review the legislative acts of the National People's Congress and its standing committee was questioned by Mainland legal experts, and the CFA needed to make a subsequent clarification judgment. The HKSAR government disagreed with the rulings of the CFA on the substantial issues concerning the right of abode of children of Hong Kong residents born in the Mainland. In the end, these rulings were overturned by the Standing Committee of the

National People's Congress (SCNPC) through a reinterpretation of the relevant provisions of the Basic Law upon a request from the CE.

These acts of the Beijing government and the CE, in turn, forced the CFA to readjust its position. As a result, the CFA's perception of the definition of winning and its perception of how to win the game had to be modified. Because of the interactions between the players, the players of the constitutional game in Hong Kong further repositioned themselves.

In Chapter one, I concluded that there would not be much change in the positioning of all the parties until 2007, after the first round of positioning and repositioning, or as the equilibrium of the game is basically achieved.

According to my understanding when I completed writing Chapter one, the next chapter should not have started until at least 2007. If the direct election of the CE were to be introduced in 2007, I suggested that the players might need to reposition themselves to adapt to the subsequent constitutional development caused by this institutional change. However, constitutional development is full of surprises. Despite everyone's expectations, people find that Hong Kong has suddenly turned to Chapter two of its constitutional development. Round two of the constitutional game has also started.

If positioning and repositioning was the central theme of the first chapter, then new players and new strategies is the theme of this unexpected second chapter. The first page of Chapter two was turned when an existing player adopted a new strategy. Unexpectedly, this new strategy had caused chain reactions, inducing a new player to join the game and forcing all existing players to adopt new strategies to strive for a new equilibrium.

The CE's new strategy

The CE was the player who turned the first page of the second chapter. When Tung became the second CE in 2002 following an uncontested election with overwhelming nominations within the Election Committee, he decided to change his governance strategy.

His governance strategy during the first term was full of ironies. He wanted to maintain continuity, so he nominated almost all the secretaries during the colonial rule to be the Principal Officials in his HKSAR government. However, he also had a lot of new policies in mind. He was a conservative, but he was also a reformer. The dilemma had weakened his governance to such an extent that there was already a general dissatisfaction about his rule when he assumed the office of the CE for the second time.[7]

To rescue himself from this poor image which he believed was caused by his lack of toughness in policy-making and implementation and the broken line of authority from his office to the bureaus under the civil service, Tung adjusted his governance strategy. His aim was to build a "strong man" image for himself and a strong government image for the HKSAR government.

To reassert his direct authority in the HKSAR government, the Principal Officials' Accountability System (POAS) was introduced in July, 2002.[8] All

Principal Officials were no longer civil servants. They were not appointed on civil service terms but on contract terms. The term of office was set for five years and will not exceed that of the CE who nominates them. Principal Officials are accountable to the CE, meaning that the CE may terminate their contracts at any time. The civil servants, who originally led the bureaus, were retitled to become the permanent secretaries of the bureaus and are now under the authority of the Principal Officials. They are responsible for assisting the Principal Officials in formulating, implementing, and marketing policies under their assigned portfolios. Some outsiders joined the team, but there were also some senior civil servants whom, after a change to their status, stayed in office. These included Regina Ip, the Secretary for Security.

Even though these changes to the whole governance mechanism of the HKSAR government are quite drastic, no amendment to the Basic Law is required. In listing the qualifications of Principal Officials, Article 61 of the Basic Law does not include the requirement of being a civil servant. Tung managed to exploit the opening left in the Basic Law which he had chosen not to do in the past years.

Immediately after its introduction, there was concern that the POAS is not really an accountability system, as the Principal Officials are not accountable directly to the Hong Kong citizens. There is no mechanism for Hong Kong people or their representatives to remove incompetent Principal Officials or Principal Officials who have committed wrongdoings. To many people, the POAS is only a mechanism for Tung to cleanse the executive authorities of the HKSAR, ensuring that his policy will be supported wholeheartedly by all officials. Not long after the launch of the POAS, it suffered a serious blow. In January, 2003, Antony Leung, the Financial Secretary, was found to have purchased a vehicle shortly before his announcement of the increase in the first registration tax of motor vehicles. Serious criticisms from the public and the media that Leung's conflict of interest generated in this incident only resulted in a letter of reprimand to Leung from Tung. The establishment and enforcement of the POAS all depended on the will and the interpretation of the CE himself.

Tung had also reformed the Executive Council and appointed the chairpersons of two major political parties in the LegCo, the Democratic Alliance on the Betterment of Hong Kong (DAB), and the Liberal Party to be members of the Executive Council. Tung believed that this ruling coalition would ensure support from the LegCo on government bills and policies. As a result, the pan-democracy camp was further marginalized.

Another pro-active move taken by Tung was to go ahead with the legislative plan to enact Article 23 of the Basic Law after five years of inaction.[9] Article 23 provides that:

> The Hong Kong Special Administrative Region shall enact laws on its own to prohibit any act of treason, secession, sedition, subversion against the Central People's Government, or theft of state secrets, to prohibit foreign political organizations or bodies from conducting political activities in the

Region, and to prohibit political organizations or bodies of the Region from establishing ties with foreign political organizations or bodies.

Tung believed that the HKSAR government had a constitutional duty to enact laws to implement Article 23.[10] A consultation paper was issued in September, 2002.[11] There may not be much dispute on whether there is such a constitutional duty, but the form, the scope, and the timing of the fulfillment of this duty were questioned by many. The Basic Law does not provide any more guidelines on legislation other than the general requirements as stated in Article 23 itself.

The consultation paper had adopted a rather expansive reading of the legislative requirements for fulfilling the constitutional duty of Article 23. A series of new offenses and old offenses to be redefined were suggested, including treason, session, sedition, and subversion. There could be definitions that might be less intrusive to individual rights, but the HKSAR government chose to provide only the lowest level of protection to Hong Kong citizens' fundamental rights, as opposed to the protection of national security. The scope of the Official Secrets Ordinance was proposed to be extended to criminalize more acts than just theft of state secrets as required by Article 23. Affiliation with illegal Mainland organizations by local organizations was also covered, though Article 23 only requires the prohibition of political organizations or bodies of the HKSAR from establishing ties with foreign political organizations or bodies. It was suggested that wide investigative powers be granted to the police in dealing with the offences under Article 23.

The proposals reflected the attitude of the HKSAR government. Insufficient attention was paid to the sensitive nature of these legislative proposals in the political and social contexts of Hong Kong and China. These so-called "crimes against the state" have been used by the Beijing government to suppress opposition in the Mainland. There was a serious concern among Hong Kong people that these new crimes, if enacted, might be manipulated to achieve a similar purpose in Hong Kong. Many proposals were not directly related to Article 23.[12] It seemed that the HKSAR government had tried to address some unspoken concerns of the Beijing government. The HKSAR government wanted to achieve too much in just one stroke.

The other matters that had caused unnecessary controversy were the performance of responsible officials, especially Regina Ip, the Secretary for Security, and some procedural decisions taken during the consultation and legislative processes. There was a three-month consultation period. However, Tung and Regina Ip did not give the public an impression that they were serious about listening to the opinions of the Hong Kong people.[13] The HKSAR government released the results of the consultation in a Compendium of Submissions,[14] showing that the majority supported legislation to implement Article 23. However, complaints were made that the government was biased in categorizing and processing the submissions.[15] There was also a strong opinion in society asking for a white bill on the national security legislation so that there could be more detailed discussion in the community on the actual wordings of all the offences before the bill went to the LegCo. However, Regina Ip refused. It seemed that there was a deadline to complete this legislation, though it was not clear whether the deadline was self-imposed or set by the Beijing government.

The LegCo started its scrutiny of the National Security (Legislative Provisions) Bill in February, 2003. The HKSAR government did make some clarifications and concessions, but its stance toward three major concerns of the public was still hard as steel. They included: (1) the provision regarding the proscription of a local organization subordinate to a Mainland organization which has been proscribed by the central authorities on national security grounds; (2) a "public interest" defense for unlawful disclosure of certain official information; and (3) the provision which confers on to the police a power to search without court warrant in the exercise of their emergency investigation powers.

With the support of the ruling coalition, Tung believed that opposition in the LegCo could be easily overcome. The legislative schedule was not disrupted by the outbreak of SARS, and Tung still demonstrated great confidence that the legislative plan could be completed before the end of the session of the LegCo in July, 2003.

No one at that time foresaw the significance of Tung's new strategies. Even Tung did not notice that the grievances of Hong Kong people against him and the HKSAR government had already accumulated to such a point that it was on the verge of outbreak.[16]

On July 1, 2003, more than half a million Hong Kong people protested in the streets. There might have been many causes to account for the people's dissatisfaction with the HKSAR government since the handover. The poor economy, the lack of accountability of the POAS, the poor performance of the officials during the SARS period, the unpopular image of Regina Ip, the undemocratic nature of the HKSAR government, and the incompetence of Tung in handling all these problems might all be secondary causes. However, there is no doubt that Article 23 triggered the deep-seated fear of Hong Kong people that the Beijing government might take away their much treasured freedom via the hands of the HKSAR government. A new player finally joined the game.

A new player: Hong Kong's civil society

At that time, Hong Kong's civil society[17] was still generally perceived as apolitical and decentralized.[18] People of Hong Kong can, and have, freely organized themselves in a web of associations functioning quite independently from the government, but there was no record of general political mobilization except during the events in 1989.[19] Political participation was fragmented and individualistic.[20] However, it is also agreed that since the 1980s and 1990s, civil society has already evolved to a state where it has acquired a certain degree of self-awareness[21] and political sensitivity.[22]

The Basic Law has provided the necessary conditions for Hong Kong's civil society to blossom. It expressly protects Hong Kong citizens' freedoms of association, of assembly, of procession, and of demonstration.[23] However,

Article 23 requires the HKSAR government to enact laws to restrict this freedom of association in Hong Kong in order to establish ties with foreign political organizations. The HKSAR government's legislative plan aimed to prohibit even ties with Mainland illegal organizations. The Basic Law is also selective in granting special recognition to certain sectors of civil society, mainly the business and professional sectors. This is reflected in the functional constituencies in the election of the LegCo and the composition of the Election Committee for the election of the CE. These groups were traditionally considered to be pro-establishment. The other sectors in the civil society were either marginalized or absorbed into peripheral organizations (consultative bodies) under the formal governance structure, allowing for a limited degree of participation in the governance process. One of the main objectives of social movements in Hong Kong's civil society in the past years was to break this institutional predilection by democratic reform.

Tung's poor governance had rejuvenated the political quest of Hong Kong's civil society, a quest which it might have suppressed since 1989. Even the more privileged sectors in civil society joined hands with the others in the July 1 rally.

The widespread participation of civil society in challenging the legislation of Article 23 was unexpected by all sectors, including the HKSAR government, the political parties, the Beijing government, and even civil society itself. No matter what caused so many people to express their dissatisfaction against the HKSAR government in such a symbolic manner, the July 1 rally is a landmark in the history of social movement in Hong Kong, indicating how a widespread people's movement could achieve significant change in major government policies.

The significance of the emergence of this new player to the constitutional game will be further analyzed in this chapter, but the joining of civil society in the game had at least disturbed the equilibrium, and every other player (maybe except for the CFA, at least at that moment) had to readjust their positions to accommodate the changing political and constitutional environment in the "post-1st-of-July-rally" era.

An immediate result of the July 1 rally was that the Liberal Party, not yet able to fully ascertain the significance of the event, decided to withdraw its support of the enactment of the Article 23 legislation according to the scheduled deadline. Without the votes from the Liberal Party, Tung had no choice but to postpone and later withdraw the enactment. Another result was the resignation of Regina Ip and Antony Leung not long after the July 1 rally, though both claimed that their resignations were unrelated to any accountability issue.

From passive to active: the new strategy of the Beijing government

After the July 1 rally and the emergence of civil society as a new game player, the Beijing government needed to review the effectiveness of its strategy toward Hong Kong. There were several considerations. After the July 1 rally, the demand for further democratic development was growing stronger. More people started to question the legitimacy of the HKSAR government in its present form. They questioned why Tung could continue to stay in office with such poor performance. It was generally recognized that there must be fundamental changes to the selection methods of the CE and the members of the LegCo before the HKSAR government could regain its legitimacy.

According to the Basic Law, there is a possibility that the third CE and all members of the LegCo will be directly elected in 2007 and 2008, respectively. Article 45 of the Basic Law provides that:

> The method for selecting the Chief Executive shall be specified in the light of the actual situation in the Hong Kong Special Administrative Region and in accordance with the principle of gradual and orderly progress. The ultimate aim is the selection of the Chief Executive by universal suffrage upon nomination by a broadly representative nominating committee in accordance with democratic procedures. The specific method for selecting the Chief Executive is prescribed in Annex I: "Method for the Selection of the Chief Executive of the Hong Kong Special Administrative Region."

Annex I of the Basic Law provides that:

> If there is a need to amend the method for selecting the Chief Executives for the terms subsequent to the year 2007, such amendments must be made with the endorsement of a two-thirds majority of all the members of the Legislative Council and the consent of the Chief Executive, and they shall be reported to the Standing Committee of the National People's Congress for approval.

Article 68 of the Basic Law provides that:

> The method for forming the Legislative Council shall be specified in the light of the actual situation in the Hong Kong Special Administrative Region and in accordance with the principle of gradual and orderly progress. The ultimate aim is the election of all the members of the Legislative Council by universal suffrage. The specific method for forming the Legislative Council and its procedures for voting on bills and motions are prescribed in Annex II: "Method for the Formation of the Legislative Council of the Hong Kong Special Administrative Region and Its Voting Procedures."

Annex II of the Basic Law provides that:

> With regard to the method for forming the Legislative Council of the Hong Kong Special Administrative Region and its procedures for voting on bills and motions after 2007, if there is a need to amend the provisions of this

Annex, such amendments must be made with the endorsement of a two-thirds majority of all the members of the Council and the consent of the Chief Executive, and they shall be reported to the Standing Committee of the National People's Congress for the record.

Reading all these provisions together, many people believed that ten years after the establishment of the HKSAR, Hong Kong people would have already had the power to decide for themselves whether direct election should be introduced as the method of election of the CE and all the members of the LegCo.[24] The HKSAR government was under pressure to put forward a timetable to review the political system so that direct elections could be introduced in 2007/2008. However, for a long time, the Beijing government has had reservations against allowing democratic reform in Hong Kong, at least not at a very fast pace. The Beijing government worries that democratic reform may affect the vested interests of the business people who have long been loyal supporters of the Beijing government and are considered to be the pillars of Hong Kong's stability and prosperity. In addition, it may encourage the demand for democratic reform in the Mainland, which may threaten the rule of the Chinese Communist Party.

However, the failure of the HKSAR government to complete the Article 23 legislation caused the Beijing government to discover that it might lose control if it continued to rely on its current strategy and the existing ruling mechanism in the HKSAR.

From the subsequent development of the July 1 rally, the Beijing government discovered that, on the one hand, Tung, though trustworthy, did not have the ability to lead the HKSAR government effectively. On the other hand, the Liberal Party was not a very trustworthy partner, especially at critical moments.

A new strategy was needed. The Beijing government had to reassert its authority within Hong Kong in a more direct and active manner. This new strategy came with several moves. First, the CE was informed that the decision on the timetable for public consultation and review on constitutional development could not be made by the HKSAR government, even though the Secretary for Constitutional Affairs had already promised the LegCo that such a decision would be made before the end of 2003.[25] This move was to call a halt to any planned action of the HKSAR government.

The second move involved four Mainland legal experts who were called to assist by suggesting that the understanding of whether "there is a need" to amend the method of selecting the CE or the forming of the LegCo must be determined by the central authorities. This move was to pave the way for the HKSAR government to formally recognize that this power must belong to the central authorities.

To coordinate with the Beijing government's move, in Tung's policy address on January 7, 2004, he announced the establishment of the Constitutional Development Task Force. This was headed by the Chief Secretary for Administration, Donald Tsang, and the other members were the Secretary for Justice and the

Secretary for Constitutional Affairs. The Task Force was to examine the relevant principles and legislative process in the Basic Law relating to constitutional development in depth, to consult the relevant departments of the central authorities, and to listen to the views of the public on the relevant issues.

To justify the stance that the central authorities have the power to decide on whether "there is a need," the previous ambiguous understanding of "One Country, Two Systems" had to be elucidated. It is very clear that the Beijing government always considers that the proper understanding of "One Country, Two Systems" must be "One Country" having primacy over "Two Systems." However, it had never explicitly stated this point clearly before. Again, through the Mainland legal experts, the correct understanding of "One Country, Two Systems" to be "One Country as the premise and foundation of Two Systems" was publicized.[26]

The next move was to use the pro-Beijing media to start a wave of patriotism debate. Referring to a statement made by Deng Xiao-ping in 1984,[27] it should be the patriots who form the main body of administrators of the HKSAR. "Patriot" was defined as one who respects the Chinese nation, sincerely supports the motherland's resumption of sovereignty over Hong Kong, and wishes not to impair Hong Kong's prosperity and stability. This move was to discredit some of the political leaders in the pan-democracy camp in Hong Kong so as to question the legitimacy of their claims for direct election in 2007/2008.

All these acts still needed a critical move that could trump any challenge from Hong Kong. On April 6, 2004, the SCNPC issued an Interpretation on Clause 7 of Annex I and Clause 3 of Annex II of the Basic Law (the Interpretation), making it clear that the procedure for making any amendment to Annex I and II can take effect only if the CE makes a report to the SCNPC regarding whether or not there is a need to make an amendment; and the SCNPC shall, in accordance with the provisions of Articles 45 and 68 of the Basic Law of the HKSAR, make a determination in the light of the actual situation in the HKSAR and in accordance with the principle of gradual and orderly progress. The bills shall be introduced by the HKSAR government to the LegCo.[28] This interpretation consolidated all the gains from the quick and overwhelming moves by the Beijing government in the constitutional game. The other players could just pass. To many people, this interpretation can hardly be called an interpretation. It looked more like an enactment or decision.

Then, again to coordinate with the Beijing government's move, the CE made a report shortly after the Interpretation and recommended that there was a need to amend Annex I and II.[29] The Task Force also issued a report recommending that direct elections should not be introduced in 2007/2008.[30] This paved the way for the SCNPC to make the final blow to direct election in 2007/2008. A decision was made by the SCNPC on April 26, 2004 that the CE and all members of the LegCo would not be directly elected by Hong Kong citizens in 2007/2008.[31] Nothing was mentioned on what would happen after 2008.

With the power of interpretation of the Basic Law, the most powerful card in this constitutional game, the Beijing government can do almost anything it likes and all the other players could hardly put up any effective resistance, not even Hong Kong's civil society. All legal arguments for direct elections in 2007/2008 were brushed aside to clear the way for the final outcome that the Beijing government desired to see. Within five months, the Beijing government had dashed whatever hopes the Hong Kong people had to see direct elections in the near future. This new strategy has achieved its objective loud and clear. If we describe the past strategy of the Beijing government as "One Country as premises and foundation of Two Systems in its passive voice", this new strategy may be described as "One Country as premises and foundation of Two Systems in the active voice".

The Beijing government adopted this active application of "One Country, Two Systems" to make it possible for resuming a more passive position later. By removing any hope for direct elections in 2007/2008, the pressure upon the HKSAR government was released. The Beijing government hoped that the HKSAR Government could refocus its efforts toward reinvigorating Hong Kong's economy.

There is a soft side to this active strategy in addition to the hard side. Taking away a political dream from the Hong Kong people was compensated for by economic gains. The Beijing government hoped that the introduction of CEPA[32] and the Individual Visit Scheme[33] would boost the economy of Hong Kong. The Beijing government still believed that the greatest grievance of Hong Kong people was economic but not political.

It is not clear whether the resignation of Tung in early 2005 was within the series of moves of the new strategy of the Beijing government. By early 2005, Hong Kong's economy was already improving and Hong Kong society also seemed to be much more stable, even though half a million people still marched in the street in the second July 1 rally in 2004. It is not clear how the resignation of Tung, if directed by the Beijing government, could be consistent with its overall plan in striving to maintain political and economic stability in Hong Kong.

After more than ten days of rumors, Tung confirmed his resignation as the CE on March 10, 2005. Tung's resignation caught many people in Hong Kong unawares, including those who believed that they had a close relationship with the HKSAR and the Beijing governments. Since the July 1 rally in 2003, there have been intense demands from the Hong Kong people for Tung's resignation. For the past 20 months, there was no sign that Tung would resign under public pressure. There was also no sign that the Beijing government would withdraw its support for Tung. Rather, many signals showed that Tung would complete his second term, which was scheduled to end on June 30, 2007, even though he might play a less active role in the governance of Hong Kong.[34]

There is much speculation on whether his resignation was a forced or a voluntary one. Tung's explanation for the resignation was his poor health, but no concrete evidence was provided on how his health situation would substantially affect his performance as the CE.

His resignation was formally accepted by the Beijing government two days later, and Donald Tsang, the Chief Secretary for Administration, was appointed as the Acting CE. Tung's resignation had caused the Beijing government to make another active move to interfere with a matter which might be a purely Hong Kong affair. The purpose again was to release the pressure upon the HKSAR government.

The cause of the controversy might also be unexpected. According to Article 52 of the Basic Law, the CE "must resign if he or she loses the ability to discharge his or her duties as a result of serious illness or other reasons." In the event that the office of CE becomes vacant, Article 53 provides that the duties of the CE will temporarily be assumed by the Chief Secretary for Administration and a new CE must be selected within six months. According to the Chief Executive Election Ordinance,[35] the by-election must be held 120 days after the date on which the office becomes vacant.[36]

The focus of the debates was the length of the term of the re-elected CE. Article 46 of the Basic Law provides that the term of office of the CE shall be five years. There is no specific provision in Article 53 and other articles of the Basic Law on the length of the term of the re-elected CE. Reading these two provisions together, it seems to be clear and unambiguous that the length of the term of the re-elected CE should also be five years.

The stance of the HKSAR government, in a written response to the LegCo by the Secretary for Constitutional Affairs on May 5, 2004, was originally in the event that the office of the CE becomes vacant, the term of office of the re-elected CE is five years.

However, after several legal experts from the Mainland expressed their opinions that the term of office should be two years, which was the remaining term of Tung's original term, the Secretary for Justice issued a statement shortly after the appointment of the Acting CE stating that the term should be two years.[37]

The change of stance of the HKSAR government caused a new wave of heated legal and political controversy. The HKSAR government introduced a bill to the LegCo to amend the Chief Executive Election Ordinance. The proposed amendment adds a proviso to the effect that a CE who fills a vacancy will serve the remainder of the term of its predecessor.

Legal actions were initiated by two Hong Kong citizens, including a legislative councilor from the pan-democracy camp, to challenge the constitutionality of the amendment to the Chief Executive Election Ordinance.

To ensure that a new CE could be elected on July 10, 2005 and would not be affected by the legal proceedings, the acting CE submitted a report to the State Council to request the SCNPC to interpret Article 53 so as to confirm that the term of the re-elected CE would only be the remaining term of his or her predecessor. On April 27, 2005, the SCNPC issued its third interpretation on the Basic Law since the handover.[38] Again by using the trump card in the constitutional game, any opposition could be removed. The Acting CE, Donald Tsang, was later elected without competition as the "new" Second CE of the HKSAR. The applications for judicial review were also withdrawn.

Following this "hard" move, the Beijing government did attempt to re-create a more harmonized game environment in Hong Kong. All legislative councilors, including the pan-democracy camp councilors who had been blacklisted owing to of their connection with the Hong Kong Alliance in Support of Democratic Movement in China, an anti-Beijing organization, were invited to visit Guangdong. The door of communication between the pan-democracy camp and the Beijing government had been reopened, though still not too wide.

This may show a pattern of the Beijing government's strategy in dealing with Hong Kong's affairs. A "hard" move must be accompanied by some following soft moves to balance the negative impact. However, one may also see that all the moves of the Beijing government share the same objective to maintain stability and prosperity in Hong Kong. What strategies and moves are needed to achieve the objective may change over time and as the social environment changes. During one time passivity might be the appropriate strategy, but during another time a hard line might be needed. At still another time a soft approach may serve the purpose better.

From the consequences, the Beijing government may see that a more active strategy in dealing with Hong Kong's internal affairs is proper because it can successfully remove all factors of instability, at least on the surface. There is no guarantee that the Beijing government will not adopt this active strategy again in the near future when it sees that there is a need. However, what it thinks is a need may not be so considered by the people in Hong Kong.

This is a unique feature of the constitutional game of Hong Kong. It is an unbalanced game in the sense that one player dominates the game. As the dominant player, the Beijing government sets the rules of the game, giving it the most favorable position and maximum room to direct the flow of the game. It also has the most powerful card in the game (i.e., the power to interpret the Basic Law). This allows the Beijing government to dominate the legal platform in addition to its immense influence in the political system.

However, even with this almost unlimited power, there are practical concerns that the Beijing government cannot ignore. If it still wants to set a constitutional game in Hong Kong and not just a purely political game, it must be constrained by the rules it has set.

In the incidents where the Beijing government had taken active moves, they were done through issuing an interpretation on relevant Basic Law articles by the SCNPC, together with other hard and soft moves to coordinate with this decisive move. The text of the Basic Law can be manipulated by the SCNPC to give meanings that conform to the objective of the Beijing government's overall strategy. Although the Beijing government has the power to make any interpretation, the actual interpretation given must be justified and legitimized by existing rules. The kind of legislative interpretation by the SCNPC is alien to Hong Kong's common law system, and the intrusion into legal interpretation by pure political concerns hurts Hong Kong's Rule of Law.

The active strategy must still be justified by using processes and reasoning that are more in line with the general principles that are acceptable in Hong Kong rather than just imposing the decision upon Hong Kong. Although the performance may still not be up to the Hong Kong standard, this reflects the fact that the Beijing government understands that this active strategy must only be used with caution. In the long run, if the Beijing government becomes more active, it will affect the degree of autonomy that Hong Kong can actually enjoy. These adverse consequences of the active approach may deter the Beijing government from using it casually.

Another new player: a new second CE

The "new" Second CE, Donald Tsang, has a civil service background. There is speculation that the Beijing government accepted Tung's resignation because it wanted to make a change in the personnel of the HKSAR government. The three main pro-Beijing camps in Hong Kong are the left-wing political groups, the business sector, and the civil service. Tung was a businessman, but he failed to handle the complex political environment within Hong Kong after the transfer of sovereignty.

The left-wing political groups have no experience in running a government. The only choice seems to be the civil service. The civil service was the ruling clique during colonial times, and there is no question of its ability to govern. However, there are reservations as to whether they can be trusted. One reason that the Beijing government insisted the term of the new CE could only be the remaining term of his or her predecessor was that Tsang had to be put on probation to test his trustworthiness. Another reason may be that the Beijing government had to pacify the other pro-Beijing groups, as they had already planned to send their representatives to run in the scheduled election for the CE in 2007.

In this two-year term, Tsang also wanted to rebuild an image of a strong, efficient, and effective government. However, there were several factors that would affect his positioning. First, Tsang does not have the general support that Tung had within the pro-Beijing camps. Second, Tsang's relationship with the Beijing government is not as close as Tung's. His support from the Beijing government is totally based on his ability to rule Hong Kong effectively and to keep the development of Hong Kong within the boundaries set by the Beijing government. Third, members of the Executive Council and the Principal Officials who were appointed by Tung were kept by Tsang in his new cabinet, which may be a condition set by the Beijing government on his appointment. How to work with them as a team was a great challenge to Tsang's governance ability and political skills.

Tsang needed to use these two years to prove his loyalty and ability. There would not be much room for him to introduce anything substantial. Maintenance was his main strategy. However, Tsang has a character very different from Tung, and he managed to attract more general support in Hong Kong. His support was kept at a relatively high level throughout these two years. He also has a better relationship with the pan-democracy camp. No matter what, he is on the same tightrope that every CE would have to walk. Balancing "One Country" and "Two Systems" well is the skill that a CE must possess. Leaning toward either side too much will cause him to fall like Tung.

New strategies for existing players?

For the existing players of the game, they may also need to adopt a new strategy to face the challenges in Chapter two.

The introduction of the POAS has ushered in a group of accountable officials to the HKSAR government. Even if they are from the civil service, their roles are different from the time during colonial rule and the first term of Tung. They are accountable to the CE. Events before and after the July 1 rally make it clear that their accountability is substantial. Although Hong Kong people have no institutional power to remove them and Tung might want to shelter them from intense public pressure, he was not successful in most cases. Even Tung himself could not stand the public pressure from the media and civil society and had to resign. Principal Officials are within the eye of any political typhoon and they must face the wind and rain. Unfortunately, each Principal Official has to face it alone.

The first batch of accountable Principal Officials came from different backgrounds. Quite a number were from the civil service; the others were from the business sector, the professional sector, and academia. The only thing in common among them is that they were all willing to serve under Tung's leadership – but their reasons might be very different. It is clear that there is no single policy vision joining them together, causing a lack of team mentality among them. As a result, whenever a Principal Official faced criticisms and challenges in his own policy portfolio, he would find himself a lone fighter, hoping for the best, and that other Principal Officials would not stab him in the back.

Under the new leadership of Tsang, there was not much change in the situation. They were all asked to stay in office, and what made them a team was, again, only that they shared the same boss.

Principal Officials also find themselves as lone fighters because they joined the HKSAR government by themselves. Within the bureau each of them leads, the Principal Officials are served by civil servants, some of whom may have originally been the top person of that bureau. The role of civil servants, especially those from the Administrative Officers' rank, has changed substantially since the introduction of the POAS. They are no longer policy-makers and in theory they should be responsible only for the implementation of policies decided by the Principal Officials. However, under the POAS system, they are also asked to fulfill the same political task as the Principal Officials to lobby support from the LegCo and answer questions from the media and the public. The only difference between civil servants and Principal Officials is that the former need not resign in the event of policy failure. This change of role has substantially affected the morale of civil servants. How far this has affected the effectiveness of the HKSAR government in governance still requires further study. The recent appointment of Tsang as the CE might give hope to some that the good old days of civil servants may come back, as Tsang himself was also a civil servant. However, bygones are bygones; the golden days of the Hong Kong civil service may never return. Unfortunately, it seems that the civil service does not have the capacity to formulate any coherent strategy to adapt to the new chapter except to simply finish their jobs at hand.

Together with the introduction to the POAS, Tung had also appointed the party leaders of the DAB and the Liberal Party to the Executive Council forming the ruling coalition. The other members of the Executive Council, like the Principal Officials, all came from different backgrounds, and there was no policy vision that united them. The political parties in the ruling coalition had already indicated dissatisfaction, since they could not have any significant input in policy-making, as all policy portfolios are in the hands of the Principal Officials. Even if they are members of the Executive Council, that privileged position very often gives them more burden than benefit. They have to defend government policies which they do not really support.

Under Tsang's new leadership, the ruling coalition was maintained. All current non-official members stay in the Executive Council. He also appointed more non-official members into the Executive Council including one from the pan-democracy camp. It is not clear whether the reform will prompt the Executive Council to be more like a real cabinet or whether it will continue to be an advisory body. Up until now, the Executive Council as a player has no independent strategy, though each of its members may have an agenda.

The result of the election in 2004 did not change the nature of the LegCo, though there are more members in the pan-democracy camp. Under the existing institutional structure, the LegCo does not have the capacity to position itself in any significant way other than putting up some form of opposition against the government. Until the time the pan-democracy camp could form the majority of the LegCo, the LegCo could not be an effective check on policy-making and implementation of the HKSAR government.

It is likely that the LegCo will continue to be divided into three wings: the left wing, the business wing, and the pan-democracy wing, with the DAB, the Liberal Party, and the Democratic Party forming the main sects of each wing respectively. Other individual members or smaller political groups fall under one of the three wings. The DAB has made it clear that its ultimate aim is to become a ruling party. Tsang's taking over of Tung's position makes it clear that the Beijing government may not believe that the DAB or the left-wing political groups in Hong Kong could have the legitimacy and ability to manage Hong Kon's complicated political environment. Therefore, in this new chapter and the coming chapters, the DAB is in rather a dilemma. To adopt a strategy which could help itself to achieve its long-term goal may conflict with its short-term duty to support the Tsang administration. Like all other players, they are walking on tightropes. If the political system of Hong Kong will develop to become more democratic, even if the pace is slow, the DAB needs the votes of the Hong Kong people. Getting only around 25 percent of the votes in the election in 2004, its road to becoming a ruling party is still long. Its coming challenge is how to get votes by supporting the HKSAR government. Ironically, Tsang's growing support makes the DAB's stance easier to justify to the public but may also further delay its dream to govern Hong Kong directly. The DAB has now adopted a strategy of maintaining the general impression of being pro-government but is also trying hard to maintain its distance from the Tsang administration.

Business people are important to the governance of Hong Kong, but it seems that after the failure of Tung, the Beijing government considers business people as a group who must be respected but cannot be trusted with the direct authority to govern Hong Kong. The Liberal Party's unfaithful track record also puts the Beijing government on alert. The Liberal Party cannot be excluded, but how far they can be trusted is a concern that cannot easily be forgotten in the minds of the officials in Beijing. The Liberal Party's main support comes from the functional constituencies in the LegCo, though it managed to win two seats in the geographical direct election in 2004. Any change in the functional constituencies will weaken its influence in the LegCo. Winning more votes in geographical direct elections must be their long-term objective if they want to maintain their share in the LegCo. The Liberal Party is in a similar dilemma to the DAB. It must strike a fine balance between supporting and keeping distance from Tsang's administration. Its greatest hope may be the office of the CE, as it is more likely that it can exert a strong influence on the Election Committee in the election for the CE. The Liberal Party must also watch closely the reaction of the Beijing government.

As for the pan-democracy camp, the chance that they could get the majority in the LegCo in the coming years is still rather remote. As the opposition in the LegCo, they find it more and more difficult to win public support by opposing the HKSAR government in light of Tsang's growing support. They must show to the public that they could be more than just a group of oppositionists. They are also in a dilemma, though of a different nature from that of the DAB and the Liberal Party.

To demonstrate their ability to govern, they must seize any chance to show that they can maintain at least a working relationship with the Beijing government and can put up some sensible alternative policies. Drawing themselves too close to the Beijing government may affect their public support, but failing to at least communicate with the Beijing government may cause them to lose votes. They must strike a balance, which is not easy to ascertain; they are also rather passive in this matter, as the Beijing government holds the key to the door of communication.

Internally, the pan-democracy camp includes political parties, groups, and individuals from very different backgrounds. They differ a lot in social policies and the only thing that joins them together is the same aspiration for democratic development in Hong Kong. It is very difficult for the pan-democracy camp to put up some joint policy platform. In addition, as they are still in the minority and lack experience in governance, their substantial social policy proposals do not enjoy the same level of legitimacy as their demands for democracy or other institutional concerns. The HKSAR government does not need to pay much attention to their concrete policy proposals, if any.

All the existing players shared the same difficulty in this new chapter. There were so many uncertainties, one of which was the baseline of the dominant player, the Beijing government. Generally, no one can have a clear direction.

Finally, we come to the CFA. During this period, unlike during the first chapter, there were not that many constitutionally sensitive cases. Even if there were, the CFA managed to play much better and has already acquired the skills to avoid sensitive issues or justify its decisions with reasons that would not arouse too much dissatisfaction from the Beijing government or the Hong Kong people. There seems to be no urgent need to develop another strategy. It can still try its best to fulfill its roles as a guardian of the rule of law, autonomy, and human rights in Hong Kong while the rule of law remains to take precedence in case of conflict between the various roles.

Can Hong Kong's civil society develop any strategy?

The active participation of Hong Kong's civil society in 2003 was unexpected. The Beijing government's main reason for adopting a more active strategy in Hong Kong affairs is the emergence of a much more politically oriented civil society following the July 1 rally. Many moves made by the Beijing government were not only to reassert its institutional control over Hong Kong, but also to convince civil society to abandon its political orientation and revert back to its traditionally more economic mind-set. The granting of CEPA status to Hong Kong and the Individual Visit Scheme were such efforts.

Civil society, by nature, is very different from the other players in the constitutional game. Civil society is not a single entity but is composed of hundreds of thousands of free associations of citizens outside the state's direct control. These associations may have a tightly organized structure or may be very loose. Relationships with members in these associations may either be relatively permanent or just temporary, even incidental. The associations can either be very big in size with thousands of members or rather small. Their objectives can be political, professional, social, religious, economic, ideological, cultural, or racial, or any of the other concerns that cause a group of people to join together. Their relationship with the government also varies from institutional, instrumental, cooperative, to confrontational.

The heterogeneity of civil society makes any analysis of its role in a constitutional game extremely difficult. It cannot be directed, only molded. This is exactly the strategy adopted by the Beijing government. The attempts by the pan-democracy camp to exert a more direct influence on civil society following the July 1 rally in 2003 only ended in failure. The best example may be seen in the result of the LegCo election in 2004. Hoping that they could utilize the anti-Tung sentiment in society to win more seats in the LegCo or even control the majority, the advancement was only very limited. Many Hong Kong people were frustrated by their poor performance in the election. There is no one association, or even a group of associations, in Hong Kong's civil society, unlike the Catholic Church and the Solidarity in the Communist Poland which could mobilize the people to join together to challenge the rulers.

Each association in the web of civil society also has its own agenda and priority. The response of each of the associations to the strategy of other parties in the constitutional game may not be static and would change over time. The sensitivity of each association to the political situation and the strategies of other players may also vary. Some may not be too sensitive to any change and their response may also be rather slow if compared with other associations. The susceptibility of each association to pressure from other players in the constitutional game is not the same. Some can stand firm on their objectives against threats, pressures or benefits while some may easily change their stance. The link to other associations in the web is also not the same. Some are very close but some may be rather isolated. All these variables make civil society a very organic but unpredictable animal.

Associations in civil society may try their best to influence others so that civil society may act as if it is a united entity against the other players in the game along a favored strategy. However, the other associations in civil society may put up counter-strategies to compete for the leading strategy for the whole of civil society. This may end with the associations working for their own strategies and it is impossible to have a coherent strategy for civil society as a whole. Even if they have such a united front, the people of Hong Kong may not respond as directed.

The other players in the game may also try to exert influence over civil society: first, through associations that are on more friendly terms, and then move to extend their influence to other associations further away from its relationship web. As the number of associations in civil society is so large, influencing associations would not be done through direct contact, except for a limited number of more influential associations. Mass media is the major tool that could influence civil society.

There is hardly any indicator to tell as to what extent the molding effort has achieved its purpose. It seems that there are no effective means to predict how civil society will react.

Judging by the weak response from civil society in the controversies over the term of the CE and the third interpretation of the Basic Law by the SCNPC, it seems that the new strategy of the Beijing government has achieved its objective to a certain degree. The small number of people participating in the third July 1 rally in 2005 confirmed this. The civil society is still more pragmatic than idealistic, more economic than political, and more cooperative than confrontational. Only if the HKSAR government or the Beijing government has done something that will cause frustration to the civil society in a continuing, immediate, and overt manner, the participation of civil society in the constitutional game will still be limited.

Conclusion: a short or long Chapter three?

After Tsang was elected as the new second CE, Chapter two closed and Chapter three has begun. He was also re-elected as the third CE and this means that

Chapter three may last for seven years. However, how Chapter three differs from the previous chapters will depend on many factors, and again all hinge on the positioning of the players in the constitutional game.

The strategy of Tsang will be critical, as he will be the focus of Chapter three. He has to maintain the trust that he has gained from the Beijing government and the Hong Kong people. There may still be all kinds of unexpected events that will put his ability to balance the interests of both sides to the test.

The most important factor is surely the strategy of the Beijing government. If we understand it correctly, and the active strategy is to allow the Beijing government to revert back to a more passive position, we foresee that the Beijing government will not be as active as in 2003 to 2005. However, it all depends on the development within Hong Kong and whether Tsang can manage to contain any conflict in Hong Kong within an acceptable range.

How active the Beijing government's strategy in Hong Kong will be will determine how much freedom Tsang could have in managing affairs in Hong Kong. We foresee that the Beijing government may have a certain degree of trust in Tsang but it would surely continue to keep a very close watch over Tsang's performance.

Within the pro-Beijing camp, the left-wing political groups and the business sector may give their half-hearted support to Tsang in the beginning. How far they will continue to give their support will depend on whether or not Tsang can handle the delicate balance between the Beijing government and the more confrontational part of civil society.

The pan-democracy camp will continue to play its role as the opposition and exert influence over civil society to mobilize the associations to push for a faster democratization pace. However, whether they can attract support from civil society will depend on whether or not they can move beyond this opposition mind-set. If they cannot put forward any concrete plan to demonstrate to the Hong Kong people that they have the ability to govern Hong Kong, their support may continue to dwindle and their prospect dim.

Another critical factor is whether civil society will be satisfied with Tsang's governance and how it will respond to the continued active strategy of the Beijing government if it decides to be more active. As no one person or group can mobilize civil society, this will be the most uncertain factor, as all parties would like to pull civil society over to their side.

If Tsang can manage to strike a balance between all of these factors, it is likely that he can complete his third term. However, the lesson of the unexpected Chapter two teaches us that in a constitutional game, there is nothing we can be too certain about. A new chapter may be turned to from interactions of old and new parties and their changing strategies generated from the ever-changing political situation.

The constitutional game continues.

Notes

1 Tai, Benny Y.T., "Chapter One of Hong Kong's New Constitution: Constitutional Positioning and Repositioning." In *Crisis and Transformation in China's Hong Kong*, ed. Ming K. Chan and Alvin Y. So. London: M.E. Sharpe, 2002.
2 Game-theoretic analysis is a methodology applied in positive political theory of law. For a detailed description of the positive political theory of law, see McCubbins, Mat, Roger Noll and Barry Weingast, "The Political Economy of Law: Decision Making by Judicial, Legislative, Executive and Administrative Agencies," Stanford Institute for Economic Policy Research Discussion Paper No. 04–35, August, 2005.
3 For an example of how different constitutional institutions interact in a constitutional game, see Segal, Jeffrey, "Separation-of-powers Games in the Positive Theory of Congress and Courts," *American Political Science Review* (1997) 91: 28–44.
4 In this understanding, there is no condition on how the constitution was made. When the constitution is respected by all players so that it has a binding effect upon their acts, a political game becomes a constitutional game. The rule of law and constitutionalism are conditions for a constitutional game.
5 See Friedman, Barry, "Taking Law Seriously," *Perspectives on Politics* (2006) 4: 261–276.
6 Friedman, Barry, "The Politics of Judicial Review," *Texas Law Review* (2005) 84: 257–337, and Jacobi, Tonja, "The Impact of Positive Political Theory on Old Questions of Constitutional Law and the Separation of Powers," *Northwestern University Law Review* (2006) 100: 259–278.
7 Tai, Benny Y.T., "Chapter One of Hong Kong's New Constitution: Constitutional Positioning and Repositioning." In *Crisis and Transformation in China's Hong Kong*, ed. Ming K. Chan and Alvin Y. So. London: M.E. Sharpe.
8 Tung had already provided some hints in his Policy Address in 2000 and in his Policy Address in 2001. See also the Address by the CE on April 17, 2002 at the LegCo and the *Code for Principal Officials under the Accountability System* (G.N. 3845, June 28, 2002).
9 It might have been the pressure from the Beijing government that caused the HKSAR government to initiate the legislation at that moment. See the view of Qiao Xiaoyang, Deputy Secretary of the Legislative Affairs Commission, National People's Congress Standing Committee, reported on September 27, 2002, *Wenweipo*.
10 For the analysis of this constitutional duty, see Tai, Benny Y.T., "The Principle of Minimum Legislation for Implementing Article 23 of the Basic Law," *Hong Kong Law Journal* 32 (2002): 579–614.
11 Consultation Document on Proposals to implement Article 23 of the Basic Law. Available at www.basiclaw23.gov.hk/english/download/reporte.pdf.
12 Tai, Note 10.
13 Peterson, Carole, "National Security Offences and Civil Liberties in Hong Kong: A Critique of the Government's 'Consultation' on Article 23 of the Basic Law," *Hong Kong Law Journal* 32 (2002): 457–470.
14 Available at www.basiclaw23.gov.hk/english/download/forward-e.pdf.
15 See "Doing Justice to Public Opinion in Public Consultations: What to Do and What NOT to Do – A Case Study of the Government's Consultation Exercise On its Proposals to Implement Article 23 of the Basic Law," a report by the Research Team on the Compendium of Submissions on Article 23 of the Basic Law, May 26, 2003. Available at www.article 23.org.hk.
16 For a detailed account of the Article 23 saga, see Peterson, Carole, "Hong Kong's Spring of Discontent: The Rise and Fall of the National Security Bill in 2003." In *National Security and Fundamental Freedoms: Hong Kong's Article 23 under Scrutiny*, ed. Fu, H.L., Peterson, Carole and Young, Simon N.M. Hong Kong: Hong Kong University Press, 2005.

17 The definition of civil society adopted in this study is the definition of the Centre for Civil Society, London School of Economics and Political Science:

> Civil society refers to the arena of un-coerced collective action around shared interests, purposes and values. Civil society commonly embraces a diversity of spaces, actors and institutional forms, varying in their degree of formality, autonomy and power.

18 The understanding of civil society adopted in this study is basically a liberal notion of civil society, emphasizing the state–civil society relationship. This relationship is not necessarily confrontational and could be cooperative, instrumental, or institutionally intertwined. This study aims to illustrate the role, capacity, capability, and autonomy of civil society in causing political and constitutional change in a constitutional system.

19 Sing, Ming, "Mobilization for Political Change – The Pro-democracy Movement in Hong Kong (1980s-1994)." In *The Dynamics of Social Movement in Hong Kong*, ed. Stephen W.K. Chiu and Lui Tai Lok. Hong Kong: Hong Kong University Press, 2000.

20 Lau, Siu-kai and Kuan Hsin-chi, "The Attentive Spectators: Political Participation of the Hong Kong Chinese," *Journal of Northeast Asian Studies* 14 (1995): 3–25.

21 Ip, Po Keung, "Development of Civil Society in Hong Kong: Constraints, Problems and Risks." In *Political Order and Power Transition in Hong Kong*, ed. Pang-kwong Li. Hong Kong: The Chinese University Press. 1997.

22 Lau and Kuan called the Hong Kong Chinese "attentative spectators." See Note 19.

23 Similar protection may be found under Article 21 of the International Covenant on Civil and Political Rights made applicable to Hong Kong via Article 39 of the Basic Law.

24 See *Explanations on "The Basic Law of the HKSAR (Draft)"* by Ji Pengfei, Chairman of the Drafting Committee for the Basic Law to the National people's Congress.

25 See the statement of the Secretary for Constitutional Affairs in a meeting of the Panel on Constitutional Affairs of the LegCo held on November 17, 2003. The Minutes of the meeting are available at www.legco.gov.hk/yr03–04/english/panels/ca/minutes/ca031117.pdf.

26 Xia Yong, Director of the Institute of Law, Chinese Academy of Social Science, is one of the four Mainland legal experts. He published an article titled "'One Country' is the premise and foundation of 'Two Systems'" on February 22, 2004 through the official Xinhua News Agency.

27 Xiaoping Deng, *Selected Works of Deng Xiaoping*. Beijing: Foreign Language Press, 1984 (Vol. III).

28 Interpretation by the Standing Committee of the National People's Congress on Clause 7 of Annex I and Clause 3 of Annex II of the Basic Law of the Hong Kong Special Administrative Region of the People's Republic of China adopted by the Standing Committee of the Tenth National People's Congress at its Eighth Session on April 6, 2004.

29 Report on whether there is a need to amend the methods for selecting the CE of the Hong Kong Special Administrative Region in 2007 and for forming the LegCo of the Hong Kong Special Administrative Region in 2008 (available at www.info.gov.hk/cab/cab-review/eng/executive/pdf/cereport.pdf).

30 The Second Report of the Constitutional Development Task Force: Issues of Principle in the Basic Law Relating to Constitutional Development (available at www.info.gov.hk/cab/cab-review/eng/report2/index.htm).

31 Decision of the Standing Committee of the National People's Congress on issues relating to the methods for selecting the CE of the Hong Kong Special Administrative Region in the year 2007 and for forming the LegCo of the Hong Kong Special Administrative Region in the year 2008 adopted by the Standing Committee of the Tenth National People's Congress at its Ninth Session on April 26, 2004.

32 CEPA stands for "Closer Economic Partnership Arrangement between Hong Kong and the Chinese Mainland." It is a free trade agreement under WTO rules and gives preferential access to the Mainland market for Hong Kong companies. It was launched on January 1, 2004.
33 The scheme allows citizens from selected cities in Mainland China to visit Hong Kong on an individual basis. In the past, Mainland people could only visit Hong Kong on business visas or in group tours.
34 One of the signals was that Tung still had many plans to achieve in his Policy Address 2005.
35 Cap. 569.
36 Section 10, Cap. 569.
37 www.info.gov.hk/gia/general/200503/12/03120310.htm.
38 Interpretation of the Standing Committee of the National People's Congress on Article 53(2) of the Basic Law of the Hong Kong Special Administrative Region Adopted at the 15th Session of the Standing Committee of the Tenth National People's Congress on April 27, 2005.

References

Carse, James P. *Finite and Infinite Games*. New York: Ballantine Books, 1986.

Chan, Ming and Alvin Y. So, eds. *Crisis and Transformation in China's Hong Kong*. London: M.E. Sharpe, 2002.

Chen, Albert H.Y. "The Constitutional Controversy of Spring 2004." *Hong Kong Law Journal* (2004) 34: 215–225.

Feldman, David. "Factors Affecting the Choice of Techniques of Constitutional Interpretation," a paper presented to the round table of the International Association of Constitutional law on Interpretation of Constitutions on October 15 and 16, 2004. The paper is available from www.law.cam.ac.uk/docs/view.php?doc=2514.

Friedman, Barry. "The Politics of Judicial Review," *Texas Law Review* (2005) 84: 257–337.

——. "Taking Law Seriously," *Perspectives on Politics* (2006) 4: 261–276.

Fu, H.L., Peterson, Carole and Young, Simon, N.M. eds. *National Security and Fundamental Freedoms: Hong Kong's Article 23 under Scrutiny*. Hong Kong: Hong Kong University Press, 2005.

Gates, Scott and D. Brian Humes. *Games, Information, and Politics: Applying Game Theoretic Models to Political Science*. The University of Michigan Press, 1997.

Ip, Po Keung. "Development of Civil Society in Hong Kong: Constraints, Problems and Risks." In *Political Order and Power Transition in Hong Kong*, ed. Pang-kwong Li. Hong Kong: The Chinese University Press, 1997, pp. 159–186.

Jacobi, Tonja. "The Impact of Positive Political Theory on Old Questions of Constitutional Law and the Separation of Powers," *Northwestern University Law Review* (2006) 100: 259–278.

Lau, Siu-kai and Hsin-chi Kuan. "The Attentive Spectators: Political Participation of the Hong Kong Chinese." *Journal of Northeast Asian Studies* 14 (1995): pp. 3–25.

McCubbins, Mat, Roger Noll, and Barry Weingast. "The Political Economy of Law: Decision Making by Judicial, Legislative, Executive and Administrative Agencies," *Stanford Institute for Economic Policy Research Discussion Paper* No. 04–35, August, 2005.

Ma, Ngok. "Civil Society in Defense: The Struggle Against National Security Legislation in Hong Kong," *Journal of Contemporary China* (2005) 14, no. 44: 465–482.

Peterson, Carole. "National Security Offences and Civil Liberties in Hong Kong: A Critique of the Government's 'Consultation' on Article 23 of the Basic Law," *Hong Kong Law Journal* (2002) 32: 457–470.

——. "Hong Kong's Spring of Discontent: The Rise and Fall of the National Security Bill in 2003." In *National Security and Fundamental Freedoms: Hong Kong's Article 23 under Scrutiny*, ed. Fu, H.L., Peterson, Carole and Young, Simon N.M. Hong Kong: Hong Kong University Press, 2005, pp. 13–62.

Porio, Emma. "Civil Society and Democratization in Asia: Prospects and Challenges in the New Millennium." In *New Challenges for Development and Modernization: Hong Kong and the Asia-Pacific Region in the New Millennium*, ed. Yeung Yue-man. Hong Kong: The Chinese University Press, 2002, pp. 225–243.

Segal, Jeffrey. "Separation-of-powers Games in the Positive Theory of Congress and Courts," *American Political Science Review* (1997) 91: 28–44.

Sing, Ming. "Mobilization for Political Change – The Pro-democracy Movement in Hong Kong (1980s-1994)." In *The Dynamics of Social Movement in Hong Kong*, ed. Stephen W.K. Chiu and Lui Tai Lok. Hong Kong: Hong Kong University Press, 2000, pp. 21–53.

Tai, Benny Y.T. "Chapter One of Hong Kong's New Constitution: Constitutional Positioning and Repositioning." In *Crisis and Transformation in China's Hong Kong*, ed. Chan Ming and Alvin Y. So. London: M.E. Sharpe, 2002, pp. 189–219.

——. "The Principle of Minimum Legislation for Implementing Article 23 of the Basic Law," *Hong Kong Law Journal* (2002) 32: 579–614.

——. "A Tale of the Unexpected: Tung's Resignation and the Ensuing Constitutional Controversy," *Hong Kong Law Journal* (2005) 35: 7–16.

Index

For Product Safety Concerns and Information please contact our EU
representative GPSR@taylorandfrancis.com
Taylor & Francis Verlag GmbH, Kaufingerstraße 24, 80331 München, Germany

9 780415 543033